Syntactic Variation and Verb Second

Linguistik Aktuell/Linguistics Today (LA)

Linguistik Aktuell/Linguistics Today (LA) provides a platform for original monograph studies into synchronic and diachronic linguistics. Studies in LA confront empirical and theoretical problems as these are currently discussed in syntax, semantics, morphology, phonology, and systematic pragmatics with the aim to establish robust empirical generalizations within a universalistic perspective.

For an overview of all books published in this series, please see
http://benjamins.com/catalog/la

General Editors

Werner Abraham
University of Vienna /
Rijksuniversiteit Groningen

Elly van Gelderen
Arizona State University

Advisory Editorial Board

Josef Bayer
University of Konstanz

Cedric Boeckx
ICREA/UB

Guglielmo Cinque
University of Venice

Liliane Haegeman
University of Ghent

Hubert Haider
University of Salzburg

Terje Lohndal
Norwegian University of Science
and Technology

Christer Platzack
University of Lund

Ian Roberts
Cambridge University

Lisa deMena Travis
McGill University

Sten Vikner
University of Aarhus

C. Jan-Wouter Zwart
University of Groningen

Volume 201

Syntactic Variation and Verb Second. A German dialect in Northern Italy
by Federica Cognola

Syntactic Variation and Verb Second

A German dialect in Northern Italy

Federica Cognola
University of Trento

John Benjamins Publishing Company
Amsterdam / Philadelphia

The paper used in this publication meets the minimum requirements of the American National Standard for Information Sciences – Permanence of Paper for Printed Library Materials, ANSI z39.48-1984.

Library of Congress Cataloging-in-Publication Data

Cognola, Federica.
  Syntactic Variation and Verb Second : A German dialect in Northern Italy / Federica Cognola.
  p.   cm. (Linguistik Aktuell/Linguistics Today, ISSN 0166-0829 ; v. 201)
 "This monograph is a fully revised version of my PhD dissertation defended in March 2010 at the University of Padua."
 Includes bibliographical references and index.
 1. German language--Dialects--Italy--Fersina River Valley. 2. German language-- Grammar--Syntax. 3. German language--Verb. I. Title.
PF5364.F4C64   2013
437.945'385--dc23   2012039316
ISBN 978 90 272 5584 6 (Hb ; alk. paper)
ISBN 978 90 272 7244 7 (Eb)

© 2013 – John Benjamins B.V.
No part of this book may be reproduced in any form, by print, photoprint, microfilm, or any other means, without written permission from the publisher.

John Benjamins Publishing Co. · P.O. Box 36224 · 1020 ME Amsterdam · The Netherlands
John Benjamins North America · P.O. Box 27519 · Philadelphia PA 19118-0519 · USA

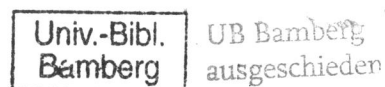

Table of contents

Acknowledgments IX
List of abbreviations XI

CHAPTER 1
Introduction 1

CHAPTER 2
Mòcheno and the V2 phenomenon 19
2.1 Introduction 19
2.2 On the V2 phenomenon 22
    2.2.1 V2 in Continental Germanic 23
    2.2.2 V2 in Old Romance languages 30
    2.2.3 Triggers for movement 39
    2.2.4 Partial conclusions 42
2.3 Mòcheno as a V2 language 43
    2.3.1 Rowley's (2003) account 43
    2.3.2 On the presence of the *Korrelate* of V2 45
    2.3.3 On the structure of Mòcheno left periphery 50
    2.3.4 Against an account in terms of optionality/grammar competition 67
2.4 Conclusions 74

CHAPTER 3
The syntax of subject pronouns 77
3.1 Introduction 77
3.2 Three classes of subject pronouns in Mòcheno 79
    3.2.1 Sentence-initial position 80
    3.2.2 The coordination test 83
    3.2.3 Focalization and isolation 84
    3.2.4 Partial conclusions 87

3.3 Distribution of subject pronouns 89
    3.3.1 Distribution of subject reduced forms in main clauses 89
    3.3.2 Reduced forms are not agreement markers 94
    3.3.3 Distribution of subject reduced forms in embedded clauses 96
    3.3.4 Distribution of strong subject pronouns 102
3.4 Conclusions 109

CHAPTER 4
Satisfaction of EPP and realization of subjects 113
4.1 Introduction 113
4.2 Fronted constituents and EPP 119
    4.2.1 Fronted operators 119
    4.2.2 The hanging-topic construction 125
    4.2.3 Simple preposing 127
    4.2.4 Left-dislocation 130
4.3 Sentences with a fronted nominative subject 132
    4.3.1 Fronted subjects and the EPP feature 133
4.4 Conclusions 136

CHAPTER 5
Mòcheno as a partial *pro*-drop language 139
5.1 Introduction 139
5.2 Mòcheno as a partial *pro*-drop language 141
    5.2.1 Properties of *pro*-drop languages 141
    5.2.2 Licensing of null referential subjects and rich agreement 144
    5.2.3 Free subject inversion and that-trace effects 145
    5.2.4 Expletive null subjects and generic pronouns 148
    5.2.5 Proposed analysis 150
5.3 The syntax of DP subjects 154
    5.3.1 DP subjects as informationally marked XPs 154
    5.3.2 DP subjects in sentences with a fronted operator 159
5.4 Conclusions 162

CHAPTER 6
Multiple access to CP and asymmetric *pro*-drop 167
6.1 Introduction 167
6.2 Multiple access to CP and EPP 170
    6.2.1 Bottleneck effects 171
    6.2.2 Combination of constituents in the left periphery 173
    6.2.3 Again on simple-preposed topics and EPP 176

       6.2.4   Grewendorf/Poletto's account   180
       6.2.5   An alternative account for main declarative clauses   181
       6.2.6   Sentences with a fronted operator   187
       6.2.7   Partial conclusions   192
   6.3   On the syntax of embedded clauses   194
       6.3.1   Position of the finite verb in embedded clauses   195
       6.3.2   Form of the complementiser and CP structure   197
       6.3.3   Realization of the subject and syntax of the finite verb   203
   6.4   Conclusions   209

CHAPTER 7
Conclusions   213

References   221
Appendix   235
Index   323

Acknowledgments

This monograph is a fully revised version of my PhD dissertation defended in March 2010 at the University of Padua.

I would like to thank Paola Benincà for her support, her suggestions over the years and for having been a model and a source of inspiration to me in her approach to linguistics. I also want to express my gratitude to my supervisor Cecilia Poletto for discussing many complex Mòcheno data with me and for helping me to shape my ideas.

I would never have been able to write this book without the constant help and support of my colleagues and friends at the University of Trento, in particular Ermenegildo Bidese, Patrizia Cordin, Lucia Galvagni and Andrea Padovan. Many thanks to Leo Toller of the Institute for the Promotion of the Mòcheno Language and Culture in Palù del Fersina for his invaluable help in collecting the data and for being my main consultant in Palù. My gratitude goes to the 45 people from all over the Fersina valley who took part in the fieldwork and to the two main informants from Fierozzo and Roveda: Cristina Moltrer and Marina Froner.

Many thanks to Werner Abraham, Birgit Alber, Paola Benincà, Kristine Bentzen, Theresa Biberauer, Ermenegildo Bidese, Walter Breu, Jan Casalicchio, Guglielmo Cinque, Patrizia Cordin, Cecilia Poletto, Roland Hinterhölzl, Andrea Padovan, Federica Ricci Garotti, Anthony Rowley, Lenka Scholze, Alessandra Tomaselli, Marit Westergaard and Chiara Zanini for discussions I have had with them on various aspects of my work. I would also like to thank the series editors, Werner Abraham and Elly van Gelderen, for accepting my monograph for publication and for their comments and suggestions on previous versions of the book. Thanks to Rachel Murphy for editing the English. All remaining errors are my own.

My work has been supported by a grant from the Caritro Foundation (Bando 2010 per progetti nell'ambito delle scienze umanistiche) from May 2011 to April 2012 and, since May 2012, by a grant from the Autonomous Province of Trento (Bandi-Post-Doc-PAT-2011). I thank them for their generous support.

This book is dedicated to my parents Carol and Guido.

List of abbreviations

All examples have been glossed according to the *Leipzig Glossing Rules* (www.eva.mpg.de/lingua/resources/glossing-rules.php). I added some specific abbreviations for Mòcheno.

Abbreviation	Meaning
ACC	accusative
AUX-FUT	future auxiliary
AUX-PASS	passive auxiliary
COND.3SG	conditional tense, third person singular
DAT	dative
EXPL	expletive element
IMP-PRON	impersonal pronoun
NEG	negation
NOM	nominative
OBJ-CL.3.SG.M	object clitic pronoun, third person singular masculine
OBJ-CL.3.SG.F	object clitic pronoun, third person singular feminine
OBJ-CL.3.SG.N	object clitic pronoun, third person singular neuter
OBJ-CL.3.PL	object clitic pronoun, third person plural
PRS.1SG	present tense, first person singular
PRS.2SG	present tense, second person singular
PRS.3SG	present tense, third person singular
PRS.3PL	present tense, third person plural
PST.3SG	past tense, third person singular
PTCP	past participle
SBJ-CL.1.SG	subject clitic pronoun, first person singular
SBJ-CL.2.SG	subject clitic pronoun, second person singular
SBJ-CL.3.SG.M	subject clitic pronoun, third person singular masculine
SBJ-CL.3.SG.F	subject clitic pronoun, third person singular feminine
SBJ-CL.1.PL	subject clitic pronoun, first person plural
SBJ-CL.2.PL	subject clitic pronoun, second person plural
SBJ-CL.3.PL	subject clitic pronoun, third person plural
SBJ-WEAK.1.SG	subject weak pronoun, first person singular
SBJ-WEAK.2.SG	subject weak pronoun, second person singular
SBJ-WEAK.3.SG.M	subject weak pronoun, third person singular, masculine
SBJ-WEAK.3.SG.F	subject weak pronoun, third person singular, feminine

Abbreviation	Meaning
SBJ-WEAK.1.PL	subject weak pronoun, first person plural
SBJ-STRONG.1.SG	subject strong pronoun, first person singular
SBJ-STRONG.2.SG	subject strong pronoun, second person singular
SBJ-STRONG.3.SG.M	subject strong pronoun, third person singular, masculine
SBJ-STRONG.3.SG.F	subject strong pronoun, third person singular, feminine
SBJ-STRONG.1.PL	subject strong pronoun, first person plural
SBJ-STRONG.2.PL	subject strong pronoun, second person plural
SBJ-STRONG.3.PL	subject strong pronoun, third person plural
SUBJ.PRS.3SG	subjunctive present tense, third person singular

CHAPTER 1

Introduction

This book investigates the syntax of the finite verb in the dialect Mòcheno (known in the German dialectological tradition as *Fersentalerisch*), a minority language (*Sprachinseldialekt*) spoken by around 580 people (Alber 2010: 33)[1] living in three villages – Palù/Palai, Fierozzo/Vlarutz and Roveda/Oachleit – in the Fersina valley in Trentino, Northern Italy.[2]

As a German dialect spoken in a linguistic island, Mòcheno has been studied by traditional dialectologists (Battisti 1925; Kranzmayer 1956; Bauer 1962; Wurzer 1977; Hornung 1979 a.o.) seeking conservative lexical and morpho-phonological characteristics lost in modern varieties of German and Romance. More recently, starting with the studies by Rowley (1982, 1986, 2003), research has focused on the actual structure of the language, which has been analysed on all linguistic levels.

One of the most striking aspects of the grammar of Mòcheno reported in the literature (Rowley 2003; Togni 1990; Cognola 2010 a.o.) is the strong presence of variation and optionality, especially at the syntactic level. These are the aspects investigated in this book.

---

1. As discussed by Alber (2010), who uses data extrapolated from the 2000 census and articles published in the local journal *Lem*, Mòcheno is still spoken by almost all families in the villages of Palù and Roveda and by only half of the families in the village of Fierozzo (see also Rowley 1986 and Cognola 2011a). Mòcheno has nearly disappeared from the village of Frassilongo, the municipality to which Roveda belongs.

2. The language island is what remains of a vast area colonised by German-speaking farmers, most of whom came from South and North Tyrol between the XII and XIII centuries. According to historians (Gerola 1929; Rogger 1979; Piatti 1996 a.o.), in the Middle Age the German-speaking area was much larger than it is today and included the linguistic island of Pinè and many villages in the Valsugana (Vignola Falesina, Ronchi, Roncegno etc.), which are nowadays fully Romance speaking. Focusing on the colonization of the Fersina valley, which took place in the form of "scattered farms" (*Hofanlagen*), the areas that were first colonised, presumably at the beginning of the XIII century, were those of Frassilongo and Roveda. Successively, around the middle of the XIII century, farmers from this area occupied the mountain of Fierozzo creating new settlements. The presence of German-speaking settlers in the village of Palù is attested from the XIV century on; it seems highly probable that a contribution to this settlement came from the nearby German-speaking colony of Pinè.

Two examples of how syntactic variation manifests itself in Mòcheno are given in (1), where two macro-phenomena central to the linguistic analysis of Germanic languages are illustrated: OV/VO word orders and the V2 phenomenon. As can be seen in (1a, b), in Mòcheno both VO and OV word orders are possible in main clauses. Analogously, the finite verb can, but does not have to, appear in the second sentence position (1c, d).[3]

(1) a. Gester   hòt=er   kaft   s puach
       yesterday has=SBJ-CL.3.SG.M   bought   the book
    b. Gester   hòt=er   s puach   kaft
       yesterday has=SBJ-CL.3.SG.M   the book   bought
    c. Gester   der Mario   hòt   kaft   a puach
       yesterday the Mario   has-PRS.3SG bought   a book
    d. Gester   hòt   der Mario   kaft   a puach
       yesterday has-PRS.3SG the Mario   bought   a book
       'Yesterday he/Mario bought a book'

The type of syntactic variation illustrated in (1) cannot be possibly ascribed to sociolinguistic variables, but is characteristic of the Mòcheno language as it is spoken in all villages and by all people.

In order to account for variation, the first studies (including Zamboni 1979: 90; Heller 1979: 119; Rowley 2003: 289, 291) emphasised the role of contact with local Romance varieties: the regional variety of Italian (Berruto 1995) spoken in Trentino and the Trentino dialect. With respect to the macro-phenomena considered above, the Romance contact varieties are, in fact, consistent VO languages with a residual V2 rule that only involves sentences with a fronted operator and pronominal subjects (Rizzi 1991; Poletto 1993). It has been suggested that all sentences divergent from the German ones owed their structure to the influence of contact Romance varieties, whereas those which adhered to the German pattern retained their original syntax. Although scholars who have conjectured that the

---

3. According to Haider's (2010b) characterization, Mòcheno must be classified as a "third-type" language, together with Yiddish and Old High German, since it does not display either strict VO or strict OV. Abraham (p.c.) suggests that the characterization as "third type" might also be used for the V2 rule: Mòcheno (and Old Romance in general) exemplify, according to this proposal, a third type, different from both strict V2 languages (as German) and non-V2 languages. Note, that the only past form available in Mòcheno is the past participle (*Partizip*), since the simple past (*Präteritum*) has disappeared. The past participle forms are reduced, i.e. the prefix *ge-* is reduced according to phonological rules (see Rowley 1986; Alber 2010; see Cognola 2011b for the hypothesis that reduction is triggered in some cases by semantics). Both facts are typical of Southern German dialects (see Abraham/Conradie 2001 and Abraham 2012 for the loss of simple past and Schirmunski 1962 for *ge-* reduction in German dialects).

syntactic variation seen in Mòcheno is the result of contact with Romance languages have never explicitly cited Kroch's (1989) "double-base hypothesis", their ideas on language variation undoubtedly resemble his. The parallel between the two theoretical approaches becomes even more apparent when we consider that a crucial tenet of the double-base hypothesis is that language variation is a direct consequence of language contact and bilingualism. In the case of Middle English, for instance, the innovative grammar was that of the Scandinavian settlers, which co-existed with the local English varieties in a bilingual environment (Pintzuk 1999; Kroch/Taylor 2000; Pintzuk/Tsoulas/Warner 2001). Mòcheno speakers have all been bilingual since at least the middle of the XVIII century, which seems to reinforce the hypothesis that language variation is a consequence of language contact in a bilingual situation.[4]

Despite its appeal and the ease with which it seems to explain the data, one of the goals of this book is to demonstrate that the double-base hypothesis cannot be applied to Mòcheno. Upon examining a more extensive range of detailed data than those presented in (1), the idea of contact is shown to be untenable. Data challenging the double-base hypothesis are discussed in detail in the following chapters and a novel account of the syntactic variation observed in Mòcheno is proposed, one which shows this variation to be generated by syntactic rules internal to a single grammar. A comprehensive discussion of the Mòcheno data confirms the conclusions arrived at in the most recent studies on language variation and change (Hinterhölzl 2009 on Old High German and Taylor/Pintzuk 2012 on Old English a.o.), which offer an explanation for syntactic variation by hypothesising the presence of a single grammar in which variation is determined by the interplay between syntax and information structure.

This study on the syntax of Mòcheno is based on the most extensive collection of syntactic data ever made for this language, carried out on two separate occasions.

In my PhD dissertation (Cognola 2010), I examined the syntax of one variety only, that spoken in the village of Palù, which I investigated in 26 interviews with one very good consultant. The decision to work with one person was determined by the need to control for sociolinguistic variables and to exclude as far as

---

4. The fact that the population of the Fersina valley has been bilingual since at least the middle of the XVIII century is evidenced by the oldest tests written in this language: the translation of the *Parable of the prodigal son* collected by Lunelli at the beginning of the XVIII century (during the collection of dialectal data from all the valleys of Trentino) and a document from 1798 written in Italian by a pedlar from the valley (*kromer* in the local language), p.c. Leo Toller. Both documents prove that around 1800 the middle-aged inhabitants of the valley had command of both languages.

possible any factors that might interfere with syntactic variation, and to obtain the most reliable data possible in order to draw accurate conclusions on the grammar of Mòcheno. The speaker who worked with me was a middle-aged man (40 when we began, 43 at the end of the study) who has always lived in the village of Palù and has always spoken Mòcheno in his family; he learnt the local Romance varieties at the kindergarden. He works for the local Institute for the Promotion of the Mòcheno Language and Culture, where he is responsible for linguistic and cultural projects. During the course of our 26 interviews, he was asked to translate sentences from Italian into Mòcheno and to give grammaticality judgments about sentences designed to test theoretical hypotheses. The fieldwork carried out in Palù for my PhD thesis provided a set of very detailed data on empirical phenomena such as the syntax of (i) finite and non-finite verb forms, (ii) DP subjects and subject pronouns and (iii) the structure of the left periphery, on the basis of which I was able to put forward a precise hypothesis which made sense of the observed syntactic variation. The theory arrived at for the Palù variety is the backbone of this work and the starting point for my subsequent hypotheses.

After the preliminary work, the next task was to deal with sociolinguistic variables, in order to ascertain whether or not the hypothesis arrived at based on the language of one speaker of one variety could be extended to the grammar of Mòcheno generally. So, I wrote a questionnaire to test the validity of these fine-grained hypotheses crucial for investigating the syntax of Mòcheno. The first four questions of the questionnaire are intended to investigate the syntax of subject pronouns and DP subjects in three syntactic contexts: wh-main interrogatives, main declarative clauses and embedded clauses. All consulted speakers were first asked to translate a stimulus sentence into Mòcheno and then to evaluate a series of alternatives selected in order to set the limits of possible variation for particular phenomena, such as the syntax of subject pronouns or OV/VO syntax. Sentences 5 to 15 aim at investigating the structure of the left periphery through a grammaticality judgment task involving single sentences or pairs of sentences. In the all questionnaires from Fierozzo and in some questionnaires from Roveda, two more sentences on the possibility of having both OV and VO in main declarative clauses might be present: for these two varieties it was, in fact, sometimes necessary to test whether both word order patterns were possible, in particular whether OV was permitted. For the Palù dialect it was not necessary to add an extra sentence, since both OV/VO orders generally appear in the responses of the consultants.

The hypotheses put forward for Palù were investigated in extensive fieldwork which involved a significant proportion of the Mòcheno-speaking population, selected according to three main sociolinguistic criteria: (i) age, (ii) gender and (iii) village/farm of residence (Labov 1966, 1972, 2001; Trudgill 1992; Berruto

Table 1.1 Sex of the informants

Village	Young	Middle-aged	Elderly
Palù	MM; FFF	MM; FFF	MM; FFF
Fierozzo	MMMM; F	MMMM; F	MMMM; F
Roveda	M; FFFF	M; FFFF	MM; FFF

1995 and references cited there, Togni 1990 for the role of the farm of residence in the specific case of Mòcheno).[5] A total of 45 people were interviewed, 15 from each municipality of the valley selected according to their age: 5 young (under 30), 5 middle-aged (between 30 and 60) and 5 elderly (over 60) speakers. I tried to include equal numbers of men and women in each group, but, as can be seen in Table 1.1, this was not always possible. In Palù, I achieved a good gender balance (2 men, 3 women) in all the groups; in Roveda only one of the young and middle-aged informants is male and two elderly men participated. It was difficult to convince men to take part in the study in these two villages: most of the men I contacted were uncooperative. It seems that all the people who refused to be interviewed were fluent speakers who had their own reasons for not wishing to participate.[6] This was not the case in Fierozzo, where some families no longer speak Mòcheno. According to Rowley (1986), only half of the families resident in Fierozzo speak the minority language, a finding also confirmed by Alber (2010) and Cognola (2011a). The reduced number of people speaking Mòcheno in the municipality of Fierozzo is reflected in the division between men and women in the table above: the young people whom I interviewed were, in fact, almost the only ones who still speak Mòcheno in Fierozzo – hence the imbalance between men and women. The situation is similar with the two other groups of speakers from Fierozzo, although not as extreme.

---

5. According to my knowledge, only the role of diatopic variables has been investigated in previous studies on Mòcheno (see Togni's (1990) observation on the role of the scattered farms and Rowley's (2003) grammar for the differences between the three varieties). As discussed below, my research shows that there is an effect of diatopic variables in the Mòcheno grammar involving both villages and scattered farms within one single village. Age plays a role too, whereas no differences connected to gender are detected. The variation due to sociolinguistic variables does not involve macro-phenomena of the Mòcheno grammar, such as the presence of OV/VO syntax or the syntax of the finite verb, but micro-phenomena.

6. The overall impression is that many very good speakers of Mòcheno did not take part in the study because they were put off by the standardization of the minority language and complained that they are no good speakers because they do not know the new rules introduced for the standardization of Mòcheno.

I had wanted to avoid the inclusion of members of the same families in the fieldwork, but this was not possible. Among the informants from Roveda, ROVE-EO and ROVE-MB are mother and daughter, as ROVE-BL and ROVE-SO. In Palù, PALÙ-MP is the son of PALÙ-MT. As far as Fierozzo is concerned, informants ROVE-MG, ROVE-CP and ROVE-GP are cousins.

In order to keep the number of relations to a minimum, I consulted speakers from different scattered farms (*Höfe*), since members of the same family tend to live in the same locality. Moreover, including people from the different micro-localities of the municipality allows the reconstruction of a much more accurate picture of Mòcheno, especially in the light of Togni's (1990: 172) observation for the Palù dialect that there may be a connection between syntactic variation and a speaker's family group. Basing the study on linguistic data from different families across the municipalities allowed me to investigate both syntactic variation and Togni's observation thoroughly.

As far as micro-toponyms are concerned, the village of Palù is split up in two main areas: *inderpòch* and *auserpòch*, and all consulted speakers agree that there is slight linguistic variation between the two areas. Lenzer, Orastòll, Simeter, Staller, Stèffener, Stelder, Tural and Vrottn are the *Höfe* "beyond" the glen (*auserpòch*), while Battister, Eckar, Jorgar, Knoppn, Tolar and Tasainer are "within" the river (*inderpòch*). As can be seen in Table 1.2, both areas of Palù and the different farms are well-represented.

Table 1.2 Informants from Palù

Village	Farm	Informant	Sex; age
Palù	Battister	PALÙ-ET	M; 60
		PALÙ-EO	F; 67
	Lenzer	PALÙ-MO	M; 38
	Orastòll	PALÙ-VL	F; 14
		PALÙ-MT	F; 75
	Simeter	PALÙ-ST	F; 18
		PALÙ-LT	M; 75
	Stèffener	PALÙ-PB	F; 31
		PALÙ-GL	F; 55
		PALÙ-MP	M; 55
		PALÙ-IP	F; 79
	Tolar	PALÙ-NI	M; 16
		PALÙ-LB	F; 29
	Jorgar	PALÙ-HN	F; 59
	Tural	PALÙ-FM	M; 24

Table 1.3 Informants from Fierozzo

Village	Farm	Informant	Sex; age
Fierozzo-S.Francesco/Auserpèrg	Gaiger	FIER-EI	M; 70
	Joppereck	FIER-PM	M; 51
	Ouberroudler	FIER-RR	F; 38
	Unterroudler	FIER-AP	M; 27
Fierozzo-S.Felice/Mittelpèrg	Boler	FIER-CP	F; 19
	Casar	FIER-GG	M; 39
	Groan	FIER-SB	M; 27
	Meidln	FIER-GM	M; 68
	Simeter	FIER-MG	M; 19
		FIER-GP	M; 20
		FIER-AM	M; 67
Fierozzo-S.Felice/Inderpèrg	Markl	FIER-GAM	F; 38
		FIER-RB	M; 47
	Soa	FIER-COP	M; 78
	Tuneger	FIER-AS	F; 77

The municipality of Fierozzo is composed of three main areas throughout which the farms are scattered: S.Francesco-*Auserperg* is the area closest to Pergine, *Inderperg* is the area on the border with Palù, and S.Felice-*Mitterperg* lies between the other two localities. S.Francesco includes the following localities: Joppern, Pletzn, Plötzer, Strapiser, Markl, Laner, Roudler and Prigln; we find the localities of Runker, Stoller, Hosler, Houver, Boler, Simeter, Kasar and Tuneger in *Mitterperg*, and Schlomper, Markl and Malzer in *Inderperg*. As already mentioned, only about half the families in the municipality of Fierozzo still speak Mòcheno; the number of speakers is particularly low in the localities of S.Francesco/Auserpèrg. Table 1.3 shows the profiles of the consulted speakers in the municipality of Fierozzo. The *Höfe* are not all represented because Mòcheno is not spoken in all of them. Unlike Palù, speakers from Fierozzo do not perceive micro-variation in the Mòcheno spoken in their municipality, but are aware of the macro-phenomena differentiating their variety from those of Palù and Roveda.

The village of Roveda (which belongs to the municipality of Frassilongo) is divided into three main areas: *Unterpèrg*, *Mittelpèrg* and *Ouberpèrg*. This last locality is now the most populated of the village and is a relatively recent settlement, characterised by new buildings and hotels, where people moved from *Unterpèrg* and *Mittelpèrg* in the sixties. For this reason, the internal micro-variation within the Roveda variety has probably seen the greatest reduction. That *Ouberpèrg* is the most densely populated area of Roveda is reflected in the figures in Table 1.4.

Table 1.4 Informants from Roveda

Village	Farm	Informant	Sex; age
Roveda/Ouberpèrg	Balschn	ROVE-CF	F; 32
		ROVE-MP	M; 38
	Kairo	ROVE-AF	F; 16
		ROVE-EF	F; 18
	Kamavrunt	ROVE-SO	F; 13
		ROVE-LF	F; 27
		ROVE-BL	F; 37
		ROVE-RF	F; 45
	Tingerla	ROVE-IP	M; 27
		ROVE-MO	M; 69
	Vrunt	ROVE-DP	M; 63
Roveda/Mittelpèrg	Mittelpèrg	ROVE-MB	F; 33
		ROVE-EO	F; 59
Roveda/Unterpèrg	Unterpèrg-Kear	ROVE-JP	F; 71
	Taufner	ROVE-RP	F; 68

I interviewed the consultants in their homes or in the Institute for the Promotion of the Mòcheno Language and Culture during the summer of 2011 (first interview 7th June, last interview 16th September). Each meeting lasted about an hour and all the responses given by the consultants were written by myself. The tasks were proposed to consultants randomly in order to avoid two or more tasks with the same phenomenon. In the Appendix, the taks are ordered according to topic. All interviews were recorded: the transcripts of each interview are given in the Appendix.

The fieldwork was followed by follow-up interviews with the informant from Palù who took part to the data collection for my PhD dissertation and two women, one from Fierozzo, and one from Roveda. The woman from Fierozzo is aged 31 and lives in Fierozzo-*Inderpèrg*; the other is 35 and lives in Roveda-*Mittelpèrg*. Mòcheno is their mother tongue and they speak it to their children, who are growing up bilingual. They are absolutely reliable speakers of Mòcheno and can be trusted. 48 consultants have been involved in the study – a number that represents nearly the 10% of the Mòcheno population.

On the basis of the data collected in my preliminary work on the Palù variety and on the extensive fieldwork carried out in the three municipalities of the valley, I propose a theoretical account for the syntactic variation observed in Mòcheno (2).

(2) a. *Gester   hòt=er   kaft   s puach*
        yesterday has=SBJ-CL.3.SG.M   bought the book
    b. *Gester   hòt=er   s puach kaft*
        yesterday has=SBJ-CL.3.SG.M   the book bought
    c. *Gester   der Mario hòt   kaft   a puach*
        yesterday the Mario has-PRS.3SG   bought a book
    d. *Gester   hòt   der Mario kaft   a puach*
        yesterday has-PRS.3SG   the Mario bought a book
        'Yesterday he/Mario bought a book'

The premise of this book is that the double-base hypothesis or indeed the contact hypothesis generally should be seen almost as a "last-resort-hypothesis", resorted to when all other explanations have failed (Svenonius 2000: 280). The first consequence of this shift in perspective on syntactic variation is that an attempt is made to account for the facts observed in (2) by starting with the idea that all word orders accepted by speakers result from the application of rules internal to one grammar. Hypotheses about speakers having access to two different grammars do not need to be applied. This shift in the way things are looked at leads to a reformulation of the starting hypothesis to be tested in the book, which is no longer that syntactic variation is due to the fact that Mòcheno speakers have access to two grammars with different parameter settings, but that Mòcheno has a V2 rule similar to that of Old Romance languages (and not to that of German), in which the movement of the finite verb to CP co-exists with multiple access to the left periphery.

That the V2 phenomenon must be understood much abstractly as the movement of the finite verb to a lower head of the left periphery in all main clauses, regardless of the linear position of the finite verb, is an idea originally proposed by Benincà (1984) for Old Romance languages and developed for other languages such as Old French by Adams (1987), Old Spanish (Fontana 1993) and Rhetoromance varieties (Poletto 2002). According to this hypothesis, the movement of the finite verb to CP is unrelated to its actual linear position within the clause, the latter being assumed to be governed by the structure of CP available in a particular language, or – if we assume that all languages share the same articulated structure of the left periphery (Rizzi 1997; Benincà 2001), by the application of some other constraints blocking multiple access to CP (such as Relativised Minimality effects, see Rizzi 1990, 2004; Poletto 2002; Roberts 2004). The suggestion is that in Old Romance languages the finite verb had to move to CP in all main clauses (as it does in modern Germanic V2 languages) giving rise to phenomena that are ungrammatical in most modern Romance varieties, such as subject-inversion, and that this movement took place within an articulated left periphery, identical to that of modern varieties. The coexistence of the V2 phenomenon with an articulated left periphery is not only a characteristic of Old Romance; it was also found in Germanic languages, at least in their older stages. Roberts (1996, 1997) noted cases of V3 or V4 in Old English, in similar syntactic/pragmatic conditions to those identified for Romance languages. The fact that the V2 rule can also coexist with an articulated left periphery in Germanic languages is very relevant to this study, since it indicates that my hypothesis that Mòcheno is a Germanic language which should be analysed as a V2 language with a split-CP is consistent with empirical facts also observed in other Germanic languages.[7]

One common aspect shared by most V2 languages with an articulated left periphery, such as Old Romance varieties and Old English, is that not all fronted constituents "count" in the same way for the V2 constraint, i.e. one does not find all typical V2 phenomena with all classes of fronted constituents (see in particular Benincà 1995, 2006; Poletto 2002; Jouitteau 2010; Holmberg 2012). For Old Romance, Benincà (1995, 2006) hypothesises that the only class of fronted XPs that "count" for the V2 rule are operators, which means that the V2 effect is caused by the finite verb moving to Focus^0 in all main declarative sentences and by the fronting of an XP to Spec,FocusP. Once Spec and head of FocusP are filled, it is possible to have topicalised XPs, which are realised syntactically as left-dislocations and are hosted in dedicated TopicPs above, as occurs in modern Romance languages (Benincà 2001). This means that operators "count" for the V2 rule, whereas left-dislocations do not; similar conclusions are reached by Poletto (2002) for Rhetoromance and by Roberts (1996) for Old English, where V3/V4 cases seem to have been restricted to sentences in which the higher constituents are left-dislocated.[8] These data on various languages in which the V2 phenomenon coexists with an articulated left periphery indicate that multiple access to the CP layer can co-occur with V2 and that this coexistence is not unsystematic or arbitrary, but is ruled by precise syntactic and pragmatic constraints. In the cases cited, V3 and V4 word orders are only allowed if the lower XP is hosted in FocusP and the higher ones are in TopicP (realised syntactically as left-dislocations).[9]

---

7. The parallel between the empirical facts detected in Mòcheno and those identified in the older stages of English runs counter to an analysis of the syntactic variation found in Mòcheno in terms of contact with modern Romance languages due to bilingualism, and supports the idea of the central role of Old and modern Romance varieties in reinforcing and supporting a Germanic system originally characterised by syntactic variation. See Benincà (1994) and Cognola (2009) for such an approach to contact in the syntactic domain.

8. For cases of V3 in Old High German, see Tomaselli (1995).

9. As extensively discussed in Holmberg (2012), the pragmatical contribution made by the fronted XP in V2 languages varies in individual languages. For convenience, I focus here on

In the first part of the book, Mòcheno is shown to be typologically very close to V2 languages with an articulated left periphery which means that most of the predictions made by Benincà's theory on Old Romance languages also hold for it. This initial result, which is supported by the wide empirical basis of this study, is the foundation for the shift proposed in this book, in which Mòcheno is no longer compared with modern Germanic languages (a comparison that led to the unproductive account of the facts in terms of the presence or absence of a phenomenon, see above), but with languages displaying the same characteristics (although they belong to a different language family). The attribution of Mòcheno to the right typological family allows us to account of the facts, describing them not in terms of the presence or absence of a phenomenon caused by the availability of two grammars with different parameter settings, but as different manifestations of V2 within one single grammar, in which V2 coexists with an articulated left periphery and obeys precise rules internal to one system.

Having demonstrated the rationale for the change of perspective from which, in the rest of the book, the empirical facts are examined, and after showing that Mòcheno belongs typologically with the Old Romance, rather than the modern Germanic, V2 languages, in the second part of the book I give a theoretical account of the particular type of V2 exhibited by Mòcheno, addressing two questions: why Mòcheno differs from Old Romance and how this asymmetry can be accounted for.

The syntax of the subject (realised as a DP and or a pronoun) is key to answering both these questions, since it interacts in a complex and intricate way with the movement of the finite verb to CP and with the licensing of *pro*. Focusing first on pronominal subjects, I demonstrate that Mòcheno has three subject pronominal forms – strong, weak (in the sense of Cardinaletti/Starke 1999) and clitic pronouns – whose distribution is linked to the syntactic nature of the fronted XP: when this is an operator or a simple-preposed XP a pronominal subject has to be realised as a clitic enclitic to the finite verb. Strong and weak pronouns cannot follow the finite verb. On the other hand, when the fronted XP is a hanging-topic or a left-dislocated XP the subject can be realised by a weak or a strong preverbal pronoun. These facts are illustrated in (3), where we can see that with a fronted operator the pronominal subject has to be realised as an enclitic pronoun (3a, b), whereas when the fronted XP is a hanging-topic, the subject pronoun has to be either a preverbal weak or a strong form (3c, d).

Old Romance languages and Old English, which are the most relevant languages for Mòcheno: Old Romance is important because of its contact with Mòcheno, and Old English because it is a Germanic language which displays similar phenomena connected to V2.

(3) a. *Benn hòt=se kaft s puach?*
when has=SBJ-CL.3SG.F bought the book
b. **Benn de /si hòt*
when SBJ-WEAK.3.SG.F/SBJ-STRONG.3.SG.F has-PRS.3SG
de /si kaft s puach?
SBJ-WEAK.3.SG.F/SBJ-STRONG.3.SG.F bought the book
'When did she buy the book?'
c. *Der Mario$_j$, de /si*
the Mario SBJ-WEAK.3.SG.F/SBJ-STRONG.3.SG.F
hòt=en tsechen der sell tepp$_j$
has=OBJ-CL.3.SG.M seen the that stupid
d. **Der Mario$_j$, hòt=se=en tsechen*
the Mario has=SBJ-CL.3.SG.F=OBJ-CL.3.SG.M seen
der sell tepp$_j$
the that stupid
'As for Mario, she has seen that stupid'

The hypothesis defended in this book is that the distribution of subject pronominal forms is linked to the fronted XP because Mòcheno is a V2 language, otherwise the relationship between a fronted XP and a class of subject pronouns would remain unclear. An important part of the hypothesis is the observation that in Mòcheno the relationship between the realization of the subject and the class the constituent belongs to follows naturally from the fact that not all XPs "count" in the same way for V2. This phenomenon has been discussed in the literature on V2 languages with an articulated left periphery. In the specific case of Mòcheno, I propose that the type of fronted XP not only has an effect on the V2, but also on the realization of the pronominal subject. That strong and weak subject pronouns "count" for V2 since they are maximal categories, whereas clitics do not because they are syntactic heads, is only part of the story. The ban on having strong and weak subject pronouns following the finite verb (no subject-verb inversion) when the fronted XP "counts" for V2, i.e. when it is either an operator (focus or interrogative wh-element) or a simple-preposed XP, is completely unexpected.

In order to account for the strong connection between the type of fronted XP and the realization of subject pronouns, which cannot be explained by the facts documented in the literature on Old Romance languages, I have decided to follow those analyses of the V2 phenomenon that link the movement of the finite verb to CP with the licensing of *pro* (Benincà 1984; Platzack 1986, 1987; Tomaselli 1990; Holmberg/Platzack 1995; Roberts 2010 a.o.). I think that the Mòcheno data, particularly those involving the realization of the pronominal subject, can only be accounted for by clearly explaining the interactions between the syntax of finite verbs, subject clitics and the licensing of *pro*.

I suggest that the connection between the movement of the finite verb, the fronting of one XP to CP (V2) and the realization of subject pronouns is that all these phenomena involve the same FP. I assume that this FP is SubjP, the existence of which has been suggested independently by Rizzi (2006), Cardinaletti (1997, 2004) and Rizzi/Shlonsky (2007), who propose that in Romance languages like Italian the realization of the subject involves two FPs: a lower FP (AgrSP) encoding all ϕ subject features and a higher FP, in the Spec of which subjects are hosted. According to Rizzi, SubjP is a criterial A-position whose head is endowed with an EPP feature: the subject has to move to the Spec position of this FP in order to satisfy the EPP feature and is "frozen in place" after satisfaction of the Subject criterion. This characterization of SubjP allows us to make sense not only of sentences with a fronted nominative DP subject, but also of quirky (non-Nominative) subjects, where the fronted XP is the pragmatic subject but does not agree with the finite verb. The theory that the realization of the subject involves two FPs in some languages is somehow reminiscent of the differentiation between pragmatic and syntactic subjects: the latter is the constituent agreeing with the finite verb, whereas the former is the XP that the sentence is about. The latter typically appears in Spec,AgrSP/TP; the former in CP. According to Rizzi's hypothesis, not all XPs appearing in the left periphery can be considered subjects, only those hosted in Spec,SubjP, which can be preceded by other constituents that are typically found in CP, like scene setters.

Another important suggestion about SubjP made by Rizzi is that the head of this FP can be realised morphologically by subject clitics in Northern Italian dialects. This view of subject clitics (see also Brandi/Cordin 1981, 1989; Haegeman 1990; Tomaselli 1990; Poletto 2000; De Crousaz/Shlonsky 2003 a.o.), which I share in this study, implies that languages with subject clitics are technically *pro-drop*, since subject clitics do not appear in AgrSP, where the presence of *pro* therefore has to be assumed.

To sum up, I suggest that in order to understand the distribution of subject pronouns in Mòcheno one must assume that in this language pragmatic and syntactic subjects are realised in two different FPs – SubjP and AgrSP – and that subject clitics are the morphological realization of $Subj^0$, whose function is to license *pro* in Spec,AgrSP. The theory that Mòcheno has to be analysed as a V2 language in which the function of subject clitic pronouns is that of licensing *pro* in Spec,AgrSP is thoroughly examined in Chapter 6, where evidence is provided that Mòcheno is a partial *pro*-drop language (Biberauer et al. 2010; Holmberg 2005 and Holmberg/Sheehan 2010).

The second aspect investigated in this study is the interaction between the realization of subjects and the V2 rule. We need to understand why subject pronouns have to appear in the clitic form whenever the fronted XP is either an operator or a simple-preposed XP, although when the fronted XP is a hanging topic or a left dislocation, both strong and weak forms are grammatical. In this book, I suggest that this connection is explained by the fact that Mòcheno is a V2 language and that SubjP is the FP involved in the two requirements of the V2 rule – movement of the finite verb and fronting of the XP.

It has been suggested (Haegeman 1997; Poletto 2002; Roberts 2004 a.o.) that the V2 rule must be captured by positing that the finite verb is moved to the lowest head of the left periphery by an EPP feature associated with the head of this FP; the EPP feature is also thought to trigger XP fronting to the Spec position of the FP hosting the finite verb. Following Rizzi (1997), it has been assumed in the literature that this FP is FinP, an FP found immediately above SubjP, where the finiteness of the clause is checked. According to this view, the difference between V2 and non-V2 languages is that in the former the finiteness of the sentence must be checked by the finite verb in every main clause, and in the latter there is no such requirement.

I put forward the hypothesis that the properties which have been attributed to FinP to account for the syntax of V2 languages are properties of SubjP: this means that in a V2 language like Mòcheno, $Subj^0$ is the head associated with the EPP feature, to which the finite verb must move in all main clauses and to the Spec of which the fronted XP has to rise. Technically, the derivation mechanism for the V2 rule that I assume for Mòcheno does not differ from previous proposals: the only change that I introduce into the theory concerns the final target of the movement of the finite verb and of XP fronting, which is not FinP but SubjP. As is clearly demonstrated in the book, $Subj^0$ is endowed with an EPP feature which forces the movement of the finite verb to its head and XP fronting to its Spec. As in Old Romance languages, only moved XPs (operators) can check the EPP feature in Spec,SubjP, hanging-topics and left dislocations cannot do so. When EPP is satisfied by a non-nominative XP, the pronominal subject has to be realised by an enclitic pronoun and the fronted XP is assumed to appear in Spec,SubjP. The finite verb moves to $Subj^0$ where it incorporates the subject clitic and *pro* is legitimated in Spec,AgrSP. EPP can be satisfied by a nominative subject only when fronted weak subjects are involved; both strong subject pronouns and DP subjects are shown to skip Spec,SubjP.

In the light of these assumptions on SubjP, the questions of what the the syntactic position of SubjP is, in particular whether it can be assumed to be in the left periphery (Cardinaletti 1997 assumes SubjP to be in IP), and whether FinP can be got rid of in the account of Mòcheno syntax must be tackled. These two questions are two sides of the same coin. In the second part of the book I propose that FinP has to be split into two different FPs: the lower one corresponds to SubjP, the higher one to an FP hosting the complementiser. These two FPs, for which

Mòcheno provides strong evidence, correspond to the two FPs assumed by Leu (2010) to be headed by the two morphological subparts of the complementiser in Germanic languages. For Mòcheno, I assume that SubjP is the subpart of FinP to the head of which the finite verb moves in all main clauses as an effect of the V2 rule (captured in terms of an EPP associated with Subj^0). SubjP corresponds to the lower head in Leu's theory, where *d-* is hosted and where the finite verb appears in main clauses. The higher FP (corresponding to FinP) hosts the *as* part of the complementiser and in the case of Mòcheno is only involved in the derivation of embedded clauses.

Returning to the two questions above, if FinP is broken down into two separate FPs, we can answer the first question positively: if SubjP corresponds to the lower FP making up FinP, then SubjP is in the left periphery, since FinP is assumed to be in CP. The answer to the second question – whether FinP can be eliminated – has to be negative: SubjP alone cannot explain the data and the presence of a higher FP connected to finiteness in embedded clauses and where a subpart of the complementiser is hosted has to be hypothesised.

The book is organised in the following way.

In Chapter 2, the V2 phenomenon is discussed from theoretical and empirical perspectives in order to establish whether or not Mòcheno displays the empirical properties generally considered to belong to V2 languages. In this chapter, I introduce the Mòcheno data investigated in the book, focusing on the syntax of the finite verb and the distribution of pronominal and nominal subjects. As discussed in detail in the chapter, Mòcheno is characterised by strong optionality at the syntactic level and displays, in an optional or reduced fashion, most of the core properties of the V2 phenomenon.

The challenge this book faces is making sense of the intriguing Mòcheno syntax introduced in Chapter 2 within the hypothesis that its syntactic variation originates from the single grammar of a V2, partial *pro*-drop language. In order to provide evidence for this theory and, most importantly, to demonstrate how the syntactic variation observed in Mòcheno can be captured through rules internal to a single grammar, in subsequent chapters I investigate the syntax of subjects, the satisfaction of the EPP feature responsible for the V2 rule and the *pro*-drop nature of Mòcheno.

In Chapter 3, I examine the syntax of subject pronouns and demonstrate that in Mòcheno there are three morphologically different subject pronominal forms (strong, weak and clitic pronouns), which have specialised for syntactic positions. Strong pronouns are shown to appear either in Topic or Focus positions, whereas weak and clitic pronouns realise the Spec and the head position of SubjP, respectively. Crucially, no subject pronoun can appear in Spec,AgrSP: I demonstrate that this position can only host *pro*.

The development of the discussion in Chapter 4 is predicated on the theory that no subject pronoun can appear in Spec,AgrSP and leads to the conclusion that there is a relationship between the distribution of subject pronouns and the fronted constituent's ability to satisfy the EPP feature responsible for the V2 effect. The subject pronoun has to be realised by an enclitic pronoun in all cases in which the fronted XP is able to satisfy EPP, and when the fronted XP cannot satisfy EPP, subject pronouns must be realised by either a strong or a weak form. I demonstrate that these constraints flow naturally from the type of V2 rule displayed by Mòcheno. Equally, the fact that EPP cannot be satisfied by all fronted constituents is shown to be a consequence of the fact that Mòcheno is an Old Romance type V2 language. In this chapter, I propose a precise hypothesis about the FP whose head is associated with the EPP feature and provide evidence that this FP is SubjP. Finally, the syntax of nominal subjects is examined and I show that when fronted, they are never able to satisfy the EPP in Spec,SubjP and, moreover, they cannot appear in Spec,AgrSP, where *pro* must again be assumed.

The type of *pro*-drop displayed by Mòcheno and its *pro* licensing mechanism are investigated in Chapter 5. I provide evidence in favour of the hypothesis that Mòcheno is a partial *pro*-drop language (Rizzi 1982; Biberauer et al. 2010 a.o.), in which free inversion is possible, along with lack of that-trace effects and expletive null subjects. In Mòcheno, licensing of referential *pro* is generally ruled out, except for the second person singular in all sentences in which the finite verb is in CP in the Fierozzo and Roveda dialects. I examine evidence supporting the theory that quasi-argumental *pro* can be licensed in Spec,AgrSP if the finite verb is in CP and a co-indexed subject appears in the sentence. In this chapter I go on to demonstrate that the way in which *pro* is licensed in Spec,AgrSP is also subject to a syntactic requirement: when there is an operator in the sentence, the presence of a subject clitic is necessary for *pro* to be licensed and the presence of a co-indexed subject (whether in the high or in the vP periphery) is not sufficient, unlike sentences with no fronted operator.

These striking data, which again point to a correlation between the satisfaction of the EPP feature (fronted operators always satisfy the EPP feature associated with Subj^0) and the realization of the subject/*pro* licensing will be explored in Chapter 6, where I tackle the derivation of sentences with multiple access to CP and that of embedded clauses. Building on the intuition that in all main declarative clauses in Mòcheno the EPP feature is satisfied by *pro*, I demonstrate that fronted constituents can skip Spec,SubjP only when the EPP feature has been satisfied by a silent category. When the EPP feature is satisfied by a moved operator, RM prevents any movement across Spec,SubjP and multiple access to CP is derived through a bi-clausal analysis with ellipsis in the higher clause (Ott 2011a, b; Merchant 2001). According to this analysis, main declarative clauses (where topics cannot be doubled by a clitic) and wh-main interrogative clauses (where all topics must be doubled by a clitic) have two different underlying structures: monoclausal and bi-clausal, respectively. This approach allows us to account for both *pro* licensing and the syntax of sentences in which several constituents appear in the left periphery. Finally, the theoretical construction arrived at for Mòcheno main declarative clauses, key to which is the assumption that Mòcheno is a partial *pro*-drop V2 language, is tested for embedded clauses and it is demonstrated that dependent clauses in Mòcheno are characterised by an absence of *pro*-drop correlated with the fact that the finite verb does not move to $Subj^0$. This examination of the syntax of embedded clauses closes the loop of the reasoning begun in Chapter 2 and developed in the subsequent chapters, with the conclusion that in Mòcheno the finite verb must move to the left periphery in all main clauses in order to license a quasi-argumental *pro* in Spec,AgrSP.

In Chapter 7, I sum up the most important results achieved in this book, discussing their relevance to both theoretical accounts of the V2 phenomenon and theories of syntactic variation. I also suggest possible future research directions in which the theory could be pursued.

CHAPTER 2

Mòcheno and the V2 phenomenon

2.1 Introduction

This chapter is devoted to a discussion of the verb-second (V2) phenomenon from an empirical and theoretical perspective, with a focus on Mòcheno, whose grammar is examined in search of the syntactic properties of the V2 rule. The aim of this discussion is, on the one hand, to deal cross-linguistically with the general empirical characteristics of the V2 rule and their theoretical accounts; on the other, to determine the syntactic behaviour of Mòcheno with respect to these characteristics. A crucial issue introduced in this chapter is that of optionality and variation at the syntactic level, which I tackle by comparing Rowley's (2003) analysis of V2 with the new one proposed in this book. The core idea of this new approach is that previous accounts failed to interpret the empirical data in the right way because they compared Mòcheno with the wrong languages: either modern German or modern contact Romance varieties. In this book, I suggest, drawing on a wide range of data, that for the syntactic phenomena under examination (the syntax of finite verbs, the V2 rule and the distribution of *pro*-drop) Mòcheno patterns like Old Romance languages and therefore must be compared with them. This approach changes the perspective from which the subject is considered and helps us to capture syntactic variation in a more objective and fruitful way.[1]

The V2 phenomenon has been studied intensively in both modern and older Germanic languages, which are all V2, except for modern English. Germanic languages demonstrate themselves to be V2 by their requirement that finite verbs be placed in second position preceded by a single arbitrary constituent; when the constituent in sentence-initial position is not the subject, it has to appear after the finite verb, leading to subject-verb inversion. In the German linguistic tradition (den Besten 1983; Tomaselli 1990, 2004; Haider 1986, 2010a a.o.), a distinction is usually made between core and correlated properties of the V2 rule (*Kerneigenschaften* and *Korrelate*). The former group includes the linear restriction (the finite verb must appear in absolute sentence-initial position, preceded by one arbitrary

---

1. As shown in Cognola (2010, 2012), Mòcheno behaves like Old Romance languages also in distribution of OV/VO word order patterns.

constituent); correlated properties are subject-verb inversion, the structural correspondence between main declarative clauses and main wh-interrogatives and the asymmetry between main and embedded clauses. All the properties of the V2 rule in German mentioned here are shared by the other Germanic languages, except for the last *Korrelat* of the V2 rule, which is typical only of Continental Germanic (see Holmberg 1986; Holmberg/Platzack 1995; Julien 2002; Heycock 2007; Bentzen et al. 2007; Westergaard 2009; Wiklund et al. 2009 for (embedded) V2 in Scandinavian and Haider/Prinzhorn 1986; Vikner 1995; Holmberg 2012 for a comparison of the Germanic languages).

As extensively discussed in Holmberg (2012), the V2 phenomenon is not only found in the Germanic languages, but is displayed by a series of languages belonging to different language families, among them the Old Romance languages. Benincà (1983, 2006) shows that the V2 phenomenon manifested itself in the Old Romance languages through three properties: (i) the possibility of having subject-finite verb inversion; (ii) the symmetry between main declarative and wh-main interrogative clauses and (iii) the asymmetry between main and embedded clauses in the distribution of *pro*-drop. Note, that these three properties are the so-called *Korrelate* of the V2 rule in the German linguistic tradition. For the Old Romance languages, the core property of the German V2, i.e. the linear restriction, does not constitute a valuable test, since the movement of the finite verb to CP in all sentences co-exists with multiple access to the left periphery in Old Romance.

The V2 phenomenon has probably been the most studied example of head movement within Generative Grammar from a theoretical perspective. The V2 rule was first formulated by den Besten (1983), who proposes that all the empirical properties of V2 languages could be accounted for by the concept that in V2 languages the CP layer is always active and the finite verb has to move to C^0 in all sentences and has to be preceded by an XP moved to Spec,CP. Within den Besten's (1983) theory, the asymmetry between main and embedded clauses observed in Continental Germanic is nicely captured by the assumption that the complementiser and the finite verb compete for the same position, C^0, and when a complementiser is hosted in CP, the finite verb cannot move to C^0 and has to remain in T^0. Recently, following the theoretical shift proposed by Kayne (1998) and Chomsky (1995, 2001) according to which all head movement has actually to be rethought of as XP movement, some scholars (Müller 2004; Biberauer/Roberts 2006; Nilsen 2003 a.o.) have proposed an alternative analysis to the V2 phenomenon in which XP movement replaces head movement.

If the technical derivation of the V2 phenomenon – in terms of either head or XP movement – offered by current syntactic theories appears to be uncontroversial, the force behind it is still a matter of debate. On the one hand, there seems to be clear evidence (the syntactic behaviour of CP expletives in German and Icelandic, Holmberg 2012; or the distribution of V1 in Breton, Jouitteau 2010, for example) that the V2 phenomenon is the result of a purely formal requirement to be understood as an EPP feature associated with the head of one FP of the left periphery (Haegeman 1997; Poletto 2002; Roberts/Roussou 2002; Roberts 2004). However, on the basis of other evidence, some scholars (Travis 1984; Zwart 1997; Koster 1994; Truckenbrodt 2006; relying on Lohnstein 2000: 145ff.; Bayer 2004: 78ff.; Brandner 2004: 107ff.; Lohnstein/Bredel 2004) have proposed that the V2 phenomenon has a semantic trigger.

After discussing the V2 phenomenon from both an empirical and a theoretical perspective, in the second part of the chapter I examine whether or not Mòcheno is a V2 language. Traditionally (Rowley 2003), Mòcheno has been considered to be a V2 language because in it finite verbs can appear in second position and be preceded by an arbitrary constituent. Note, that the properties that Rowley cites in order to establish that Mòcheno is a V2 language are the core properties of the V2 phenomenon in Germanic languages. As discussed in detail below, the tests proposed by Rowley for classifying Mòcheno as a V2 language prove to be unsatisfactory when further data are considered. The main weakness is the position of the finite verb, which may appear in second position but does not have to; moreover, when the two tests are applied to Mòcheno and a non-V2 language such as Italian, both languages can be seen to behave in the same way. This leads to the paradoxical conclusion that Mòcheno is not a V2 language.

In the remainder of the chapter, I show that the conclusion that Mòcheno is not a V2 language is incorrect. In fact, when one also considers the correlated properties of the V2 phenomenon the picture changes radically: Mòcheno displays all the *Korrelate* of the V2 rule: (i) subject-verb inversion, (ii) structural symmetry between main declarative clauses and wh-questions and (iii) asymmetry between main and embedded clauses. However, all these properties are optional and variation is found according to the type of subject (DP or pronominal). Leaving the problem of optionality/variation aside for the moment, the fact that all *Korrelate* of the V2 phenomenon are present in Mòcheno, although in an optional or reduced fashion, constitutes a first difference between Mòcheno and Italian, since in the latter the correlated properties of the V2 rule are always excluded, as expected in a non-V2 language. I therefore suggest that one has to look at the correlated properties of V2 in order to establish reliable tests for detecting the phenomenon in a language such as Mòcheno. This conclusion is backed up by the comparison with Old Romance languages, which are considered V2 languages on the basis of the *Korrelate* of V2 (Benincà 1984, 1994, 2006).

The last part of the chapter lays out convincing evidence against an analysis of the syntactic variation of Mòcheno in terms of contact. The first evidence given is based on the observation that, contrary to the predictions made by the contact hypothesis, a phenomenon like subject-verb inversion, which (according to the contact hypothesis) has to be seen as an instance of the finite verb being in C^0 as a consequence of the application of the abstract rules of the conservative German type grammar, does not correlate with other German syntactic properties. For example, subject-verb inversion can coexist with multiple access to CP and VO syntax and, conversely, the absence of subject-verb inversion can coexist with the *Satzklammerstruktur*, which is not possible in the Romance contact varieties. The points noted above run counter to an explanation of V2 in terms of an "optionality" allowed by the availability to speakers of different grammars with different parameter settings. If this were the case, the movement or the lack of movement of the finite verb to CP would correlate with other syntactic properties of German and Romance respectively. In Mòcheno, there is no such correlation.

The second set of arguments against an explanation of Mòcheno syntactic variation in terms of the presence of two competing grammars comes from the observation that optionality is not found in all syntactic domains, but seems to be restricted to main declarative clauses. For example, subject-verb inversion with nominal subjects is (apparently) optional in main declarative clauses but not permitted in main interrogatives; analogously, both OV and VO word orders are permitted in main declarative clauses, whereas only VO syntax is grammatical in sentences with a fronted operator (Cognola 2012). The lack of complete optionality in all syntactic environments is very problematic for the contact hypothesis and suggests it is almost untenable in the case of Mòcheno.

2.2 On the V2 phenomenon

In this section I examine the core properties of the V2 phenomenon from both an empirical and a theoretical perspective in order to introduce the tools necessary for a discussion of the Mòcheno data and their analysis. A comprehensive discussion of the V2 phenomenon is beyond the scope of this book; instead, I focus on those aspects of the phenomenon and those Germanic and Romance languages that are closest to Mòcheno and are therefore most useful in making the comparisons (for a comprehensive study on V2 see Holmberg 2012 and references cited there).

First, I consider the empirical properties of the V2 phenomenon, distinguishing between core and correlated properties and focusing on German and Old Romance languages. Then, I discuss the most influential theoretical attempts to understand the derivation of V2 sentences, focusing on the work of den Besten (1983), Travis (1984) and Müller (2004). In the second part of the section, I examine the hypotheses that have been put forward to account for the movement of both the finite verb and an XP to the left periphery in V2 languages, focusing on work by Haegeman (1997) and Roberts (2004), who call for the presence of a finiteness feature, to be checked by the finite verb only in V2 languages, and by Truckenbrodt (2006), who links the movement of the finite verb to CP with the semantics of the sentence and the need in V2 languages to check the illocutionary force in CP.

2.2.1 V2 in Continental Germanic

A V2 language is defined as a language in which the finite verb has to show up in second position in main clauses, preceded by an arbitrary single constituent. This is illustrated in (4) with German.

(4) a. *Hans hat ein Buch gekauft*
    Hans has-PRS.3SG a book bought
 b. *Gestern hat Hans ein Buch gekauft*
    yesterday has-PRS.3SG Hans a book bought
 c. *Ein Buch hat Hans gekauft*
    a book has-PRS.3SG John bought
    'Hans bought a book yesterday'

In a V2 language, the finite verb can only be preceded by a single fronted constituent, as shown by the ungrammaticality of the sentences in (5).

(5) a. **Gestern ein Buch hat Hans gekauft*
    yesterday a book has-PRS.3SG Hans bought
 b. **Gestern Hans hat ein Buch gekauft*
    yesterday Hans has-PRS.3SG a book bought

In studies on standard German (den Besten 1983; Tomaselli 2004; Haider 2010a a.o.), the above properties are considered to be at the core of the V2 rule: "(i) the finite verb has to be the second sentence constituent, (ii) following an arbitrary, single, clause-initial constituent" (Haider 2010a: 1).

The two core properties of the V2 phenomenon in standard German correlate with three other sub-properties, called *Korrelate* in the literature. The first sub-property is subject-verb inversion. When the fronted constituent is not the subject, it has to appear after the finite verb.[2]

(6) a. *Gestern   kaufte   Hans   ein Buch*
       yesterday bought-PST.3SG Hans   a book
   b. **Gestern Hans   kaufte   ein Buch*
       yesterday Hans   bought-PST.3SG a book
   c. *Ein Buch kaufte   Hans   gestern*
       a book   bought-PST.3SG Hans   yesterday
   d. **Ein Buch Hans   kaufte   gestern*
       a book   Hans   bought-PST.3SG yesterday
       'Yesterday Hans bought a book'
   e. *Nachdem er   das Zimmer verlassen hatte, ging   Hans*
       after   he   the room   left-PTCP had,   went-PST.3SG Hans
       sofort   nach Hause
       immediately to home
   f. **Nachdem er   das Zimmer verlassen hatte, Hans ging*
       after   he   the room   left-PTCP had,   Hans went-PST.3SG
       sofort   nach Hause
       immediately to home
       'After leaving the room, Hans went immediately home'

According to den Besten (1983) and Tomaselli (2004), the second *Korrelat* of the V2 rule in German is the structural identity between main declarative clauses and wh-main interrogatives. As illustrated in (7), in wh-questions the finite verb has to appear in second position (7a); only the wh-element can show up in CP, as expected from the linear restriction (7b). Subject-verb inversion is obligatory (7c).[3]

---

[2]. As discussed in Frey (2004a), subject-oriented adverbs can intervene between the finite verb (or the complementiser) and the DP subject in German. See also Pittner (1999), Frey/Pittner (1999) and Grewendorf (2005) on this.

[3]. This argument relies on Chomsky (1977), who first theorises that wh-movement targets the CP layer. In some non-V2 languages (including English), movement of the finite verb to CP forces movement of the finite verb to C^0: Rizzi (1991) speaks of "residual V2" languages in order to refer to the restricted movement of the finite verb to C^0 in correspondence with a fronted operator. As we will see in this chapter, Mòcheno cannot be considered a residual V2 language, since a number of syntactic properties connected with the movement of the finite verb to C^0 take place in main declarative clauses.

(7) a. *Wann haben   deine Freunde einen Film im Kino   gesehen?*
       when have-PRS.3PL your friends a film-ACC in-the cinema seen
   b. **Im Kino   wann haben   deine Freunde einen Film gesehen?*
       in-the cinema when have-PRS.3PL your friends a film-ACC seen
   c. **Wann deine Freunde haben   einen Film im Kino   gesehen?*
       when your friends   have-PRS.3PL a film-ACC in-the cinema seen
      'When did your friends see a movie in the cinema?'

The last *Korrelat* of the V2 rule in standard German is the asymmetry between main and embedded clauses with respect to the position of the finite verb. As is well known, the V2 phenomenon is a root phenomenon in continental Germanic: this means that the finite verb has to appear in the second sentence-position (V2) in main clauses, whereas in embedded clauses it appears in sentence-final position (OV, (8)). This is illustrated in the following examples.

(8) a. *Ich weiß   nicht, ob meine Freunden einen Film*
       I   know-PRS.1SG NEG   if my friends   a film-ACC
       im Kino   gesehen haben
       in-the cinema seen   have-PRS.3PL
   b. **Ich weiß   nicht, ob meine Freunden haben*
       I   know-PRS.1SG NEG   if my friends   have-PRS.3PL
       einen Film im Kino   gesehen
       a film-ACC in-the cinema seen
       'I don't know if my friends have seen a film in the cinema'
   c. **Ich habe   gehört, dass Hans kaufte*
       I   have-PRS.1SG heard that Hans bought-PST.3SG
       gestern   ein Buch
       yesterday a book
   d. **Ich habe   gehört, dass ein Buch kaufte*
       I   have-PRS.1SG heard that a book   bought-PST.3SG
       Hans gestern
       Hans yesterday
   e. *Ich habe   gehört, dass Hans gestern   ein Buch*
       I   have-PRS.1SG heard that Hans yesterday a book
       kaufte
       bought-PST.3SG
      'I heard that Hans bought a book yesterday'

In continental Germanic, embedded V2 is possible only in a very restricted number of cases, in which the complementiser can be dropped, such as in reported speech (9a). As can be inferred from the contrast between (9b) and (9c), the movement of the finite verb in embedded clauses is subject to the absence of the complementiser (see Vikner 1995; Heycock 2006; Bentzen et al. 2007).

(9) a. Es   ist   berichtet worden, gestern   sei
       EXPL is-PRS.3SG reported AUX-PASS yesterday is-PRS.CONG.3SG
       der Präsident angekommen
       the president arrived

   b. *Es   ist   berichtet worden, dass gestern   sei
       EXPL is-PRS.1SG reported AUX-PASS that yesterday is-PRS.CONG.3SG
       der Präsident angekommen
       the president arrived

   c. Es   ist   berichtet worden, dass gestern   der Präsident
       EXPL is-PRS.1SG reported AUX-PASS that yesterday the president
       angekommen sei
       arrived   is-PRS.CONG.3SG
       'It was reported that the president arrived yesterday'

The empirical properties of the V2 phenomenon in Continental Germanic illustrated in the previous examples are captured by the classical formulation of V2 given in (10), originally proposed by den Besten (1983), who offers the first theoretical account of this phenomenon within the framework of Generative Grammar.

(10) a. One Verb Preposing rule moves the finite verb to the complementizer in root sentences;
   b. Two or one root transformations transferring a constituent into the leftmost position of COMP.   (den Besten 1983:60)

Den Besten's formulation of the V2 rule in continental Germanic intriguingly captures the asymmetry between the position of the finite verb in main and embedded clauses: it assumes that the finite verb and the complementiser compete for the head of CP.

In (11), I show the structure of a main (declarative or interrogative, there is no difference between them in V2 languages) clause according to den Besten's (1983) analysis. The finite verb is assumed to move to the head of CP, followed by the movement of one XP to Spec,CP; the linear OV word order arises from the assumption that in German VP is head final.[4]

---

4. In this structure, I adhere to the standard view on German, according to which I(nfl) does not project in German but tense and finite features (with the syntactic subject, as proposed by Koopman/Sportiche 1991) are present in VP (see Abraham 1992 and Haider 2010a a.o.). For the hypothesis of the presence of IP (or TP) in German, see Tomaselli (1990, 2004),

(11)
```
                    CP
                   /  \
         das Buch/wasⱼ  C'
                       /  \
                   kaufteₖ  VP
                           /  \
                        Hans   V'
                              /  \
                            tⱼ    tₖ
```

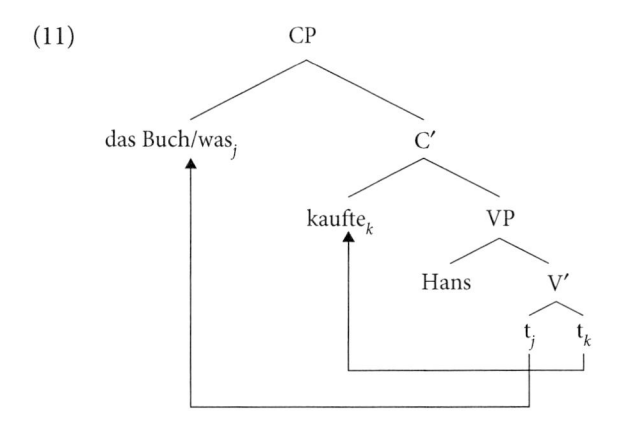

The above structure allows us to explain the core properties of V2 (CP is composed of one FP only, no split-CP, therefore only one single constituent can be fronted) and to derive subject-verb inversion (when the finite verb goes up to C^0, the subject remains in Spec,VP) and the structural correspondence between main declarative and main interrogative clauses.

In order to make sense of the last correlated property of V2, the asymmetry between embedded and main clauses, den Besten (1983) proposes that complementiser and finite verb compete for the same C^0 position: therefore the movement of the finite verb to CP cannot take place if a complementiser is present.[5] The derivation of an embedded clause is given in (12).

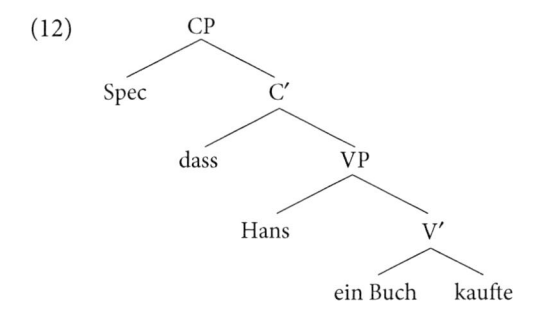

(12)
```
              CP
             /  \
          Spec   C'
                /  \
             dass   VP
                   /  \
                Hans   V'
                      /  \
                 ein Buch  kaufte
```

Müller (2004), Hinterhölzl (2006) a.o. For the hypothesis that V-to-C is actually V-to-I-to-C, see Holmberg/Platzack (1995). For an attempt to account of the syntax of German within Kayne's (1994) antisymmetric approach, see Zwart (1997), Haegeman (2000) and Hinterhölzl (2006) a.o.

5. See Reis (1985) for a critical discussion of den Besten's analysis of embedded clauses in German, where a series of counterexamples of his generalization on embedded clauses is given.

Den Besten (1983:55) explicitly assumes that the derivations proposed above apply to all sentences in V2 languages, including those in which movement of the finite verb to C^0 is not immediately obvious, such as sentences with a fronted subject ("symmetrical analysis" of V2).

The theory that in V2 languages sentences with a fronted subject involve movement of the finite verb to CP was first challenged by Travis (1984). Her "asymmetrical V2" hypothesis contends that in Continental Germanic languages the finite verb moves to CP only when non-nominative constituents are fronted to CP and nominative subjects always appear in Spec,IP in both main and embedded clauses. Travis's hypothesis has been further developed using an asymmetric approach (Kayne 1994) by Zwart (1997) and Koster (1994) for Dutch, Röngvaldsson and Thráinsson (1990) for Icelandic and Santorini (1995) for Yiddish, all of whom have provided evidence for the head-initial character of IP in Continental-Germanic OV-languages. This hypothesis is generally accepted today (and is adopted in this book). Recently, van Craenenbroeck and Haegeman (2007) provided evidence to support the "symmetrical" analysis based on the distribution of clitics in some Flemish dialects.

In conclusion, I would like to briefly mention some recent modifications to den Besten's theory of V2. Following the shift in the theory proposed by Kayne (1998) and Chomsky (1995, 2001), according to which all movement is remnant XP movement, it has been proposed (Nilsen 2003; Biberauer/Roberts 2006; Biberauer/Richards 2006; Müller 2004 a.o.) that V2 must be technically derived via remnant XP movement. How head movement can be replaced by remnant XP movement in the derivation of sentences in V2 languages is shown by Müller (2004) with a German sentence with a fronted subject (*Maria hat ein Buch gekauft*, (13)). The linear word order is derived by assuming that the VP layer, where the lexical verb is found, moves to Spec,TP (for EPP reasons in Biberauer/Roberts 2006); vP, in Spec of which the subject is found and in whose head appears the finite verb, is moved to CP.

(13) [Tree diagram:

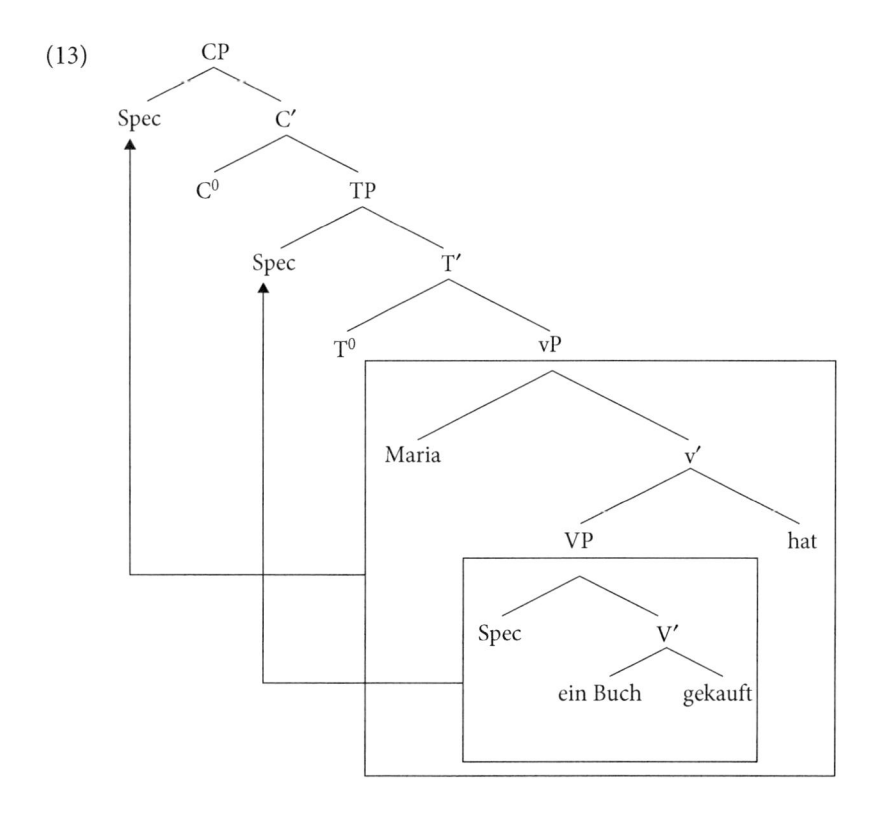

CP
├── Spec
└── C'
    ├── C⁰
    └── TP
        ├── Spec
        └── T'
            ├── T⁰
            └── vP
                ├── Maria
                └── v'
                    ├── VP
                    │   ├── Spec
                    │   └── V'
                    │   ├── ein Buch
                    │   └── gekauft
                    └── hat

with movement arrows from VP region up to Spec,TP and from vP up to Spec,CP]

In the case of sentences with a fronted adverb, such as *Gestern hat Maria ein Buch gekauft*, Müller (2004: 190) proposes that TP has multiple Specs: VP moves to the lowest Spec of TP and the subject moves to the highest Spec of TP and the vP, whose edge is the AdvP, goes up to Spec,CP. According to Müller (2004), only adverbs and subjects can be merged on the edge of vP. The derivation of sentences involving a fronted verb argument, e.g. *Ein Buch hat Maria gekauft*, first involves movement of the XP to be fronted to Spec,vP as an effect of scrambling. The DP subject follows in Spec,vP, in a lower Spec position. Again, multiple Specs are allowed in this theory.

In this book, I adhere to the traditional theory that V2 is head movement, since I think that the head-movement analysis offers a superior description of the empirical facts of a less studied language such as Mòcheno. In the following subsection, I examine the properties of Old Romance languages which have been defined as V2 languages in the literature like the Germanic ones.

2.2.2 V2 in Old Romance languages

Several studies (Benincà 1984, 1994, 1995, 2006; Vanelli 1987; Adams 1987; Vance 1989; Salvi 1990; Fontana 1993; Roberts 1993; Ribeiro 1995; Hirschbühler/Junker 1988; Poletto 1995 a.o.) have shown V2 not to be restricted to Germanic language, but to have been a syntactic characteristic of all Old Romance languages until at least the beginning of the XIV century.

The V2 character of all Old Romance languages is less "rampant" than that of the Germanic languages, since in Old Romance languages the finite verb does not have to appear in second sentence position. The lack of a linear restriction, paradoxical as it seems for the characterization of a language family as V2, is the only property of V2 languages that is missing from Old Romance languages, where we find a series of syntactic phenomena that are absolutely ruled out in the modern varieties and are typical of V2 languages: (i) subject-verb inversion; (ii) symmetry between wh-questions and main clauses and (iii) asymmetry between main and embedded clauses.

Subject-verb inversion in Old Romance languages is illustrated in the following examples, all taken from Benincà (2006: 66f., her examples (19) to (23)). The sentences in (14) illustrate subject-verb inversion in Old French (14a, b) and in Provençal (14c, d).

(14) a. *Autre chose   ne   pot   li roi   trouver*
        other things NEG could-PST.3SG the king find
                                                                                                   Old French (Artù, 101)
        'The king could not find anything else'
   b. *Un pou aprés eure de prime   fu   Mador venuz   a cort*
        a bit   after hour of first   was-PST.3SG Mador arrived to court
                                                                                            Old French (Artù, 103)
        'Mador arrived at court a little after the hour of first hour (i.e., 6 AM)'
   c. *Mal cosselh donet   Pilat*   Provençal (Venjansa, 106)
        bad advice gave-PST.3SG Pilatus
        'Pilatus gave bad advice'
   d. *Si sai   eu la meillor razon*   Provençal (Gaucelm Faidit, 47)
        so know-PRS.1SG I the best reason
        'So I know the best reason'

In (15a) an example of V2 in Old Spanish and in (15b) of V2 in Old Portuguese.

(15) a. *Este logar mostro   dios a Abraam*
       this place showed-PST.3SG God   to Abraham
                                    Old Spanish (Fontana 1993: 64)
       'God showed Abraham this place'
    b. *Con tanta paceenca   sofria   ela esta enfermidade*
       with so much patience suffered-PST.3SG she this disease
                                    Old Portuguese (Ribeiro 1995: 114)
       'She suffered this disease so patiently'

Finally, in (16) three examples of subject-verb inversion in Old Northern Italian varieties.

(16) a. *Bon vin   fa   l'uga negra*   Old Milanese (Bonvesin, 96)
       good wine makes-PRS.3SG the grape black
       'Black grapes make good wine'
    b. *Et così lo mis   e' ço*   Old Venetian (Lio Mazor, 31)
       and so it put-PST.1SG I down
       'And so I put it down'
    c. *Ciò tenne   il re a grande maraviglia*
       this held-PST.3SG the king to great marvel
                                    Old Florentine (Novellino, Tale 2)
       'The king was astonished at that'

Subject-verb inversion was possible, not obligatory, in Old Romance languages. As shown in (17), a DP subject can appear in the left periphery followed by another XP, giving rise to V3 word order.

(17) a. *Et [chi facesse   contra]$_j$ [la prima volta] gli$_j$*
       and who do-COND.3SG contrarily, the first time   to him
       sia imposta penitenca, e   la seconda sia cacciato
       be imposed penance, and the second be expelled
                                    Old Florentine (Testi fiorentini, 46)
       'And anyone who may act contrarily, the first time should be fined and the second time he should be expelled'
    b. *E [Perp Capel] [en la fiata] branchà   uno uiger de pes*
       and Pero Capel immediately seised-PST.3SG a hamper of fish
                                    Old Venetian (Lio Mazor, 35)
       'And Pero Capel immediately seised a hamper of fish'

The distribution of subject-verb inversion illustrated above for main declarative clauses is also found in wh-main interrogatives: in the examples in (18a, all taken from Munaro 2010: 1148ff.), a DP subject can either appear in subject-verb inversion (18a, b), or in the construction known as free-inversion (18c), in which the DP subject follows the non-finite verb form. In Old Italian, a DP subject could also precede the interrogative wh-element (18d): in this case, the DP subject is analysed as a left-dislocation (from now on: LD).

(18) a. *Dimmi, verace maestra, in che modo fa   Ira*
       tell-me true mistress   in what way makes-PRS.3SG Anger
       le sue operazioni   per le dette vie?
       the her operations for the mentioned ways
                                          (Bono Giamboni, Trattato, cap. 25, par. 4)
       'Tell me true mistress how does Anger make her operations?'
   b. *Perché semo noi venuti a queste donne?*
       why   are we come   to those women
                                          (Dante, Vita Nuova, cap. 14, par. 2)
       'Why did we go to those women?'
   c. *In che modo è   obligato l'un uomo a l'altro*
       in what way is-PRS.3SG bound   one man to another
       naturalmente per via di veritade?
       naturally   by the way of truth
                                          (Bono Giamboni, Libro, cap. 71, par. 23)
       'How is one man bound naturally to another because of the truth?'
   d. *Messere, voi quale avete   più cara?*   (Novellino, 2, r. 31)
       Sir,   you what have-PRS.3PL most dear
       'What is the dearest to you, sir?'

The data discussed so far have shown that in Old Romance varieties, unlike in the modern ones, subject-verb inversion in main declarative clauses and wh-questions was possible, though not obligatory, since it coexisted with other strategies for the realization of subjects (free inversion and LD).

The last asymmetry between Old and modern Romance varieties reported in the literature concerns the distribution of *pro-drop* in main and embedded clauses (see Benincà 1984; Adams 1987 a.o.). In Old Romance languages, which, like the modern ones, were all *pro-drop*, *pro* subjects appeared more frequently in main clauses, whereas in embedded clauses the subject pronoun tended to be realised. This phenomenon, called "asymmetric pro-drop" by Benincà, is illustrated in (19, from Benincà 2006: 68).[6]

---

6. The same asymmetry in the distribution of pro-drop has been reported for Old High German (Axel 2007; Axel/Weiß 2011).

(19) a. *Quand tu veniss al mondo, se tu voliss*
when you came-PST.2SG to-the world, if you want-COND.2SG
pensar, negota ge portassi, negota n
think, nothing there brought-PST.2SG nothing from-there
poi portar (Old Mil.; Bonvesin, 179)
can-PRS.2SG take
'When you came into the world, if you think about it, you didn't bring anything and nothing you can take away'

b. *et levà lo rem et de- me sulo col et*
and raised-PST.3SG the oar and hit-PST.3SG me on-the neck and
menà- me zo per lo brazo, sì ch' el me
stroke-PST.3SG me down on the arm, so that he to me
lo scavezà (OldVen.; Lio Mazor, 18)
it broke-PST.3SG
'And he raised the oar and hit me on the neck, and struck my arm so that he broke it'

c. *E così ne provò de' più cari ch' elli avea*
and so of them tested-PST.3SG of the most dear that he had-PST.3SG
(Old Flor.; Testi fiorentini, 74)
'So he tested some of the best friends he had'

So far, we have seen that Old Romance displays three properties that have been connected in the literature with the V2 phenomenon: subject-verb inversion, structural identity between main declarative clauses and wh-questions and asymmetry between main and embedded clauses in the distribution of *pro-drop*. The fact that none of these properties is obligatory is typical of Old Romance languages. It has never been suggested that variation within the V2 phenomenon in Old Romance languages can be accounted for by the hypothesis of true optionality in the syntactic domain, or through the idea of the presence of two competing grammars; variation has, instead, been related to the presence of a split-CP (Benincà 1984, 2006). The possibility of having multiple access to CP makes the movement of the finite verb to CP opaque, leading to V3 or V4 word orders. These word orders, however, are not to be considered violations of the V2 rule, but rather effects of a split CP. From this perspective, the V2 phenomenon must be understood as the requirement that the finite verb appears in a head of the left periphery and establishes a Spec/head relation with a constituent. In some V2 languages, other XPs can precede the lowest XP and the finite verb, but this does not preclude the classification of such languages as V2.

The possibility of having multiple access to CP in Old Romance languages (especially in Old Italian varieties) is illustrated in (20, from Benincà 2006: 76, her (49)).

(20) a. [La mia gran pena   e   lo gravoso affanno c'   ho
the my great sorrow and the grievous pain that have-PRS.1SG
lungiamente per amor patuto]$_j$ [madonna] lo$_j$ m'   ha
long   for love suffered, my lady   it to me has-PRS.3SG
in gioia ritornato   Old Sicilian (Scremin, 89, Guido delle Colonne)
into joy turned
'The great sorrow and grievous pain that I have suffered for a long time my lady turned into joy for me'

b. [La vertude ch'   illa ave   d'aduciderme e   guarire]$_j$
the virtue that she has-PRS.3SG to kill-me and heal
[a lingua   dir] non l$_j$' auso   Old Sicilian (Scremin, 88, Re Renzo)
to tongue say NEG it dare-PRS.1SG
'I do not dare to tell the virtue that she has to kill me and heal me'

c. [A lè] [per tug li tempi] me   rend   e   me
to her for all the times myself surrender-PRS.1SG and myself
consegno   Old Milanese (Bonvesin, 163)
deliver-PRS.1SG
'I surrender and submit myself to her forever'

Multiple access to CP cannot be considered a late development of Old Italian, since it occurs in the oldest Italian text, the *Placitum* from Capua, 960 (cited from Benincà 2006: 78).

(21) Sao   ko   [kelle terre per kelle fini   que ki
know-PRS.1SG that those lands for those boundaries that here
contene]$_j$,   [trenta anni] le$_j$ possette   parte
contains-PRS.3SG thirty years   them owned-PST.3SG party
Sancti Benedicti
Saint Benedict
'I know that the party of Saint Benedict owned for thirty years those lands between the boundaries that are here contained'

Let us sum up the empirical properties of the V2 phenomenon in Old Romance and German. As illustrated in Table 2.1, Old Romance languages and German share all the so-called correlated properties of the V2 phenomenon, although in the former these properties are optional. This correlates with the fact that Old Romance languages, unlike Germanic languages, had a split-CP and therefore allow multiple access to CP, which resulted in a violation of the linear restriction.

Table 2.1 Properties of V2 in German and Old Romance

Language	Core properties		Correlated properties		
	V in 2nd position	XP-V	subj-V inversion	decl=wh	main vs embedded
German	✓	✓	✓	✓	✓
Old Romance	*	✓	✓ (optional)	✓	✓ (pro)

As already mentioned above, the syntactic properties of Old Romance languages have been explained by the hypothesis that these languages have a V2 rule fully comparable to that of V2 Germanic languages, which has been lost in modern Romance varieties. In Old Romance, the movement of the finite verb to CP in all main clauses (assumed to be the core of the V2 rule) took place within an articulated structure of the left periphery, which made the V2 phenomenon opaque. Benincà (2006) demonstrates that Old and modern Romance varieties share a very close structure of the left periphery (Rizzi 1997, refined by Benincà 2001; Benincà/Poletto 2004; Frascarelli 2000, 2009; Frascarelli/Hinterhölzl 2007).[7] The structure of the left periphery is given in (22, from Benincà/Poletto 2004: 78). The highest area of the left periphery hosts the frame, where FPs for hanging topics (from here on HT) and scene setters are found. All topics and LDs can appear in the area dedicated to the themes and operators are positioned in the lowest area of CP.

(22) [$_{FRAME}$ [HT – Scene Setter] [$_{THEME}$ [Shift Topic – Contrastive Topic Familiarity Topic] [$_{FOCUS}$ [Contrastive Focus – Information Focus/wh]]]]

The only difference between Old and modern Romance varieties is that in the former the finite verb had to move to a head hosted in the left periphery in all main clauses, whereas in modern varieties this movement is restricted to a few special cases (like main interrogative clauses).

Let us consider the derivation of a sentence with subject-verb inversion, in which it must be assumed that the finite verb has moved to CP, such as (23).

(23) Ciò tenne   il re   a grande maraviglia
     this held-PST.3SG the king to great marvel *Old Florentine (Novellino, Tale 2)*
     'The king was astonished at this'

---

7. Rizzi's (1997) and Benincà's (2001) structures of the left periphery differ with respect to the position of TopicPs, which Rizzi assumes to be recursive and allowed to show up either before or after FocusP, according to the structure *ForceP – TopicP* – FocusP – TopicP* – FinP*. Benincà shows TopicPs to occupy fixed positions above and not below FocusP. For a detailed discussion of the data supporting Benincà's structure of CP, I refer the reader to her work; for cross-linguistic evidence against the sequence *Focus-Topic*, see Puskas (2000) and Aboch (2004).

According to Benincà, sentences with subject-verb inversion involve the fronting of an XP to the Spec position of FocusP, followed by the movement of the finite verb to Focus^0; the subject is assumed to appear in Spec,AgrSP.[8] The derivation is given in (24).

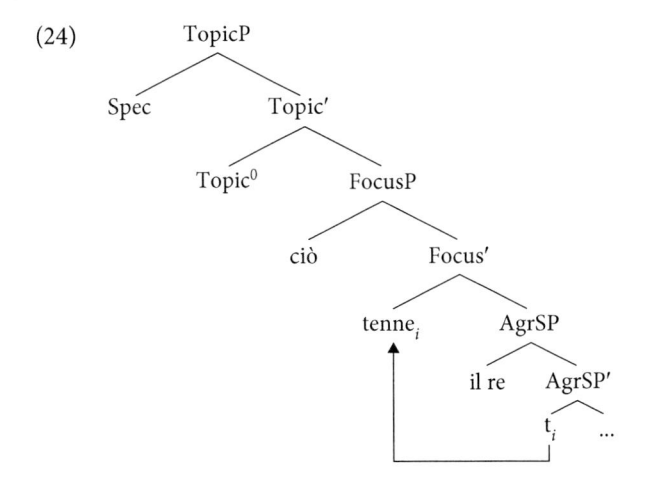

(24)
```
              TopicP
             /      \
          Spec      Topic'
                   /      \
                Topic⁰    FocusP
                  |      /      \
                 ciò   Focus'
                      /      \
                  tenne_i    AgrSP
                            /      \
                          il re   AgrSP'
                                    |
                                    t_i   ...
```

One of Benincà's most important contributions has been to demonstrate, through the analysis of the distribution of enclisis and proclisis in Old Romance languages, that in a V2 language with a split-CP not all constituents "count" in the same way for V2 (see also Jouitteau 2010 on this). In particular, left-dislocated constituents which can be recognised syntactically by the presence of pronominal doubling do not "count" for V2.[9] Let us consider the examples in (25, from Benincà 2006: 81), where an instance of multiple access to the left periphery is given. As shown by Benincà, in this configuration the highest constituent has to be analysed as a theme (either an HT or an LD), since it is doubled by a clitic in IP as it is in the modern varieties and the doubler and all other clitics present in the clause have to be proclitic to the finite verb.

---

8. Benincà (2006: 80) assumes that XPs that are fronted through the "anaphoric anteposition" construction (Benincà 1988, 2001) are also hosted in the Spec of an FP dedicated to operators in the lowest portion of CP, though the possibility that these XPs are hosted in TopicP is left open. In the latter case, one has to assume the presence of a silent operator in Spec,Focus in order to satisfy the requirement imposed by the V2 rule.

9. As discussed in the previous note, anaphoric antepositions, which pragmatically realise a topic, are treated by Benincà as constructions targeting an operator position in the Focus field.

(25) a. [*La mia gran pena e lo gravoso affanno c' ho*
 the my great sorrow and the grievous pain that have-PRS.1SG
 lungiamente per amor patuto]$_j$ [madonna] lo$_j$ m' ha
 long   for love suffered, my lady   it to me has-PRS.3SG
 in gioia ritornato   Old Sicilian (Scremin, 89, Guido delle Colonne)
 into joy turned
 'The great sorrow and grievous pain that I have suffered for a long time my lady turned into joy for me'
 b. [*La vertude ch' illa ave   d'aduciderme e   guarire]$_j$*
 the virtue that she has-PRS.3SG to kill-me and heal
 [*a lingua dir] non l$_j$' auso*   Old Sicilian (Scremin, 88, Re Renzo)
 to tongue say NEG it   dare-PRS.1SG
 'I do not dare to tell the virtue that she has to kill me and heal me'

Clitics in main clauses of Old Romance, however, are not always proclitic, unlike in the modern varieties. As illustrated in (26a, from Benincà 2006:72, 26b from Benincà 2010:55), when the thematised constituent is not followed by another XP, all pronouns present in the sentences must follow the finite verb.

(26) a. *Lo primo modo$_j$ chiamo=lo$_j$ estato temoruso*
 the first mode   call-PRS.3SG-it state timorous
                                          Old Umbrian (Jacopone)
 'I call the first type (of love) timorous state'
 b. *A voi, le mie poche parole ch' avete   intese*
 to you, the my few words   that have-PRS.2PL understood
 hol=le   dette con grande fede
 have-PRS.1SG=them said with great faith
                            (Matteo de' Libri, Dicerie volgari, p. 15 rr. 9–10)
 'To you, the words that you understood, I said in great faith'

The distribution of pronouns in Old Romance, which has been described as the effect of morphophonological constraints by Tobler/Mussafia, has been given a syntactic account by Benincà.[10] According to Benincà, proclisis is obligatory in all cases in which the Spec of the FP responsible for the V2 phenomenon (in her system Spec,FocusP) hosts an XP, as illustrated in (27).

---

10. For a syntactic account, see also Uriagereka (1995), Rivero (1986), Barbosa (1995), Roberts (2010). For a recent phonological approach to the Tobler/Mussafia law, see Fischer (2002).

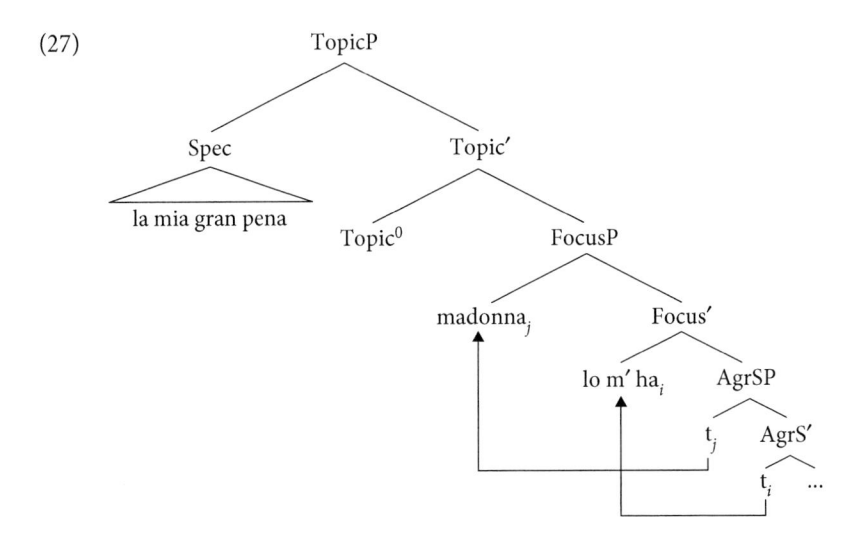

(27) [Tree diagram:
TopicP
├── Spec: la mia gran pena
└── Topic'
    ├── Topic⁰
    └── FocusP
        ├── madonna$_j$
        └── Focus'
            ├── lo m' ha$_i$
            └── AgrSP
                ├── t$_j$
                └── AgrS'
                    └── t$_i$ ...]

Enclisis is obligatory when FocusP is empty and the fronted constituent is a theme (an HT or an LD): in this configuration the finite verb has to move to the head of the TopicP hosting the fronted XP, leaving its doubler behind. The structure of sentences with pronoun enclisis is shown in (28).

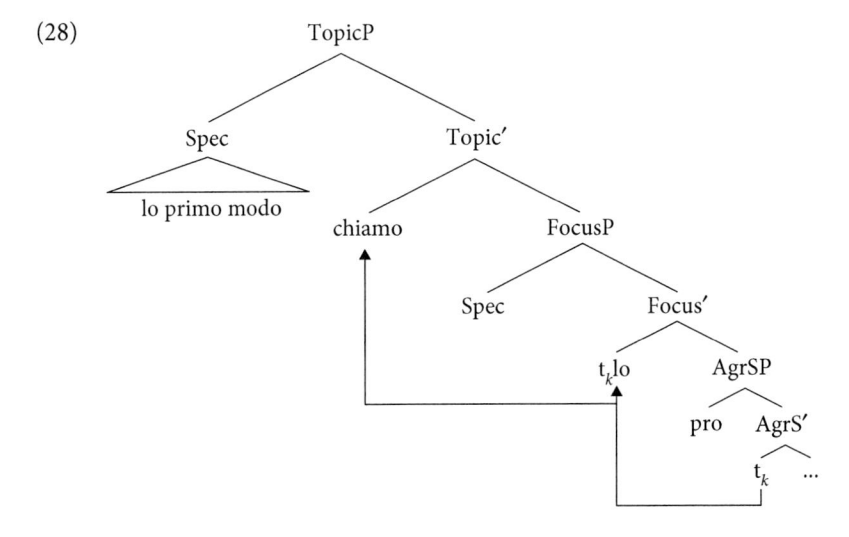

(28) [Tree diagram:
TopicP
├── Spec: lo primo modo
└── Topic'
    ├── chiamo
    └── FocusP
        ├── Spec
        └── Focus'
            ├── t$_k$lo
            └── AgrSP
                ├── pro
                └── AgrS'
                    └── t$_k$ ...]

The only case in which two arguments can co-occur in the left periphery without a clitic copy is when the higher one of the two is the subject, as in (29) from Benincà (2006: 78). In this case, it is assumed that the subject is topicalised in the left periphery and doubled by a silent *pro* in Spec,AgrSP; the requirements imposed by the V2 phenomenon are satisfied by the lowest XP.

(29) [La mia cattivanza] [l'alma]   ha   menata
     the my wickedness the soul has-PRS.3SG led
                                                    Old Umbrian (Jacopone)
     'My wickedness led my soul'

This examination of the V2 rule has so far focused only on its empirical properties in German and Old Romance languages, and on the technical derivation of V2 sentences. Below, I consider the hypotheses that have been put forward to explain what triggers V2.

2.2.3 Triggers for movement

In the previous section, we saw that there is a consensus on how the V2 phenomenon manifests itself in Continental Germanic and how V2 sentences have to be technically derived within current syntactic theory. It remains unclear why only V2 languages display the two core properties summarised below (from Holmberg 2012:39) and what the forces behind the movement of the finite verb and the fronting of an XP are.

(30) a. A functional head in the left periphery attracts the finite verb;
     b. This functional head wants a constituent moved to its specifier position.

Focusing first on the movement of the finite verb to C^0, a fruitful line of research has linked the need to have the finite verb in CP with the realization of the subject. Platzack (1986, 1987), Koopman (1984), Holmberg and Platzack (1995) propose that in V2-languages nominative-case assignment can only take place if the finite verb is in CP (through government), whereas in non-V2 languages the nominative case can be assigned through a Spec/head agreement relation in TP. More recently, the connection between V2 and the realization of the subject has been reconsidered in terms of an EPP feature associated either with the head of CP (in V2 languages) or with the head of TP (in non-V2 languages). Haegeman (1997), Rizzi/Roberts (1989) and Roberts (1996, 2004) propose, following Rizzi's (1997) split-CP hypothesis, that the CP-head associated with EPP is the lowest projection of CP, Fin^0, which has strong features in V2 languages and weak features in non-V2 languages (Haegeman 1997:150). In discussing this line of research on the force behind the movement of the finite verb to the left periphery in V2 languages, a series of studies pointing to a connection between licensing of *pro* and the movement of the finite verb to CP has to be mentioned (Benincà 1982; Tomaselli 1990; Brandi/Cordin 1989; Poletto 2000; Platzack 1987; Franco 2009; Roberts 2010 a.o.). All these studies share the hypothesis that in different *pro*-drop languages, the possibility of having *pro* is somehow subject to the syntactic position of the finite verb in the clause and in particular that the presence of a null silent pronoun is favoured when the finite verb appears in the left periphery.

Common to all the theoretical accounts briefly discussed so far is the assumption that the movement of the finite verb to the left periphery in V2 languages is a formal requirement imposed by grammar with no semantic nor pragmatic motivation. Truckenbrodt (2006) recently put forward an articulated theory of V2 in German (a theory which seems to be valid for all Germanic languages, see Holmberg 2012), in which he assumes a connection between the movement of the finite verb to CP and the semantics of the clause. According to Truckenbrodt, in V2 languages the finite verb moves to the left periphery in order to check the illocutionary force of the sentence; within a split-CP framework this FP corresponds to ForceP.

The tension between the two views on V2 – the first considering it to result from a purely formal requirement imposed by the grammar of V2 languages to be explained in terms of EPP, the second an interface phenomenon involving syntax and semantics/pragmatics – is also found between the theoretical accounts proposed for the second requirement of the V2 rule: XP fronting.

Evidence supporting the idea that XP fronting is a purely formal requirement fully comparable to EPP come from the distribution of expletive pronouns in V2 languages, which has been discussed by several scholars (Cardinaletti 1990; Holmberg 2012; Biberauer 2010 a.o.). As illustrated in the examples in (31, from Holmberg 2012: 35), in a V2 language such as Icelandic the expletive pronoun must appear in sentence-initial position if no other XP is fronted: when another XP is fronted in the left periphery, the expletive is ruled out.

(31) a. *Θαδ rignir*
EXPL rain
'It is raining'

b. *Rignir (*Θαδ)?*
rain EXPL
'Is it raining?'

c. *Nú rignir (*Θαδ)*
now rain EXPL
'It is raining now'

The same restriction is found in German with the expletive *es* (see Cardinaletti 1990; Cardinaletti/Giusti 1996).[11]

---

11. As is well known, in German, unlike in Icelandic, the expletives appearing with passive/impersonal constructions or with unaccusative verbs are considered as CP-expletives, whereas

(32) a. *Es   wurde   getanzt*
         EXPL AUX-PASS danced
         'There was dancing'
     b. *In der Kneipe wurde   (*es) getanzt*
         in the bar   AUX-PASS EXPL danced
         'There was dancing in the bar'

Conversely, for many V2 languages belonging to different language families it has been reported (Travis 1984, 1994; Zwart 1997; Koster 1994; Benincà 1984, 2006; Poletto 2002) that XP fronting has a semantic/pragmatic effect, differing from language to language, on a sentence (see Holmberg 2012 for an overview of the effects of XP-fronting in different V2 languages). This again confuses the whole picture of V2, since it seems to indicate that XP fronting has a semantic effect in V2 languages. It might also lead to the hypothesis that the pragmatically-marked interpretation of the fronted XP is responsible for the movement of the finite verb. This hypothesis does not appear to be unreasonable given that a reduced version of the V2 rule still exists in some non-V2 languages (the so-called "residual-V2 languages", Rizzi 1991) applying to certain pragmatically-marked constituents, typically operators. Moreover, diachronic investigations on the development of V2 in Germanic languages (Longobardi 1994; Fuß 2008 a.o.) have pointed to a clear correspondence between the movement of the finite verb to CP and the type of fronted XP: in particular, V2 seems to have diffused in the grammars of Old Germanic languages from precisely those sentences with a fronted negation and a fronted operator.

The whole discussion so far indicates how complicated both the V2 phenomenon and the theoretical interpretation of data, even within a single language family, are. In order to deal comprehensively with the subject and because of its relevance to the account of V2 in Mòcheno that is developed in this book, I have to face one last theoretical issue: how the empirical data from Continental Germanic V2 languages, in particular the linear restriction discussed above, can be reconciled both with the split-CP hypothesis (Rizzi 1997) and also with the broader assumption that all languages share a universal structure (UG).

The most influential account of this problem is given in terms of Relativised Minimality (from here on: RM, Rizzi 1990, 2004) by Branigan (1996), Haegeman (1997), Poletto (2002) and Roberts (1997, 2004). According to these scholars, once an XP has been fronted to Spec,FinP in order to satisfy the EPP feature

---

those showing up with weather verbs are assumed to be IP expletives. In Icelandic, on the other hand, weather verbs also require CP expletives.

associated with Fin⁰ responsible of the V2 effect, nothing more can be moved through Spec,FinP. This is clearly stated by Haegeman (1997):

> In root clauses the finite verb moves to Fin⁰. One maximal projection will move to (and sometimes through), the specifier of FinP to satisfy the EPP associated with finite Fin⁰. The relevant maximal projection may, for instance, be a subject, a topicalized constituent, or a wh constituent. […] Fin⁰ is occupied by the inflected verb which carries agreement features. If no constituent is topicalized or wh-moved, the subject will move to [Spec,FinP] to satisfy the EPP on Fin⁰. Its specifier is the subject, which, by hypothesis, carries matching agreement features. Recall that Rizzi (1991) assumes that A-positions are specifier positions containing a constituent which can be construed as agreeing with the head in terms of phi features. According to this definition, [Spec,Fin] […] will be construed as an A position. […] The fact that [Spec,FinP] can host weak pronoun subjects […], and expletive and quasi argument subjects […] is unproblematic.
>
> (Haegeman 1997: 17f.)

As discussed by Roberts (1997), this account of XP-fronting in V2 languages does not rule out the base-generation of some XPs in the left periphery in Spec positions of TopicPs.

An alternative account is proposed by Frascarelli/Hinterhölzl (2007), who put forward the hypothesis, fully compatible with Truckenbrodt's (2006) account discussed above, that in German the finite verb does not target the lowest head of the left periphery (Fin⁰) in sentences with V2-word order, but the highest one, Force⁰.

2.2.4 Partial conclusions

In this section, I have dealt with the empirical properties of the V2 phenomenon and with the theoretical accounts of it offered within the framework of Generative Grammar, focusing mainly on German and Old Romance languages.

The general impression that emerges from the above discussion is that the empirical properties of the V2 phenomenon are straightforward and can be described using the technical tools offered by current syntactic theory. However, the picture is less coherent at the explicative level, where there are conflicting data supporting different theoretical accounts. In particular, at the explicative level there seem to be strong asymmetries between different languages belonging to the same language family (German vs. Scandinavian) and even within the same language (Scandinavian where there is evidence for both the theory that V2 is a purely formal requirement and for the opposite theory that it is an effect of semantics/pragmatics).

With this background in mind, I now focus on the Mòcheno data, first considering whether or not we have empirical evidence for defining it a V2 language. There is a general consensus on this definition (Rowley 2003; Cognola 2008, 2010 a.o.), based, however, on different analyses. I also discuss whether the hypothesis of contact-induced change and of the presence of two competing grammars both available to the speakers of Mòcheno could be a valid explanation for syntactic variation in this language.

2.3 Mòcheno as a V2 language

2.3.1 Rowley's (2003) account

In his comprehensive grammar of the Mòcheno language, Rowley (2003: 281) characterises Mòcheno as a V2 language on the basis of the following empirical facts:

> Im Aussagesatz steht das finite Verb in der Regel an zweiter Stelle. Davor steht gerne das Thema des Satzes, das Satzglied, von dem die Rede ist, oder das Element, das zur Einbindung der Äußerung in den Redekontext wichtig ist. Das kann jedes Satzglied sein, das in seiner Bedeutung für das Thema herausgestellt und [...] gekennzeichnet worden soll.[12]

According to Rowley, Mòcheno must be considered a V2 language on the basis of two grammatical characteristics: the finite verb is generally (*in der Regel*) found in second position and any constituent can take the first sentence position and be followed by the finite verb. These are the two core properties of the V2 phenomenon in German, discussed above. In (33), I give some examples from Rowley (2003: 281) supporting his analysis of V2: in all the examples the finite verb is found in second position preceded by one single arbitrary constituent.[13]

---

12. "In a main declarative clause the finite verb generally appears in second position, preceded by the theme of the sentence, that is the constituent the speaker is talking about, or by an element that is preposed due to its relevance in the utterance and that functions as a connection between the concrete sentence and the outside context. This element can be any constituent that is highlighted due to its relevance for the theme and that therefore needs to be highlighted", my translation.

13. The facts illustrated in these examples are representative of all varieties, even when the relevant example is missing for a single variety. For a complete list of examples, I refer the reader to Rowley (2003).

(33) a. *Bir ondera miasn   gia*
         we other   have-PRS.1PL go
         'We have to go'
    b. *S proat   hom=sa   nèt gahòp de sèlln jor   nèt*
         the bread have-PRS.3PL=SBJ-CL.3.PL NEG had   the those years NEG
         'They did not have bread in those years'
    c. *En Palai stea   i   za schloven*
         in Palù stay-PRS.1SG SBJ-STRONG.1.SG to sleep
         'I sleep in Palù'

When we take a closer look at the data, we immediately discover that Rowley's characterization of V2 does not really seem to properly account for the properties of the V2 phenomenon in Mòcheno, since the finite verb can, but does not have to, appear in second position. Moreover, the fact that any constituent can take the sentence-initial position is a core property of the V2 rule only when in co-occurrence with linear restriction. That the finite verb does not have to appear in the absolute second position is illustrated by the example in (34, from Rowley 2003: 283).

(34) *Vriarer en Palai de schualkinder   en summer   hom*
     once   in Palù the school-children in summer have-PRS.3PL
     gia gamiast   za hiatn   de kia
     go PTCP-must-PTCP to look after the cows
     'Once in Palù schoolchildren had to spend their summer looking after the cows'

Crucially, the same syntax as (34) is also found in Italian, a non-V2 language, which allows several constituents to appear before the finite verb, as illustrated in (35).

(35) *Una volta a Palù i bambini   l'estate   dovevano   andare*
     once   in Palù the children in summer must-PST.3PL   go
     a tenere   le vacche
     to look after the cows
     'Once in Palù schoolchildren had to spend their summer looking after the cows'

Moreover, the possibility of having any constituent in first position, which Rowley takes to be a diagnostic of V2, is also characteristic of modern Italian (36): this property can be considered typical of a V2 language only if it correlates with the linear restriction.

(36) a. *Noi dobbiamo   andare*
         we have-PRS.3PL go
         'We have to go'
     b. *Pane non ne avevamo   in quegli anni*
         bread NEG of it have-PST.3PL in those years
         'We did not have any bread in that time'
     c. *A Palù mi   fermo   a dormire*
         in Palù myself stay-PRS.1PL to sleep
         'I sleep in Palù'

Therefore, the two properties of its grammar assumed by Rowley to show that Mòcheno must be analysed as a V2 language do not seem to adequately describe the empirical facts, since, with respect to these properties, Mòcheno behaves exactly as Italian, a non-V2 language.

In the following section, I demonstrate that the conclusion arrived at through the discussion of Rowley's syntactic tests – that Mòcheno is not a V2 language – is wrong: Mòcheno has to be considered a V2 language, since it has all the correlated properties of V2 and therefore patterns like Old Romance languages.

2.3.2 On the presence of the *Korrelate* of V2

In order to establish whether Mòcheno is a V2 language, Rowley (2003) only focuses on the so-called core properties of the V2 rule. These, as discussed at the beginning of this chapter, are characteristic only of the Germanic type of V2 and not of the V2 phenomenon in other languages. It is thus necessary to examine the syntactic behaviour of Mòcheno in relation to the correlated properties of V2: subject-verb inversion in main declarative clauses; structural identity between main declarative and main interrogative clauses and the asymmetry between main and embedded clauses.

Let us focus first on subject-verb inversion in main declarative clauses. As shown in (37), in main declarative clauses in which a constituent different from the subject is fronted (with different pragmatic readings), NP subject-verb inversion is possible, though not obligatory.

(37) a. *Van Nane hòt   der Mario niamer klofft*
         of-the John has-PRS.3SG the Mario never spoken
     b. *Van Nane der Mario hòt   niamer klofft*
         of-the John the Mario has-PRS.3SG never spoken
         'Of John Mario never spoke'

c. Gester   hòt   der Mario en de Maria a puach gem
    yesterday has-PRS.3SG the Mario to the Mary a book given
d. Gester   der Mario hòt   en de Maria a puach gem
    yesterday the Mario has-PRS.3SG to the Mary a book given
    'Yesterday Mario gave Mary a book'

The fact that NP subjects can follow the finite verb is noted by Rowley (2003, (38), from Rowley 2003: 287), even though he does not consider this to be connected to the V2 rule.[14]

(38) Haier   aa   sai   bolten vremma en inser tol kemmen
     this year also are-PRS.3PL many strangers in our valley come
     'Also this year many tourists have come to our valley'

A similar pattern of optionality in subject-verb inversion can be detected for main declarative clauses with subject pronouns, although this is less evident because in Mòcheno three different classes of subject pronouns which have specialised for syntactic positions are available in the paradigm (see next chapter). As illustrated in (39a, b), subject-verb inversion is always obligatory with subject clitics, whereas strong subject pronouns have specialised for the preverbal position (39c, d).

(39) a. Van   Nane hòt=se   niamar klofft
         of-the John has=SBJ-CL.3.SG.F   never   spoken
     b. *Van   Nane se=hòt   niamar klofft
         of-the John SBJ-CL.3.SG.F=has   never   spoken
     c. Van   Nane si   hòt niamar klofft
         of-the John SBJ-STRONG.3.SG.F   has never   spoken
     d. *Van   Nane hòt si   niamar klofft
         of-the John has SBJ-STRONG.3.SG.F never   spoken
         'Of John she has never spoken'

The fact that subject-verb inversion is always possible in Mòcheno main declarative clauses is a strong asymmetry with respect to contact Romance languages, where subject-verb inversion is absolutely ruled out, for both NP subjects and strong pronouns (40a, b) and subject clitic pronouns (40c).[15]

---

14. Rowley (2003: 287) also reports the presence of the so-called "free-inversion" typical of Romance (see, for instance, Kayne 1975 on French; Belletti 2001, 2004 on Italian), where the NP subject follows the past participle and not the finite verb. For an analysis of free-inversion in Mòcheno and its connection with the pro-drop parameter, see Chapter 5.

15. Subject-verb inversion with subject clitic pronouns can only be tested in the Trentino dialect, since Italian lacks subject clitics. As discussed in the previous footnote, the only subject-

(40) a. *Ieri   Mario/lui   ha   (*Mario/lui) dato   un libro a Maria*
         yesterday Mario/he   has-PRS.3SG   Mario/he   given a book   to Mary
     b. *Algeri   el Mario/elo l'=ha   (*el Mario/elo) dat*
         yesterday Mario/he   SBJ-CL.3.SG.M=has Mario/he   given
         en libro a la Maria
         a book   to the Mary
         'Yesterday Mario gave Mary a book'
     c. *Del   Mario no   la=ha=(*la)   mai   parlà*
         of-the John   NEG SBJ-CL.3.SG.F=has=SBJ-CL.3.SG.F   never spoken
         'Of Mario she has never spoken'

The data discussed so far allow us to conclude that, for the moment, what we must consider an optional rule of subject-verb inversion is operative in Mòcheno main declarative clauses.

Let us now consider the second correlated property of V2, the structural identity between main declarative and main interrogative clauses, focusing on subject-verb inversion in main interrogatives. As illustrated in (41), in the main interrogative clauses of Mòcheno an NP subject cannot follow the finite verb in subject-verb inversion (41a) or precede it (41b), but can appear in the sentence only if it is (either right- or left-) dislocated (41c).

(41) a. **Benn hòn   daine kamaroten tsechen a film?*
         when have-PRS.3PL   your friends   seen   a film
     b. **Benn daine kamaroten hòn   tsechen a film?*
         when your friends   have-PRS.3PL   seen   a film
     c. *(Daina kamaroten$_j$), benn hòn=sa$_j$ tsechen a film*
         your friends   when have=SBJ-CL.3.PL   seen   a film
         (daine kamaroten)$_j$?
         your friends
         'When did your friends see a film?'

When the subject is realised by a pronoun, as in the examples in (42), the enclitic form is the only way to realise it, whereas the strong forms are excluded from both preverbal and postverbal positions.

(42) a. *Benn (*sa)=hòn=sa   /(*sei)   tsechen a film?*
         when SBJ-CL.3.PL=have=SBJ-CL.3.PL   /SBJ-STRONG.3.PL seen   a film

---

verb inversion available in Romance is "free-inversion", where the subject follows the non-finite verb form and not the finite one.

b. *Benn sei   hòn   tsechen a film?
   when SBJ-STRONG.3.PL have seen   a film
   'When did they see a film?'

As illustrated in (43), Mòcheno shares the same syntax as Romance contact varieties, in which NP subject-verb inversion is ruled out in wh-main interrogatives (43a, b, c) and is obligatory with subject clitics (43d, e).

(43) a. *Cosa hanno   i tuoi amici   comprato?
        what have-PRS.3SG the your friends bought
     b. I tuoi amici,   cosa hanno   comprato (i tuoi amici)?
        the your friends what have-PRS.3SG bought   the your friends
     c. *Che ha=i   i to amizi   tolt?
        what have=SBJ-CL.3.PL the your friends bought
     d. Che ha=i   tolt, i to amizi?
        what have=SBJ-CL.3.PL bought the your friends
     e. Che (*la)=ha=la   tolt?
        what SBJ-CL.3.SG.F=has=SBJ-CL.3.SG.F bought

The empirical data concerning the syntax of wh-main interrogatives point to a clear absence of structural identity between declarative and interrogative clauses when the subject is realised by an NP and to a partial identity when the subject is a pronoun (subject-verb inversion is obligatory). These facts call for an explanation, which I propose in this book, but also seem to indicate that in V2 languages (as Mòcheno is argued to be) the empirical properties connected with the V2 phenomenon might manifest themselves in different forms, since the movement of the finite verb to CP can interfere with specific grammatical traits of the specific V2 language. This is important from a comparative perspective because it strongly indicates that the Germanic V2 rule is one subtype of V2.

Finally, let us consider the last correlated property of the V2 rule, the asymmetry between main and embedded clauses with respect to the position of the finite verb, which is a characteristic German only. As exemplified in (44), Mòcheno, especially in the variety spoken in Palù, can be said to display an asymmetry between main and embedded clauses similar to that found in standard German, since in embedded clauses strict OV is possible (44a, b), though not obligatory (44c, d).

(44) a. I   boas   nèt, benn as   de maina
        SBJ-STRONG.1.SG know-PRS.1SG NEG when that the my
        kamaroten a film tsechen hom
        friends   a film seen   have-PRS.3PL

b. *I   boas   nèt, benn as   de maina*
    SBJ-STRONG.1.SG know-PRS.1SG NEG when that   the my
    kamaroten hom   a film tsechen
    friends   have a film seen
    'I don't know when my friends have seen a film'
c. *Er   hòt mer tsòk, as=o   du*
    SBJ-STRONG.3.SG.M has to me said, that=SBJ-CL.2.SG you
    a puach kaft   hòst
    a book   bought have-PRS.2SG
d. *Er   hòt mer tsòk, as=o   du*
    SBJ-STRONG.3.SG.M has to me said, that=SBJ-CL.2.SG you
    hòst   a puach kaft
    have-PRS.2SG a book   bought
    'He told me that you have bought a book'

In contact Romance languages, both strict OV syntax and the *Satzklammerstruktur* are always ungrammatical, as can be seen in (45).

(45) a. **Non so   quando i miei amici   un film visto hanno*
         NEG know-PRS.1SG when   the my friends   a film   seen have-PRS.3PL
     b. **Non so   quando i miei amici   hanno*
         NEG know-PRS.1SG when   the my friends   have-PRS.3PL
         un film visto
         a film   seen
     c. *Non so   quando i miei amici   hanno   visto*
         NEG know-PRS.1SG when   the my friends   have-PRS.3PL seen
         un film
         a film
     d. **No so   quando che i me amizi   en cinema vist ha*
         NEG know-PRS.1SG when that the my friends a film   seen have
     e. **No so   quando che i me amizi   ha en cinema vist*
         NEG know-PRS.1SG when that the my friends have a film   seen
     f. *No so   quando che i me amizi   i=ha*
         NEG know-PRS.1SG when that the my friends SBJ-CL.3.PL=have
         vist en cinema
         seen a film

In Table 2.2, I sum up what we have seen so far in this section, comparing the syntactic behaviour of Mòcheno, German and Old Romance languages with respect to the relevant phenomena. Unlike German, but like Old Romance, Mòcheno lacks a core property of V2 – linear restriction – but can be said to have subject-verb inversion and asymmetry between main and embedded clauses,

Table 2.2 Properties of V2 in German and Mòcheno

Language	Core properties		Correlated properties		
	V in 2nd position	XP-V	subj-V inversion	decl=wh	main vs embedded
German	✓	✓	✓	✓	✓
Old Romance	*	✓	✓ (opt)	✓	✓ (pro)
Mòcheno	*	✓	✓ (opt)	?	✓ (opt)

although these properties are optional. With respect to the structural symmetry between main declarative and main interrogative clauses, an analysis of the data in terms of presence/absence is misleading. I prefer not to take a position on the question at this point, but to wait until the issue can be dealt with in all its complexity (see the subsequent chapters).

The comparison between the three languages undertaken for this study has shown that Mòcheno patterns with V2 languages in important respects and its V2 system is much closer to that of Old Romance languages. I hypothesised above, relying on Benincà's analysis, that the asymmetries between Old Romance and German are due to the fact that only the former language family has an articulated structure of the left periphery (or has no restrictions blocking multiple access to CP, see above). Therefore, it can be predicted that, if Mòcheno patterns with Old Romance with respect to empirical manifestations of the V2 rule, it must also share the articulated structure of the left periphery with Old Romance languages. This prediction is tested in the next section.

2.3.3 On the structure of Mòcheno left periphery

The aim of this subsection is to demonstrate that in Mòcheno the V2 phenomenon (movement of the finite to CP followed by XP fronting) takes place within an articulated structure of the left periphery comparable to that identified for Old and modern Romance languages and that the asymmetries between Mòcheno and German are to be expected in a V2 language with a split-CP.

In order to demonstrate the above, I examine the syntax and the syntactic position of the different pragmatic constructions hosted in the left periphery: this description of the facts is relevant not only to the present discussion, but also to my subsequent analysis of V2.

Hanging topics
The hanging-topic construction, also known as *nominativus pendens* or *freies Thema* in the German linguistic tradition, is a structure present in both German (Altmann 1981; van Riemsdijk 1997; Frey 2004b; Grewendorf 2008; Ott 2011 a.o.)

and Romance (Benincà 1988, 2001, 2006 a.o.) languages. The construction allows a given constituent to be thematised in the left periphery.

The HT construction in German is illustrated in (46, the first two examples from Bidese/Tomaselli 2005: 73). In it the fronted XP must be in the nominative case (and is therefore somehow unconnected to the main clause) and must be doubled in IP by either a pronoun or an epithet.

(46) a. *Der neue Lehrer$_j$,   die Studenten haben   *(ihn$_j$) schon*
       the new teacher-NOM the students have-PRS.3PL him   already
       kennengelernt
       met
   b. **Den neuen Lehrer$_j$, die Studenten   haben   ihn$_j$ schon*
       the new teacher-ACC the studentsNOM have-PRS.3PL him   already
       kennengelernt
       met
       'As for the new teacher, the students have already met him'
   c. *Der neue Lehrer$_j$,   die Studenten haben   *(diesen Genie$_j$)*
       the new teacher-NOM the students have-PRS.3PL this genius
       schon   kennengelernt
       already met
   d. **Den neue Lehrer$_j$, die Studenten haben   diesen Genie$_j$*
       the new teacher-ACC the students have-PRS.3PL this genius
       schon   kennengelernt
       already met
       'As for the new teacher, the students have already met this genius'

In German, which has maintained the case morphology on DPs, the identification of the HT is straightforward; this cannot be said for Romance languages, which have lost the case morphology on nouns. As Mòcheno does not have case morphology on DPs either, it is worth consulting Benincà's (1988, 2001) and Benincà/Poletto's (2004) work, as they give a detailed analysis of HTs in Italian.

In languages with no case morphology on DPs, an HT cannot always be distinguished from other thematizations in the left periphery, such as LDs. This is because in both constructions the fronted XP has the same morphological shape and doubling is also possible for LDs.[16] Benincà (1988, 2001) proposes the

---

16. See Cardinaletti (2002) and Cruschina (2010) for the idea that the presence or absence of pronominal doubling in the LD construction is not due to optionality, but to the instantiation of different constructions. This point is irrelevant to the present discussion, since we are discussing the tests used to distinguish HTs from other constructions requiring a doubler in IP. The point made by Cardinaletti (2002) and Cruschina (2010) is discussed below and in Chapter 4 in the case of Mòcheno.

following syntactic properties to distinguish HTs from LDs: only HTs require obligatory resumption; only HTs can be doubled by an epithet, HTs are not recursive and have to appear in the highest portion of CP.

The first property is illustrated in (47, from Benincà 2001: 44), where, for the sake of clarity, PPs are considered. When a DP appears in the left periphery without a case-assigning preposition (47a, c) resumption is obligatory; when a fronted XP appears together with a preposition (47c, d), doubling is possible, but not obligatory. According to Benincà, in the former case the construction appearing in the left periphery must be analysed as an HT, in the latter case it is considered an LD.

(47) a. *Mario$_j$, non *(ne$_j$) parla   più   nessuno*
Mario   NEG of-him speak-PRS.3SG anymore no one
'Mario, nobody talks of him anymore'

b. *Di Mario$_j$, non (ne$_j$) parla   più   nessuno*
of Mario NEG of-him speak-PRS.3SG anymore no one
'Of Mario, nobody talks anymore'

c. *Mario$_j$, gli amici   *(gli$_j$) hanno   fatto   un brutto scherzo*
Mario   the friends to him have-PRS.3PL made a bad   joke
'Mario, his friends made him a nasty trick'

d. *A Mario$_j$, gli amici (gli$_j$) hanno   fatto un brutto scherzo*
to Mario the friends to him have-PRS.3PL made a bad   joke
'To Mario, his friends made a nasty trick'

Another property distinguishing HTs from LDs is the type of resumption permitted by the construction: as shown in (48a, c), an HT can be doubled by an epithet or by a tonic pronoun, whereas an LD can only be doubled by a clitic (48b, d).

(48) a. *Gianni$_j$ ho   parlato ieri   [a quel cretino]$_j$*
Gianni have-PRS.1SG spoken yesterday to that stupid

b. **A Gianni$_j$ ho   parlato ieri   [a quel cretino]$_j$*
to Gianni have-PRS.1SG spoken yesterday to that stupid
'As for Gianni, I met that stupid thing yesterday'

c. *Gianni$_j$ sono   uscita   ieri   [con lui]$_j$*
Gianni am-PRS.1SG gone out yesterday with him

d. **Con Gianni$_j$ sono   uscita   ieri   [con lui]$_j$*
with Gianni am-PRS.1SG gone out yesterday with him
'As for Gianni, I went out yesterday with him'

HTs are not recursive: as shown in (49) below (both adapted from Benincà/ Poletto 2004: 69), there can only be only one HT in a sentence (49a), whereas LDs can be recursive (49b).

(49) a. *Gianni$_j$ questo libro$_i$, non ne$_i$ hanno più
 Gianni this book NEG of-it have-PRS.1PL anymore
 parlato a lui$_j$
 spoken to him
 b. A Gianni$_j$ di questo libro$_i$, non glie$_j$ne$_i$ hanno
 to Gianni of this book NEG to him-of-it have-PRS.1PL
 più parlato
 anymore spoken
 'They have not talked to John about this book anymore'

Finally, as illustrated in (50), in Italian the HT has to precede all other constructions hosted in the left periphery.

(50) a. Giorgio, ai nostri amici, chi non parla più di lui?
 Giorgio, to-the our friends who NEG speaks-PRS.3SG anymore of him
 b. *Ai nostri amici, Giorgio, chi non parla più di lui?
 to-the our friends Giorgio who NEG speaks-PRS.3SG anymore of him
 c. *Chi ai nostri amici Giorgio non parla più di lui?
 who to-the our friends Giorgio NEG speaks-PRS.3SG anymore of him
 'As for Giorgio, to our friends who never talks of him anymore?'

Let us now move to consider whether or not the HT construction exists in Mòcheno, a language, as has already been noted, without morphological cases on NPs. I will first examine the fronted XPs in relation to doubling in IP. As illustrated in the examples in (51), when an indirect object (from now on: IO) appears in the left periphery with a case-assigning preposition, no resumption in IP is required (51a); when the IO is not preceded by a preposition, and only the fronted XP bears nominative case, resumption is obligatory (51b, c). The former construction has to be analysed as an LD, whereas the latter one is an HT: as in Romance and German, HTs require obligatory doubling.

(51) a. En de Maria hòt niemand klofft
 to the Mary has-PRS.3SG no one spoken
 b. *De Maria hòt niemand klofft
 the Mary has-PRS.3SG no one spoken
 c. De Maria$_j$, niemand hòt=en$_j$ klofft
 the Mary no one has=OBJ-CL.3.SG.F spoken
 'No one spoke to Mary'

As in German and modern Italian, also in Mòcheno a DP can be doubled by a pronominal form or by an epithet (52a, c); doubling with an epithet is ruled out when the fronted constituent bears case, that is when the preposition is present

(52b, d). The XP that can be doubled by an epithet has to be analysed as an HT, whereas the XP doubled by the pronominal for is an LD.

(52) a. *Der Nane$_j$, i   hòn   gester   klofft*
        the John, SBJ-STRONG.1.SG have yesterday spoken
        va im$_j$/ van sell tepp$_j$
        of him/ of that stupid
    b. **Van Nane$_j$, i   hòn   gester   klofft*
        of-the John, SBJ-STRONG.1.SG have yesterday spoken
        va im$_j$/ van sell tepp$_j$
        of him/ of that stupid
        'As for John, I spoke yesterday of him/of that stupid'
    c. *Maria$_j$, i   hòn   gester   a puach kaft*
        Maria, SBJ-STRONG.1.SG have yesterday a book   bought
        pet ir$_j$/ pet de sell bai$_j$
        with her/with that woman
    d. **Pet de Maria$_j$, i   hòn   gester   a puach kaft*
        with the Maria, SBJ-STRONG.1.SG have yesterday a book   bought
        pet ir$_j$/ pet de sell bai$_j$
        with her/with that woman
        'As for Maria, yesterday I bought a book with her/that woman'

When the fronted XP is a subject, a direct object (from now on: DO) or an IO, in Mòcheno the epithet has to co-occur with an obligatory clitic pronoun referring back to the fronted XP. This is illustrated in the examples in (53a, b, c).

(53) a. *Der Mario$_j$, er$_j$ hòt mer trog   a puach*
        the Mario SBJ-STRONG.3.SG.M has to me brought a book
        der sell tepp$_j$
        the that stupid
    b. **Der Mario$_j$, hòt mer   trog   a puach der sell tepp$_j$*
        the Mario   has-PRS.3SG brought a book   the that stupid
        'As for Mario, that stupid brought me a book'
    c. *Der Mario$_j$, i   hòn=en$_j$ nou net tsechen*
        the Mario, SBJ-STRONG.1.SG have=OBJ-CL.3.SG.M yet not seen
        hait der sell tepp$_j$
        today the that stupid
    d. **Der Mario$_j$, i   hòn   nou net tsechen*
        the Mario, SBJ-STRONG.1.SG have-PRS.1SG yet not seen
        hait der sell tepp$_j$
        today the that stupid
        'As for Mario, I have not seen that stupid yet today'

e. *Der Mario$_j$, i   hòn=en$_j$ gem*
   the Mario   SBJ-STRONG.1.SG have=OBJ-CL.3.SG.M given
   a puach en sell tepp$_j$
   a book   to that stupid
f. **Der Mario$_j$, hòn   gem   a puach en sell tepp$_j$*
   the Mario   have-PRS.1SG given a book   to that stupid
   'As for Mario, I gave a book to that stupid'

Recursion is another property of HTs that needs to be tested: according to the analysis of Romance languages given by Benincà (2001) and Benincà/Poletto (2004), HTs are not recursive. The same seems to be true for Mòcheno, as can be seen from the ungrammaticality of (54a). Notice, that HT's lack of recursion is a pertinent test, since multiple access to CP is generally possible in Mòcheno, as illustrated in (54b).

(54) a. **Der Mario$_k$, der Luca$_j$ gester   hòt=er$_j$ klofft*
         the Mario, the Luca yesterday has=SBJ-CL.3.SG.M spoken
         der sell tepp$_j$ va im$_k$
         the that stupid   of him
         'As for Mario, Luca spoke of him yesterday'
     b. *Der Mario$_k$, der Luca$_j$ gester   hòt-er$_j$ klofft*
        the Mario, the Luca yesterday has=SBJ-CL.3.SG.M spoken
        van der sell tepp$_k$?
        of that stupid
        'As for Mario, did Luca speak of that stupid yesterday?'

The last property that I will consider is the structural position of HTs within the fine structure of the left periphery; in order to determine where HTs are hosted within CP, I combine an HT with all other constructions appearing in the left periphery, detecting their relative order.

Let us first consider the combination of an HT and operators. As illustrated in the sentences in (55), an HT must precede a focused item (55a, c); the inverted order is ungrammatical (55b, d).

(55) a. *Der Mario$_j$, GESTER hòn=e=en$_j$*   *tsechen*
        the Mario, yesterday have=SBJ-CL.1.SG=OBJ-CL.3.SG.M seen
        der sell tepp$_j$, ont net hait
        the that stupid and not today
     b. **GESTER der Mario$_j$, hòn=e=en$_j$*   *tsechen*
        yesterday the Mario   have=SBJ-CL.1.SG=OBJ-CL.3.SG.M seen
        der sell tepp$_j$, ont net hait
        the that stupid and not today
        'As for Mario, it was yesterday that I saw that stupid thing, not today'

c. *Der Mario$_j$ ÒLLBE   hòn=sa   klofft   van sell tepp$_j$*
   the Mario   always   have=SBJ-CL.3.PL spoken   of-that stupid
d. **ÒLLBE der Mario$_j$ hòn=sa   klofft   van sell tepp$_j$*
   always   the Mario   have=SBJ-CL.3.PL spoken   of-that stupid
   'As for Mario, they have always spoken of that stupid'

In (56), I exemplify that an HT must also precede an interrogative wh-element.

(56) a. *Der Mario$_j$ ber   hòt=en$_j$ tsechen   der sell tepp$_j$?*
         the Mario   who   has=OBJ-CL.3.SG.M   seen   the that stupid
     b. **Ber der Mario$_j$ hos=o=en$_j$ tsechen*
         who the Mario   have=SUBJ-CL.2.SG=OBJ-CL.3.SG.M   seen
         der sell tepp$_j$?
         the that stupid
         'As for Mario, who saw that stupid?'
     c. *Der Mario$_j$ benn   hos=o   klofft   van sell tepp$_j$?*
         the Mario   when   have=SUBJ-CL.2.SG spoken   of-the that stupid
     d. **Benn der Mario$_j$ hos=o   klofft   van sell tepp$_j$?*
         when the Mario   have=SUBJ-CL.2.SG spoken   of-the that stupid
         'As for Mario, when did you speak of that stupid?'

The data discussed so far clearly indicate that in Mòcheno HTs have to precede operators.

Let us look now at the relative order of HTs and topics. As discussed below, Mòcheno displays two topic constructions: simple preposing (from now on: SP) and LD. In the former construction the topicalised XP is destressed, realises old/given information and lacks doubling in IP; in the latter, it is old/given information and is syntactically doubled by a clitic pronoun in IP. Beginning with SP, in (57) I show that an HT must also be followed by a simple-preposed constituent.

(57) a. *Der Mario$_j$, petn Nane   hom=sa   klofft*
         the Mario   with-the John have=SBJ-CL.3.PL   spoken
         van sell tepp$_j$
         of-that stupid
     b. **Petn Nane   der Mario$_j$ hom=sa   klofft*
         with-the John the Mario   have=SBJ-CL.3.PL   spoken
         van sell tepp$_j$
         of that stupid
         'As for Mario, with John they have already spoken of that stupid'
     c. *Der Mario$_j$ s puach   hòn=e=en$_j$ gem*
         the Mario   the book   have=SBJ-CL.1.SG=OBJ-CL.3.SG.M   given
         en sell tepp$_j$
         to that stupid

d. *S puach der Mario$_j$ hòn=e=en$_j$ gem
the book the Mario have=SBJ-CL.1.SG=OBJ-CL.3.SG.M given
en sell tepp$_j$
to that stupid
'As for Mario, I have given the book to that stupid'

In (58), I provide evidence that an HT must also be followed by a left-dislocated constituent.

(58) a. *Der Mario$_j$, en de Maria$_k$ hòn=e=en$_k$*
the Mario, to the Mary have=SBJ-CL.1.SG=OBJ-CL.3.SG.M
klofft van sell tepp$_j$
spoken of-the that stupid
b. **En de Maria$_k$ der Mario$_j$ hòn=e=en$_k$*
to the Mary the Mario have=SBJ-CL.1.SG=OBJ-CL.3.SG.M
klofft van sell tepp$_j$
spoken of-the that stupid
'As for Mario, I have spoken with Mary of that stupid'

Scene setters, which according to Benincà/Poletto (2004) form a special class among the elements appearing in the left periphery, must also follow an HT.

(59) a. *Der Mario$_j$ en 2006/gester hòn=sa=nen$_j$*
the Mario in 2006/yesterday have=SBJ-CL.3.PL=OBJ-CL.3.SG.M
gem a praiz en sell tepp$_j$
given a price to that stupid
b. **En 2006/gester der Mario$_j$ hon=(sa)=en$_j$*
in 2006/yesterday the Mario have=SBJ-CL.3.PL=OBJ-CL.3.SG.M
gem a praiz en sell tepp$_j$
given a price to that stupid
'As for Mario, in 2006/yesterday that stupid was given a price'

As summarised in Table 2.3, all combinatorial tests carried out in this section indicate that in Mòcheno an HT has to precede all other constructions hosted in the left periphery: we can therefore conclude that HTs occupy the left-most projection of CP.

Other topic constructions
In this subsection, I examine two other constructions that express topicality in Mòcheno: SP and LD. Comparisons between German and Romance languages (particularly Italian) are also key for topic constructions other than HTs: I will first examine the topic constructions in these languages.

Table 2.3 Combinatorial properties of HTs

HT	wh/focus
*wh/focus	HT
HT	SP
*SP	HT
HT	LD
*LD	HT
HT	scene setter
*scene setter	HT

As is well known (Altmann 1981; Bidese/Tomaselli 2005; Ott 2011 a.o.), in German topicality can be expressed through two constructions other than the HT-construction. The first is *Topikalisierung*, illustrated in (60a) and characterised by the fact that the fronted XP appearing in the left periphery is given a topic reading and is not doubled in IP. In (60b), I illustrate German *Linksversetzung*, in which the fronted XP has a contrastive topic reading and is doubled by a d-pronoun immediately following the fronted constituent.

(60) a. *Das Buch habe ich gestern gekauft*
the book have-PRS.1SG I yesterday bought
'The book, I bought yesterday'

b. *Den neuen Lehrer$_j$ den$_j$ haben die Studenten*
the new teacher-ACC him-ACC have-PRS.3PL the students
schon kennengelernt
already met
'The new teacher, the students have already met him'

Let us consider topic constructions in Italian, focusing on those encoded in the high left periphery and relevant for the V2 pheonomenon.[17] In Italian, a fronted constituent can be given a topic reading through two constructions: SP, illustrated in (61a, from Benincà 1988: 142) and LD (61b). SP involves a topic-comment articulation in which the fronted XP is not doubled by a clitic.[18] If the fronted XP in

---

17. For an analysis of these constructions, which is not offered in this book, I refer the reader to Cecchetto (1999, 2000), Cardinaletti (2002), Frey (2004a), Belletti (2006), Ott (2011) a.o.

18. This construction has been labelled in different ways in the Italian linguistic tradition. Benincà (1988) calls it "anaphoric anteposition", because in Italian only given (i.e. "anaphoric") constituents are compatible with this construction (see also Cruschina 2010). Rizzi (1997: 285) distinguishes between fronted constituents and calls the construction "topicalization" when the fronted XP is an argument and SP when non-arguments such as PPs are fronted. Here, I opt for the term SP, which captures the facts of Mòcheno in the best way. In Mòcheno, unlike Italian, both [+/–given (anaphoric)] XPs can be fronted, which makes the label "anaphoric

the topic-comment articulation is doubled by a clitic pronoun in IP, the construction is known as LD (Benincà 1988; Cinque 1977, 1990; Rizzi 1997; Frascarelli 2000, 2004; Cruschina 2010; 61b). Note, that in Italian it is not obligatory to give left-dislocated constituents a contrastive reading, as in German *Linksversetzung*, although a contrastive interpretation is generally possible (see, Frascarelli/ Hinterhölzl 2007).

(61) a. *La stessa proposta   fece   anche il partito di maggioranza*
        the same proposal made-PST.3SG also   the party of majority
        'The same proposal made also the party of majority'
   b. *La stessa proposta$_j$ la$_j$ fece   anche il partito di maggioranza*
        the same proposal   it   made-PST.3SG also   the party of majority
        'The same proposal was made by the party of majority, too'

This brief introduction has shown that in the languages closest to Mòcheno, topics can be expressed through two constructions other than HTs, which in both languages require (LD) or lack (SP) pronominal doubling in IP. Let us now consider Mòcheno and try to establish whether these two constructions are grammatical and, if they are, what their properties are. For the sake of clarity and in order to detect minimal pairs in the two constructions, I focus here on verb arguments, all of which have a clitic doubling.[19]

The first thing to be noted is that in Mòcheno, German *Linksversetzung* is ruled out, as shown in (62). This is due to the process of reduction that both d-pronouns and demonstratives have undergone, which in Mòcheno cannot be either topicalised or focused and must therefore be analysed as weak forms (see next chapter). As illustrated in (62b), only strong pronominal forms (which can be focused and topicalised) can appear in constructions similar to German *Linksversetzung*. However, consultants claim that these are very unnatural in Mòcheno. The most spontaneous construction is the one shown in (62c), where the fronted XP is doubled by a clitic in IP.

---

anteposition" misleading in the case of Mòcheno. The distinction between "topicalization" and "simple preposing" seems redundant to me and I find the label SP much more appropriate to describe the construction in Mòcheno. I therefore use this term when referring to the Mòcheno construction.

19. As discussed in Cognola (2010), in Mòcheno it is possible to double some constituents, such as PPs with semi-argumental status, with a P+pronoun, but this possibility is not shared by all semi-arguments. For the sake of clarity, I have decided not to discuss these complex cases and to focus on verb arguments, which display a more coherent pattern.

(62)   a.   *Der Nane$_j$, der/der sell$_j$ hòn=e   pakemmp
             the John   him-that one   have=SBJ-CL.1.SG met
       b.   Der Nane$_j$, im$_j$ hòn=e   pakemmp
             the John   him   have=SBJ-CL.1.SG met
             'As for John, it was him who I met'
       c.   Der Nane$_j$, i   hòn=en$_j$ pakemmp
             the John   SBJ-STRONG.1.SG have=OBJ-CL.3.SG.M met
             'As for John, I met him'

The data discussed in (62) clearly indicate that Mòcheno relies on a single construction to express topics that are doubled by a pronoun in IP, which immediately recalls the Romance LD construction rather than the German one.

In order to investigate the properties of topics in Mòcheno, I start out from the assumption that all topics are D-linked (Pesetzky 1987) and are either accessible (+given or anaphoric) or non accessible (−given or −anaphoric) in the context (Reinhart 1981; Chafe 1987; Vallduví 1992; Frascarelli/Hinterhölzl 2007; Lopez 2009; Cruschina 2010).

In (63a), I show that in Mòcheno SP can express non-accessible D-linked constituents, whereas LD (63b) cannot do so.

(63)   Context: my friend was supposed to buy a book, but was always finding an excuse for not buying it. Finally he buys the book and I can say to another friend who knows the facts:
       a.   S puach   hòt=er   gester   kaft
             the book has=SBJ-CL.3.SG.M   yesterday bought
       b.   #S puach$_j$ er   hòt=s$_j$ gester   kaft
             the book   SBJ-CL.3.SG.M   has=OBJ-CL.3.SG.N yesterday bought
             'He bought the book yesterday'

Accessible and D-linked constituents can be realised either through an SP (64a) or an LD (64b). In this construction the fronted topic is not given a contrastive reading, which, according to consultants, is given to the strong subject pronoun instead.

(64)   Someone asks: Benn   hòt=er   kaft   s puach?
                       when   has=SBJ-CL.3.SG.M   bought   the book
       a.   S puach   hòt=er   gester   kaft
             the book has=SBJ-CL.3.SG.M   yesterday bought
       b.   S puach   er   hòt=s   gester   kaft
             the book SBJ-CL.3.SG.M   has=OBJ-CL.3.SG.N yesterday bought
             'He bought the book yesterday'

The data above, far from representing a complete discussion of SP and LD in Mòcheno, show that in this language a topic can be realised in the left periphery by either an SP or an LD. Unlike Italian, SP has a wider range of usages, since it is compatible with both accessible and non-accessible D-linked consituents, whereas in Italian SP is restricted to accessible topics. Conversely, LD in Mòcheno is compatible only with [+given] constituents, whereas in Italian it can realise both [+/–given] XPs. In contrast to German, LD in Mòcheno does not have a contrastive reading, which is an effect of its morphological realization (the lack of strong d-pronouns in Mòcheno). Mòcheno SP, on the other hand, shares most of the properties of German topicalization.

After describing the two constructions that realise topics in the left periphery of Mòcheno, I now examine the combination of these constructions with operators. The prediction to be tested is that topics, realised syntactically as SP or LD, precede operators, as they do in Romance languages. Beginning with topics realised by an SP, in (65), I consider the combination of simple-preposed topics and interrogative wh-elements. As is evident from the examples below, an SP can never precede an interrogative wh- pronoun.

(65) *Context: Last class I asked the students to buy the textbook; in the next class I ask:*
Someone says: Uans hòt s puach kaft (someone has bought a book)
a. **S puach ber hòt kaft?*
the book who has bought

Context: In the conversation it was said that he had met someone's mother; after a while, I ask:
Someone says: Er hòt de sai muam pakemmp (he has met her aunt)
b. **De sai muam bo hòt=er pakemmp?*
the her aunt where has=SBJ-CL.3.SG.M met

Context: The teacher tells us to buy a book; after one hour I see that a school friend of mine already has the book, and I say:
Someone says: Der Mario hòt schua s puach kaft (Mario has already bought the book)
c. **Der Mario benn hòt kaft s puach?*
the Mario when has-PRS.3SG bought the book

As illustrated in (66), a [+/–given] D-linked constituent realised syntactically by an SP cannot follow the operator either.

(66) *Context: Last class I asked the students to buy the textbook; in the next class I ask:*
Someone says: Uans hòt s puach kaft (someone has bought the book)

a. *Ber s puach   hòt   kaft?
   who the book has-PRS.3SG bought

Context: In the conversation it was said that he had met someone's mother; after a while, I ask:
Someone says: Er hòt de sai muam pakemmp (he met his aunt)

b. *Bo   de dai muam hòt=er   pakemmp?
   where the his aunt has=SBJ-CL.3.SG.M   met

Context: The teacher tells us to buy a book; after one hour I see that a school friend of mine already has the book, and I say:
Someone says: Der Mario hòt schua s puach kaft (Mario has already bought the book)

c. *Benn   der Mario hòt   kaft   s puach?
   where the Mario has-PRS.3SG bought the book

As shown in (67), the same facts hold when foci are considered: a simple-preposed verb argument can neither precede (67a, c, e) nor follow a focused item (67b, d, f).

(67) *Context: My brother says he is going to buy the book for Maria's birthday in the bookshop, which would take him at least one hour; after ten minutes he is back with the book and says he bought it in the village shop. My mum is amased that he was so quick, since she thinks he had gone to the far-away bookshop. I say:*
Someone says: Ah, s puach hòt=er en de libreria kaft (the book he bought in the shop)

a. *S puach EN DE BOTEIG hòt=er   kaft,   ont net
   the book in the shop   has=SBJ-CL.3.SG.M bought and not
   en de libreria
   in the bookshop

b. *EN DE BOTEIG s puach hòt=er   kaft,   ont net
   in the shop the book has=SBJ-CL.3.SG.M bought and not
   en de libreria
   in the bookshop

Context: Mario was supposed to go today to buy a book for Mary's birthday, but had done it yesterday. My mother, who thinks that Mario still has to buy the book, says that Mario has to go to town today. I say:
Someone says: Ah, Mario hòt hait kaft s puach en de Maria (Mario bought Mary a book today)

c. *En de Maria GESTER   hòt=er   kaft   s puach,
   to the Mary yesterday has=SBJ-CL.3.SG.M bought the book
   ont net hait
   and not today

d. *GESTER en de Maria hòt=er   kaft   s puach,
   yesterday to the Mary has=SBJ-CL.3.SG.M bought the book
   ont net hait
   and not today

The data discussed so far would not have been predicted from either Beninca's (2001) or Rizzi's (1997) maps of the articulated structure of the left periphery, since they indicate that in Mòcheno topics realised by an SP cannot either precede (which is predicted by Benincà's theory) or follow (which is the prediction of Rizzi's system, where TopicPs are recursive above and below FocusP) a fronted operator. In the following chapters, it will be shown that this situation directly depends on the V2 rule of Mòcheno.[20]

Let us now examine topics realised syntactically as LD, which in main declarative clauses are compatible only with accessible, D-linked constituents. As shown in (68), an interrogative wh-element can co-occur with a left-dislocated verb argument: all ungrammatical sentences involving a simple-preposed verb argument preceding a wh-element given in (68) above become grammatical if the verb argument is doubled by a pronoun, that is if it is syntactically an LD and not an SP. Note that in interrogative clauses LD expresses both [+/–given] constituents, as it is the only construction compatible with operators.

(68) Context: last class, I asked the students to buy the textbook. In the next class, I ask:
Someone says: Uans hòt s puach kaft (someone bought the book)

a. S puach$_j$ ber hòt=s$_j$ kaft?
   the book who has=OBJ-CL.3.SG.N bought
   'Who bought the book?'

Context: I know that a friend of mine was supposed to buy a book for Maria's birthday. I offer to go with him, since he does not have a car and you must drive to the shops. He answers that he has already bought the book, and I suppose that he went with someone. I ask:

---

20. Note, that the incompatibility between a fronted topic (realised syntactically by an SP) and a fronted operator is not explained by Rizzi's (2004) latest version of RM, according to which a topic (SP) and an operator do not give rise to RM because they have a different featural make-up (Topic vs. Focus features).

Someone says: Er hòt gester s puach en de Maria kaft (He bought Mary a book yesterday)
    b. En de Maria$_j$ pet bem   hòt-=er=en$_j$
       to the Mary with whom has=SBJ-CL.3.SG.M=OBJ-CL.3.SG.F
       kaft   s puach?
       bought the book
       'With whom did you buy the book for Mary?'

Context: The teacher tells us to buy a book; after one hour I see that a school friend of mine already has the book, and I say:
Someone says: Der Mario hòt schua s puach kaft (Mario has already bought the book)
    c. Der Mario$_j$ benn hòt=er$_j$ kaft   s puach?
       the Mario when has=SBJ-CL.3.SG.M bought the book
       'When did Mario buy the book?'

As shown in (69), a left-dislocated topic can only precede, never follow, an interrogative wh-element.

(69) *Context: Last class I asked the students to buy the textbook; in the next class I ask:*
      Someone says: Uans hòt s puach kaft (someone bought a book)
      a. *Ber s puach$_j$ hòt-s$_j$ kaft?
         who the book has=OBJ-CL.3.SG.N bought

Context: I know that a friend of mine was supposed to buy a book for Maria's birthday. I offer to go with him, since he does not have a car and you must drive to the shops. He answers that he has already bought the book, and I suppose that he went with someone. I ask:
Someone says: Er hòt gester s puach en de Maria kaft (He bought yesterday Mary a book)
      b. *Pet bem   en de Maria$_j$ hos=o=en$_j$
         with whom to the Mary have=SBJ-CL.2.SG=OBJ-CL.3.SG.F
         kaft   s puach?
         bought the book

Context: The teacher tells us to buy a book; after one hour I see that a school friend of mine already has the book, and I say:
Someone says: Der Mario hòt schua s puach kaft (Mario has already bought the book)
      c. *Benn der Mario$_j$ hòt=er$_j$ kaft   s puach?
         where the Mario has=SBJ-CL.3.SG.M bought the book

The distribution of left-dislocated verb arguments in the left periphery does not change when a focus is involved either: as can be seen in (70), a focus can be preceded by a [+/−given] constituent realised syntactically by an LD; an LD must precede the operator and can never follow it.

(70) Context: *My brother says he is going to buy the book for Maria's birthday in the bookshop, which would take him at least one hour. After ten minutes he is back with the book and says he bought it in the village shop. My mum is amased that he was so quick, since she thinks he had gone to the far-away bookshop. I say:*
Someone says: Ah, s puach hòt=er en de libreria kaft *(The book he bought in the bookshop)*

   a. S puach$_j$ EN DE BOTEIG hòt=er=s$_j$
       the book in the shop   has=SBJ-CL.3.SG.M=OBJ-CL.3.SG.N
       kaft,   ont net en de libreria
       bought and not in the bookshop
   b. *EN DE BOTEIG s puach$_j$ hòt=er=s$_j$
       in the shop   the book has=SBJ-CL.3.SG.M=OBJ-CL.3.SG.N
       kaft,   ont net en de libreria
       bought and not in the bookshop

Context: *Mario bought a book for Mary's birthday yesterday. His mother, who thinks that he still has to buy the book, says that Mario has to go buy the book today. I say:*
Someone says: Ah, Mario hòt hait kaft s puach en de Maria *(Today Mario has bought Mary the book)*

   c. En de Maria$_j$ GESTER   hòt=er=en$_j$
       to the Mary   yesterday has=SBJ-CL.3.SG.M=OBJ-CL.3.SG.M
       kaft   s puach, ont net hait
       bought the book and not today
   d. *GESTER en de Maria$_j$ hòt=er=en$_j$
       yesterday to the Mary has=SBJ-CL.3.SG.M=OBJ-CL.3.SG.M
       kaft   s puach, ont net hait
       bought the book and not today

The data discussed so far are summarised in Table 2.4, where the combinatorial properties of SPs and LDs are reexamined. The conclusion arrived at on the basis of the different tests is that SPs are never compatible with fronted operators, whereas LDs can co-occur with operators, but only if they precede them. In sentences with a fronted operator, LDs realise both [+/−given] constituents, as they are the only grammatical construction in this configuration.

Table 2.4 Combinatorial properties of SPs and LDs

*SP	wh/focus
*wh/focus	SP
LD	wh/focus
*wh/focus	LD

The discussion of data carried out in this section has allowed us to reconstruct the structure of the left periphery sketched in (71) for Mòcheno: HTs and scene setters precede topics (realised syntactically by LD or SP) and operators. Nothing can yet be said with respect to the CP position targeted by the finite verb.

(71) [$_{FRAME}$ [HT – Scene Setter] [$_{THEME}$ [LD/SP] [$_{FOCUS}$ [wh/focus]]]]

The constructions hosted in the left periphery can co-occur, as shown in (72); their order is that given in the structure in (71), as the ungrammaticality of (72b–d) shows.

(72) a. Der Mario$_j$, gester   s puach$_k$ ber
       the Mario   yesterday the book   who
       hòt=s$_k$=en$_j$ gem   en sell tepp$_j$?
       has=OBJ-CL.3.SG.N=OBJ-CL.3.SG.M given to that stupid

   b. *Der Mario$_j$, s puach$_k$ gester   ber
       the Mario   the book   yesterday who
       hòt=s$_k$=en$_j$ gem   en sell tepp$_j$?
       has=OBJ-CL.3.SG.N=OBJ-CL.3.SG.M given to that stupid

   c. *S puach$_k$ der Mario$_j$ gester   ber
       the book the Mario   yesterday who
       hòt=s$_k$=en$_j$ gem   en sell tepp$_j$?
       has=OBJ-CL.3.SG.N=OBJ-CL.3.SG.M given to that stupid

   d. *S puach$_k$ der Mario$_j$ ber   gester
       the book the Mario   who   yesterday
       hòt=s$_k$=en$_j$ gem   en sell tepp$_j$?
       has=OBJ-CL.3.SG.N=OBJ-CL.3.SG.M given to that stupid
       'Mario, yesterday who gave a book to that stupid?'

In Table 2.5, I sum up the syntactic behaviour of the three languages discussed in this chapter: German, Old Romance (in particular Old Italian) and Mòcheno, with respect to the properties necessary for the detection of the V2 rule. From the table, it can be seen that Mòcheno patterns like Old Romance languages in all important respects, since in both languages the lack of linear restriction correlates with the presence of a split-CP.

Table 2.5 Properties of V2 in German, Old Romance and Mòcheno

Language	Core properties		Correlated properties		
	V in 2nd position	XP-V	subj-V inversion	decl=wh	main vs embedded
German	✓	✓	✓	✓	✓
Old Romance	*	✓	✓ (opt)	✓	✓ (pro)
Mòcheno	*	✓	✓ (opt)	?	✓ (opt)

My initial prediction that, if Mòcheno patterns like Old Romance with respect to the V2 rule, then it must also share the articulated structure of the left periphery with Old Romance, has been fully validated. On the basis of the strong evidence given in this chapter, I propose in the remainder of the book a cartographic account of the syntax of Mòcheno, starting from the premise that we are dealing with an Old Romance type V2 language. But first, I would like to briefly discuss some evidence against the contact hypothesis as an explanation of the empirical facts included in this chapter.

2.3.4 Against an account in terms of optionality/grammar competition

The aim of this book is to provide evidence for a categorization of Mòcheno as a V2 language in which the observed syntactic variation follows naturally from the type of V2 displayed by the language. I do not believe it to be the result of either optionality in the application of the syntactic rules, or of the availability to Mòcheno speakers of competing grammars with different parameter settings. I challenge the contact hypothesis by pointing out that the characteristics of V2 in Mòcheno can be explained by demonstrating that Mòcheno patterns like V2 Old Romance languages. This I have tried to do in this chapter. The approach adopted in this work is therefore completely antithetical to the idea that variation depends on optionality; instead, it regards it as the result of the internal rules of a single grammar. In this final subsection, I finish the discussion by adding some further evidence against the account of Mòcheno syntax that uses the double-base/contact hypothesis.

As we have seen above, in Mòcheno main declarative clauses, DP subject-verb inversion appears to be optional, as repeated in (73) below.

(73) a. Van   Nane hòt   der Mario niamer klofft
        of-the John has-PRS.3SG the Mario never   spoken
     b. Van   Nane der Mario   hòt   niamer klofft
        of-the John the Mario has-PRS.3SG never   spoken
        'Of John Mario never spoke'

c. Gester   hòt   der Mario   en de Maria a puach gem
   yesterday has-PRS.3SG the Mario   to the Mary a book   given
d. Gester   der Mario   hòt   en de Maria a puach gem
   yesterday the Mario   has-PRS.3SG   to the Mary a book   given
   'Yesterday Mario gave Mary a book'

An alternative analysis to the one proposed in this book (subject-verb inversion is not optional, but, since Mòcheno is a V2 with a split-CP, the finite verb moves to CP in all sentences and the DP subject can itself be topicalised or remain below in the clause) is that the examples given are the result of optionality or of the application of the abstract rules of competing Romance and a German grammars. According to this hypothesis, sentences with subject-verb inversion have to be derived according to the structure in (74): the finite verb moves to CP; the DP subject remains in Spec,TP (or in VP, according to the adopted theory).

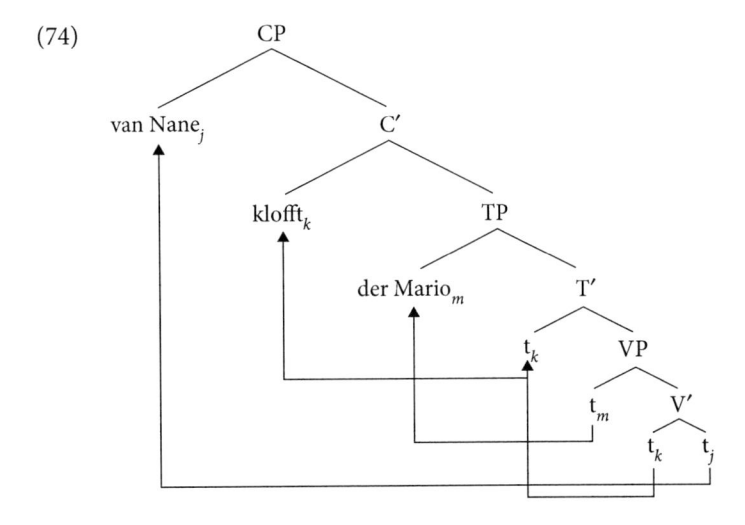

(74)
```
              CP
            /    \
     van Nane_j   C'
                 /  \
              klofft_k   TP
                        /  \
                 der Mario_m   T'
                              /  \
                           t_k   VP
                                /  \
                             t_m   V'
                                  /  \
                                t_k   t_j
```

The version without inversion, on the other hand, would correspond to the structure in (75): the finite verb remains in T⁰ and is preceded by the fronted XP and the DP subject, in Spec,CP and Spec,TP respectively.

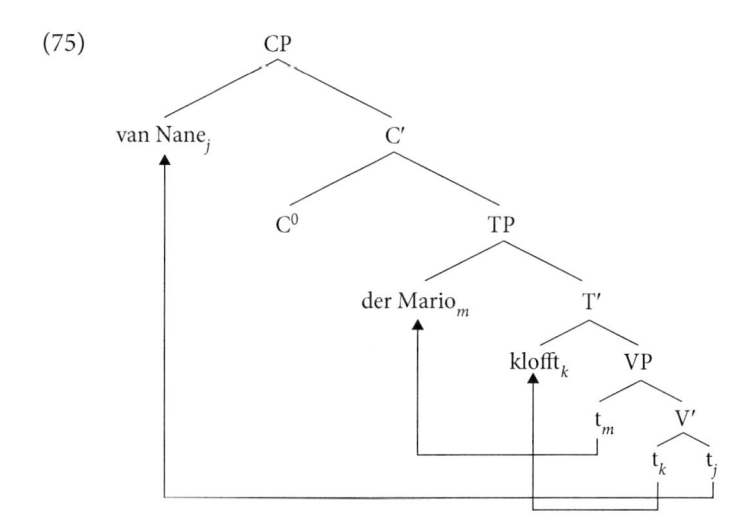

(75)
```
                    CP
                   /  \
          van Nane_j   C'
                      /  \
                    C⁰    TP
                         /  \
                der Mario_m  T'
                            /  \
                       klofft_k  VP
                               /  \
                             t_m   V'
                                  /  \
                                t_k   t_j
```

I think that there is strong evidence for the hypothesis that the distribution of subject-verb inversion in Mòcheno is not determined by the availability to the speakers of two grammars with different parameter settings, but must be the result of factors internal to a single grammar. Let us consider the examples in (76). Sentences (76a) and (76b) differ only in the syntax of the NP subject: in the first sentence subject-inversion has taken place, in the second one it has not. The hypothesis of contact would account for the observed syntactic variation through the assumption that (76a) is the output of the abstract rules of the conservative Germanic grammar, whereas (76b) is created by the abstract rules of the innovative Romance grammar. This hypothesis proves to be incorrect when we consider the position of the past participle: in both sentences, the past participle appears in sentence-final position giving rise to the so-called *Satzklammerstruktur* typical of German but completely ungrammatical in the contact Romance varieties (76c, d).

(76) a. Gester   hòt   der Mario a puach en de Maria gem
        yesterday has-PRS.3SG the Mario a book   to the Mary given
     b. Gester   der Mario hòt   a puach en de Maria gem
        yesterday the Mario has-PRS.3SG a book   to the Mary given
     c. *Ieri   Mario ha   un libro a Maria dato
        yesterday Mario has-PRS.3SG   a book   to Mary given
     d. *Algeri   el Mario l'ha   en libro ala Maria
        yesterday the Mario SBJ-CL.3.SG.M=has a book to-the

The presence of the OV structure in both the sentences with and those without subject-verb inversion runs counter to the double-base hypothesis. If a sentence without subject-verb inversion was the output of the abstract rules of Romance, the whole sentence would be expected to follow the rules of the Romance grammar. A sentence without subject-verb inversion would be expected to have VO syntax – as in Romance – and a sentence with subject-verb inversion should correlate with OV word order – as in German.

Another counterexample to the hypothesis that the syntactic variation observed in Mòcheno depends on the availability to speakers of Mòcheno of two grammars with different parameter setting can be found in (77). In (77a), I show that subject-verb inversion can coexist in Mòcheno with multiple access to CP: this would not be the case if the V2 property were the result of the application of the abstract rules of standard German, since subject-verb inversion would then be expected to co-occur with the linear restriction, as in German (77b, c).[21]

(77) a. *Gester   en de Maria hòt   der Mario a puach gem*
       yesterday to the Mary has-PRS.3SG the Mario a book   given
   b. **Gestern   der Maria   hat   der Mario   ein Buch*
       yesterday the Mary-DAT has-PRS.3SG the Mario-NOM a book
       gegeben
       given
   c. *Gestern   hat   der Mario   der Maria   ein Buch*
       yesterday has-PRS.3SG the Mario-NOM the Mary-DAT a book
       gegeben
       given
       'Yesterday Mario gave Mary a book'

Focusing on subject-verb inversion with pronominal subjects, we again find evidence against both the optionality and the contact hypotheses. As discussed above, in Mòcheno the distribution of subject pronouns varies according to the class (strong, weak and clitic, see next chapter) to which the pronominal forms belong. As shown again in (78a), a subject clitic must always follow the finite verb, whereas the strong pronominal forms can only appear before the finite verb (78b), a position that is ruled out for the clitic pronoun.

---

21. As discussed in Chapters 4 and 5, the two versions (with or without subject-verb inversion) are not identical from the point of view of semantics/pragmatics. This would not be expected within the optionality/contact hypothesis, but is predicted by the theory that variation takes place within a single grammar.

(78) a. Gester   hòt=se/   *si   kaft   a puach
         yesterday has=SBJ-CL.3.SG.F/ SBJ-STRONG.3.SG.F bought a book
     b. Gester   si/   *se=hòt   kaft   a puach
         yesterday SBJ-STRONG.3.SG.F SBJ-CL.3.SG.F=has bought a book
         'Yesterday she bought a book'

The syntax of subject pronouns illustrated by the examples in (78) is unexpected if one start from the hypothesis of two competing grammars, but fully predicted by the theory of a single grammar with specific rules independent of both German and Romance contact varieties. In German, there is no evidence for a system similar to that of Mòcheno: the reduced pronominal forms that appear in the *Wackernagelposition* are homophonous with the strong forms (Tomaselli 1990; Poletto/Tomaselli 1995), indicating that German has not developed a morphologically different class of weak pronouns, unlike Mòcheno. The pattern displayed by Mòcheno subject pronouns is also unexpected from the perspective of those Germanic languages which have developed a morphologically different class of reduced pronouns, such as West Flemish (Haegeman 1990, 1992) and Bavarian dialects (Bayer 1984; Gruber 2008). In West Flemish weak forms are never obligatory, but can appear either alone or together with the strong form in a doubling construction. This is very different from Mòcheno, where, on the one hand, the reduced form *se* is obligatory, and, on the other, its presence rules out the appearance of the corresponding strong form *si* in subject-verb inversion. In Bavarian, reduced pronominal forms are not found in all persons of the paradigm but are limited to the second persons. In the second singular, moreover, the reduced form enclitic to finite verb and complementiser is realised by the second person suffix *-st*. In the Romance contact dialect Trentino, a language that has subject clitics (see Vanelli/Renzi/Benincà 1985; Brandi/Cordin 1981; Poletto 2000 a.o.), these have to precede the finite verb in main declarative clauses. A strong pronominal form must precede the finite verb and can only appear together with the clitic form (doubling).

(79) a. Algeri   l'ha=(*la)   tolt   en libro
         yesterday SBJ-CL.3.SG.F=has=SBJ-CL.3.SG.F bought a book
     b. *Gester   se=hòt   kaft   a puach
         yesterday SBJ-CL.3.SG.F=has   bought   a book
     c. Algeri   ela *(l)'ha   tolt   en libro
         yesterday she SBJ-CL.3.SG.F=has bought   a book
     d. *Gester   si   se=hòt   kaft   a puach
         yesterday SBJ-STRONG.3.SG.F SBJ-CL.3.SG.F=has bought   a book

The syntax of Mòcheno subject pronouns also diverges from that of Italian. As is well-known (Rizzi 1982 a.o.) and as illustrated in the example in (80a, b), Italian is a consistent *pro-drop* language, which means that "a silent, referential, definite subject" (Holmberg/Roberts 2010: 16) can be licensed in all finite clauses. In consistent *pro*-drop languages, a strong subject pronoun appearing in a sentence gets a pragmatically-marked reading. Mòcheno behaves differently from standard Italian: as shown in (80c), "a silent, referential, definite subject" cannot be licensed in Mòcheno main clauses.²²

(80) a. *Ieri   ha   comprato un libro*
        yesterday has-PRS.3SG bought   a book
     b. *Ieri   lei ha   comprato un libro*
        yesterday she has-SBJ-CL.3.SG.F bought a book
     c. **Gester hòt   kaft   a puach*
        yesterday has-SBJ-CL.3.SG.F bought a book

The last argument against a treatment of the syntactic variation found in Mòcheno in terms of optionality/contact that I want to mention is a general one unrelated to the phenomena dealt with in this book. It is, however, very relevant to the present discussion. As pointed out by Svenonius (2000: 280), the hypothesis of contact is tenable only when optionality is "rampant", that is when it is found in all syntactic environments. As discussed by Cognola (2010, 2012) and illustrated in (81) below, this fact does not hold for Mòcheno. In this language, characterised by the co-existence of both OV and VO word orders as shown again in (81a), VO syntax is obligatory in all sentences with a fronted operator (81b–e). This behaviour is not predicted at all by the hypothesis that syntactic variation is due either to optionality or to the presence of two competing grammars.

(81) a. *Gester   hòn=e   (kaft)   s puach (kaft)*
        yesterday have=SBJ-CL.1.SG bought   the book bought
        'Yesterday I bought the book'
     b. *Benn   hos=o   kaft   s puach?*
        when   have=SBJ-CL.2.SG bought   the book
     c. **Benn   hos=o   s puach kaft?*
        when   have=SBJ-CL.2.SG the book bought
        'When did you buy the book?'

---

22. As will be shown in Chapter 5, Mòcheno must actually be considered a partial *pro*-drop language (in Holmberg's 2005, 2012 sense); a fact, however, which does not contradict the argument presented in this last section, since the *pro*-drop system of Mòcheno is not shared by the other languages considered in this subsection.

d. KA PERSEN hòn=e   kaft   s puach, ont net ka Trient
    in Pergine have=SBJ-CL.1.SG bought the book, and not in Trento
e. *KA PERSEN hòn=e   s puach kaft,   ont net ka Trient
    in Pergine have=SBJ-CL.1.SG the book bought, and not in Trento
    'It was in Pergine where I bought the book, not in Trento'

The distribution of OV and VO syntax in main declarative and main interrogative clauses was investigated in sentences 1 and 4 of the questionnaire. The results are summarised in Table 2.6, which shows that in main declarative clauses both OV and VO syntax are used and judged grammatical by all the speakers of all three varieties; the same is true for VO syntax in main interrogative clauses. The possibility of having OV syntax drops when wh-main interrogatives are considered. Only two consultants (ROVE-DP and PALÙ-FM, 2/42, see Appendix) produced OV word order when asked to translate the stimulus Italian wh-main interrogative into Mòcheno; 19/42 judge OV grammatical in wh-interrogatives, but do not actively use it and 21/42 reject it. For most of the speakers who rejected OV word order in wh-interrogatives, OV word order is only possible in these sentences if the interrogative is a special one (in Obenauer's 1994 sense), a judgment that is also shared by the consultant from Palù who took part to the research reported in Cognola (2010). Given that many of the speakers clearly said that OV word order is possible only in special interrogative clauses, it cannot be excluded that those who accepted OV but did not use this word pattern actively in unmarked sentences had this special interpretation in mind.[23]

Let me finish the discussion of the distribution of OV/VO by considering the distribution of the word orders according to the variable "age". In the variety of Palù, OV in wh-interrogative clauses is rejected by 3/5 of the middle-aged speakers (PALÙ-MP; PALÙ-MO and PALÙ-PB), by a young speaker (PALÙ-LB)

Table 2.6 OV/VO word orders in main declarative and interrogative clauses

	VO in main decl	OV in main decl	VO in wh-interr	OV in wh-interr
Palù	15/15	15/15	14/14	8/14
Fierozzo	15/15	13/15	15/15	7/15
Roveda	14/14	12/14	14/14	6/13
Total	44/44	40/44	43/43	21/42
Percentage	100%	90%	100%	50%

---

23. In the interviews, I obviously tried to verify whether OV syntax was accepted because the wh-interrogative was interpreted as a special rather than a real interrogative, but a straightforward result was only achieved for some speakers (see questionnaires in the Appendix).

and by the elderly PALÙ-MT. Considering that PALÙ-LB is aged 29 and is therefore very close to the group of the middle-aged speakers and also that the key informant from Palù (aged 40) patterns like the other people of his age, it has to be concluded that rejection of OV in wh-main interrogatives is a trait of the Palù dialect spoken by the middle-aged. In Fierozzo we have a different picture, since OV in wh-interrogatives is rejected by 3/5 of elderly speakers (FIER-AM; FIER-COP and FIER-EI), by 3/5 of middle-aged (FIER-GG, FIER-RB and FIER-RR) and by two young people, who do not accept OV in main declaratives either (FIER-AP and FIER-MG). Finally, in Roveda OV in wh-main interrogatives is rejected by 3/5 of young speakers (ROVE-IP, ROVE-LF and ROVE-SO), by two middle-aged (ROVE-MP and ROVE-MB) and two elderly speakers (ROVE-JP and ROVE-EO). These data seem to indicate that the presence of OV word orders cannot necessarily be considered a conservative grammatical property, preserved by elderly speakers and lost in the language used by the younger generation; all empirical facts indicate that the picture is much more intricate than this. Unfortunately, examining these sociolinguistic factors in detail is beyond the scope of this book.

In this subsection, I have provided evidence against an explanation for the syntactic variation observed in Mòcheno in terms of optionality or contact and in favour of an analysis that treats it as the result of rules internal to a single grammar characterised by a V2 rule, which is explored in the following chapters. This discussion is crucial to my thesis, since it shows that, on close examination, the two analyses generally adopted in an attempt to understand the Mòcheno data (see above) are actually implausible and must therefore be abandoned in favour of a new account.

2.4 Conclusions

In this chapter, which has focused on German and Old Romance languages, I have discussed the empirical properties of the V2 phenomenon and the theoretical accounts put forward to make sense of them. In the second part of the chapter, Mòcheno was examined for the syntactic properties of the V2 rule identified for Germanic and Old Romance languages, in order to show that the V2 phenomenon also exists in this language.

I suggest that Mòcheno must be considered a V2 language, despite the fact that the V2 phenomenon manifests itself only through correlated properties, unlike German and V2 Germanic languages in general. I propose that this is because Mòcheno does not pattern like Germanic V2 languages, but like the Old

Romance V2 languages, a theory supported by the comparisons illustrated in this chapter. On the one hand, I show that Old Romance languages only have the *Korrelate* of the V2 phenomenon, like Mòcheno, on the other that in both Old Romance and Mòcheno this is associated with the presence of an articulated left periphery of the clause. My proposal is thus that the empirical facts observed in Mòcheno naturally follow from its characterization as a V2 language of Old Romance type, in which the lack of the linear restriction should not be understood as an instantiation of a non-V2 grammar, but as the result of the fact that several XPs can be topicalised in the left periphery of a language with a split-CP. Within this framework, the V2 phenomenon is to be understood in a much more abstract way as the obligation that the finite verb move to CP in all sentences, irrespective of the linear position of the finite verb.

This new view of V2 in Mòcheno introduces a shift in the way things are looked at in the language's grammar, since it allows us to account for its version of V2, by treating it as a unitary and coherent phenomenon that manifests within a single grammar and through properties typical of Old Romance languages. Therefore, what was necessarily treated in previous accounts as the effect of contact and the instantiation of the abstract rules of a grammar in competition, is understood simply as part of the V2 system of Mòcheno and no longer needs to be seen as an exception. This conclusion is corroborated by the data discussed in the last section of the chapter, where I have shown that the syntactic facts of Mòcheno cannot be accounted for in terms of optionality or through the hypothesis of two competing grammars, since "Romance" and "Germanic" traits can coexist in a single sentence (subject-verb inversion in a sentence with VO syntax) and optionality is not available in all syntactic environments (distribution of subject pronouns, OV/VO in wh-main interrogative clauses).

On the basis of the conclusions laid out in this chapter, according to which Mòcheno must be considered a V2 language of Old Romance type and the observed syntactic variation has to be understood as the result of rules internal to a single grammar and not in terms of optionality or competing grammars, I now proceed to investigate the nature of these rules. The movement of the finite verb to CP in all main clauses is investigated initially through an analysis of the syntax of subject pronouns. Mòcheno has a very complex system of subject pronouns which must be examined in detail and which is closely connected to the V2 rule. I demonstrate that the distribution of the three classes of subject pronouns in Mòcheno depends on the type of fronted XP: when the fronted XP is an operator, for instance, pronominal subjects have to be realised as clitics, whereas when it is an HT it must be realised by either a strong or a weak form. The syntactic distribution of the different forms pre- or postverbally depending on the fronted XP allows us to advance an initial theoretical hypothesis to account for V2 in Mòcheno, in particular for XP fronting and the movement of the finite verb to CP. The rest of the hypothesis is set out in Chapter 4. Chapters 5 and 6 are dedicated to refining the proposed hypothesis.

CHAPTER 3

The syntax of subject pronouns

3.1 Introduction

In the previous chapter, I tackled the V2 phenomenon from both a theoretical and an empirical point of view, in an attempt to answer the question whether Mòcheno can be considered a V2 language.

We saw that if one compares the empirical facts of Mòcheno syntax with the properties of V2 in Continental Germanic, the answer is no. Mòcheno only has the correlated properties of V2, and even these are optional or reduced; moreover, it lacks the linear restriction. In Mòcheno V3/V4 word orders are possible, which is totally incompatible with the definition of V2 that relies on the linear position of the finite verb used for V2 Germanic languages. However, if a comparison is made with Old Romance languages, which many scholars consider to have been V2 languages until the XIV century, the picture changes drastically. The empirical facts reported for Mòcheno are shared by Old Romance languages, which only had the so-called correlated properties of Germanic V2 and were also characterised by optionality. The lack of the core properties of the V2 phenomenon and the optionality in the correlated properties in Old Romance languages have been explained (Benincà 2006) by the hypothesis that Old Romance languages had a split-CP, just like the modern ones, and that the finite verb could move to two different positions within the periphery and be preceded by topicalised XPs. Benincà's valuable contribution has been showing that in V2 Old Romance languages not all fronted constituents "count" for V2, unlike in V2 Germanic languages, where all fronted XPs can satisfy the EPP feature connected with one head of CP. For Old Romance, Benincà proposes that only fronted operators (foci and wh-elements), not topics, "count" for V2: in this language family, FocusP is the FP actually targeted by the movement of the finite verb to CP in all main clauses and by XP fronting.

In the previous chapter, we saw that Mòcheno behaves like an Old Romance language as far as the properties correlated to V2 are concerned, and also with respect to the structure of its left periphery. This makes the parallel between Old Romance and Mòcheno even more striking. Below (82a), I repeat the structure of the left periphery proposed for Old Romance languages (Benincà 2006) and for Mòcheno.

(82) [$_{FRAME}$ [HT – Scene Setter] [$_{THEME}$ [Topic][V+fin] [$_{FOCUS}$ [Focus/wh] [V+fin]]]]

In this book, I propose and defend the theory that in Mòcheno the finite verb must move to CP in all sentences, according to the language's V2 rule. In order to demonstrate that Mòcheno is a V2 language and that the finite verb has to move to the head of an FP in the left periphery in all sentences, even in cases where we have no clear evidence for the movement (lack of subject-verb inversion or presence of V4 word orders…), the first step is to consider the morphosyntactic properties of subject pronouns.

The aim of this chapter is to provide evidence through several syntactic tests that Mòcheno has three classes of subject pronouns: clitic, weak and strong pronouns, which have specialised for different syntactic positions. Clitics can only appear in the *Wackernagelposition*, weak pronouns can only precede the finite verb, and strong subject pronouns have specialised for the realization of topic and focus readings. The distribution of the three classes of subject pronouns is shown to interact with the two requirements of the V2 rule: the movement of the finite verb to CP and XP fronting in all sentence.

The data discussed in this chapter come mainly from interviews with three key informants, a speaker of each of the three varieties (see Introduction). These interviews were a preliminary to the fieldwork carried out with 45 speakers from all over the valley. The information collected in the preliminary work with the three consultants has been integrated with material from the questionnaires given in the Appendix, where I tested the conclusions arrived at in the interviews. In the fieldwork with 45 informants, I could not ask my consultants for every form of all the persons of the paradigm, instead I focused on the most representative personal pronouns, i.e. third person pronouns. These forms were examined in different syntactic contexts: wh-main interrogatives, sentences with fronted adverbial and embedded clauses.

In the first section of the chapter, I provide syntactic evidence to support the classification of Mòcheno subject pronouns into three classes: clitic, weak and strong. The tests considered are the classic ones (described in Cardinaletti/Starke 1999) and concern the distribution of the different forms in sentence-initial position, in coordination, in isolation and in their compatibility with focalization. Section two is devoted to investigating the distribution of the three subject pronominal forms. I focus particularly on the fact that the different forms can appear in the *Wackernagelposition* in main and embedded clauses and in the left periphery.

3.2 Three classes of subject pronouns in Mòcheno

According to Rowley (2003: 179ff.), Mòcheno displays two morphologically different classes of pronouns: personal pronouns and demonstratives, both of which are composed of a strong and a weak form. The two forms are distinguished on the basis of their phonological properties: weak pronouns bear no accent, whereas strong pronouns are stressed. The classification of the forms according to these criteria is given in Table 3.1.

In this book, building on the syntactic tests first proposed by Kayne (1975), Jaeggli (1982), Brandi/Cordin (1981, 1989), Vanelli/Renzi/Benincà (1985), Rizzi (1986), Vanelli (1987), Holmberg (1991), Poletto/Tomaselli (1995) and summarised in Cardinaletti/Starke (1999), I propose a new classification of Mòcheno subject pronouns in strong, weak and clitic forms. As summarised in Table 3.1, Rowley (2003: 179) assumes that Mòcheno displays the strong masculine form *der*, homophonous with the weak *der*, and the strong feminine *di*, homophonous with the weak *de*. As discussed in Cognola (2010: 56ff.), the form *der* is absent from the paradigm of the Palù dialect (where only the form *ar* is attested) and is found only in the varieties of Fierozzo and Roveda. Moreover, *der*, *ar* and *de* all consistently behave as weak subject pronouns in all syntactic tests (see below), which makes the hypothesis of the presence of two (strong and weak) homophonous forms untenable. In the data collected for this book I have never come across the form *di*.[1] When I explicitly asked the informants whether or not they accepted this form in their variety, they rejected it. Therefore, in my new classification I propose that there is only one demonstrative form (*de* or *der*), which behaves syntactically as a weak pronoun and has no strong homophone. Finally, the new data

Table 3.1 Classification of subject pronouns in Rowley (2003: 179ff.)

	Pronouns		Demonstratives	
	Strong	Weak	Strong	Weak
1.SG	i	e	–	–
2.SG	du	de (F/R), o (P)	–	–
3.SG-masc.	er	er	der	der
3.SG-fem.	si	se, sa	di	de
1.PL	bir, biar	der, ber	–	–
2.PL	ir	er	–	–
3.PL	sei	sa, se	di	de

---

[1] I attested the use of the form *di* in the language of the small children from Fierozzo (Cognola 2011a).

Table 3.2 Novel classification of subject pronouns in Mòcheno

	Strong form	Clitic form	Weak form
1.SG	i	e (F/P/R)	e (R/F)
2.SG	du	o (P)	de (R/F)
3.SG-masc.	er	er	der (R/F)/ar (P)
3.SG-fem.	si	se	de
1.PL	bir, biar (P)	ber, bar (P)	bar (P), ber (F,P), der (R)
2.PL	ir	er	–
3.PL	sei	sa	de

point to the fact that the second plural forms *biar* and *der* given by Rowley are not shared by all varieties: the former is only found in Palù, the latter only in Roveda. The complete list of the subject pronominal forms discussed in this chapter and their classification are given in Table 3.2.

3.2.1 Sentence-initial position

The aim of this section is to try and determine whether or not the subject pronominal forms listed above are all compatible with the absolute sentence-initial position. This test allows us to make a first distinction between strong and weak pronouns on the one hand, and clitic pronouns on the other. As is well known (Cardinaletti/Starke 1999 on the South Tyrolean dialect spoken in the village of Olang), in those V2 languages displaying all three classes of subject pronouns only strong and weak pronouns can appear in sentence-initial position, whereas clitics cannot be fronted.[2]

Let us consider now the subject pronominal forms listed above in Table 3.1 and test what forms are compatible with the sentence-initial position.

As shown in (83a, b), the two pronominal forms for the first person singular can both show up in sentence-initial position in the varieties of Palù and Roveda, whereas in the variety of Fierozzo, *e* cannot be fronted. For the first person plural, we find three forms that can show up in sentence-initial position: *bir* can be fronted in all varieties (83c), *biar* and *bar* are the forms of Palù (83c); *ber* can be

---

2. Old Romance languages (but not modern Northern Italian dialects) pattern like German dialects with subject clitics: the restriction on the sentence-initial position is known as the *Tobler and Mussafia law*. For an analysis of this restriction within the Generative framework, see Benincà (1995), Uriagereka (1995) and references cited there.

fronted in the variety of Fierozzo (83e) but not in the other two and *der* is a form only found in Roveda (83f).³

(83) a. I (P/F/R)   hòn   a puach kaft
     b. E (P/R)   hòn   a puach kaft
         I   have-PRS.1SG a book bought
     c. Bir (P/F/R)   hom   a puach kaft
     d. Biar/Bar (P) hom   a puach kaft
     e. Ber (F)   hom   a puach kaft
     f. Der (R)   hom   a puach kaft
         we   have-PRS.1PL a book bought

Moving to the second person plural, in (84) I show that one of the two forms can show up in sentence-initial position, whereas the other one cannot.

(84) a. Ir (P/F/R)   hòt   a puach kaft
     b. *Er (P/F/R)   hòt   a puach kaft
         you   have-PRS.2PL a book bought

As for the second person singular, *du* can appear in sentence-initial position in all varieties (85a). The form *o* (found only in the dialect of Palù) cannot be fronted (85b), whereas *de* can (85c).

(85) a. Du (P/F/R)   hòst   kaft   a puach
     b. *O (P)   hòst   kaft   a puach
     c. De (F/R)   hòst   kaft   a puach
         you   have-PRS.2SG bought a book

In (86a, b) I illustrate the distribution of third person singular feminine pronouns. In sentence-initial position two forms are possible, whereas the form *se* is ungrammatical in this position.

(86) a. Si (P/F/R)   hòt   kaft   a puach
     b. De (P/F/R)   hòt   kaft   a puach
     c. *Se (P/F/R)   hòt   kaft   a puach
         she   has-PRS.3SG bought a book

For the third person masculine, all forms listed above are compatible with the sentence-initial position, as illustrated in (87a, b).

---

3. The strong forms of the first plural *bir* and the strong second plural *ir* can also be reinforced by *òndera*, "others": *biròndera* and *iròndera*. These two pronouns behave in all tests (focalization, isolation, first position, coordination…) as strong pronouns. In the variety of Roveda, also the form *der* (to be analysed as a weak form) can be modified by *òndera*.

(87) a. Er (P/F/R) hòt   kaft   a puach
     b. Ar (P)   hòt   kaft   a puach
     c. Der (F/R) hòt   kaft   a puach
        he   has-PRS.3SG bought a book

Finally, in (88) I consider the distribution of third person plural pronouns. The two forms that can show up in first position are *sei* and the demonstrative *de*, whereas the form *sa* is not grammatical in this position.

(88) a. Sei (P/F/R) hom   a puach kaft
     b. De (P/F/R)   hom   a puach kaft
     c. *Sa (P/F/R) hom   a puach kaft
        they   have-PRS.3PL   a book bought

In Table 3.3, I summarise the results of the first test, which has shown that not all subject pronominal forms are compatible with the sentence-initial position. The forms that are not compatible with this position have to be classified as subject clitic pronouns.

This first test has allowed us to separate clitics from strong and weak pronouns. In the following subsection, I focus on these two latter classes and I carry out the tests proposed in the cited literature to distinguish strong from weak pronominal forms: (i) coordination, (ii) focalization and (iii) isolation. The prediction to be tested is that among those subject pronominal forms that are compatible with the sentence-initial position, only strong pronouns pass all three tests.

Table 3.3 Subject pronouns compatible with the sentence-initial position

	Forms	First position
1.SG	i	✓
	e	✓ (P;R); *(F)
2.SG	du/de (R/F)	✓
	o (P)	*
3.SG-masc.	er/ar (P)/der (R/F)	✓
3.SG-fem.	si/de	✓
	se	*
1.PL	bir; biar/bar (P); /der (R)	✓
	ber	*(P;R); ✓ (F)
2.PL	ir	✓
	er	*
3.PL	sei/de	✓
	sa	*

3.2.2 The coordination test

In this subsection, I examine all subject pronominal forms listed in Table 3.2 above in order to establish what forms can be coordinated.

As exemplified in (89a), only one form of the two present for the first person singular can be coordinated, namely *i*. Of the five forms for the first plural, *bir* can be coordinated in all varieties (89b) together with *biar* (only found in the Palù dialect) (89c). All other forms are ungrammatical when coordinated (89d, e).

(89) a. *I/*E ont sei (P/F/R)* hòm   *a puach kaft*
       I and they   have-PRS.3PL a book bought
    b. *Bir ont de sèlln der nem (P/F/R)* hom   *a puach kaft*
    c. *Biar/*Bar ont de sèlln der nem (P)* hom   *a puach kaft*
    d. **Ber ont de sèlln der nem (P/F/R)* hom   *a puach kaft*
    e. **Der ont de sèlln der nem (R)* hom   *a puach kaft*
       we and the those near   have-PRS.1PL a book bought

In the third person singular, one form can be coordinated, whereas the other cannot, as illustrated in (90).

(90) a. *Er/Si ont i (P/F/R)* hom   *a puach kaft*
       he/she and I   have a book bought
    b. **Ar ont i (P)* hom   *a puach kaft*
    c. **Der ont i (F/R)* hom   *a puach kaft*
       he and I   have-PRS.1PL a book bought
    d. **De ont i (P/F/R)* hom   *a puach kaft*
       she and I   have-PRS.1PL a book bought

The same distribution is found in the third person plural: one form can be coordinated, the other cannot (91a, b).

(91) a. *Sei ont der sèlln (P/F/R)* hom   *a puach kaft*
       they and the those   have-PRS.3PL a book bought
    b. **De ont der sèlln (P/F/R)* hom   *a puach kaft*
       they and the those   have-PRS.1PL a book bought

The third person forms ruled out in sentence-initial position cannot be coordinated either. This is illustrated in the examples in (92).

(92) a. **Se ont de sèll (P/F/R)* hom   *a puach kaft*
       she and the that   have-PRS.3PL a book bought
    b. **Sa ont de sèlln (P/F/R)* hom   *kaft*   *a puach*
       they and the those   have-PRS.3PL bought a book

In (93), I exemplify that only the forms *du* and *ir* for the second person singular and plural can be coordinated.

(93) a. *Du ont i (P/F/R) hom   a puach kaft*
    b. **O ont i (P)   hom   a puach kaft*
    c. **De ont i (F/R) hom   a puach kaft*
       you and I   have-PRS.1PL a book bought
    d. *Ir ont de sèlln (P/F/R)   hòt   kaft   a puach*
    e. **Er ont de sèlln (P/F/R) hom   kaft   a puach*
       you and the those   have-PRS.1PL bought a book

Table 3.4 summarises the results of the coordination test. It shows that only one form of the paradigm – assumed to be the strong one – can be coordinated and all forms classified as clitics are ungrammatical in coordination. Moreover, some forms allowed to appear in sentence-initial position fail the coordination test and are therefore to be considered as weak pronouns.

In the next subsection I consider the focalization and isolation tests.

Table 3.4 Subject pronominal forms that can be coordinated

	Forms	Coordination
1.SG	i	✓
	e	*
2.SG	du	✓
	o (P)/de (F/R)	*
3.SG-masc.	er	✓
	ar (P)/der (F/R)	*
3.SG-fem.	si	✓
	de	*
	se	*
1.PL	bir; biar (P)	✓
	bar (P); ber; der (R)	*
2.PL	ir	✓
	er	*
3.PL	sei	✓
	de	*
	sa	*

3.2.3 Focalization and isolation

In the literature it has been noticed that only strong pronouns can be focused and appear in isolation. In what follows, I test the prediction that only those forms that can both be coordinated and fronted can also be focused and appear in isolation.

Beginning with the first person forms, in (94) I show that only the form *i* can be focused (94a). In (94b, c) can be seen that only the first plural forms *bir* (present in all varieties) and *biar* (found only in the dialect of Palù) can be focused, whereas all other four forms are ungrammatical when focused (94d, e, f).

(94) a. I/*E (P/F/R) hòn kaft s puach (ont nèt du)
I have-PRS.1SG bought the book and not you
b. BIR (P/F/R) hom a puach kaft (ont nèt ir)
c. BIAR (P) hom a puach kaft (ont nèt ir)
d. *Ber (P/F/R) hom a puach kaft (ont nèt ir)
e. *Der (R) hom a puach kaft (ont nèt ir)
f. *Bar (P) hom a puach kaft (ont nèt ir)
we have-PRS.1PL a book bought and not you

Of the third person forms, only only one can be focused (95).

(95) a. ER/SI (P/F/R) hòt kaft s puach (ont nèt du)
he/she has-PRS.3SG bought the book and not you
b. *AR (P) hòt kaft s puach (ont nèt du)
c. *DER (F/R) hòt kaft s puach (ont nèt du)
he has-PRS.3SG bought the book and not you
d. *DE (P/F/R) hòt kaft s puach (ont nèt du)
she has-PRS.3SG bought the book and not you
e. SEI (P/F/R) hom a puach kaft (ont nèt bir)
f. *DE (P/F/R) hom a puach kaft (ont nèt bir)
they have-PRS.3PL a book bought and not we

As expected, third person clitics are incompatible with focalization, as exemplified in (96).

(96) a. *SE (P/F/R) hòt a puach kaft (ont nèt du)
she has-PRS.3SG a book bought and not you
b. *SA (P/F/R) hom a puach kaft (ont nèt du)
they have-PRS.3PL a book bought and not you

The same distribution of focalization is found with the second person forms: one form (assumed to be the strong one) can be focused, whereas the other one cannot, (97).

(97) a. DU (P/F/R) hòst kaft a puach (ont nèt i)
b. *O (P) hòst kaft a puach (ont nèt i)
c. *DE (F/R) hòst kaft a puach (ont nèt i)
you have-PRS.2SG bought a book and not I

c. IR (P/F/R)   hòt   kaft   a puach (ont nèt bir)
d. *ER (P/F/R) hòt   kaft   a puach (ont nèt bir)
   you   have-PRS.2PL bought a book   and not we

Moving to the isolation test, in (98) I show that all pronouns that cannot be focused or coordinated cannot appear in isolation.

(98) a. *Ber hòt   kaft   a puach?*
       who has-PRS.3SG bought a book
   b. *I (P/F/R)/ *e (P/F/R)*
   c. *Du (P/F/R)/ *o (P)/ *de (R/F)*
   d. *Er (P/F/R)/ *ar (P)/ *der (F/R)*
   e. *Si (P/F/R)/ *de (P/F/R)/ *se (P/F/R)*
   f. *Bir (P/F/R)/ biar (P)/ *bar (P)/ *ber (P/F/R)/ *der (R)*
   g. *Ir (P/F/R)/ *er (P/F/R)*
   h. *Sei (P/F/R)/ *de (P/F/R)/ *sa (P/F/R)*
      I/you/he/she/we/you/they did

The results of the focalization and isolation tests are summarised in Table 3.5.

Table 3.5 Subject pronouns that can be focused and appear in isolation

	Forms	Focalization	Isolation
1.SG	i	✓	✓
	e	*	*
2.SG	du	✓	✓
	o (P)/de (R/F)	*	*
3.SG-masc.	er	✓	✓
	ar (P)/der (R/F)	*	*
3.SG-fem.	si	✓	✓
	de	*	*
	se	*	*
1.PL	bir; biar (P)	✓	✓
	bar (P); ber; der (R)	*	*
2.PL	ir	✓	✓
	er	*	*
3.PL	sei	✓	✓
	de	*	*
	sa	*	*

3.2.4 Partial conclusions

In Table 3.6 I summarise the syntax of the subject pronouns. Despite the complexity of the data and the availability of several forms in the different dialects, some regularities can be detected.

In the third person singular feminine and in the third person plural three forms (strong, weak and clitic) are present. The second person plural does not display variation: all three dialects have the same forms that behave syntactically as strong and clitic pronouns. In the first person singular, the two forms available must be analysed as strong and weak forms in the varieties of Palù and Roveda, whereas in the variety of Fierozzo the reduced form *e* behaves syntactically as a clitic, since it cannot appear in absolute sentence-initial position. In the second person plural we find five morphologically different forms: *bir* is the strong from in all dialects, together with *biar* present only in the variety of Palù; *bar* and *der* are the weak forms in Palù and Roveda respectively, whereas in Fierozzo the weak form is *ber*. The latter form has to be classified as a clitic in the other dialects. The strong second person singular form *du* is present in all dialects; in Fierozzo and Roveda the reduced form is the weak *de*, whereas in Palù we find the clitic *o*.

Table 3.6 Classification of the subject pronominal forms according to the tests

	Forms	Fronting	Coordination	Focalization	Isolation	Type
1.SG	i	✓	✓	✓	✓	strong
	e (P;R)	✓	*	*	*	weak
	e (F)	*	*	*	*	clitic
2.SG	du	✓	✓	✓	✓	strong
	de (R/F)	✓	*	*	*	weak
	o (P)	*	*	*	*	clitic
3.SG-m.	er	✓	✓	✓	✓	strong
	ar (P)/der (R/F)	✓	*	*	*	weak
3.SG-f.	si	✓	✓	✓	✓	strong
	de	✓	*	*	*	weak
	se	*	*	*	*	clitic
1.PL	bir; biar (P)	✓	✓	✓	✓	strong
	bar (P); ber (F); der (R)	✓	*	*	*	weak
	ber (P;R)	*	*	*	*	clitic
2.PL	ir	✓	✓	✓	✓	strong
	er	*	*	*	*	clitic
3.PL	sei	✓	✓	✓	✓	strong
	de	✓	*	*	*	weak
	sa	*	*	*	*	clitic

Finally, all varieties have a strong and a weak form for the third person singular masculine: *ar* in the Palù dialect, *der* in the Roveda and Fierozzo dialects.

The subject pronouns distribute in the paradigm according to three patterns. In the first one, exemplified by third and first person forms, three morphologically distinct forms are available. Of these forms, one can be classified as strong (it passes all tests), one as weak (it fails all tests, except for fronting) and one as clitic (it fails all tests). The second pattern is that of the second person (singular and plural). These persons only display two morphologically different forms: one has to be classified as a strong pronoun and the other as a clitic (but see the case of *de*). Finally, the last type is that of the first person singular and the third person singular masculine where two morphologically different forms are present: one is strong, the other is weak.[4]

In this section, I proposed a new classification of Mòcheno subject pronominal forms building on the results of the syntactic tests on the morphologically different forms available in the paradigm of subject pronouns. So far, very little has been said with respect to the distribution of the three forms. In what follows, I consider the syntax of the forms belonging to the three classes of subject pronouns with the aim of investigating whether all types of subject pronouns can appear in all positions of the clause. In particular, I focus on the

---

4. In Cognola (2010: 62f.), I noted that the third person plural has developed a complex form, *sa sei*, formed by the third person clitic (*sa*) and the strong form (*sei*). As shown below, this form cannot (i) be focused, (ii) appear in isolation or (iii) in sentence-initial position. However, *sa sei* can be coordinated, like the strong form *sei* (iv).

    a. **SA SEI   hom a puach kaft   ont nèt bir*
       SBJ-CL.3.PL SBJ-STRONG.3.PL have a book bought and not we
    b. *Ber hòt   kaft   a puach?*
       who has-PRS.3SG bought a book?
       Sei/*sa sei
       SBJ-STRONG.3.PL/SBJ-CL.3.PLSBJ-STRONG.3.PL
    c. **Sa sei   hom a puach kaft*
       SBJ-CL.3.PL SBJ-STRONG.3.PL have a book bought
    d. *Sa sei/   sei ont de sèlln   hom a puach kaft*
       SBJ-CL.3.PL SBJ-STRONG.3.PL/ SBJ-STRONG.3.PL and the those have a book bought

The outstanding syntactic behaviour of this third person plural form seems to indicate that this person is developing a proclitic form. This recalls an observation made for Cimbrian by Bidese (2008: 103) in his diachronic study of the syntax of Cimbrian, where he notes that in a period in which Cimbrian had only strong and weak subject pronominal forms, a subject clitic form developed just for the third person plural. Only in the later texts, subject clitic forms appear for all persons of the paradigm. Therefore, Bidese concludes that the third person plural has an "innovative" character in the diachronic development of Cimbrian, since the shift from weak forms to clitic forms started precisely with the third person plural.

Wackernagelposition, the area between IP and CP (Thiersch 1978; Lenerz 1985; Poletto/Tomaselli 1995; Bidese 2008 a.o.), that I investigate in both main and embedded clauses.

3.3 Distribution of subject pronouns

In this section, I examine the distribution of the strong, weak and clitic subject pronominal forms of Mòcheno summarised in Table 3.7.

In the first part of this section, I focus on the distribution of subject pronouns in the *Wackernagelposition* in both main and embedded clauses. In the dialect spoken in Palù this position can only host clitic pronouns in both main and embedded clauses, whereas in the varieties of Roveda and Fierozzo, subject clitics must appear in the *Wackernagelposition* in main clauses and in the embedded ones only weak and strong forms can show up. In the second part of the section, I consider the distribution of strong subject pronouns, concentrating mostly on pronominal doubling.

Table 3.7 Classification of Mòcheno subject pronouns

	Strong form	Weak form	Clitic form
1.SG	i	e	–
2.SG	du	de (R/F)	o (P)
3.SG-masc.	er	ar (P)/der (R/F)	–
3.SG-fem.	si	de	se
1.PL	bir; biar (P)	bar (P); der (R); ber (F)	ber (P,R)
2.PL	ir	–	er
3.PL	sei	de	sa

3.3.1 Distribution of subject reduced forms in main clauses

In this section, I consider the distribution of reduced subject pronominal forms – weak pronouns and clitics – in main clauses, addressing the issue of whether the forms belonging to this class have specialised for one clausal position.

Let us consider the distribution of first person reduced forms in sentences with a fronted adverbial. As exemplified in (99), the weak form *e* must follow the finite verb (99a, b); the postverbal position is ruled out for the strong form (99c).

(99) a. Gester   hòn=e (P/F/R)   kaft   a puach
           yesterday have=SBJ-CL.1.SG bought a book
       b. *Gester   e=hòn (P/F/R)   kaft   a puach
           yesterday SBJ-CL.1.SG=have bought a book
       c. *Gester   hòn i (P/F/R)   kaft   a puach
           yesterday have SBJ-STRONG.1.SG bought a book
           'Yesterday I bought the book'

In the first person plural, *ber* follows the finite verb in all varieties (100a, b); this is ruled out for strong forms (100c). In the variety of Palù, the from *bar* must follow the finite verb, whereas *biar* cannot (100d, e, f). Finally, the form *der* found in the variety of Roveda is incompatible with the postverbal position (100g).

(100) a. Gester   hòn=ber (P/F/R)   kaft   s puach
           yesterday have=SBJ-CL.1PL bought the book
       b. *Gester   ber=hòn (P/F/R)   kaft   s puach
           yesterday SBJ-CL.1PL=have bought the book
       c. *Gester   hòn bir (P/F/R)   kaft   s puach
           yesterday have SBJ-STRONG.1PL bought the book
       d. Gester   hòn bar (P)   kaft   s puach
           yesterday have SBJ-WEAK.1PL bought the book
       e. *Gester   bar   hòn (P) kaft   s puach
           yesterday SBJ-WEAK.1PL have   bought the book
       f. *Gester   hòn biar (P)   kaft   s puach
           yesterday have SBJ-STRONG.1PL bought the book
       g. *Gester   hòn der (R)   kaft   s puach
           yesterday have SBJ-WEAK.1PL bought the book

In (101), I examine the distribution of the second person forms. The clitic *o* (only found in the Palù dialect) must show up in enclisis to the finite verb (101a, b), whereas the postverbal position is ruled out for its strong counterpart (101c).

(101) a. Gester   hos=o (P)   kaft   s puach
           yesterday have=SBJ-CL.2SG bought the book
       b. *Gester   o=host (P)   kaft   s puach
           yesterday SBJ-CL.2SG=have bought the book
       c. *Gester   hòst   du (P/F/R)   kaft   s puach
           yesterday have-PRS.2SG SBJ-STRONG.2SG bought the book

The form *de*, found in the Fierozzo and Roveda dialects, cannot follow the finite verb and appear in the *Wackernagelposition*, but must drop (102). This represents an example of pure *pro-drop*.

(102) a. Gester   hòst (F/R)   kaft   s puach
         yesterday have-PRS.2SG bought   the book
     b. *Gester   hòst   de (F/R) kaft   s puach
         yesterday have-PRS.2SG SBJ-WEAK.2.SG bought the book

In the second person plural, the clitic form *er* must show up in the *Wackernagel-position* (103a, b), which is ruled out for the strong *ir*.

(103) a. Gester   hòt=er (P/F/R)   kaft   s puach
         yesterday has=SBJ-CL.2.PL bought the book
     b. *Gester   er=hòt (P/F/R)   kaft   s puach
         yesterday SBJ-CL.2.PL=hòt bought the book
     c. *Gester   hòt ir (P/F/R)   kaft   s puach
         yesterday has SBJ-STRONG.2.PL bought the book

Let us consider the third person singular feminine forms, the distribution of which has also been tested in the fieldwork with 45 informants. According to the three consultants, the form *se* has specialised for enclisis (104a, b). The weak subject pronominal form cannot follow the finite verb in any variety, as can be seen in (104c), whereas it can precede it only in the dialect of Fierozzo (104d, e).

(104) a. Gester   hòt=se (P/F/R)   kaft   s puach
         yesterday has=SBJ-CL.3.SG.F bought the book
     b. *Gester   se=hòt (P/F/R)   kaft   s puach
         yesterday SBJ-CL.3.SG.F=has bought the book
     c. *Gester   hòt de (P/F/R)   kaft   s puach
         yesterday has SBJ-WEAK.3.SG.F bought the book
     d. *Gester   de   hòt (P/R) kaft   s puach
         yesterday SBJ-WEAK.3.SG.F has   bought the book
     e. Gester   de   hòt (F)   kaft   s puach
         yesterday SBJ-WEAK.3.SG.F has   bought the book

The judgments and the intuitions of the three informants considered in the preliminary study are confirmed by the speakers consulted in the recent fieldwork. As can be seen in the first two columns of Table 3.8, all informants but one (44/45) agree that the subject clitic form *se* must be enclitic to the finite verb and proclisis is always ruled out. Moreover, the enclitic form is the one used by all informants for expressing the subject pronoun in unmarked sentences.[5] All informants reject (and never produce) sentences in which *de* follows the finite verb (fourth

---

5. According to FIER-AP, the only informant who does not accept subject clitics enclitic to the finite verb in main declarative clauses, the subject pronouns have to appear in their weak form (*de*) before the finite verb, as in (104e).

Table 3.8 Third person singular feminine subject forms in the questionnaires

	gester hòt-se	gester se-hòt	gester de hòt	gester hòt de
Palù	15/15	0/15	9/15	0/15
Fierozzo	14/15	0/15	12/15	0/15
Roveda	15/15	0/15	4/15	0/15
Total	44/45	0/45	25/45	0/45
Percentage	98%	0%	55%	0%

column): this fully confirms the judgments of the single informants given in (104). Less straightforward are the judgments on the sentences in which the weak pronoun precedes the finite verb. As can be seen in the third column, a preverbal weak subject pronoun is accepted by the majority of speakers in Palù (9/15) and Fierozzo (12/15), whereas it is rejected by most speakers in Roveda (11/15). This gives rise to a percentage of acceptance at chance level.

The data discussed in Table 3.8 confirm the judgments provided by the three informants involved in the preliminary work on the syntax of Mòcheno, except for the variety of Palù, where we find a contrast between the single informant, who rejects the order adverbial – weak pronoun, and the majority of consulted speakers, who accept it. The disagreement between the informant from Palù and the majority of speakers from his village might suggest that he cannot be trusted. This conclusion is immediately shown to be wrong when the sociolinguistic variables are examined. In Table 3.9, I consider the data from the questionnaires focusing on the age of the informants. As can be seen in the section dedicated to the informants from Palù, preverbal weak subject pronouns are accepted by 3/5 young speakers, by 1/5 middle-aged and by all elderly speakers. Considered the data in this table and that the single informant from Palù is a middle-aged man, his judgments turn out to be fully coherent with those of the speakers of his age.[6] Therefore, it can be concluded that the disagreement between his judgments and those of the other speakers from Palù follows from sociolinguistic variables. Instead of disproving the reliability of the informant from Palù, the reported asymmetries reinforce the fact that he is a good informant and has to be trusted.

Let us consider the third person singular masculine forms. In (105) I show that the weak pronouns *ar* (used in the Palù dialect) and *der* (found in the Fierozzo and Roveda dialects) cannot follow the finite verb (105a, b). The strong form *er* can follow the finite verb (105c). The weak pronoun *der* is only accepted in the preverbal position by speakers of the Fierozzo dialect.

---

6. As already pointed out in Chapter 2, Table 2.6, with respect to the distribution of OV/VO word order patterns, the middle-aged speakers from Palù represent an independent group with respect to both young and elderly speakers.

Table 3.9 Distribution of clitic and weak third person singular feminine subject forms in the questionnaires

	Younger speakers					Middle-aged speakers					Elderly speakers			
Palù	FM	LB	NI	ST	VL	GL	HN	MP	MO	PB	ET	EO	IP	LT	MT
gester hòt-se	✓	✓	✓	✓	✓	✓	✓	✓	✓	✓	✓	✓	✓	✓	✓
gester se-hòt	*	*	*	*	*	*	*	*	*	*	*	*	*	*	*
gester de hòt	*	*	✓	✓	✓	✓	*	*	*	*	✓	✓	✓	✓	✓
gester hòt-de	*	*	*	*	*	*	*	*	*	*	*	*	*	*	*
Fierozzo	AP	CP	GP	MG	SB	GG	GM	PM	RB	RR	AS	AM	COP	EI	GM
gester hòt-se	*	✓	✓	✓	✓	✓	✓	✓	✓	✓	✓	✓	✓	✓	✓
gester se-hòt	*	*	*	*	*	*	*	*	*	*	*	*	*	*	*
gester de hòt	✓	✓	*	✓	✓	*	✓	✓	✓	*	✓	✓	✓	✓	✓
gester hòt-de	*	*	*	*	*	*	*	*	*	*	*	*	*	*	*
Roveda	AF	EF	IP	LF	SO	BL	CF	MP	MB	FR	DP	JP	MO	RP	EO
gester hòt-se	✓	✓	✓	✓	✓	✓	✓	✓	✓	✓	✓	✓	✓	✓	✓
gester se-hòt	*	*	*	*	*	*	*	*	*	*	*	*	*	*	*
gester de hòt	✓	*	*	*	*	*	✓	*	*	✓	*	✓	*	*	*
gester hòt-de	*	*	*	*	*	*	*	*	*	*	*	*	*	*	*

(105) a. *Gester   hòt ar (P)   kaft   s puach
         yesterday has SBJ-WEAK.3.SG.M bought the book
     b. *Gester   hòt der (F/R)   kaft   s puach
         yesterday has SBJ-WEAK.3.SG.M bought the book
     c. Gester   hòt er (P/F/R)   kaft   s puach
         yesterday has SBJ-STRONG.3.SG.M bought the book

In (106), I examine the distribution of the third person plural forms. The clitic form must be enclitic to the finite verb (106a, b), whereas the weak one is ruled out from the postverbal position (106e) in all varieties. The weak form can precede the finite verb (106d), but not for all speakers and not in all dialects (see above). The strong forms cannot follow the finite verb.

(106) a. Gester   hom=sa (P/F/R)   kaft   s puach
         yesterday have=SBJ-CL.3.PL bought the book
     b. *Gester   sa=hom (P/F/R)   kaft   s puach
         yesterday SBJ-CL.3.PL=have bought the book
     c. *Gester   hom=sei (P/F/R)   kaft   s puach
         yesterday have=SBJ-STRONG.3.PL bought the book
     d. Gester   de   hom kaft   s puach
         yesterday SBJ-WEAK.3.PL   have bought the book

e. *Gester   hom   de (P/F/R)   kaft   s puach
   yesterday have SBJ-WEAK.3.PL   bought   the book

So far, we have seen that in main clauses with a fronted adverbial the subject pronoun can be expressed either through an enclitic subject pronoun (which on the basis of the data collected in the fieldwork is the preferred variant used and accepted by almost all speakers, 44/45) or through a preverbal weak pronoun (accepted by most speakers, but not by all of them, especially in the village of Roveda). In this section it has also been shown that subject clitics must be enclitic to the finite verb and that weak and strong subject pronouns are always ruled out from the *Wackernagelposition*, with the only exception of the strong pronoun *er*.

In this section, I have classified the reduced subject pronominal forms following the finite verb as subject clitics. This claim is not obvious. For other close varieties spoken in other German-speaking linguistic islands, in fact, it has been proposed that subject clitics have developed into agreement markers (Kolmer 2005; Bidese 2008), that is into verbal suffixes hosted in TP/AgrSP. An analysis of subject clitics as elements realising an IP head obviously runs counter to the theory proposed in this book that Mòcheno is a V2 language. Therefore, in the following subsection I consider some evidence against an analysis of Mòcheno subject clitics as agreement markers.

3.3.2 Reduced forms are not agreement markers

It has been proposed (Kolmer 2005 for Walser dialects and Bidese 2008: 120 for the variety of Cimbrian spoken in the village of Roana) that in languages similar to Mòcheno and spoken in other German-speaking linguistic islands of Northern Italy, reduced subject pronouns have developed into agreement markers, that is they have nearly acquired the status of verbal suffixes.

This proposal is supported by the fact that in unmarked main declarative clauses of these languages, NP subjects must be doubled by a co-indexed subject clitic pronoun enclitic to the finite verb (107a, b) for Walser and the Cimbrian variety spoken in Roana (107a from Kolmer 2005: 175, quoting from Zürrer 1999 and 107b from Bidese 2008: 119). The co-occurrence of NP subjects and co-indexed subject pronominal forms in unmarked main declarative clauses is found in non-V2 languages such as Northern Italian dialects, with the only difference that in Northern Italian dialects the clitic is proclitic and not enclitic, as illustrated in (107c).

(107) a. *De bruder$_j$ wont=er$_j$* z Turiin un ds wääti$_i$
 the brother lives=SBJ-CL.3.SG.M in Turin and the sister
 wont-dsch$_i$ z Meiland
 lives in Milan
 'The brother lives in Turin and the sister lives in Milan'
 b. *Hoite de muutar$_j$ hat=*(se$_j$) gakhoofet de ojar in merkaten*
 today the mum has=SBJ-CL.3.SG.F bought the eggs in the market
 'Today the mum bought the eggs at the market'
 c. *Ancoi la mama l'ha tolt el pan*
 today the mum SBJ-CL.3.SG.F=has bought the bread
 'Today the mum bought the bread'

In (108), I show that NP subjects cannot co-occur with a coindexed subject clitic pronoun in an unmarked main declarative clause in any variety of Mòcheno.

(108) a. **Der Mario$_j$ hòt=er$_j$ kaft s puach*
 the Mario has=SBJ-CL.3.SG.M bought the book
 b. *Der Mario hòt kaft s puach*
 the Mario has-PRS.3SG bought the book
 c. **I$_j$ hòn=e$_j$ kaft s puach*
 SBJ-STRONG.1.SG have=SBJ-CL.1.SG bought the book
 d. *I$_j$ hòn kaft s puach*
 SBJ-STRONG.1.SG have-PRS.1SG bought the book

An NP subject or a strong subject pronoun can only be doubled by a clitic if they are thematised in the left periphery, as in the examples in (109).

(109) a. *Der Mario$_j$, hòt=er$_j$ kaft s puach?*
 the Mario has=SBJ-CL.3.SG.M bought the book
 'Did Mario buy the book?'
 b. *I$_j$, bo hòn=e$_j$ kaft s puach?*
 SBJ-STRONG.1.SG where have=PRS.1SG bought the book
 'Where did I buy the book?'

The above data (108) and (109) clearly indicate that the Mòcheno subject clitic forms cannot be analysed as agreement markers, since they cannot co-occur with a co-indexed NP subject in an unmarked main clause. This conclusion is also supported by the data discussed in the next subsection, where I consider the distribution of subject pronouns in embedded clauses. I show that subject pronouns have to be realised through clitics enclitic to the complementiser in the embedded clauses of the Palù dialect and that they can never encliticise to the finite verb in any Mòcheno dialect. Both facts run counter to the analysis of subject clitic pronouns as agreement markers.

3.3.3 Distribution of subject reduced forms in embedded clauses

In this subsection, I examine the distribution of the subject pronominal forms in embedded clauses providing further evidence for the hypothesis that subject clitics are not agreement markers in Mòcheno.[7]

Let us begin with the second person forms in the Palù dialect. As exemplified in (110), the subject pronoun must be realised by the clitic form *o*, which encliticises to the complementiser (110b–d). The strong form is ruled out, as exemplified in (110e).

(110) a. Er hòt mer pfrok
 SBJ-STRONG.3.SG.M has me-DAT asked
 b. abia as=o der compito gamocht hòst
 how that=SBJ-CL.1.SG the homework done have-PRS.2SG
 c. *abia as der compito gamocht hòs=o
 how that the homework done have=SBJ-CL.1.SG
 d. *abia as (der compito) hòs=o (der compito) gamocht
 how that the homework have=SBJ-CL.1.SG the homework done
 e. *abia as du der compito gamocht hòst
 how that SBJ-STRONG.2.SG the homework done have-PRS.2SG
 'He asked me how you did your homework'

The realization of the second person singular subject pronouns in embedded clauses has been investigated in the fieldwork carried out for this book (see questionnaires in the Appendix, sentence 3). As summarised in Table 3.10, the judgments of the informant given in (110) are fully confirmed by the consultants from Palù. When asked to translate the Italian sentence corresponding to (110) into Mòcheno, all speakers produce a clitic enclitic to the complementiser. In the grammaticality judgment task, 9/10 informants claim that the clitic is obligatory

Table 3.10 Second person singular pronouns in embedded clauses in the Palù dialect

	compl+cl	compl+cl+strong	compl+strong
	as-o	as-o du	as du
Total	15/15	9/10	1/10
Percentage	100%	90%	10%

---

7. In this book, I do not explore the connections between the syntax of Mòcheno subject pronouns and the phenomenon of complementiser agreement (Bennis/Haegeman 1984; Haegeman 1990, 1992; Carstens 2003; van Koppen 2005; Gruber 2008 a.o.), although the two phenomena are surely correlated.

and cannot be substituted by the strong form (PALÙ-NI is the only speaker who accepts the embedded clause without the clitic and with the strong pronoun *du*).

In the other two varieties of Mòcheno, the preferred strategy for realising the second person subject pronoun in embedded clauses is through the weak form *de* (111b). The strong form *du* can also show up (111c) and note that, differently from the variety of Palù, the strong form can appear without the reduced form.[8]

(111) a. Er   hòt mer   pfrok
         SBJ-STRONG.3.SG.M has me-DAT asked
    b. abia as   de   hòst   gamocht
       how that SBJ-WEAK.2.SG have-PRS.2SG done
       der/en compito
       the-NOM/ACC homework
    c. abia as   du   hòst   gamocht
       how that SBJ-STRONG.2.SG have-PRS.2SG done
       der/en compito
       the-NOM/ACC homework
       'He asked me how you did your homework.'

The data given in (111) are confirmed by the majority of the speakers consulted in the fieldwork, as summarised in Table 3.11 (see questionnaires in the Appendix, sentence 3).

Summing up, the data discussed for second person singular subject pronouns point to a variation between the Mòcheno dialects in the distribution of the strong form *du*. This variation might be due to the absence of a clitic form for the second person singular in the Fierozzo and Roveda dialects, or, conversely, of a weak pronoun in the Palù dialect. In what follows, I investigate the behaviour of third person singular feminine pronouns, which have all three forms in all varieties.[9]

Table 3.11 Second person singular pronouns in embedded clauses in the Fierozzo and Roveda dialects

	compl+weak	compl+strong
	as de	as du
Total	15/15	9/12
Percentage	100%	75%

8. The form *en* is the accusative form of the masculine article which only appears in the variety of Roveda. Note, that differently from the dialect spoken in Palù, in Fierozzo and Roveda VO syntax is the preferred word order in embedded clauses (see below).

9. In Chapters 5 and 6, it will be shown that this variation is due to the type of *pro*-drop displayed by the Mòcheno dialects.

As illustrated in (112), a third person singular feminine subject pronoun has to be realised by the clitic form *se* enclitic to the complementiser (112b) in the Palù dialect. Weak and strong subject pronominal forms are ruled out from the *Wackernagelposition* in embedded clauses, as can be seen in (112c).

(112) a. *Er   hòt   mer   pfrok*
         SBJ-STRONG.3.SG.M has-PRS.3SG   me-DAT   asked
   b. *abia as=se   der compito   gamocht hòt*
      how that=SBJ-CL.3.SG.F   the homework   done   has
   c. **abia as si/de   der compito*
      how that SBJ-STRONG.3.SG.F/SBJ-WEAK.3.SG.F   the homework
      gamocht hòt
      done   has
      'He asked me how she did her homework'

These data are confirmed by the speakers interviewed in the fieldwork. 15/15 speakers produce a subject clitic enclitic to the complementiser in their translation of the Italian sentence corresponding to (112). Both weak and strong subject pronominal forms are rejected by 7/8 speakers.[10]

In the two other Mòcheno dialects, the unmarked way of realising the third person feminine subject pronoun is through the weak form *de*, as exemplified in (113b). In these two varieties the subject pronoun can also be realised by a strong form (113c), but not by a clitic (113d).

(113) a. *Er   hòt   mer   pfrok*
         SBJ-STRONG.3.SG.M has   me-DAT   asked

Table 3.12 Third person singular pronouns in embedded clauses in the Palù dialect

	compl+cl	compl+strong
	as-se	as de/si
Total	15/15	1/8; 1/8
Percentage	100%	12%; 12%

---

10. The only informant who accepts weak and strong pronouns after the complementiser is again PALÙ-NI, who is the only informant who claims that the clitic *o* is not obligatory with the second person singular. This might indicate that this young speaker has a different grammar (much closer to that of the other two variants).

b. abia as   de   hòt   gamocht
    how that SBJ-WEAK.3.SG.F has-PRS.3SG done
    der/en compito
    the-NOM/ACC homework

c. abia as   si   hòt   gamocht
    how that SBJ-STRONG.3.SG.F has-PRS.3SG done
    der/en compito
    the-NOM/ACC homework

d. *abia as=se   hòt gamocht der/en compito
    how that=SBJ-CL.3.SG.F has done   the-NOM/ACC homework
    'He asked me how she did her homework'

The data collected in the questionnaires confirm the pattern discovered for the Fierozzo and Roveda dialects. Most informants (14/15 from Roveda and 10/12 from Fierozzo) use the weak form for realising the subject pronoun in their translations of the Italian sentence into Mòcheno. They also judge strong pronouns grammatical (6/7 in Fierozzo and 5/7 in Roveda), whereas subject clitics are rejected by 5/8 speakers in Fierozzo and by 8/13 in Roveda. Only one speaker from Roveda (ROVE-LF) uses the subject clitic form in the translation.

The data discussed above for the third person feminine singular forms confirm the presence of variation in the realization of subject pronouns between the Palù dialect and the other two Mòcheno varieties. In the former, subject pronouns must be realised by the clitic form enclitic to the complementiser, whereas in the latter they must be realised by either the weak or the strong form. Although a theoretical analysis of this variation cannot be given here (see Chapters 5 and 6), the data discussed above are further evidence that subject clitics are not agreement markers, since they encliticise to the complementiser. Subject clitics encliticise to the complementiser only in the Palù dialect; however, the fact that subject clitics are not agreement markers can also be demonstrated for the other two dialects. As shown in (114), in the Fierozzo and Roveda dialects a subject clitic cannot encliticise to the finite verb in embedded clauses and this is fully expected within the hypothesis that they are not agreement markers.

Table 3.13 Third person singular pronouns in embedded clauses in the Fierozzo and Roveda dialects

	compl+cl	compl+weak	compl+strong
	as-se	as de	as si
Total	8/19	24/27	11/14
Percentage	42%	89%	78%

(114) a. *Er   hòt mer   pfrok*
        SBJ-STRONG.3.SG.M has me-DAT asked
    b. **abia as de mama_j hòt-se_j   gamocht*
        how that the mum has=SBJ-CL.3.SG.F done
        der/en compito
        the-NOM/ACC homework

In (115), I examine the syntax of third person singular masculine forms. As exemplified in (115b), subject pronouns can be realised by the weak forms *ar* and *der*; the strong form *er* is only grammatical in the Fierozzo and Roveda dialects (115c, d).

(115) a. *Er   hòt   mer   pfrok*
        SBJ-STRONG.3.SG.M has-PRS.3SG me-DAT asked
    b. *abia as   ar/der   der compito   gamocht hòt*
        how that SBJ-WEAK.3.SG.M the homework done has-PRS.3SG
    c. **abia as   er   der compito   gamocht hòt*
        how that SBJ-STRONG.3.SG.M the homework done has-PRS.3SG
    d. **abia as   er   der/en compito   gamocht*
        how that SBJ-STRONG.3.SG.M the-NOM/ACC homework done
        hòt
        has-PRS.3SG
        'He asked me how he did his homework'

Third person plural forms behave as third person singular forms. In the Palù dialect only subject clitics can appear in embedded clauses (116b, c); in the other varieties clitics are ruled out (116d).

(116) a. *Er   hòt   mer   pfrok*
        SBJ-STRONG.3.SG.M has-PRS.3SG me-DAT asked
    b. *abia as=sa   der compito   gamocht hòn (P)*
        how that=SBJ-CL.3.PL the homework done   have-PRS.3PL
    c. **abia as   sei/de   der compito (P)*
        how that SBJ-STRONG.3.PL/SBJ-WEAK.3.PL the homework
        gamocht hòn
        done   have-PRS.3PL
    d. *abia as   sei/de   hòn (F/R)*
        how that SBJ-STRONG.3.PL/SBJ-WEAK.3.PL have-PRS.3PL
        gamocht der/en compito
        done   the-NOM/ACC homework
        'He asked me how they did their homework'

In (117), I give the examples of the first person singular. In the Palù dialect the only form allowed is the reduced form *e* (117b, c); in the other varieties both strong and weak forms are grammatical in embedded clauses (117d).

(117) a. *Er   hòt   mer   pfrok*
         SBJ-STRONG.3.SG.M has me-DAT asked
      b. *abia as   e   der compito   gamocht hòn (P)*
         how that SBJ-WEAK.1.SG the homework   done   have-PRS.1SG
      c. *??abia as i   der compito   gamocht hòn (P)*
         how   that SBJ-STRONG.1.SG the homework done   have-PRS.1SG
      d. *abia as   e   /i   hòn (F/R)*
         how that SBJ-WEAK.1.SG /SBJ-STRONG.1.SG have-PRS.1SG
         gamocht en/der compito
         done   the-ACC/NOM homework
         'He asked me how my exam was'

Finally, in (118) I consider the first person plural in the Palù dialect. As exemplified in (118b), both clitic (*ber*) and weak (*bar*) forms must appear next to the complementiser, a position that is ungrammatical for the strong forms (118c).

(118) a. *Er   hòt   mer   pfrok*
         SBJ-STRONG.3.SG.M has-PRS.3SG me-DAT asked
      b. *abia as   ber   /bar   der compito   gamocht*
         how that SBJ-CL.1.PL /SBJ-WEAK.1.PL the homework done
         hòn
         have-PRS.3PL
      c. **abia as   bir   /biar   der compito*
         how   that SBJ-STRONG.1.PL /SBJ-STRONG.1.PL the homework
         gamocht hòn
         done   have-PRS.3PL
         'He asked me how our exam was'

In the two other varieties, the subject pronoun must be realised by the weak or the strong form (119).

(119) a. *Er   hòt   mer   pfrok*
         SBJ-STRONG.3.SG.M has-PRS.3SG me-DAT asked
      b. *abia as   ber   hòn   gamocht der compito*
         how that SBJ-WEAK.1.PL have-PRS.1PL done   the homework
      c. *abia as   der   hòn   gamocht en compito*
         how that SBJ-WEAK.1.PL have-PRS.1PL done   the-ACC homework

d. *abia as bir hòn gamocht*
how that SBJ-STRONG.1.PL have-PRS.1PL done
en/der compito
the-ACC/NOM homework
'He asked me how our exam was'

The data examined in this subsection have shown that subject clitic pronouns have specialised for the *Wackernagelposition* of both main and embedded clauses in the variety of Palù, whereas in the latter dialects subject clitics must show up in the *Wackernagelposition* in main declarative and not in embedded clauses. In no variety do we find evidence for the analysis of reduced subject pronouns as agreement markers. In the following section, I conclude this chapter dedicated to the syntax of subject pronouns by taking into consideration the distribution of strong subject pronouns.

3.3.4 Distribution of strong subject pronouns

As illustrated in (120) for the first person singular and plural, the strong forms *i* and *bir/biar* must precede the finite verb. According to the judgments of the informants, the sentences in which a strong subject pronoun precedes the finite verb have all a pragmatically marked reading: the strong pronoun is generally focussed. Note, that the fact that strong subject pronouns convey a pragmatically-marked reading is typical of *pro*-drop languages (Holmberg/Roberts 2010).

(120) a. *Gester i hòn kaft a puach*
yesterday SBJ-STRONG.1.SG have-PRS.1SG bought a book
b. **Gester hòn i kaft a puach*
yesterday have-PRS.1SG SBJ-STRONG.1.SG bought a book
'Yesterday it was me who bought the book'
c. *Gester bir /biar hòn*
yesterday SBJ-STRONG.1.PL /SBJ-STRONG.1.PL have-PRS.1SG
kaft s puach
bought the book
d. **Gester hòn bir kaft s puach*
yesterday have-PRS.1PL SBJ-STRONG.1.PL bought the book
'Yesterday it was us who bought the book'

Let us consider now the second persons. As expected, the strong forms *du* and *ir* must appear before the finite verb and convey a pragmatically-marked topic or focus reading.

(121) a. Gester   du   hòst   kaft   s puach
          yesterday SBJ-STRONG.2.SG   have-PRS.2SG bought the book
     b. *Gester   hòst   du   kaft   s puach
          yesterday have-PRS.2SG   SBJ-STRONG.2.SG bought the book
          'Yesterday it was you who bought the book'
     c. Gester   ir   hòt   kaft   s puach
          yesterday SBJ-STRONG.2.PL   have-PRS.2PL bought the book
     d. *Gester   hòt   ir   kaft   s puach
          yesterday have-PRS.2PL   SBJ-STRONG.2.PL bought the book
          'Yesterday it was you who bought the book'

The third person feminine and plural forms follow the general rule: as exemplified in (122), the strong forms *si* and *sei* have to show up before the finite verb and have a marked reading. This fact is confirmed by the consultants interviewed in the fieldwork, see the questionnaires in the Appendix, sentence 2.

(122) a. Gester   si   hòt   kaft   s puach
          yesterday SBJ-STRONG.3.SG.F   has-PRS.3SG bought the book
     b. *Gester   hòt   si   kaft   s puach
          yesterday has-PRS.3SG   SBJ-STRONG.3.SG.F bought the book
          'Yesterday it was she who bought the book'
     c. Gester   sei   hom   kaft   s puach
          yesterday SBJ-STRONG.3.PL   have-PRS.3PL bought the book
     d. *Gester   hom   sei   kaft   s puach
          yesterday have-PRS.3PL   SBJ-STRONG.3.PL bought the book
          'It was them who bought the book yesterday'

The only apparent exception is the third person masculine form *er*, which can both precede or follow the finite verb (123).

(123) a. Gester   er   hòt   kaft   s puach
          yesterday SBJ-STRONG.3.SG.M   has-PRS.3SG bought the book
          'Yesterday it was he who bought the book'
     b. Gester   hòt   er   kaft   s puach
          yesterday has-PRS.3SG   SBJ-CL.3.SG.M bought the book
          'Yesterday he bought the book'

The syntax of the strong *er* is not necessarily a counter-argument to the whole account, but might depend on the availability of a clitic form homophonous with the strong pronoun. This hypothesis is supported by the pragmatic interpretation of the forms according to their position: when the pronoun *er* precedes the finite verb, it gets a pragmatically-marked focus or topic reading (like all strong subject pronouns), when it follows the finite verb, it is pragmatically unmarked (like all subject clitics). Further evidence for the presence of a subject clitic homophonous with the strong subject pronoun *er* is represented by the fact that the subject pronoun *er* can be separated from the finite verb by intervening material when it precedes the finite verb (124a) and not when it follows it (124b). As exemplified in (124c, d) with the third person feminine forms this asymmetry is typical of strong vs clitic forms (see Brandi/Cordin 1981; Vanelli 1987; Poletto 2000 a.o.).

(124) a. *Er,   gester   hòt   a puach kaft*
         SBJ-STRONG.3.SG.M yesterday has-PRS.3SG a book bought
      b. **Gester   hòt   s puach er   kaft*
         yesterday has-PRS.3SG the book SBJ-CL.3.SG.M bought
         'Yesterday he bought the book'
      c. *Si,   gester   hòt   a puach kaft*
         SBJ-STRONG.3.SG.F yesterday has-PRS.3SG a book bought
      d. **Gester   hòt s puach se   kaft*
         yesterday has the book SBJ-CL.3.SG.F bought
         'Yesterday she bought the book'

Therefore, I propose that the third person masculine subject pronoun displays three forms: the strong *er*, the weak *der/ar* and the clitic *er* homophonous with the strong form.[11]

We have seen so far that in Mòcheno main declarative clauses strong pronouns occupy a fixed position in the clause and must precede the finite verb. Moreover, they always receive a pragmatically-marked reading in all varieties. I put forward the hypothesis that strong subject pronouns are hosted in the Spec of either a TopicP or a FocusP of the left periphery and not in the Spec of IP (or TP/AgrSP), i.e. in an A'-position and not in an A-position. Evidence for this hypothesis comes from the sentences in (125), where I show that material, such as the high adverbial *za en gluck*, "luckily" (assumed to mark the border between IP and CP, see Cinque 1999), can intervene between the strong pronoun and the finite verb. This indicated that the subject pronoun is not in Spec,TP/Spec,AgrSP, but higher in the high left periphery.

(125) a. *Gester   er   za en gluck hòt   a puach kaft*
         yesterday SBJ-STRONG.3.SG.M fortunately has-PRS.3SG a book bought

---

11. Note, that in the Palù dialect the form *ar* appears next to the complementiser in embedded clauses (see above). I assume that the form *ar* appearing in embedded clauses is a clitic homophonous with the weak form.

b. *Gester   si   za en gluck hòt   a puach kaft*
    yesterday SBJ-STRONG.3.SG.F fortunately has-PRS.3SG a book bought
c. *Gester   sei   za en gluck hòm   a puach kaft*
    yesterday SBJ-STRONG.3.PL fortunately have-PRS.3PL a book bought
    'Yesterday it was he/she/them who fortunately bought the book'

The above data have shown that, in main clauses, strong subject pronouns are always ruled out from the *Wackernagelposition*, which can only host clitic forms. Strong subject pronouns can only appear in the clause when either a focus or a topic reading must be expressed and in this case I propose that they occupy a position in the high left periphery.

I conclude this subsection by examining the syntax of strong subject pronouns in the embedded clauses of the Palù dialect, where, as repeated in (126), only the enclitic forms are permitted. Recall, that in the Fierozzo and Roveda dialects both weak and strong forms can appear in embedded clauses, whereas clitics are ruled out.

(126) a. *Er   hòt   mer   pfrok*
         SBJ-STRONG.3.SG.M has-PRS.3SG me-DAT asked
     b. *abia as=se   der compito   gamocht hòt*
         how that=SBJ-CL.3.SG.F the homework done   has-PRS.3SG
     c. **abia as   de   /si   der compito*
         how that SBJ-WEAK.3.SG.M /SBJ-STRONG.3.SG.F the homework
         gamocht hòt
         done   has-PRS.3SG
         'He asked me how she did her homework'

In the Palù dialect, strong pronouns can only appear in embedded clauses in the doubling construction with the clitic form illustrated in (127). This is confirmed by 12/12 consulted speakers from Palù (see Appendix, question 3).

(127) a. *Er   hòt   mer   pfrok*
         SBJ-STRONG.3.SG.M has-PRS.3SG me-DAT asked
     b. *abia as=o   du   der compito*
         how that=SBJ-CL.2.SG SBJ-STRONG.2.SG the homework
         gamocht hòst
         done   have-PRS.2SG
     c. *abia as=er   ir   der compito*
         how that=SBJ-CL.2.PL SBJ-STRONG.2.PL the homework
         gamocht hòt
         done   have-PRS.2PL

d. *abia as=se   si   der compito*
how that=SBJ-CL.3.SG.F SBJ-STRONG.3.SG.F the homework
gamocht hòt
done   has-PRS.2SG

e. *abia as=ar   er   der compito*
how that=SBJ-CL.3.SG.M SBJ-STRONG.3.SG.M the homework
gamocht hòt
done   has-PRS.2SG

f. *abia as=sa   sei   der compito*
how that=SBJ-CL.3.PL SBJ-STRONG.3.PL the homework
gamocht hon
done   have-PRS.3PL

g. *abia as=e   i   der compito*
how that=SBJ-CL.1.SG SBJ-STRONG.1.SG the homework
gamocht hòn
done   have-PRS.1SG

h. *abia as=bar   bir   der compito*
how that=SBJ-CL.1.PL SBJ-STRONG.1.PL the homework
gamocht hom
done   have-PRS.1PL

Leaving aside the analysis of sentences with strong subject pronouns in the Fierozzo and Roveda dialects, for the Palù dialect I propose that strong pronouns are hosted in the vP periphery (Jayaseelan 2001; Belletti 2001, 2004) and can, therefore, never appear in the *Wackernagelposition*. This claim is supported by the data in (128), where I show that a DO can intervene between the clitic and the strong pronoun.[12]

---

12. Note that in (128h) the only grammatical form is *biar*; conversely, *bir* is the only grammatical form when the clitic and the strong pronouns are not separated by intervening material. This distribution of the strong forms is also found in main declarative clauses, as exemplified in the sentences below from Cognola (2010:70):

a. *Gester   hòn=bar   bir   kaft   s puach*
yesterday have=SBJ-CL.1.PL SBJ-STRONG.1.PL bought the book

b. **Gester hòn=bar   biar   kaft   s puach*
yesterday have=SBJ-CL.1.PL SBJ-STRONG.1.PL bought the book

c. *Gester   hòn=bar   s puach   biar   kaft*
yesterday have=SBJ-CL.1.PL the book   SBJ-STRONG.1.PL bought

d. **Gester hòn=bar   s puach   bir   kaft*
yesterday have=SBJ-CL.1.PL the book   SBJ-STRONG.1.PL kaft

(128) a. *Er   hòt   mer   pfrok*
        SBJ-STRONG.3.SG.M has-PRS.3SG me-DAT asked
   b. *abia   as=o   der compito   du*
        how that=SBJ-CL.2.SG the homework SBJ-STRONG.2.SG
        gamocht   hòst
        done   have-PRS.2SG
   c. *abia   as=er   der compito   ir*
        how that=SBJ-CL.2.PL the homework SBJ-STRONG.2.SG
        gamocht   hòt
        done   have-PRS.2SG
   d. *abia   as=se   der compito   si*
        how that=SBJ-CL.3.SG.F the homework SBJ-STRONG.3.SG.F
        gamocht   hòt
        done   have-PRS.2PL
   e. *abia   as=ar   der compito   er*
        how that=SBJ-CL.3.SG.M the homework SBJ-STRONG.3.SG.M
        gamocht   hòt
        done   have-PRS.2PL
   f. *abia   as=sa   der compito   sei*
        how that=SBJ-CL.3.PL the homework SBJ-STRONG.3.PL
        gamocht   hon
        done   have-PRS.2PL
   g. *abia   as=e   der compito   i*
        how that=SBJ-CL.1.SG the homework SBJ-STRONG.1.SG
        gamocht   hom
        done   have-PRS.1SG
   h. *abia   as=bar   der compito   biar*
        how that=SBJ-CL.1.PL the homework SBJ-STRONG.1.SG
        gamocht   hom
        done   have-PRS.1PL

The last piece of evidence supporting the hypothesis that strong subject pronouns appear in the vP periphery comes from the distribution of the strong forms with respect to sentential adverbs. As demonstrated by Cognola (2012), the low left periphery is found in Mòcheno below sentential adverbs, which – following Cinque (1999) – I assume to occupy a fixed position in the clause. In (129), I show that the sentential adverb *òllbe* must precede the strong subject pronoun: this indicates

---

In Cognola (2010), following a suggestion by Cecilia Poletto (p.c.), I proposed that the two strong forms for the first person plural underwent a specialization process, with one form realising topic features and the other focus features.

that the strong form can never move passed sentential adverbs, i.e. must remain in a Spec position of the vP periphery (where it gets its pragmatically-marked reading).

(129) a. *Er   hòt   mer   pfrok*
         SBJ-STRONG.3.SG.M has-PRS.3SG me-DAT asked

   b. *abia as=o   òllbe   du*   (**òllbe*)
      how that=SBJ-CL.2.SG always SBJ-STRONG.2.SG always
      der compito   gamocht hòst
      the homework done   have-PRS.3SG

   c. *abia as=er   òllbe   ir*   (**òllbe*)
      how that=SBJ-CL.2.PL always SBJ-STRONG.2.SG always
      der compito   gamocht hòt
      the homework done   has-PRS.3PL

   d. *abia as=se   òllbe   si*   (**òllbe*)
      how that=SBJ-CL.3.SG.F always SBJ-STRONG.3.SG.F always
      der compito   gamocht hòt
      the homework done   has-PRS.3SG

   e. *abia as=ar   òllbe   er*   (**òllbe*)
      how that=SBJ-CL.3.SG.M always SBJ-STRONG.3.SG.M always
      der compito   gamocht hòt
      the homework done   has-PRS.3SG

   f. *abia as=sa   òllbe   sei*   (**òllbe*)
      how that=SBJ-CL.3.PL always SBJ-STRONG.3.SG.F always
      der compito   gamocht hon
      the homework done   have-PRS.3PL

   g. *abia as=e   òllbe   i*   (**òllbe*)
      how that=SBJ-CL.1.SG always SBJ-STRONG.1.SG always
      der compito   gamocht hom
      the homework done   have-PRS.1SG

   h. *abia as=bar   òllbe   bir*   (**òllbe*)
      how that=SBJ-CL.1.PL always SBJ-STRONG.1.PL always
      der compito   gamocht hom
      the homework done   have-PRS.1PL

In embedded clauses, subject doubling is also possible in the other Mòcheno dialects, where it involves the weak and the strong forms, as shown in (130). The doubling construction exemplified below is also accepted or produced by 23/23 consultants interviewed in the fieldwork (see Appendix).

(130) a. Er   hòt   mer   pfrok
         SBJ-STRONG.3.SG.M has-PRS.3SG me-DAT asked
     b. abia as   de   hòt   si   gamocht
         how that SBJ-WEAK.3.SG.F has   SBJ-STRONG.3.SG.F   done
         de compiti
         the homework
     c. *abia as   hòt si   gamocht de compiti
         how that has SBJ-STRONG.3.SG.F   done   the homework

In this subsection, we have seen that strong subject pronouns are ruled out from the *Wackernagelposition* in main clauses in all dialects, whereas in the Fierozzo and Roveda varieties they can appear, along with the weak forms, in embedded clauses. In the Palù dialect, strong subject pronouns are disallowed in embedded clauses, where only clitics enclitic to the complementiser can appear, except for the doubling construction, in which they co-occur with the clitic showing up in the *Wackernagelposition* and appear in the vP periphery. The doubling construction is also permitted in the other two varieties, where it involves the weak and the strong forms.

3.4 Conclusions

The aim of this chapter was to consider the morphologically different subject pronominal forms present in Mòcheno in order to classify them on an empirical base and to establish whether the different classes of subject pronouns underwent a process of specialization in the expression of features connected to subjecthood which is now manifested in the fact that they can only appear in one area of the clause. The latter aspect of this discussion is clearly very important for the book's aim to demonstrate that Mòcheno is a V2 language, since the correct classification of subject pronominal forms and their position in the clause is crucial to the analysis of subject-verb inversion.

The application of the syntactic tests proposed in the literature for identifying the different classes of pronouns (compatibility with the sentence-initial position; possibility of being coordinated, focused and appearing in isolation) has led to the proposal of a novel classification of Mòcheno subject pronouns, given in Table 3.14.

The main difference between the classification of subject pronouns shown in Table 3.14 and the one proposed by Rowley (2003) lies in the treatment of pronouns deriving from demonstratives, which have been shown to behave coherently as weak pronouns and to display only one form (no strong homophonous

Table 3.14 Novel classification of subject pronouns in Mòcheno

	Strong form	Clitic form	Weak form
1.SG	i	e (F/P/R)	e (R/F)
2.SG	du	o (P)	de (R/F)
3.SG-masc.	er	er	der (R/F)/ar (P)
3.SG-fem.	si	se	de
1.PL	bir, biar (P)	ber, bar (P)	bar (P), ber (F,P), der (R)
2.PL	ir	er	–
3.PL	sei	sa	de

form). I therefore integrated them into the paradigm of subject pronominal forms. The tests applied in the first part of the chapter did not allow us to classify all the forms; some of the subject clitics, in particular, remain unclassified. This applies, for instance, to the third person singular masculine forms. I suggest that the *er* form behaves as a strong pronoun when it precedes the finite verb or appears in the doubling construction, and as an enclitic when it immediately follows the finite verb. The presence of homophonous forms was not detected in the tests applied to the forms, but was discovered by analysing their distribution within the clause.

All forms classified as clitics on the basis of the tests applied in the first part of the chapter have been shown to have specialised for the *Wackernagelposition*; they appear in enclisis to the finite verb or to the complementiser (only in the Palù dialect). In only a few cases (first person singular and third person singular masculine) is the form following the finite verb or the complementiser either strong or weak: these do not constitute a counter-example to the generalization that clitics have specialised for the *Wackernagelposition*, but are simply cases of homophonous clitics with strong or weak forms. In this chapter it has also been shown that both weak and strong pronouns are excluded from the *Wackernagelposition*, which is dedicated to clitics. The strong forms can only appear in the Spec position of FocusPs or TopicPs of the high or vP periphery, since they have specialised for the expression of pragmatically-marked readings, whereas weak pronouns can only precede the finite verb in absolute sentence-initial position.

Now that the forms have been accurately classified and their distribution has been established, in the next chapter I propose a comprehensive analysis of the syntax of subject pronouns which can account for both grammatical and ungrammatical word orders. The proposed account relies on two central ideas. The first is that Mòcheno is a V2 language, which must be technically captured through the hypothesis that a lower head of CP is associated with an EPP feature which is responsible for the movement of the finite verb and XP fronting, as discussed in Chapter 2. The second is that the classification of subject pronouns into three classes actually reflects structural differences: clitics are syntactic heads, whereas strong and weak pronouns are maximal categories. Weak pronouns are unstressed, whereas strong pronouns bear accent. On the basis of these two assumptions, I put forward a specific hypothesis as to which CP head is associated with an EPP feature in Mòcheno and which constituents can be fronted to its Spec in obedience to the V2 rule. I go on to put forward detailed hypotheses on the position and the function of clitics, with a particular focus on their relation to AgrSP and CP.

CHAPTER 4

Satisfaction of EPP and realization of subjects

4.1 Introduction

In the previous chapter, I made a detailed analysis of the syntax of the subject pronominal forms present in the paradigms of the three varieties of Mòcheno and proposed a novel system for their classification. The aim of this chapter is to put forward a theoretical account that explains the distribution of these forms in main clauses (embedded clauses will be considered in Chapter 6).

The distribution of the different forms is summarised in the examples below. Strong and weak pronouns are compatible with the absolute sentence-initial position, which is ruled out for clitics (131a). When an adverbial is fronted, strong and weak (not for all speakers, see previous chapter) pronouns can precede the finite verb, but the most natural word order is that in which the clitic is enclitic to the finite verb; strong and weak forms cannot follow the finite verb in the *Wackernagelposition* (131b). Finally, as is shown in this chapter, when the fronted constituent is an operator, as in (131c), the enclitic form is obligatory and all other forms are ruled out.

(131) a. *Si* /*de* /*se *hòt*
SBJ-STRONG.3.SG.F /SBJ-WEAK.3.SG.F /SBJ-CL.3.SG.F has-PRS.3SG
kaft a puach
bought a book
'She bought a book'

b. *Gester si* /*de* *hòt=se*
yesterday SBJ-STRONG.3.SG.F /SBJ-WEAK.3.SG.F has=SBJ-CL.3.SG.F
/*si /*de *kaft a puach*
SBJ-STRONG.3.SG.F /SBJ-WEAK.3.SG.F bought a book
'Yesterday she bought a book'

c. *Benn* *si /*de
when SBJ-STRONG.3.SG.F /SBJ-WEAK.3.SG.F
**se=hòt=se* /*si
SBJ-CL.3.SG.F=has=SBJ-CL.3.SG.F /SBJ-STRONG.3.SG.F
**de kaft a puach?*
SBJ-WEAK.3.SG.F bought a book
'When did she buy a book?'

In this chapter, I propose that the syntax of subject pronouns in (131) can only be captured, if one assumes that Mòcheno is a V2 language, in which the head of an FP found in CP is associated with an EPP feature triggering movement of the finite verb to its head and XP fronting to its Spec in all main clauses. Therefore, the hypothesis I start from is that Mòcheno is a V2 language, where the movement of the finite verb and the fronting of a constituent are required in all main clauses.

Detecting these two assumed movements, however, is not as easy as it might seem. As discussed in Chapter 2, Mòcheno is a V2 language of Old Romance type, which means that all properties of the V2 phenomenon coexist with multiple access to CP. Moreover, in "relaxed" V2 languages not all fronted constituents "count" in the same way for V2: in Old Romance, for instance, topics do not "count" for V2, whereas operators do. The empirical problem that we have to face is, therefore, that in a V2 language with multiple access to CP fronting of an XP does not automatically indicate satisfaction of the requirements imposed by the V2 rule. A single fronted constituent might be a topic appearing in Spec,TopicP fully unaffected by V2 and EPP, but it could equally be an operator and therefore able to satisfy EPP. The difficulties, encountered in the Old Romance language, of investigating the V2 phenomenon in a language with multiple access to CP decrease when studying a modern language such as Mòcheno, where the pragmatic conditions of sentences can be controlled for. Pragmatics and information structure, both of which are dealt with in this book, are not the only conditions through which the V2 character of Mòcheno can be tested and (hopefully) proved. This must be borne in mind when considering V2 from a cross-linguistic perspective: as discussed in Chapter 2 (see Holmberg 2012), the V2 phenomenon certainly interacts with pragmatics, but also shows the properties of a purely formal grammatical constraint. I, therefore, I try to investigate the V2 phenomenon from a syntactic point of view.

In doing this, I rely on Benincà's intuition that for establishing whether or not a fronted constituent "counts" for V2 in V2 languages with multiple access to CP, the syntactic realization of pronouns has to be taken into account. In her work on Old Romance, Benincà focuses on object clitics, as the varieties she deals with did not have subject clitics (these have since developed in some modern varieties, including Northern Italian dialects). As shown in the examples in (132), in Old Romance proclisis is obligatory in all cases in which several XPs appear in CP (132a), whereas pronouns must be enclitic when a constituent is topicalised in the left periphery (132b). This leads Benincà to propose that when Spec,FocusP hosts a constituent, proclisis is obligatory; when Spec,FocusP is empty, enclisis is the only way to express object clitics. Foci "count" for V2 (since they can be preceded by other constituents obligatorily doubled by a clitic in IP), whereas topics do not (see Chapter 2).

(132) a. *[La vertude ch' illa ave   d'aduciderme e   guarire]ⱼ,*
the virtue that she has-PRS.3SG to kill-me   and heal
[a lingua dir] non lⱼ' auso Old Sicilian (Scremin, 88, Re Renzo)
to tongue say NEG it dare-PRS.1SG
'I do not dare to tell the virtue that she has to kill me and heal me'
b. *Lo primo modoⱼ chiamo=loⱼ   estato temoruso*
the first mode   call-PRS.3SG-it state timorous
Old Umbrian (Jacopone)
'I call the first type (of love) timorous state'

Here, capitalising on Benincà, I focus on the syntax of subject clitics, an analysis of which I contend constitutes a reliable test for demonstrating that Mòcheno is a V2 language. My thesis is that in all cases in which the fronted constituent "counts" for V2, subject pronouns have to be realised by a subject clitic, which must be enclitic to the finite verb; when the fronted XP does not "count" for V2, subject pronouns must be realised by preverbal strong or weak forms. This hypothesis implies that if the fronted XP does not "count" for V2, another constituent satisfies the requirements of V2, as will be demonstrated in this and in the following chapters. That this account allows us to make sense of variation within a single grammar, thus obviating the need for the use of the double-base hypothesis, is a very welcome result.

On the basis of the intuition that in a language with multiple access to CP the V2 has to be investigated indirectly by looking at the syntax of pronouns, I examine all the constructions hosted in the left periphery in order to determine the constituents with which enclisis is possible or obligatory. Two predictions are tested in the chapter. The first is that when a fronted constituent forces enclisis it "counts" for V2; conversely, when it does not trigger enclisis, it does not "count" for V2. The second is that if a constituent forces enclisis, it necessarily forms a Spec/head configuration with the finite verb, whereas if the fronted XP does not "count" for V2, it does not. These two predictions are prompted by fact that Mòcheno is a language with multiple access to CP, but, nevertheless, a V2 language, in which the V2 rule is assumed to manifest itself as it does in all other V2 languages, see Holmberg (2012: 39).

(133) a. A functional head in the left periphery attracts the finite verb;
b. This functional head wants a constituent moved to its spec position.

As I lay out the results of my empirical investigation into the distribution of subject pronouns in relation to fronted constituents, I attempt to give a theoretical account of the data through a precise hypothesis on the FP involved in the V2 phenomenon. In the light of the evidence presented in this chapter, I suggest that the starting point for determining which FP is involved in V2 in Mòcheno is to formulate a precise hypothesis on the syntactic position of subjects and subject clitics. Following Cardinaletti (1997, 2004), Cardinaletti/Roberts (2002), Rizzi (2006), Rizzi/Shlonsky (2007) a.o., I propose that the realization of subjects involves two different FPs: a lower projection – AgrSP (Pollock 1989; Belletti 1990 and Cardinaletti 1997) – is responsible for the realization of the case/agreement relation in terms of nominative case assignment and the checking of ϕ features (gender, number and person) between subject and finite verb. The head of a higher FP – SubjP – is associated with the classical EPP feature (Chomsky 2001) according to which all sentences must have a subject realised in Spec,SubjP. The XP satisfying the EPP feature in Spec,SubjP can be considered the "pragmatic subject" and the constituent agreeing with the finite verb and appearing in Spec,AgrSP is the "syntactic subject".

Within the articulation of SubjP and AgrSP, I assume, in accordance with established studies on Romance clitics (Kayne 1975; Brandi/Cordin 1981, 1989; Rizzi 1986; Benincà/Cinque 1993; Sportiche 1996, 1998; Poletto 2000; Roberts 2010 a.o.), that Mòcheno subject clitics are syntactic heads: this proposition is fully supported by the evidence discussed in the previous chapter, where we saw that clitics in Mòcheno display all those properties generally ascribed to their head status (they cannot be focused and cannot appear in coordination or in isolation, they need a host). Following Rizzi (2006), I assume that subject clitics realise the head of SubjP (for the idea that clitics are hosted in an A position found above a lower Agr head, see also De Crousaz/Shlonsky 2003). As is generally accepted (Brandi/Cordin 1981; Rizzi 1986; Tomaselli 1990; Poletto 2000; De Crousaz/Shlonsky 2003; Roberts 2010 a.o.), I suppose that the subject clitic in Subj^0 licenses a *pro* in Spec,AgrSP. Consequently, languages with subject clitics must be considered to be technically *pro*-drop. All the assumptions on the FPs involved in the realization of the subject are summarised in the structure in (134).[1]

---

1. Cardinaletti (1997) suggests that the two FPs involved in the realization of pragmatic and syntactic subjects are not adjacent, but are separated by a position for parentheticals. The issue of the adjacency of the two FPs dedicated to the subject is not relevant here and will be discussed below with respect to Mòcheno. Following Kayne (1994) and Cinque (1999), I assume that the underlying VP word order in Mòcheno is VO.

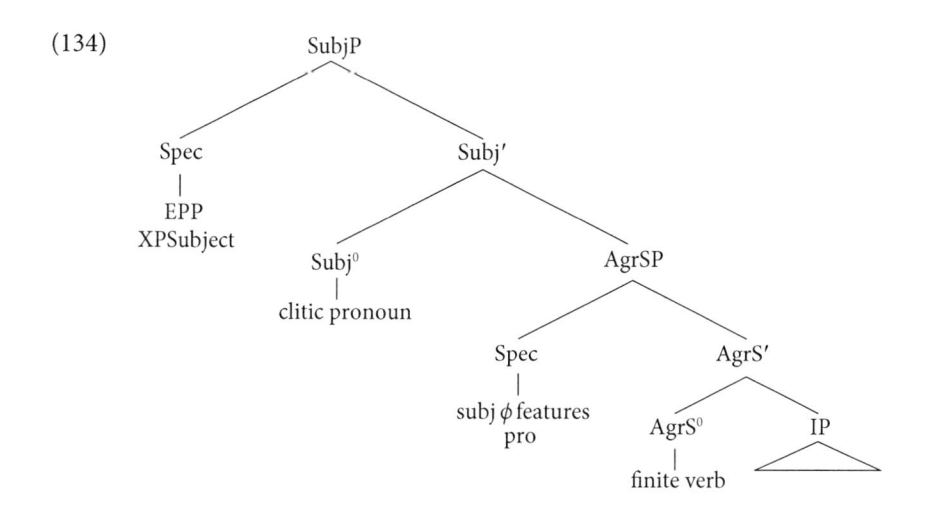

(134)
```
                    SubjP
                   /     \
                Spec      Subj'
                 |       /    \
                EPP    Subj⁰   AgrSP
              XPSubject  |    /     \
                    clitic pronoun  Spec    AgrS'
                                     |     /    \
                                 subj φ features AgrS⁰   IP
                                     pro      |
                                          finite verb
```

According to the structure in (134), SubjP is a projection whose head is associated with an EPP feature and hosts fronted constituents in its Spec position (pragmatic subjects). Its head can be lexicalised by subject clitic pronouns in those languages that have developed these elements, whose function is to license *pro* in Spec,AgrSP. The silent category realises all ϕ features connected with the syntactic subject.

Given this characterization of SubjP and the empirical facts of Mòcheno, I propose that in this language the FP associated with the EPP feature responsible for V2 is actually SubjP: this means that in Mòcheno the finite verb has to move to Subj⁰ in all main clauses and a constituent has to be fronted to Spec,SubjP, as is generally accepted (Haegeman 1997; Poletto 2002; Roberts 2004; Holmberg 2012 a.o.). When the head of SubjP is lexicalised by subject clitics, the finite verb moves to Subj⁰ where it serves as a host for the clitic. Enclisis is derived through incorporation (Backer 1985; Brody 2000; Sportiche 1996).[2] The derivation of sentences in which the EPP feature has been satisfied by the fronted XP is given in (135). Note, that I assume that the finite verb moves to Subj⁰, in line with the standard characterization of the V2 phenomenon, although this is not proven in the

---

[2]. As we saw in Chapter 3, in Mòcheno proclisis is always ruled out. According to my analysis this is due to the fact that Mòcheno is a V2 language in which the finite verb moves to Subj⁰ in all main declarative clauses, incorporating the subject clitic pronoun (if present). Within the theory proposed in this book, proclisis (found in Northern Italian dialects) has to be derived through adjacency, with the subject clitic realising the head of SubjP and the finite verb appearing in the head of AgrSP. In this study, I do not take a position about the exact derivation of subject clitics, particularly about an account in terms of base-generation in the head of SubjP or movement to that position. For some theories on this subject, see Cecchetto (1999, 2000), Belletti (2006) and references cited there.

current chapter. Convincing evidence of this movement is provided in Chapter 6, where the syntax of embedded clauses is considered.

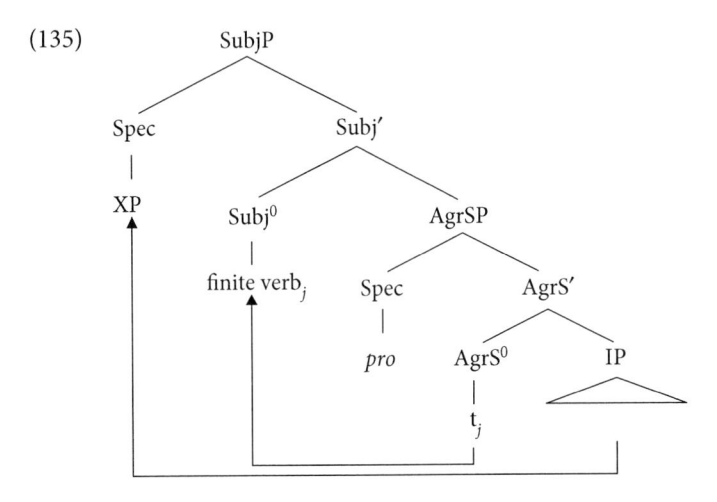

(135)

```
                    SubjP
                   /     \
                Spec     Subj'
                 |      /     \
                 XP   Subj⁰   AgrSP
                       |      /    \
                 finite verbⱼ Spec  AgrS'
                              |     /    \
                             pro  AgrS⁰   IP
                                    |
                                   tⱼ
```

Now, the mechanism for the satisfaction of the EPP feature associated with Subj⁰ allows us to explain the distribution of subject pronouns, in particular the impossibility of having a weak and a strong subject pronoun following the finite verb in sentences with a fronted operator. In this chapter I do not give a formal account of those sentences in which the fronted constituent is unable to satisfy the EPP associated with Subj⁰; to do so, I would need to introduce further relevant arguments. A proposal for the derivation of sentences involving constituents unable to satisfy EPP is put forward in Chapter 6.

Building on the results obtained through the analysis of sentences in which EPP is satisfied by a fronted operator, in the second part of this chapter I examine the syntax of sentences with a fronted subject, focusing on subject DPs and strong pronouns. I demonstrate that, surprisingly, in sentences with a fronted nominative NP and pronominal subject a *pro* is licensed in Spec,AgrSP. This conclusion leads to a more precise formulation of the licensing conditions of a *pro* in Spec,AgrSP.

The chapter is organised in the following way. In Section 4.2, I examine all types of fronted constituents (operators, HTs, SPs and LD), in order to establish whether or not they satisfy the EPP feature associated with Subj⁰. My criteria for identifying the satisfaction of EPP by the fronted constituent are the distribution of enclisis and the presence of a Spec/head configuration between the fronted XP and the finite verb. When these two conditions are met, I assume that EPP has been satisfied. As will be seen below, fronted operators and SPs are able to satisfy EPP, whereas HTs and LDs are not. In Section 4.3, I focus on the syntax of sentences with a fronted NP subject, showing that fronted NP subjects cannot satisfy EPP and behave like LDs, despite the lack of pronominal doubling in IP. In the following chapter, the partial *pro*-drop character of Mòcheno is discussed: the empirically-supported hypothesis of the presence of *pro* allows a reevaluation of data and the completion of my analysis.

4.2 Fronted constituents and EPP

4.2.1 Fronted operators

In this subsection, I examine the interaction between a fronted operator and the realization of the subject pronominal form and I show that in Mòcheno operators are able to satisfy the EPP associated with Subj^0, since they form a Spec/head configuration with the finite verb and force the realization of the subject pronoun through the clitic form.

The fact that in sentences with a fronted operator the fronted XP and the finite verb form (at some level) a Spec/head configuration is evidenced by the examples in (136). In these sentences is shown that no material (a verb argument, an adverb or an adverbial PP) can intervene between the fronted operator and the finite verb.

(136) a. *Benn s puach hòt=er kaft en Nane?
       when the book has=SBJ-CL.3.SG.M bought to John
   b. Benn hòt=er kaft s puach en Nane?
       when has=SBJ-CL.3.SG.M bought the book to John
       'When did he buy John the book?'
   c. *Bos en de Maria /za en gluck hòt=se kaft?
       what to the Mary /luckily has=SBJ-CL.3.SG.F bought
   d. Bos hòt=se kaft en de Maria /za en gluck?
       what has=SBJ-CL.3.SG.F bought to the Mary /luckily
       'What did she buy Mary/luckily?'
   e. *A PUACH en de boteig hòn=e kaft (ont net a penna)
       a book in the shop have=SBJ-CL.1.SG bought and not a pen
   f. A PUACH hòn=e kaft en de boteig (ont net a penna)
       a book have=SBJ-CL.1.SG bought in the shop and not a pen
       'It was a book that I bought in the shop, not a pen'

In sentences with a fronted operator, the subject pronoun cannot be realised by the weak form, as shown in (137).

(137) a. *Benn (de) hòt (de) kaft s puach?
       when SBJ-WEAK.3.SG.F has SBJ-WEAK.3.SG.F bought the book

b. *Benn (der/ar)   hòt (der/ar)   kaft   s puach?
   when SBJ-WEAK.3.SG.M has SBJ-WEAK.3.SG.M bought the book
   'When did she/he buy the book?'
c. *A PUACH (der/ar)   hòt (der/ar)   kaft
   a book SBJ-WEAK.3.SG.M has SBJ-WEAK.3.SG.M bought
   en de boteig (ont net a penna)
   in the shop and not a pen
   'It was a book that he/she bought in the shop, not a pen'

As illustrated in (138), the strong subject forms are also ruled out from sentences with a fronted operator.

(138) a. *Pet bem   (si)   hòt (si)   kaft
         with whom SBJ-STRONG.3.SG.F has SBJ-STRONG.3.SG.F bought
         s puach?
         the book
         'With whom did she buy the book?'
      b. *Benn (bir)   hòn (bir)   kaft   s puach?
         when SBJ-STRONG.2.PL have SBJ-STRONG.2.PL bought the book
         'When did we buy the book?'
      c. *Bos (du)   host (du)   kaft
         what SBJ-STRONG.2.SG have SBJ-STRONG.2.SG bought
         en de Maria?
         to the Mary
         'What did you buy Mary?'
      d. *PETN LUCA (si)   hòt (si)   kaft
         with-the Luca SBJ-STRONG.3.SG.F has SBJ-STRONG.3.SG.F bought
         s puach   (ont net petn Nane)
         the book and not with-the John
         'It was with Luca that he bought the book, and not with John'
      e. *A PUACH (i)   hòn (i)   kaft
         a book SBJ-STRONG.1.SG have SBJ-STRONG.1.SG bought
         en Nane (ont net a penna)
         to John and not a pen
         'It was a book that I bought John, not a pen'

The data above indicate that in sentences with a fronted operator the subject pronoun must be realised by the clitic form and the fronted XP and the finite verb must form a Spec/head configuration.

The syntax of subject pronouns in sentences with a fronted operator has been tested in the fieldwork carried out with 45 informants (sentence 1, see Appendix). The results are summarised in Table 4.1, where I examine the realization of the

Table 4.1 Third singular feminine forms in object wh-interrogative

	wh-V-cl	wh-cl-V	wh-weak/strong V	wh-V-weak/strong
Palù	15/15	0/15	1/15; 0/15	0/14; 1/14
Fierozzo	15/15	0/15	2/15; 1/15	0/15; 1/15
Roveda	15/15	0/15	1/15; 0/15	0/15; 0/15
Total	45/45	0/45	4/45; 1/45	0/44; 2/44
Percentage	100%	0%	8%; 2%	0%; 4%

Table 4.2 Third singular masculine forms in adverbial wh-interrogative

	wh-V-cl	wh-cl-V	wh-weak V	wh-V-weak
Palù	14/14	0/14	0/12	0/13
Fierozzo	15/15	0/15	0/15	0/15
Roveda	15/15	0/14	0/14	0/13
Total	44/44	0/44	0/41	0/43
Percentage	100%	0%	0%	0%

third person singular feminine subject pronouns. As shown in the second column, 45/45 informants agree that in sentences with a fronted operator the subject pronoun must be realised by the clitic form enclitic to the finite verb. The subject clitic cannot be proclitic (third column). Weak and strong forms are ruled out from both the preverbal and the postverbal position for almost all informants (over 90%).

The same pattern of distribution of third person singular feminine subject pronouns is found with third person singular masculine pronouns investigated in the second sentence of the questionnaire. As summarised in Table 4.2, all informants agree that subject pronouns must be realised by the enclitic form *er*, homophonous with the strong form, and the weak forms *der* (Fierozzo and Roveda) and *ar* (Palù) are ruled out.

The data collected in the questionnaires confirm that in sentences with a fronted operator the subject pronoun must be realised by the clitic form. According to the hypothesis put forward in this chapter, the realization of the subject pronoun as a clitic should correlate with the presence of an obligatory Spec/head correlation between the fronted operator and the finite verb, as repeated in (139).

(139) a. *Bos hòt=er   kaft?*
       what has=SUBJ-CL-3.SG.M bought
   b. **Bos gester   hòt=er   kaft?*
       what yesterday has=SUBJ-CL-3.SG.M bought
       'What did he buy yesterday?'

c. A PUACH hòt=er   kaft,   ont net a penna
    a book   has=SUBJ-CL-3.SG.M bought   and NEG a pen
d. *A PUACH gester   hòt=er   kaft   ont net a penna
    a book   yesterday has=SUBJ-CL-3.SG.M bought and NEG a pen
    'It was a book that he bought yesterday, not a pen'

The sentences in (139) above have been investigated through a grammaticality judgment task in sentences 6 and 7 of the questionnaire. The results of this task are summarised in Table 4.3. As shown in the second and the third columns, almost all informants agree that nothing can intervene between a fronted interrogative wh-element and the finite verb. When the fronted operator is a contrastive focus, all consultants agree that the unmarked word order is that in which focus and finite verb are adjacent, but 16/44 also accept an intervening constituent.[3]

All the data collected point to the fact that in sentences with a fronted operator the subject pronoun must be realised by the clitic form (enclitic to the finite verb) and nothing can intervene between the fronted operator and the finite verb (Spec/head configuration). I take this to mean that fronted operators satisfy the EPP feature associated with the head of SubjP and nothing can be moved through that position (due to classical RM). The finite verb moves to Subj⁰ where it incorporates the subject clitic. *Pro* is licensed in Spec,AgrSP. This is illustrated in the structure in (140).

Table 4.3 Spec/head configuration in sentences with a fronted operator

	wh-V	wh-adv/direct-obj-V	Focus-V	Focus-adv-V
Palù	15/15	1/15; 1/15	15/15	5/15
Fierozzo	15/15	0/15; 1/15	15/15	7/15
Roveda	15/15	0/15; 0/15	14/14	4/14
Total	45/45	1/45; 2/45	44/44	16/44
Percentage	100%	2%; 4%	100%	36%

---

3. This last piece of data is extremely interesting in the light of the analysis of sentences with multiple access to CP that will be given in Chapter 6. Those sentences will be shown to be V2 sentences in which EPP is satisfied by *pro*: the presence of a silent category permits movement of constituents to be topicalised from the clause to the left periphery without interfering with EPP and Spec,SubjP. These multiple topics are not doubled by a clitic and obviously do not satisfy EPP. The data discussed in Table 4.3, in particular the asymmetry between wh- interrogative clauses and sentences with a fronted focus, might indicate that Mòcheno is developing a contrastive left dislocation construction, similar to the one of Romance languages (Benincà 2001; Bocci 2007; Frascarelli/Hinterhölzl 2007 a.o.).

(140)

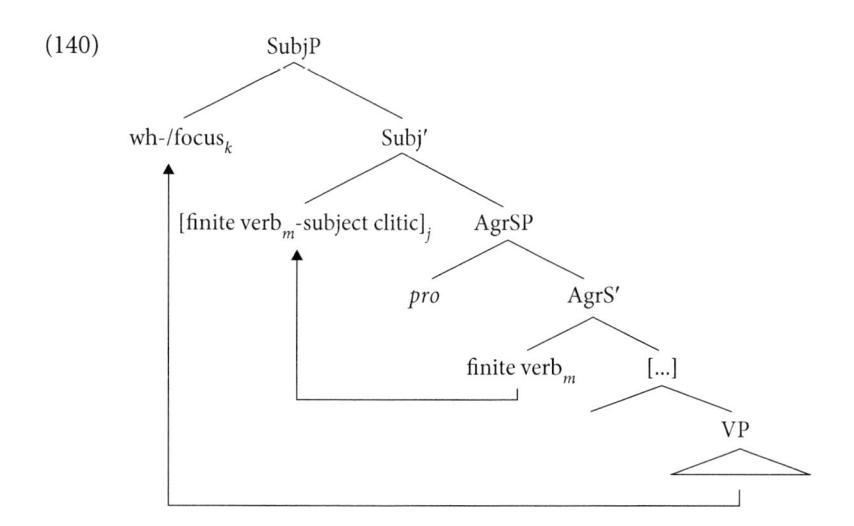

```
                        SubjP
                       /     \
              wh-/focus_k    Subj'
                           /      \
         [finite verb_m -subject clitic]_j   AgrSP
                                         /      \
                                       pro      AgrS'
                                              /      \
                                      finite verb_m   [...]
                                                        \
                                                         VP
```

The structure (140) builds on the hypothesis that subject pronominal forms cannot be hosted in AgrSP in Mòcheno.[4] There are two arguments for rejecting the hypothesis that Mòcheno subject pronouns can appear in AgrSP. The first is the syntax of subject clitics in unmarked declarative clauses. As we saw in the previous chapter and as repeated in (141), a DP subject cannot be doubled by a co-indexed clitic in Mòcheno: I take this to indicate that subject clitics do not lexicalise the head of AgrSP.

(141) a. *De mama_j hòt=se_j   a puach kaft
           the mum   has=SBJ-CL.3.SG.F a book   bought
       b. *De mai kamaroten_j hòn=sa_j   de Maria pakemmp
           the my friends   have=SBJ-CL.3.PL the Mary met

---

4. The hypothesis that both clitic and weak pronouns are hosted in AgrSP (head and Spec position respectively) could be maintained if one assumed that AgrS⁰ is associated with an EPP feature, as proposed by Homlberg/Platzack (1995) for Scandinavian languages. This idea implies that the mechanism assumed for FinP (SubjP in my account) would in reality affect AgrSP. There are three shortcomings in this proposal. The first one is that EPP and subject agreement are reunified again in the same FP, which is an unwelcome result in the light of the work pointing to the presence of two FPs involved in the realization of the subject (Cardinaletti 1997, 2004; Rizzi 2006). The second one is that the assumption that AgrS⁰ is associated with an EPP feature leads to postulate another trigger for the movement of the finite verb to CP, maybe the presence of an operator (along the lines of Travis 1994; Benincà 2006). Finally, the idea that weak and clitic subjects are hosted in AgrSP leads to an analysis of Mòcheno as a non-pro-drop language, which is contrary to the evidence that we have.

Strong and weak subject pronouns cannot be assumed to be hosted in Spec,AgrSP on the basis of the data repeated in (142), where I show that subject-verb inversion is ruled out with these subject pronominal forms.

(142) a. *Gester   hòt   de   /si   a puach kaft
         yesterday has   SBJ-WEAK.3.SG.F   SBJ-STRONG.3.SG.F a book bought
      b. *Gester   hòn   de   /sei   a puach kaft
         yesterday have SBJ-WEAK.3.PL   SBJ-STRONG.3.PL   a book bought

Since no subject pronoun can show up in AgrSP in Mòcheno, I put forward the hypothesis that weak and clitic forms realise Spec and head of SubjP, respectively, as illustrated in (143). I assume that the strong forms are hosted in the Spec of an FP of the high or low left periphery (see below).

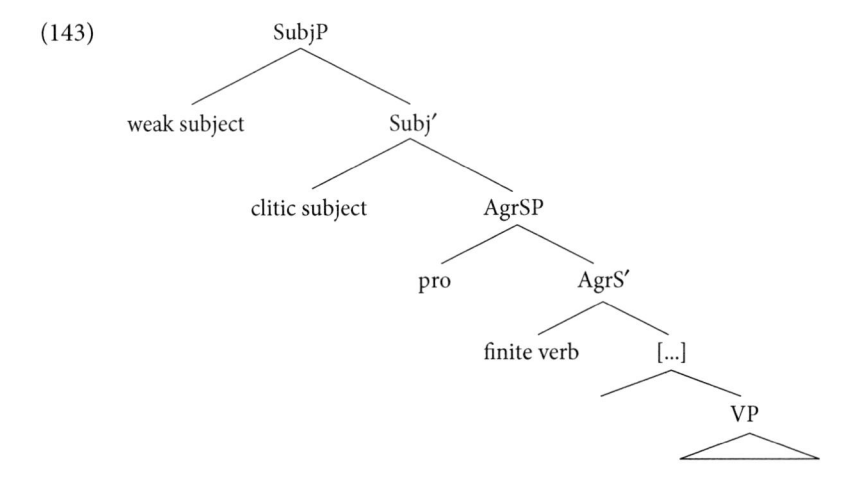

(143)

```
              SubjP
             /     \
       weak subject  Subj'
                    /    \
            clitic subject  AgrSP
                           /    \
                          pro    AgrS'
                                /    \
                          finite verb  [...]
                                        \
                                         VP
```

The structure in (143) implies that the weak subjects pronominal forms appearing in sentence-initial position are always able to satisfy the EPP feature in Spec,SubjP. As shown in (144), this prediction is borne out: the fronted weak subject pronoun must form a Spec/head configuration with the finite verb.

(144) a. *E   gester   hòn   kaft   s puach
         SBJ-WEAK.1.SG yesterday have   bought the book
      b. *Bar/ber/der   gester   hòn   kaft   s puach
         SBJ-WEAK.1.PL yesterday have   bought the book
      c. *De   gester   hòt   kaft   s puach
         SBJ-WEAK.3.SG.F yesterday have bought the book
      d. *De   gester   hòn   kaft   s puach
         SBJ-WEAK.3.PL   yesterday have bought the book

In this subsection, I have taken into consideration the syntax of sentences with a fronted operator, examining the realization of subject pronouns and showing that fronted operators must form a Spec/head configuration with the finite verb and subject pronouns must be realised by the clitic form (enclitic to the finite verb). I interpreted these facts by putting forward the hypothesis that fronted operators are able to satisfy the EPP feature associated with Subj^0 which is responsible for the V2 rule in Mòcheno. According to my analysis, fronted operators must move through Spec,SubjP for EPP reasons and by doing so block the possibility for the other subject pronominal forms to show up. The finite verb moves to Subj^0, where it incorporates the subject clitic, the function of which is to license *pro* in Spec,AgrSP.

In the next subsection I examine the first topic construction to be investigated: the hanging-topic construction, testing whether fronted HTs can satisfy the EPP feature associated with Subj^0.

4.2.2 The hanging-topic construction

As discussed in Chapter 2, in Mòcheno HTs can be distinguished from other types of thematizations such as LDs only iff a PP is involved and/or the thematised XP is doubled by an epithet. In (145), I repeat the relevant examples: note that the obligatory subject pronoun must be realised by the strong form and enclisis is impossible.

(145) a. *Der Mario$_j$,* *(er)$_j$*   hòt   mer   trog
       the Mario   SBJ-STRONG.3.SG.M   has-PRS.3SG   me-DAT   brought
       a puach der sell tepp$_j$
       a book   the that stupid
    b. **Der Mario$_j$, hòt=er$_j$*   mer   trog   a puach
       the Mario   has=SBJ-CL.3.SG.M   me-DAT   brought   a book
       der sell tepp$_j$
       the that stupid
       'As for Mario, that stupid brought me a book'
    c. *Der Mario$_j$,* *(i)*   hòn=en$_j$ nou net
       the Mario,   SBJ-STRONG.1.SG   have-PRS.1SG=him   yet   NEG
       tsechen hait   der sell tepp$_j$
       seen   today   the that stupid
    d. **Der Mario$_j$, hòne=en$_j$*   nou net tsechen hait   der sell tepp$_j$
       the Mario,   have=SBJ-CL.1.SG   yet not seen   today the that stupid
       'As for Mario, I have not seen that stupid yet today'

e. *Der Mario$_j$, *(i) hòn=en$_j$ gem a puach
the Mario SBJ-STRONG.1.SG have-PRS.1SG=him given a book
en sell tepp$_j$
to that stupid

f. *Der Mario$_j$, hòn=e=en$_j$ gem a puach en sell tepp$_j$
the Mario have=SBJ-CL.1.SG=him given a book to that stupid
'As for Mario, I gave a book to that stupid'

More examples of the HT construction involving a PP are given in (146). In these senteces can be seen that the realization of the subject pronoun through the enclitic form is ruled out and the strong or the weak forms must appear in the clause.

(146) a. Der Mario$_j$ si/ de hòt
the Mario SBJ-STRONG.3.SG.F SBJ-WEAK.3.SG.F has-PRS.3SG
nia klofft van sell tepp$_j$
never spoken of-the that stupid

b. *Der Mario$_j$ hòt=se nia klofft van sell tepp$_j$
the Mario has=SBJ-CL.3.SG.F never spoken of-the that stupid
'As for Mario, I have never spoken of that stupid'

c. Sei$_j$ der Nane hòt klofft der gonze tog
SBJ-STRONG.3.PL the John has-PRS.3SG spoken the whole day
van selln teppn$_j$
of-the those stupids

d. *Sei$_j$ hòt der Nane klofft der gonze tog
SBJ-STRONG.3.PL has-PRS.3SG the John spoken the whole day
van selln teppn$_j$
of-the those stupids
'As for them, John spoke the whole day of those stupids'

The above data show that when the fronted XP is an HT, the subject pronoun cannot be realised by the clitic form, which I take to mean that HTs are not able to satisfy the EPP feature associated with Subj^0.

In (147) I examine the syntactic behaviour of HTs with respect to the second property connected with the V2 phenomenon: the creation of a Spec/head configuration between the fronted XP and the finite verb. The following examples show that an HT can be separated by the finite verb by intervening material.

(147) Der Mario$_j$ pet de sai mama hòn=e nia klofft
the Mario with the his mum have=SBJ-CL.1.SG never spoken
van sell tepp$_j$
of-the that stupid
'As for Mario, I have never spoken of that stupid with his mum'

The data discussed in this subsection have shown that when the fronted constituent is an HT, the subject pronoun cannot be realised by the clitic form (enclitic to the finite verb) and that HTs cannot form a Spec/head configuration with the finite verb. Both properties follow straightforwardly from the hypothesis that HTs are not able to satisfy the EPP feature associated with $Subj^0$, unlike fronted operators.

In what follows, I consider the simple-preposing and the left-dislocation constructions discussed in Chapter 2 with the aim of establishing whether or not SPs and LDs can satisfy the EPP feature in Spec,SubjP.

4.2.3 Simple preposing

In Chapter 2, we saw that in Mòcheno main declarative clauses, both accessible and non-accessible D-linked constituents can be thematised through the simple-preposing construction. SP involves fronting of a constituent not doubled by a clitic in IP.

As exemplified in the sentences given in (148), fronted SPs establish a Spec/head configuration with the finite verb: no material can intervene between the fronted constituent and the finite verb.

(148) *Context: My friend was supposed to buy a book, but was always finding an excuse for not buying it. Finally he buys the book and I can say to another friend who knows the facts:*
Someone asks: Benn hòt=er kaft s puech? (When did he buy the book?)
a. *S puach gester hòt=er kaft
   the book yesterday has=SBJ-CL.3.SG.M bought
b. S puach hòt=er gester kaft
   the book has=SBJ-CL.3.SG.M yesterday bought
'He bought the book yesterday'

Context: In a school there is a very problematic class; the teachers are supposed to report to the school master (a woman) on the problems they have with each child. A teacher leaves the teachers' room and heads for the school master's office; the other teacher, who had already spoken of the case of one single child (John) with the school master says:
Someone asks: Pet bem hòs=o schua klofft van Nane?
(With whom have you already spoken of John?)
c. *Van Nane pet ir hòn=e schua klofft
   of-the John with her have=SBJ-CL.1.SG already spoken

    d.   Van Nane   hòn=e   schua   klofft   pet ir
       of-the John have=SBJ-CL.1.SG already spoken with her
       'I have already spoken of John with her'

As expected, the presence of a Spec/head configuration between the simple-preposed constituent and the finite verb correlates with the realization of subject pronouns. As shown in (149), in sentences with an SP, both strong and weak subject pronouns are ruled out and the subject pronoun must be realised by the clitic form.

(149) *Context: My friend was supposed to buy a book, but was always finding an excuse for not buying it. Finally he buys the book and I can say to another friend who knows the facts:*
     Someone asks: Benn hòt=er kaft s puech? (When did he buy the book?)
    a.   *S puach   si   /de   hòt*
       the book SBJ-STRONG.3.SG.F SBJ-WEAK.3.SG.F has-PRS.3SG
       si   /de   kaft   en de boteig
       SBJ-STRONG.3.SG.F SBJ-WEAK.3.SG.F bought in the shop
    b.   *S puach   hòt=se   kaft   en de boteig*
       the book has=SBJ-CL.3.SG.F bought in the shop
       'The book she bought in the shop'

     Context: In a school there is a very problematic class; the teachers are supposed to report to the school master (a woman) on the problems they have with each child. A teacher leaves the teachers' room and heads for the school master's office; the other teacher, who had already spoken of the case of one single child (John) with the school master says:
     Someone asks: Hòs=o schua klofft van Nane pet ir?
     (Have you already spoken of John with her?)
    c.   *Van Nane   bir/biar   hom bir/biar   schua*
       of-the John SBJ-STRONG.1.PL have SBJ-STRONG.1.PL already
       klofft   pet ir
       spoken with her
    d.   *Van Nane   hom=ber   schua   klofft   pet ir*
       of-the John have=SBJ-CL.1.PL already spoken with her
       'We have already spoken of John with her'

The simple-preposing construction was investigated in the fieldwork with 45 informants (see Appendix, sentence 5). The consultants were asked to judge the grammaticality status of a sentence with a simple-preposed DO followed by the finite verb (SP-V) and two more sentences in which the SP is followed by an adverb (*gester*, SP-Adv-V) and a nominal subject (*der Mario*, SP-SUBJ-V) respectively. The results of this task are summarised in Table 4.4. In the second column I show

Table 4.4 SP and Spec/head configuration in sentences with a fronted SP

	SP-V	SP-adv-V	SP-SUBJ-V
Palù	15/15	2/15	3/15
Fierozzo	15/15	4/15	3/15
Roveda	15/15	0/15	0/15
Total	45/45	6/45	6/45
Percentage	100%	13%	13%

that all informants judge the simple-preposing construction perfectly grammatical when the fronted constituent is immediately followed by the finite verb.[5] Only a few speakers from Palù and Fierozzo accept the sentences in which the fronted SP is followed by an adverb (third column) or the subject (fourth column).[6]

I take the data discussed above to indicate that sentences with a simple-preposed XP pattern like sentences with a fronted operator. Both SPs and operators are able to satisfy the EPP feature associated with $Subj^0$ and this manifests itself in the obligatory realization of subject pronouns through the clitic forms and in the presence of a Spec/head configuration between fronted SP and the finite verb. The structure of sentences with a fronted SP is given in (150).

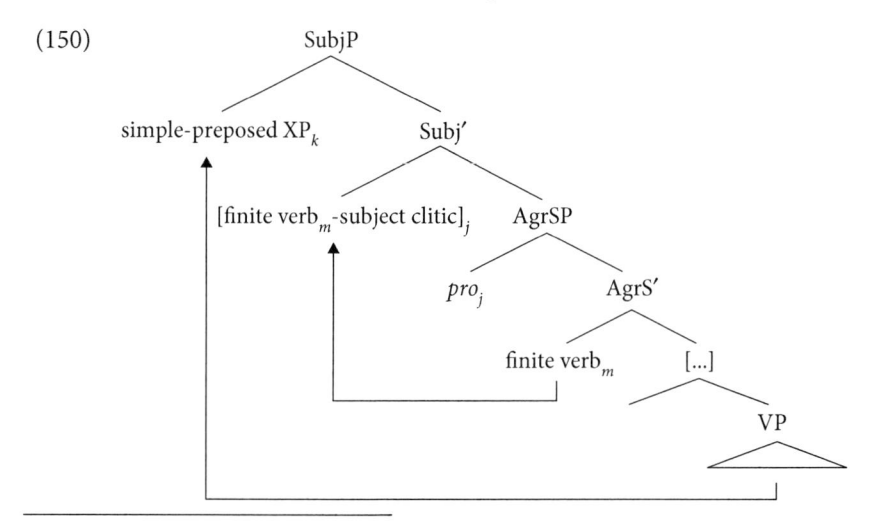

(150)
```
                    SubjP
                   /     \
   simple-preposed XP_k   Subj'
                         /     \
   [finite verb_m-subject clitic]_j   AgrSP
                                     /     \
                                   pro_j   AgrS'
                                          /     \
                                    finite verb_m   [...]
                                                     \
                                                      VP
```

5. This sentence was read out to the informants by myself with the intonational pattern typical of SPs (the fronted XP is unstressed). As can be seen in the Appendix, this construction has always been interpreted as an SP by the consulted speakers and never as an instance of a focalization.

6. Note that in one an the same variety we do not find coherence among speakers. For instance, FIER-CP accepts sentences with an intervening subject, but not those with an intervening adverb; conversely, FIER-COP rejects an intervening subject and accepts an intervening adverb.

In the following subsection, I examine the syntactic behaviour of left-dislocated constituents.

4.2.4 Left-dislocation

As discussed in Chapter 2, in Mòcheno main declarative clauses accessible (but not non-accessible) D-linked constituents can be thematised through the left-dislocation construction. LD involves fronting of a constituent doubled by a clitic in IP.

Let us examine whether the left-dislocated XP can establish a Spec/head configuration with the finite verb. As shown in (151), material can intervene between the LD and the finite verb; the fact that the XP in first position is a PP (151b, c) ensures that the construction under examination is an LD and not an HT.

(151) a. *S puach$_k$ en de boteig hòt=se=s$_k$*   *gester*
the book in the shop   has=SBJ-CL.3.SG.F=OBJ-CL.3.SG.N yesterday
kaft
bought
'As for the book, she bought it yesterday in the shop'
b. *Van Nane$_k$ gester   hòn=e   klofft va im$_k$*
of-the John yesterday have=SBJ-CL.1.SG spoken of him
'As for John, I spoke yesterday of him'
c. *En de Maria$_j$ gester   hòn=e=en$_j$*   *a puach*
to the Mary   yesterday have=SBJ-CL.1.SG=OBJ-CL.3.SG.F a book
kaft
bought
'As for Mary, I bought her a book yesterday'

In the examples in (152) I show that the lack of a Spec/head configuration between LD and finite verb correlates with the realization of the subject pronoun: as expected, this must be realised by the strong or the weak forms. Enclisis is ruled out.

(152) *Someone asks: Benn hòt=er kaft s puech? (When did he buy the book?)*
a. *S puach$_k$ si   /de*
the book SBJ-STRONG.3.SG.F SBJ-WEAK.3.SG.F
hòt=s$_k$ kaft   en de boteig
has-PRS.3SG=OBJ-CL.3.SG.N bought in the shop
b. **S puach$_k$ hòt=se=s$_k$ kaft   en de boteig*
the book has=SBJ-CL.3.SG.F=OBJ-CL.3.SG.N bought in the shop
'The book she bought in the shop'

Someone asks: Bos hos=o kaft en de Maria? (What did you buy for Mary?)
c. En de Maria$_j$ i hòn=en$_j$
 to the Mary SBJ-STRONG.1.SG have-PRS.1SG=OBJ-CL.3.SG.F
 a puach kaft
 a book bought
d. *En de Maria$_j$ hòn=e=en$_j$ a puach kaft
 to the Mary have=SBJ-CL.1.SG=OBJ-CL.3.SG.F a book bought
 'I bought Mary a book'

The above data show that left-dislocated constituents cannot satisfy the EPP feature associated with Subj^0, according to the tests followed in this book.

The LD construction was also investigated in the fieldwork with 45 informants. In sentence 8, consultants were asked to judge the grammaticality of the LD construction. The results summarised in Table 4.5 show that this construction is accepted only by a few speakers (30%) of the Palù and Fierozzo dialects. This fact contrasts with the judgments on the SP-construction, which is accepted by all informants.

The data collected in the fieldwork indicate that LD is marginally possible in Mòcheno (except for the Roveda dialect, where it is ruled out). The main consultant from Palù (Cognola 2010) is one of the speakers who accept the construction, along with five speakers from his village interviewed in the fieldwork. Note that these five speakers (PALÙ-ST, 18; PALÙ-LT, 75; PALÙ-MP, 55; PALÙ-GL, 55; PALÙ-NI, 16) and the main informant (LT) all stem from the same farms. LT, PALÙ-ST and PALÙ-LT come from the farm *Simeter*; PALÙ-MP and PALÙ-GL live in the farm *Steffener*, in the houses that are closest to *Simeter*. PALÙ-NI lives in another farm, but his father grew up in *Steffener*. The fact that the LD construction is only accepted by those speakers who live in or have some connection with *Simeter* and *Steffener* confirms Togni's (1990) observation that there may be a connection between syntactic variation and a speaker's family group. The data discussed in this book demonstrate that this connection exists but is restricted to a micro-phenomenon (the syntax of LD) and not to macro-phenomena (the syntax of the finite verb, i.e. of V2).

Table 4.5 LD in main declarative clauses

	LD-subj-V-cl	SP-SUBJ-V	SP-V
Palù	5/13	3/15	15/15
Fierozzo	7/15	3/15	15/15
Roveda	1/14	0/15	15/15
Total	13/43	6/45	45/45
Percentage	30%	13%	100%

Table 4.6 LD and SP in wh-main interrogative clauses

	LD-wh-V	SP-wh-V
Palù	15/15	1/15
Fierozzo	14/15	1/15
Roveda	12/15	0/15
Total	41/45	2/45
Percentage	91%	4%

In Chapter 2, we saw that in wh-main interrogative clauses, SP is ruled out and the only way in which both accessible and non-accessible D-linked constituents can be thematised in the left periphery is through the left-dislocation construction (or through HT). This was investigated in sentences 12 and 15 of the questionnaire, where I tested whether an interrogative wh-element can be preceded by both SP and LD. As shown in Table 4.6, nearly all speakers (91%) accept LD in wh-main interrogatives, whereas almost no one (2/45) accepts that an operator is preceded by a simple-preposed constituent.

The data indicate a complex pattern of variation for LD. This construction is accepted only by a few speakers (30%) in main declarative clauses. The data collected from these speakers show that LDs do not "count" for V2, i.e. they do not form a Spec/head configuration with the finite verb and do not force the presence of a subject clitic pronoun. In wh-main interrogative clauses, LD is accepted by almost all consultants (91%), also by those who reject it in main declarative clauses. This asymmetry is dealt with in Chapter 6, where sentences with multiple access to CP are examined. Here suffices it to say, that LDs cannot satisfy the EPP feature associated with $Subj^0$ and behave like HTs.

In what follows, I take into consideration the syntax of sentences with a fronted nominative subject, trying to determine whether fronted nominative subjects are able to satisfy the EPP feature in Spec,SubjP.

4.3 Sentences with a fronted nominative subject

In the previous section, I examined the distribution of subject pronouns in Mòcheno main declarative clauses showing that there is a clear connection between the distribution of the subject pronominal forms and the type of fronted constituent. My hypothesis is that the link between subject pronouns and fronted constituent can be captured if one assumes that Mòcheno is a V2 language and that the FP associated with the EPP feature responsible for V2 is SubjP. Following Rizzi (2006),

I assume that SubjP is an A-position headed by subject clitic pronouns; the finite verb moves to Subj⁰ in all sentences for EPP reasons and an XP has to move to (or through) Spec,SubjP in order to satisfy the EPP feature associated with the head of SubjP. In the case in which EPP has been satisfied by a non-nominative fronted constituent, subject pronouns must be realised by an enclitic pronoun, whose function is to license *pro* in Spec,AgrSP.

As we known from the literature discussed in Chapter 2, some scholars (Travis 1984, 1994 a.o.) have proposed that sentences with a fronted nominative subject do not involve an underlying V2 structure. This means that both subject and finite verb remain in IP and do not move to CP. According to the "asymmetric analysis" of V2, the finite verb only moves to CP when a non-nominative constituent is fronted. The issue of the position occupied by the subject and the finite verb in sentences with a fronted subject correlates with the question of the A/A' character of subjects. Benincà/Cinque (1993), Contreras (1991), Branigan (1996) among others propose that fronted NP subjects occupy the Spec of an A' position; Cardinaletti (1997, 2004), Rizzi (2006) and Rizzi/Shlonsky (2007) among others assume that the position hosting fronted NP subject (that is SubjP) is an A-position.

In what follows, I try to establish what the position of fronted NP subjects is and to determine whether they can satisfy the EPP feature in Spec,SubjP.

4.3.1 Fronted subjects and the EPP feature

In this subsection I examine the syntax of sentences with a fronted subject trying to establish where fronted subjects are hosted (a Spec position of CP, Spec,SubjP or Spec,AgrSP) and, therefore, whether they can or must satisfy the EPP feature responsible for V2.

I rely on the possibility of having a Spec/head configuration between the fronted subject and the finite verb for establishing whether fronted subjects "count" for V2. Let us consider sentences involving an NP subject or a strong subject pronoun appearing in the absolute sentence-initial position. As shown in (153), a fronted NP/strong subject pronoun can be separated from the finite verb by both a parenthetical (153a) and other constituents (153b).

(153) a. *De mama moan=e   hòt   a puach kaft*
         the mum think=SBJ-CL.1.SG has-PRS.3SG a book bought
         'The mum, I think, bought a book'

b. *Der Mario /er gester /en de boteig hòt*
   the Mario /SBJ-STRONG.3.SG.M yesterday /in the shop has
   kaft s puach
   bought a book
   'Mario/he bought a book in the shop yesterday'
c. *Gester der Mario /er en Luca$_j$*
   yesterday the Mario /SBJ-STRONG.3.SG.M to Luca
   hòt=(en$_j$) gem a puach
   has-PRS.3SG=OBJ-CL.3.SG.M bought a book
   'As for Luca, Mario bought him a book yesterday'

The above data indicate that unmarked fronted subjects do not have to establish a Spec/head configuration with the finite verb, which I take to mean that they do satisfy the EPP feature associated with Subj^0.

As shown in (154), fronted subjects must only form a Spec/head configuration with the finite verb when they are focused, i.e. when they behave as operators.

(154) a. **DE MAMA gester hòt kaft a puach ont net der tata*
   the mum yesterday has-PRS.3SG bought a book and not the dad
b. *Gester DE MAMA hòt kaft a puach ont net der tata*
   yesterday the mum has-PRS.3SG bought a book and not the dad
   'It was mum who bought the book yesterday, not dad'
c. **DER MARIO en Luca hòt kaft a puach ont net der tata*
   the Mario to Luca has-PRS.3SG bought a book and not the dad
d. *DER MARIO hòt kaft a puach en Luca ont net der tata*
   the Mario has-PRS.3SG bought a book to Luca and not the dad
   'It was Mario who bought a book for Luca, not dad'

Summing up, fronted subjects must satisfy the EPP feature only when they are focused, but not when they are pragmatically unmarked. In this latter case, they appear in a Spec position of the left periphery, since they are separated from the finite verb by intervening material. Therefore, in unmarked sentences, fronted subjects behave like left-dislocated XPs and HTs, despite they lack any pronominal resumption in IP. As shown in (155), fronted subjects cannot be doubled by a subject clitic not even when they are separated from the finite verb by a parenthetical or a constituent. This indicates that Kolmer's (2005) generalization is not valid for Mòcheno.

(155) a. **De mama$_j$ /si$_j$ moan=e*
   the mum SBJ-STRONG.3.SG.F think=SBJ-CL.1.SG
   hòt-sa$_j$ a puach kaft
   has=SBJ-CL.3.SG.F a book bought

b. *Der Mario_j /er_j   gester   /en de boteig
   the Mario/ SBJ-STRONG.3.SG.M yesterday /in the shop
   hòt-er_j   kaft   s puach
   has=SBJ-CL.3.SG.M   bought a book
c. *Gester   der Mario_k/ er_k   en Luca_j
   yesterday the Mario SBJ-STRONG.3.SG.M to Luca
   hòt=er_k=(en_j)   gem   a puach
   has=SBJ-CL.3.SG.M=OBJ-CL.3.SG.M given a book

The syntax of sentences with a fronted subject was tested in the questionnaire (sentences 9, 10, 11). As summarised in Table 4.7, all informants agree that in an unmarked sentence the subject can be followed by an adverbial PP (second column). In this configuration, all judge pronominal doubling of the fronted subject ungrammatical.

All data collected indicate that fronted NP subjects and strong subject pronouns are not able to satisfy the EPP feature in Spec,SubjP, unless they are focused. In main declarative clauses, fronted nominative subjects behave therefore as HTs and LDs, although they do not require pronominal doubling. Note, that the syntactic behaviour of NP subjects and strong subject pronoun points to a striking asymmetry with that of weak subject pronouns. As shown in (156), in fact, the weak forms always create a Spec/head configuration with the finite verb, unlike the strong pronouns and NP subjects.

(156) a. *De   moan=e   hòt   a puach kaft
         SBJ-WEAK.3.SG.F think=SBJ-CL.1.SG has-PRS.3SG a book   bought
      b. De mama/ si   moan=e   hòt
         the mum SBJ-STRONG.3.SG.F   think=SBJ-CL.1.SG has-PRS.3SG
         a puach kaft
         a book bought
         'She/the mum, I think, bought the book'

I suggest that the data in (156) indicate that NP subjects and strong pronouns never show up in Spec,SubjP (unless they are focused) and that this position can

Table 4.7 LD and SP in wh-main interrogative clauses

	Subj-PP-V	Subj_j-PP-V-clitic_j
Palù	15/15	0/15
Fierozzo	15/15	0/15
Roveda	15/15	0/15
Total	45/45	0/45
Percentage	100%	0%

only host weak pronouns (differently from Rizzi 2006 and Cardinaletti 1997, 2004).

This result allows us to take a position with respect to Cardinaletti's (1997) proposal that SubjP, assumed to host all types of subjects, and AgrSP, assumed to host *pro*, are not adjacent but are separated by a position for parentheticals, as sketched in (157, from Cardinaletti 1997:77).

(157) [SubjP NP/strong/weak pronouns [XP parenth. [AgrSP *pro* Vfin]]]

The Mòcheno data indicated straightforwardly that the structure in (157) is not valid for this language, and that SubjP can only host weak pronouns and focused fronted subjects.[7] Unmarked strong pronominal subjects and NP subjects appear in a Spec position of the left periphery and skip Spec,SubjP, like other topicalizations. I come back to this in Chapter 6.

4.4 Conclusions

This chapter has focused on the mechanism by which fronted constituents satisfy the EPP feature in Mòcheno. As discussed in the introduction, it is not as easy to determine whether or not a fronted XP satisfies the EPP feature responsible for V2 as it is in V2 languages without multiple access to CP. In relaxed V2 languages, in fact, not all fronted constituents are able to satisfy the EPP feature responsible for V2.

I used two tests to establish which fronted constituents satisfy EPP. Following Benincà (1984, 2006), who shows that in V2 Old Romance languages the distribution of enclisis and proclisis depends on whether the fronted constituent counts for V2, I proposed that the syntax of subject pronouns described in the previous chapter has to be directly linked with the V2 phenomenon and particularly with the satisfaction of the EPP feature responsible for V2. I suggest that in all cases in which subject pronouns must be realised by a clitic form, the fronted constituent satisfies the EPP feature. I have shown that all fronted operators and simple-preposed constituents trigger the realization of the subject pronoun as a clitic enclitic to the finite verb, whereas when the fronted constituent is an HT or an LD, subject pronouns have to be realised by weak or strong forms.

The second test I used for establishing whether fronted XPs can satisfy the EPP feature is whether or not it is possible to have a Spec/head configuration

---

7. Focused XPs probably move through Spec,SubjP before reaching their landing site, Spec,FocusP. See Haegaman (1997) on this.

Table 4.8 EPP and realization of the subject pronoun

Fronted XP	Subject pron	Spec/head config.	EPP on Subj^0
wh-element	enclitic/*strong/*weak	✓	✓
focus	enclitic/*strong/*weak	✓	✓
simple preposing	enclitic/*strong/*weak	✓	✓
left dislocation	strong/weak/*enclitic	*	*
hanging topic	strong/weak/*enclitic	*	*
NP/strong subj	–	*	*

between the fronted constituent and the finite verb. When the fronted XP must form a Spec/head configuration with the finite verb, I take this as evidence that it has satisfied EPP. The creation of the Spec/head configuration is obligatory with all constituents that trigger the realization of subject pronouns as clitics, fronted operators and simple-preposed topics, and optional with fronted HTs and LDs.

According to the tests carried out in this chapter and as summarised in Table 4.8, all fronted constituents that do not require a pronominal doubling in IP are able to satisfy the EPP feature responsible for V2, whereas those constructions in which the fronted XP is doubled by a clitic in IP (HT and LD) do not "count" for V2. Note, that fronted nominative DP subjects are included among the latter class: the evidence discussed above shows that they have to be analysed as left-dislocated XPs doubled in IP by *pro*.

I have tried to capture the empirical facts by assuming that in Mòcheno the FP associated with the EPP feature is SubjP. In the literature, the Spec of this FP is assumed to host the pragmatic subjects (Cardinaletti 1997, 2002; Rizzi 2006; Rizzi/Shlonsky 2007; De Crousaz/Shlonsky 2003 a.o.) whereas its head is assumed to be lexicalised by subject clitics (Rizzi 2006). In all cases in which the EPP feature is satisfied, I assume that the fronted XP is moved to (or through) Spec,SubjP, forcing the movement of the finite verb to Subj^0 and the realization of the subject pronoun through the clitic form. Weak pronouns are ruled out in sentences in which the fronted XP satisfies EPP because they are both thought to compete with the fronted XP for Spec,SubjP. When the fronted constituent cannot satisfy the EPP feature in Spec,SubjP, it is assumed to "skip" Spec,SubjP, whose EPP feature has to be satisfied by another constituent. HTs, LDs and fronted (non-focused) strong pronouns and NP subjects are all unable to satisfy the EPP feature. The derivation of sentences with constituents which cannot satisfy the EPP feature in Spec,SubjP is given in Chapter 6.

This empirically-based theoretical account relies entirely on the classification of Mòcheno as a *pro*-drop language, meaning that nothing except the silent category *pro* can appear in Spec,AgrSP. The syntax of all subject pronominal forms, which have been shown to have no links with AgrSP, requires that a *pro* in

Spec,AgrSP be hypothesised. Weak and strong forms can never appear in subject-verb inversion, which would be very surprising if they were hosted in AgrSP, as would be the case if Mòcheno were a non-*pro*-drop language.

In the next chapter, I examine the hypothesis that Mòcheno is a *pro*-drop language, investigating the properties of *pro*-drop languages discussed in the literature and reaching the conclusion that Mòcheno must be considered a partial *pro*-drop language.

CHAPTER 5

Mòcheno as a partial *pro*-drop language

5.1 Introduction

In Chapters 3 and 4, I advanced the hypothesis that Mòcheno is a *pro*-drop language – a thesis arrived at on the basis of both theory-internal considerations (according to the standard analysis, subject clitic pronouns have the function of licensing *pro*) and empirically-based arguments (the syntax of weak and strong subject pronouns and that of DP subjects). The aim of this chapter is to corroborate the hypothesis that Mòcheno is a *pro*-drop language by considering the syntactic properties shown in the literature to be linked to the *pro*-drop phenomenon and investigating whether Mòcheno has these properties. Establishing whether Mòcheno is *pro*-drop is crucial to this book's central hypothesis that Mòcheno must be analysed as a V2 language, since theoretically nothing prevents us from hypothesising that the silent maximal category can satisfy EPP.

As discussed in Holmberg/Roberts (2010), the best-studied case of *pro*-drop languages is that of consistent *pro*-drop languages (Perlmutter 1971; Rizzi 1982; 1986 a.o.) which have long been taken to be the only null subject languages. Consistent null subject languages, including Italian and Northern Italian dialects, allow for non-referential *pro* in all sentences, permit free-inversion, do not display that-trace effects and have rich agreement morphology on finite verbs. It is assumed that the null subject in consistent *pro*-drop languages is licensed by just the presence of rich verbal agreement morphology (Holmberg/Roberts 2010; Roberts 2010).

Work by Shlonsky (2009) on Hebrew, Holmberg (2005) on Finnish, Sheehan (2007) on the whole Romance language family and the papers collected in Biberauer (2008) and Biberauer et al. (2010) have shown that the *pro*-drop system found in consistent null subject languages is only one of the possible *pro*-drop systems. When other languages and language families are included in the investigation, we find examples of referential *pro* being licensed in some contexts but not in all. Holmberg (2005), Sheehan (2007) and Holmberg/Sheehan (2010) define the languages in which the referential *pro* is only licensed in some syntactic contexts as "partial null subject languages".[1]

Partial *pro*-drop languages are more difficult to describe theoretically than consistent null-subject languages, since, unlike the latter group, they do not have a coherent set of specific properties that can be ascribed to them generally. For instance, in the partial *pro*-drop language Finnish (Holmberg 2005), first and second person pronouns can drop in all contexts, whereas in the partial *pro*-drop language Brazilian Portuguese (Tarallo 1983; Figueiredo Silva 2000; Sheehan 2007) *pro*-drop is not permitted in sentences with a fronted operator. Therefore, partial *pro*-drop languages are each *pro*-drop in their own particular way, with the only constant being that null referential subjects are allowed in some, but not all, contexts.

German, Dutch and Afrikaans (Cardinaletti 1990 and Biberauer 2010) are classified as partial *pro*-drop languages, because they allow expletive null subjects under certain conditions. Since these languages never permit referential null subjects, Holmberg/Roberts (2010) propose to classify them as expletive null subject languages.

Building on the literature discussed, in what follows, I go on to provide further evidence for the analysis of Mòcheno as a partial *pro*-drop language. In particular, I show that in Mòcheno, as in German, it is possible to license expletive null subjects in passive constructions; although, Mòcheno behaves like consistent null subject languages in having no that-trace effects and permitting free-inversion. Mòcheno, unlike consistent null-subject languages, does not allow for referential null subjects, except for the second person singular in the main clauses of the Fierozzo and Roveda dialects. These empirical properties, far from appearing randomly in Mòcheno, are shown to form a cluster typical of partial *pro*-drop languages. As pointed out by Holmberg/Roberts (2010), all languages that allow for the free inversion of overt subjects, also manifest that-trace effects and all have developed expletive *pro*: Mòcheno can be said to have reached the highest level of this implicational scale, since it has developed all three properties. As discussed in the second part of the chapter, Mòcheno has actually gone beyond the implicational scale proposed by Holmberg/Roberts (2010), since it also allows for the licensing of referential *pro* (possible in two varieties but very restricted) and of quasi-argumental *pro*. The conditions governing the licensing of quasi-

---

1. A third type of *pro*-drop languages is identified in the literature: discourse or radically *pro*-drop languages, in which null subjects appear without any kind of agreement marking (Huang 1984; Rizzi 1986; Holmberg/Roberts 2010 and references cited there). Since this type of null subject language is not relevant to the present discussion, I only mention it briefly, referring the reader to the cited literature.

argumental *pro* in main clauses with pronominal and nominal subjects are explored in the second part of the chapter.

The chapter is organised in the following way. In Section 5.2, I discuss the properties ascribed to *pro*-drop languages in the literature, investigating the syntactic behaviour of Mòcheno in terms of these properties and reaching the conclusion that Mòcheno must be considered a partial *pro*-drop language. In Section 5.3, I examine the syntax of DP subjects in all syntactic contexts in order to investigate the interaction between fronted nominative subjects and licensing of *pro* in Spec,AgrSP. In 5.4 I sum up the results reached in the chapter, focusing on how *pro* can be licensed in Mòcheno.

5.2 Mòcheno as a partial *pro*-drop language

5.2.1 Properties of *pro*-drop languages

As discussed by Rizzi (1982) and Holmberg/Roberts (2010: 2ff.), consistent null subject languages share the cluster of properties listed in (158).

(158) a. The possibility of a silent, referential, definite subject of finite clauses;
       b. free subject-verb inversion;
       c. absence of complementiser-trace effects;
       d. rich agreement inflection on finite verbs.

In (158), I exemplify properties (158a, d) with data from Italian. In this language, subject pronouns can drop in all persons and this correlates with the presence of rich agreement inflection on all persons of the paradigm (examples from Holmberg/Roberts 2010).

(159) a. (Io) compr-o, "I buy"
       b. (Tu) compr-i, "you buy"
       c. (Lui/lei) compr-a, "he/she buys"
       d. (Noi) compri-a-mo, "we buy"
       e. (Voi) compr-a-te, "you buy"
       f. (Loro) Compr-a-no, "they buy"

In (160), I show that in Italian an overt subject can be realised in the postverbal position (free inversion), where it usually gets a focus reading (see Belletti 2004). In Italian, free inversion is permitted with all classes of verbs and with all types of subjects (QPs or NPs).

(160) a. *Hanno   telefonato molti studenti*
           have-PRS.3PL phoned   many students
       b. **Have telephoned many students*
           'Many students phoned'
       c. *Ha   telefonato Mario*
           has-PRS.3SG phoned   Mario
       d. **Has phoned Mario*
           'Mario phoned'

Finally, in (161), I consider the last property of *pro*-drop languages: the that-trace effect. This constraint blocks only in *pro*-drop languages wh-movement of a subject from an embedded finite clause to the matrix clause if the complementiser introducing the embedded clause is present (161b, d).

(161) a. *Chi hai   detto che ha   scritto*
           who have-PRS.2SG said that hasPRS.3SG written
           questo libro?
           this   book
       b. *Who did you say (*that) had wrote this book?*
           'Who did you say wrote this book?'
       c. *Chi pensi   che sia   il più intelligente?*
           who think-PRS.2SG that is-SUBJ.3SG the most intelligent
       d. *Who do you think (*that) is the most intelligent?*
           'Who do you think is the most intelligent?'

As discussed in the introduction, in partial *pro*-drop languages the properties of consistent null-subject languages appear in some contexts but not in all. Moreover, it is typical of partial null-subject languages that "generic pronouns can and must be null" (Holmberg 2005: 540), whereas in consistent null-subject languages either a clitic form (as Italian *si*) or a special verb form are required. This asymmetry between consistent null-subject languages and partial null-subject languages is exemplified with Finnish and Italian data in (162a, from Holmberg 2005: 540).

(162) a. *Täällä ei saa polttaa*
           here   NEG may smoke
       b. *Qui non *(si)   può   fumare*
           here NEG IMP-PRON can-PRS.3G smoke
           'It is not allowed to smoke here'

Most Germanic languages (German, Afrikaans, Dutch, see Biberauer 2010) and several creoles (Nicolis 2008) are analysed as expletive null-subject languages. This classification implies that these languages are not *pro*-drop or partial *pro*-drop, that is they do not display any of the properties listed in (158), but may license *pro* with non-referential expletives (Cardinaletti 1990 a.o.). This is illustrated in (163) with German. As shown in (163a, b), when the neuter pronoun *es* is referential and refers back to a neuter noun (*das Kind*, *das Mädchen* oder *das Buch*) it cannot be dropped, as expected in a non-null-subject language. When *es* is used as an expletive pronoun in an impersonal passive construction, as in 163c), it must be dropped when another constituent is fronted to the left periphery, as shown in (163d). In this last sentence, the presence of *pro* must be assumed in Spec,AgrSP.

(163) a. *Es   ist   gestern   angekommen*
         SBJ-PRON.3.SG.N is-PRS.3SG yesterday arrived
     b. *Gestern   ist   *(es)   angekommen*
         yesterday is-PRS.3SG SBJ-PRON.3.SG.N arrived
        'He/She/It arrived yesterday'
     c. *Es   wurde   gestern   getanzt*
         EXPL AUX-PASS yesterday danced
     d. *Gestern   wurde   (*es)   getanzt*
         yesterday AUX-PASS EXPL   danced
        'Yesterday there was dancing'

As discussed by Cardinaletti (1990) among others, in German (differently from Icelandic, Holmberg 2012) the expletive pronoun *es* behaves as a referential pronoun with weather verbs. This is exemplified in (164).[2]

(164) a. **Es   hat   gestern   geregnet*
         EXPL has-PRS.3SG yesterday rained
     b. *Gestern   hat   *(es)   geregnet*
         yesterday has-PRS.3SG EXPL   rained
        'It rained yesterday'

In this subsection, I have introduced all the empirical properties of null-subject, partial null-subject and expletive null-subject languages. In what follows, I examine the syntactic behaviour of Mòcheno with respect to these properties.

---

2. I do not see this as a problem for the analysis of German as an expletive null-subject language, but simply as an indication that in order for *pro* to be licensed in this language the passive morphology has to be present. Therefore, also for German and expletive-null subject languages it might be assumed that *pro* licensing depends on verbal agreement morphology, with the passive morphology being somehow "richer" than the active morphology.

5.2.2 Licensing of null referential subjects and rich agreement

As discussed in the previous section, consistent null-subject languages are characterised by the cluster of properties listed in (158) and repeated below in (165).

(165) a. The possibility of a silent, referential, definite subject of finite clauses;
   b. free subject-verb inversion;
   c. absence of complementiser-trace effects;
   d. rich agreement inflection on finite verbs.

Let us examine the properties (165a, d) in Mòcheno. As illustrated in (166), in this language it is not possible to have a silent, referential, definite subject in finite clauses, but the strong subject pronoun must be present. Note, that in this case the strong subject pronoun is not given a pragmatically-marked reading. This correlates with an agreement verbal system composed of three different agreement forms (-st, -t, -n; the first singular has no ending) for six persons of the paradigm. According to the classification proposed by Koeneman/Zeijlstra (2012), this agreement system (the same as that of Yiddish) has to be classified as rich,[3] but is poorer than that of a consistent null-subject language such as Italian.

(166) a. *(i) kav, "I buy"
   b. *(du) kavst, "you buy"
   c. *(er/si/de) kavt, "he/she buys"
   d. *(bir) kavn, "we buy"
   e. *(ir) kavt, "you buy"
   f. *(sei) kavn, "they buy"

The above data show that Mòcheno patterns like a non-*pro*-drop language with respect to properties (165a, d) and differs, therefore, from both standard Italian (see previous section) and the contact Trentino dialect. In this Romance dialect, *pro* is licensed in all persons (see Brandi/Cordin 1981, 1989; Poletto 2000) and strong pronouns only appear when a pragmatically-marked reading has to be conveyed.

(167) a. (mi) togo, "I buy"
   b. (ti) *(te) toi, "you buy"
   c. (elo/ela) *(el/la) tol, "he/she buys"
   d. (noaltri) tolen, "we buy"

---

3. "A language exhibits rich subject agreement if agreement involves at least the same featural distinctions as those manifested in the smallest (subject) pronoun inventories universally possible" Koeneman/Zeijlstra (2012: 4).

e. (voaltri) tolé, "you buy"
f. (lori) *(i) tol, "they buy"

The data discussed above show that null referential pronouns cannot be licensed in main declarative clauses in Mòcheno – a result that runs counter to my hypothesis that Mòcheno is a *pro*-drop language

Let us examine sentences in which the fronted XP is not the subject. As shown (168), in wh-interrogative clauses referential *pro* cannot be licensed, and subject clitics (enclitic to the finite verb) must show up. The only exception is represented by the second person singular in the Fierozzo and Roveda dialects, where *pro* is licensed by the finite verb in CP.

(168)   a. Benn kav-*(e) s puach? "When do I buy the book?" ...
        b. Benn kavst (F/R)/kavs(t)-*(o, P) s puach?
        c. Benn kavt-*(er/se) s puach?
        d. Benn kavn-*(ber) s puach?
        e. Benn kavt-*(er) s puach?
        f. Benn kavn-*(sa) s puach?

The same distribution of referential *pro* and subject clitics is found in the case in which the fronted XP is an adverb, as shown in (169).

(169)   a. Morm kav-*(e) s puach "Tomorrow I buy the book" ...
        b. Morm kavst (F/R)/kavs(t)-*(o, P) s puach
        c. Morm kavt-*(er/se) s puach
        d. Morm kavn-*(ber) s puach
        e. Morm kavt-*(er) s puach
        f. Morm kavn-*(sa) s puach

The data discussed above have shown that, according to the characterization of partial *pro*-drop languages given in the introduction, Mòcheno can be classified as a partial *pro*-drop language, since *pro* licensing is possible in some but not in all syntactic contexts. In the next subsection, I examine free-subject inversion and that-trace effects.

5.2.3 Free subject inversion and that-trace effects

In Mòcheno, NP subjects can appear in two inversion constructions. The first one, exemplified in (170a, c), is the standard subject-finite verb inversion typical of V2 Germanic languages. In this construction, the NP subject follows the finite verb and precedes the non-finite verb form. As shown in (170b, d), Mòcheno NP subjects can also appear in the free-subject inversion construction, in which the

NP subject follows the non-finite verb form and is not doubled by any type of pronominal resumption.

(170) a. *(S) hòt   der Mario telefoniert
            EXPL has-PRS.3SG the Mario phoned
       b. *(S) hòt   telefoniert der Mario
            EXPL has-PRS.3SG phoned   the Mario
            'Mario phoned'
       c. *(S) hòn   viele studenten telefoniert
            EXPL have-PRS.3PL many students   phoned
       d. *(S) hòn   telefoniert viele studenten
            EXPL have-PRS.3PL phoned   many students
            'Many students phoned'

As illustrated in (171), both types of subject inversions are found with unaccusative and inergative verbs too.

(171) a. *(S) ist   de mama kèmen
            EXPL is-PRS.3SG the mum come
       b. *(S) ist   kèmen de mama
            EXPL is-PRS.3SG come the mum
            'The mum has arrived'
       c. *(S) hòt   der Mario schlòvn
            EXPL has-PRS.3SG the Mario slept
       d. *(S) hòt   schlòvn der Mario
            EXPL has-PRS.3SG slept   the Mario
            'Mario slept'

Unlike V2 Germanic languages, in Mòcheno both inversion constructions are marked: in both, the NP subject receives a pragmatically-marked focus reading. As shown in (172a, b, c), when the overt subject precedes the past participle, the most natural reading is the narrow-focus reading, whereas when the subject follows the past participle, it naturally gets a wide-focus reading (172d, e, f).[4] These readings are ruled out when the subject appears in sentence-initial position.

(172) a. Ber hòt   telefoniert?
           who has-PRS.3SG phoned
           'Who phoned?'

---

4. The presence of two FocusPs in the lower portion of the clause recalls the data from Yiddish discussed by Diesing (1997).

b. S   hòt   der Mario telefoniert
    EXPL has-PRS.3SG the Mario phoned
c. #Der Mario hòt   telefoniert
    the Mario   has-PRS.3SG   phoned
    'Mario phoned/It was Mario who phoned'
d. Bos   ist   passiert?
    what   is-PRS.3SG   happened
    'What happened?'
e. S   hòt   telefoniert der Mario
    EXPL has-PRS.3SG   phoned   the Mario
f. #Der Mario hòt   telefoniert
    the Mario   has-PRS.3SG   phoned
    'Mario phoned'

The above examples show that free subject inversion is possible in Mòcheno and involves an overt subject with a pragmatically-marked reading and the expletive pronoun *s* appearing in sentence-initial position. I suggest that the expletive pronoun *s* must be considered a CP-expletive, a maximal category that shows up in the clause in order to satisfy one of the requirements of the V2 rule (one XP in Spec,SubjP). The fact that *s* is hosted in the left periphery in sentences with (free) subject-verb inversion is evidenced by the examples in (173), where I show that the expletive disappears in all cases in which other XPs are fronted.

(173) a. *(S) hòt   telefoniert der Nane
          EXPL has-PRS.3SG   phoned   the Mario
          'Mario phoned'
      b. Hait   hòt   (*s)   telefoniert der Nane
          today has-PRS.3SG   EXPL   phoned   the John
          'Mario phoned today'
      c. Hòt   (*s)   telefoniert der Nane?
          has-PRS.3SG   EXPL   phoned   the John
          'Has John phoned?'

I take the examples in (173) to indicate that in the free subject-verb-inversion construction, the fronted expletive has to be analysed as a maximal category realising a Spec position of CP (presumably Spec,SubjP). The ϕ features of the subjects are realised by *pro* appearing in Spec,AgrSP. This hypothesis finds further confirmation in the data in (174), where I show that the finite verb must agree with the overt subject and not with the fronted expletive. This allows us to rule out that *s* is hosted in Spec,AgrSP – a position in which I assume that only *pro* can be found.

(174) a. S   hòn   schlofen de kinder
          EXPL have-PRS.3PL slept   the children
     b. *S   hòt   schlofen de kinder
          EXPL has-PRS.3SG   slept   the children
          'The children slept'

The data above show that free-subject inversion of overt subjects is possible in Mòcheno and that this construction interacts with both the V2 rule (*s* must appear in Spec,SubjP for EPP reasons) and the licensing of *pro* (the finite verb must move to Subj⁰ for *pro* to be licensed).

In (175), I consider that-trace effects in Mòcheno. The examples show that Mòcheno does not display that-trace effects and the complementiser must be present in all syntactic contexts.

(175) a. Ber hòs=o   zok, *(as) schrim hòt   s   doi puach?
          who have=SBJ-CL.2.SG   said that   written has-PRS.3SG   the this book
          'Who did you say has written this book?'
     b. Ber muas=o,   *(as) ist der tschaiste?
          who think-PRS.2SG that   is the most intelligent
          'Who do you think is the most intelligent one?'

Summing up, in this subsection I have provided evidence that Mòcheno displays both free inversion of overt subjects and absence of that-trace effects. Both properties are assumed to coexist with the V2 rule, as evidenced by the data on the distribution of the expletive pronoun *s* in the free subject-verb inversion construction.

In what follows, I consider the behaviour of Mòcheno with respect to two more properties that have been connected in the literature to partial *pro*-drop languages: the possibility of having both expletive null subjects and null generic pronouns. The investigation of these two last properties will allow us to complete the examination of the empirical facts and to reach a conclusion with respect to its *pro*-drop system.

5.2.4 Expletive null subjects and generic pronouns

As discussed above, German allows for a very restricted type of *pro*-drop that only involves expletive pronouns. In this language, referential pronouns cannot be dropped (176a, b), which is typical of non-*pro*-drop languages. Unexpectedly, expletive pronouns can drop, as shown in (176c, d), and *pro* must be assumed in Spec,AgrSP.

(176) a. *Es   ist   gestern   angekommen*
         SBJ-PRON.3.SG.N is-PRS.3SG yesterday arrived
    b. *Gestern   ist   *(es)   angekommen*
         yesterday is-PRS.3SG SBJ-PRON.3.SG.N arrived
        'He/She/It arrived yesterday'
    c. *Es   wurde   gestern   getanzt*
         EXPL AUX-PASS yesterday danced
    d. *Gestern   wurde   (*es) getanzt*
         yesterday AUX-PASS EXPL   danced
        'Yesterday there was dancing'

In (177), I show that Mòcheno behaves like standard German, since it allows for expletive null-subjects in passives.

(177) a. *S   ist   finz spat   tonzt   ont sungn kemmen*
         EXPL is-PRS.3SG   until late danced and sung   AUX-PASS
    b. *Finz spat ist   (*-s) tonzt   ont sungn kemmen*
         until late is-PRS.3SG EXPL   danced and sung   AUX-PASS
        'Last night there were dancing and singing until late'
    c. *Benn ist   (*-s) tonztn ont sungn kemmen?*
         when is-PRS.3SG EXPL   danced and sung   AUX-PASS
        'When was there dancing and singing?'
    d. *S   ist   galesen kemmen*
         EXPL is-PRS.3SG read   AUX-PASS
        'People/We read'
    e. *Hait   ist   (*s) galesen kemmen*
         today is-PRS.3SG EXPL read   AUX-PASS
        'Today people/we read'
    f. *Benn ist   (*s) galesen kemmen?*
         when is-PRS.3SG EXPL read   AUX-PASS
        'When did people/we read?'

In Mòcheno, as in German, expletive null-subjects can only be licensed in passive sentences. As shown in (178), in an active sentence the presence of the expletive *s* and the fact that the finite verb is in CP are not sufficient conditions for *pro* to be licensed.

(178) a. **S   hòt   telefoniert*
         EXPL has-PRS.3SG phoned
    b. **(S)   hòt   telefoniert der Nane*
         EXPL has-PRS.3SG phoned   the John
        'John phoned'

The last phenomenon that I consider is the licensing of generic pronouns. As observed by Holmberg (2005) and Holmberg/Roberts (2010) and as shown in (179a, from Holmberg 2005: 540 and 179b from Sheehan 2007: 6), generic pronouns can or must be null in partial-null-subject languages.

(179) a. *Täällä ei saa polttaa*
 here NEG may smoke
 'Smoking is not allowed here'
 b. *Aqui vende sapato*
 here sells-PRS.3SG shoes
 'Shoes are sold here'

In Mòcheno there are two ways through which the generic pronoun corresponding to Italian *si* can be expressed: either through the passive construction with the expletive *s* or through the pronoun *man*, identical to the corresponding German form. As illustrated in (180), both pronouns cannot be dropped in Mòcheno.

(180) a. **(S) mu net garacht kemmen*
 EXPL can-PRS.3SG NEG smoked AUX-PASS
 'Smoking is not permitted'
 b. *Do mu *(s) net garacht kemmen*
 here can EXPL NEG smoked AUX-PASS
 'Smoking is not permitted here'
 c. *Man mua net rachen*
 IMP-PRON can-PRS.3SG NEG smoke
 'One is not allowed to smoke'
 d. *Do mua *(man) net rachen*
 here can-PRS.3SG IMP-PRON NEG smoke
 'One is not allowed to smoke here'

In the following subsection I sum up the results reached in this section the and put forward a specific hypothesis for Mòcheno.

5.2.5 Proposed analysis

The results reached so far are summarised in Table 5.1. The comparison with the expletive null subject language German and the consistent *pro*-drop language Italian shows that Mòcheno sets itself between these two extremes. Like Italian, Mòcheno allows for that-trace violations and free-inversion; like German it does not permit generic null-subjects. Both Mòcheno and German have a poorer

Table 5.1 *Pro*-drop properties

	pro$_{EXPL}$	pro$_{REF}$	rich agr	that-t violations	free inversion	generic null-pro
German	✓	*	–	*/✓	*	*
Italian	✓	✓	+	✓	✓	*
Mòcheno	✓	*	–	✓	✓	*

verbal morphology than that of Italian, but, still rich according to the criteria proposed by Koneman/Zeijstra (2012).[5]

On the basis of comparative work (see Gilligan 1987 and Nicolis 2008), Holmberg/Roberts (2010:38) propose the implicational scale in (181) for the phenomena related to *pro*-drop discussed so far. If a language has free-inversion, it also allows for that-trace violations and expletive null subjects. Therefore, the properties in (181) can be seen as a cluster of correlated properties.

(181) Free inversion > allow that-trace violations > expletive null subjects.

As summarised in Table 1, Mòcheno displays all three properties of Roberts/Holmberg's implicational scale.

As is typical of partial null-subject languages, in Mòcheno it is also possible to license a referential *pro* in some cases but not in all. The cases in which *pro* must be licensed are more restricted than those reported in the literature on partial *pro*-drop languages, since the condition governing *pro* licensing in Mòcheno is the syntactic position of the finite verb: when the verb is in CP, *pro* can be licensed.

As repeated in (182), referential *pro* is licensed by the finite verb in CP in the second person singular in the Roveda and Fierozzo dialects (182a, b).

(182) a. *Benn kavst   s puach?*
         when buy-PRS.2SG the book
         'When do you buy the book?'
     b. **(Du)   kaft   s puach*
         SBJ-STRONG.2.SG buy-PRS.2SG the book
         'You buy the book'

---

5. As discussed by Featherston (2005), the issue whether German has that-trace effects is rather controversial. According to Haider (1983, 1993), Grewendorf (1988), von Stechow and Sternefeld (1989), Bayer (1990), Lutz (1996) standard German does not display that-trace effects, along with Southern German dialects (Bayer 1984). Featherston (2005) provides experimental evidence for the presence of that-trace effects in all varieties of German. That-trace effects can be absent from V2 non-*pro*-drop languages is also evidenced by some Scandinavian dialects, see Lohndal (2009).

The above examples indicate that the crucial condition for referential *pro* to be licensed is that the finite verb appears in a head of the left periphery: this fact fully confirms Benincà's (1984, 2006) and Adam's (1987) findings for Old Romance languages. Moreover, *pro* can be licensed in the same contexts also in Bavarian dialects, as pointed out by Bayer (1984) and Poletto/Tomaselli (2002) a.o.

The mechanism of licensing of referential *pro* is summarised in the structure in (183). The finite verb moves to Subj^0; no clitic lexicalises this head and *pro* is licensed in Spec,AgrSP.[6]

(183)

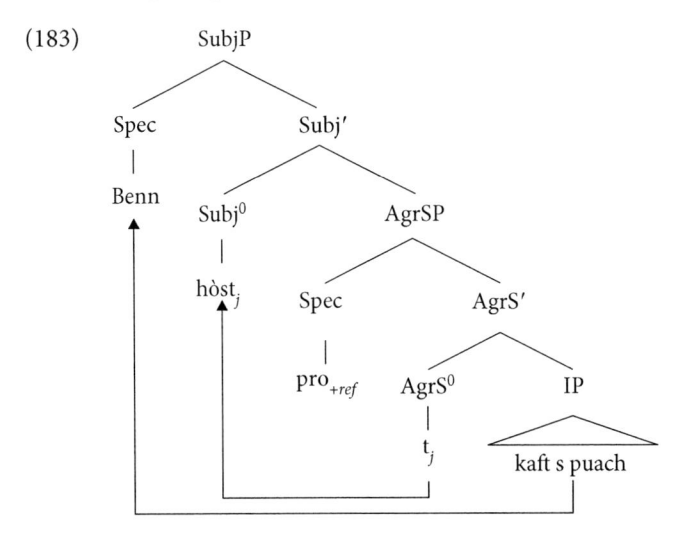

```
                SubjP
               /     \
            Spec      Subj'
             |       /     \
           Benn   Subj⁰    AgrSP
                   |      /     \
                  hòst_j Spec    AgrS'
                          |     /     \
                        pro_+ref AgrS⁰  IP
                                  |    /\
                                  t_j  kaft s puach
```

We have seen that referential *pro* can be licensed directly by the finite verb appearing in CP in the second person singular in the Roveda and Fierozzo dialects. This *pro* licensing strategy co-exists with another strategy, exemplified in (184), that is shared by all Mòcheno dialects. *Pro* can be licensed in Spec,AgrSP if the finite verb is in CP and the (pronominal or NP) subject co-indexed with *pro* appears in the sentence.

(184) a. Benn hòt=*(er)   kaft   s puach?
         when has=SBJ-CL.3.SG.M bought the book
         'When did he buy the book?'
     b. S   hòn   telefoniert *(der Mario ont der Luca)
         EXPL have-PRS.3PL phoned   the Mario   and the Luca
         'Mario and Luca phoned'

---

6. The fact that referential *pro* can be licensed only with the second person singular may be due to fact that only this person displays a specific agreement form (*-st*).

I put forward the hypothesis that the two strategies available in Mòcheno for licensing *pro* actually instantiate the licensing of two types of null subjects. I suggest that in the examples in (184), the *pro* appearing in Spec,AgrSP is a quasi-argumental *pro*. Adapting Rizzi's (1986) original proposal (see Borer 1989; Cabredo-Hofherr 2006 a.o.), I put forward the hypothesis that referential *pro* identifies the features person, number (+/−singular) and gender; quasi-argumental *pro* identifies the features person and number (+/−singular), but not the feature gender, which has to be identified by the co-indexed subject pronoun or by the overt subject. Finally, I assume that non-referential *pro* only identifies the features person and number (+singular). In Mòcheno, therefore, quasi-argumental *pro* can reach the status of referential *pro* when either a pronominal or an NP co-indexed subject appears in the sentence, the role of which is to realise the gender features not identified by quasi-argumental *pro*.

The theory proposed above allows us to account for the cases in which *pro* is licensed simply by the finite verb in CP or by the finite verb in CP and the subject clitic. The hypothesis does not account for the examples in which the subject cannot be dropped such as (169b) discussed at the beginning of this section. There are two possible analysis for those sentences. Either we assume that in main clauses with a fronted subject the finite verb is not in CP which means that *pro* cannot be licensed and the subject must show up in Spec,AgrSP, as shown in (185). This analysis must be rejected in the light of the data discussed in the previous and in this chapter. In the previous chapter, we saw that in sentences with a fronted NP subject, the subject is hosted in a TopicP of the left periphery and is doubled by *pro* in Spec,AgrSP. Considered that *pro* can only be licensed if the finite verb is in the left periphery (see above), the analysis in (185) is not valid for Mòcheno main clauses.

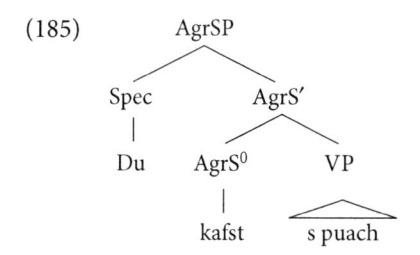

(185)
```
         AgrSP
        /     \
     Spec    AgrS'
      |      /    \
     Du   AgrS⁰    VP
           |      /  \
          kafst  s puach
```

The second analysis is the one given in the structure in (186). The fronted subject is in the Spec of a TopicP of the left periphery; the finite verb has moved to Subj⁰ and *pro* is licensed in Spec,AgrSP. This structure is in line with the findings discussed in the previous chapter, but it does not account for the satisfaction of the V2 constraint, since it is not clear what satisfies the EPP feature in such a sentence. This is tackled in the following chapter.

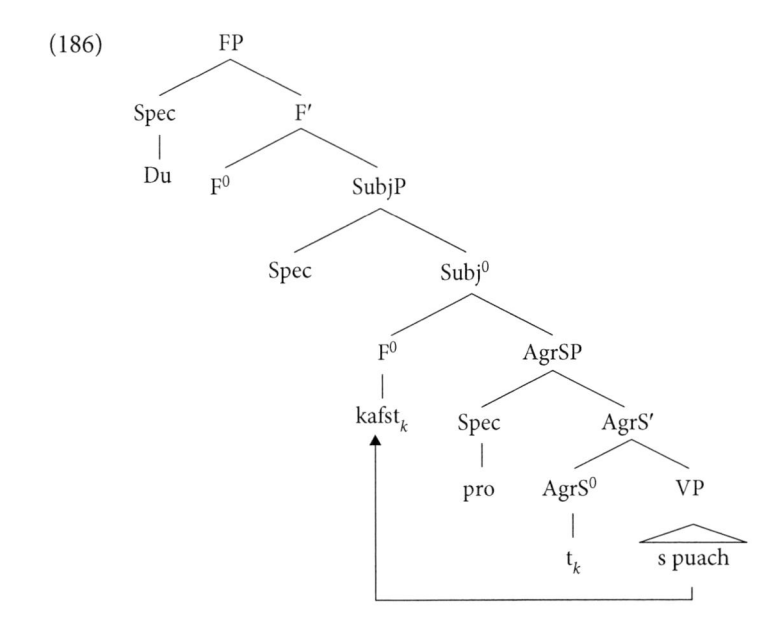

(186)
```
              FP
           /      \
         Spec      F'
          |      /    \
          Du    F⁰    SubjP
                |    /     \
                   Spec    Subj⁰
                          /      \
                         F⁰      AgrSP
                         |      /     \
                       kafstₖ  Spec   AgrS'
                               |     /    \
                              pro  AgrS⁰   VP
                                    |     /\
                                    tₖ   s puach
```

Summing up, so far I have provided evidence for considering Mòcheno a partial *pro*-drop language, in which expletive *pro* and quasi-argumental *pro* can be licensed. The possibility of having referential *pro* is restricted to one person of the paradigm of two varieties.

In the following section, I provide evidence that the licensing of quasi-argumental *pro* with overt subjects is not an optional operation, but an obligatory one. This has already been implicitly demonstrated for subject clitics, whose presence is assumed to be necessary for licensing of *pro* in Spec,AgrSP, but not for nominal overt subjects. The analysis of the syntax of nominal subjects completes the investigation of the realization of the syntactic subject in Mòcheno, which I started in Chapter 3 and due to the complexity of the empirical data can only be completed in this chapter.

5.3 The syntax of DP subjects

5.3.1 DP subjects as informationally marked XPs

The aim of this subsection is to examine the syntax of DP subjects and to provide evidence supporting the fact that in Mòcheno main clauses NP subjects are always given a pragmatically-marked topic/focus reading in all positions within the sentence. This means that in Mòcheno quasi-argumental *pro* must be licensed not only when subject enclitic pronouns show up in the clause, but also when a DP subject is present.

In main declarative clauses, NP subjects can appear in two positions: either before the finite verb (187a) or after it and before the non-finite verb form (187b).[7]

(187) a. *Gester   der Mario hòt   a puach kaft*
         yesterday the Mario has-PRS.3SG a book   bought
     b. *Gester   hòt   der Mario a puach kaft*
         yesterday has-PRS.3SG the Mario a book   bought
         'Mario bought a book yesterday'

The two word orders in (187) have been tested in the fieldwork with 45 informants (sentence 4, see Appendix). As summarised in Table 5.2, the word order pattern with preverbal subject is judged grammatical by all informants, whereas subject-verb inversion is accepted by 38/45 consultants (84%). Most informants who accept subject-verb inversion agree on the fact that this word order is marked: see for instance the judgments given by informants PALAI-MO and ROVE-IP among others.

The data from the questionnaires indicate that the word order patterns in (187) are found in the three varieties and represent a domain of the Mòcheno grammar characterised by variation. In what follows, I provide evidence in favour of the fact DP subjects preceding the finite verb are topics, whereas when they follow it, they are given a focus reading.

Beginning with topics, in (188), I examine the case in which the DP subject is a given and accessible constituent (see Chafe 1987; Frascarelli/Hinterhölzl 2007 and Cruschina 2010 a.o.), identified as such because it is introduced by a wh-main

Table 5.2 DP subjects in main declarative clauses with a fronted adverbial

	Adv-DPsubj-V	Adv-V-DPsubj
Palù	14/14	15/15
Fierozzo	15/15	10/15
Roveda	15/15	9/15
Total	44/44	38/45
Percentage	100%	84%

---

7. I do not consider here the syntax of free inversion, which has been dealt with in the previous section. Recall that in the free subject-verb inversion construction, subjects are given a focus reading.

interrogative clause (188a, Antinucci/Cinque 1977; Benincà 1988).⁸ As can be seen in (188b), the DP subject is not compatible with subject-verb inversion, but has to precede the finite verb (188c, d). Moreover, clitic doubling is ruled out.

(188) a. Bos hòt=er$_j$ kaft gester der Mario$_j$?
what has=SBJ-CL.3.SG.M bought yesterday the Mario
'What did Mario buy yesterday?'
b. #Gester hòt der Mario a puach kaft
yesterday has-PRS.3SG the Mario a book bought
c. Der Mario$_j$ gester hòt=(*er$_j$) a puach kaft
the Mario yesterday has=SBJ-CL.3.SG.M a book bought
d. Gester der Mario$_j$ hòt=(*er$_j$) a puach kaft
yesterday the Mario has=SBJ-CL.3.SG.M a book bought
'Yesterday Mario bought a book'

Subject-verb inversion is ruled out also in the case in which the DP subject is a contrastive topic (Valldují 1992; Benincà/Poletto 2004; Frascarelli/Hinterhölzl 2007; Cruschina 2010).

(189) a. Bos hòn=se òllbe kaft en de boteig?
what have=SBJ-CL.3.PL always bought in the shop
'What have they always bought in the shop?'
b. #En de boteig hòt de mama òllbe s mel kaft
in the shop has-PRS.3SG the mum always the flour bought
ont der tata de zaitung
and the father the newspaper
c. En de boteig de mama$_j$ hòt=(*sa$_j$) òllbe s mel
in the shop the mum has=SBJ-CL.3.SG.F always the flour
kaft ont der tata de zaitung
bought and the father the newspaper
'In the shop, mum has always bought the flour and dad the newspaper'

Let us consider now the case in which the DP subject is a non-accesible D-linked constituent. As illustrated in (190), also in this case the only grammatical position for the overt subject is before the finite verb.

(190) *Context: my friend was supposed to buy a book, but was always finding an excuse for not buying it. Finally he buys the book and I can say to another friend who knows the facts:*

---

8. Here, I limit myself to assuming that the given and accessible constituents appearing in the examples (188) are topics, without going into the details of the exact semantic characterization of the topics construction.

a. #Boas=o   (as) gester   hòt   der Mario
   know=SBJ-CL.2.SG that yesterday has-PRS.3SG the Mario
   s puach   kaft
   the book bought
b. Boas=o   (as) gester   der Mario_j hòt=(*er_j)
   know=SBJ-CL.2.SG that yesterday the Mario has=SBJ-CL.3.SG.M
   s puach   kaft
   the book bought
   'Do you know that Mario bought the book yesterday?'

The data above show that DP subjects must precede the finite verb when they are given a topic reading.

Let us consider now the context in which DP subjects are new information foci (Belletti 2004 and Cruschina 2006). As shown in (191b), when the DP subject is a new information focus, it cannot precede the finite verb in the left periphery, but has to follow it and precede the past participle, as in (191c).

(191) a. Ber hòt   kaft   s puach gester?
         who has-PRS.3SG bought the book yesterday
         'Who bought the book yesterday?'
      b. #Der Mario hòt   s puach gester   kaft
         the Mario has-PRS.3SG the book yesterday bought
      c. S puach gester   hòt   der Mario kaft
         the book yesterday has-PRS.3SG the Mario bought
         'Mario bought the book yesterday'

As illustrated in (192, from consultant PALÙ-MO, see Appendix), a DP subject following the finite verb is also compatible with the the contrastive-focus reading (192b), which is ruled out if the DP subject precedes the finite verb (192c).⁹

(192) a. Hòt   der tata a puach kaft   gester?
         has-PRS.3SG the dad a book bought yesterday
         'Did dad buy a book yesterday?'
      b. Na, gester   hòt   de mama   a puach kaft   (net der tata)
         no, yesterday has-PRS.3SG the mum a book bought NEG the dad
      c. #Na, gester   de mama hòt   a puach kaft   (net der tata)
         no, yesterday the mum has-PRS.3SG a book bought NEG the dad
         'No, it was mum who bought the book yesterday'

---

9. Note that DP subject-verb inversion is possible in yes/no questions, whereas it is ruled out in sentences with a fronted operator, see below and Cognola (2008) on this.

The above data indicate that a DP subject can (and must) follow the finite verb only when it is a new-information or contrastive focus. Within a cartographic approach (Rizzi 1997; Cinque 1999 a.o.), this fact implies that an NP subject following the finite verb does not appear in Spec,AgrSP, but in the Spec of an FP of the low left periphery.

This supposition is corroborated by the data on the syntactic position of the focalised DP subject with respect to sentential adverbs, which constitute a border between the lower and the higher portions of the clause (Kratzer 1989; Diesing 1992, 1997; Hinterhölzl 2006 a.o.). As shown in (193), an NP subject following the finite verb must follow sentential adverbs, which is expected within the hypothesis that NP subjects can only appear after the finite verb when they are focused in the vP periphery.

(193) a. *Ber hòt òllbe kaft s mel en de boteig?*
who has-PRS.3SG always bought the flour in the shop
'Who has always bought the flour in the shop?'
b. #*S mel en de boteig hòt de mama òllbe kaft*
the flour in the shop has-PRS.3SG the mum always bought
c. *S mel en de boteig hòt òllbe de mama kaft*
the flour in the shop has-PRS.3SG always the mum bought
'It was mum who always bought the flour in the shop'

The same holds for contrastively focused DP subjects, which as shown in (194, from informant PALÙ-MO) have to follow the adverb *schua*.

(194) a. *Hòt der tata schua s puach kaft?*
has-PRS.3SG the father already the book bought
'Has dad already bought the book?'
b. #*Na, gester hòt de mama schua s puach kaft*
no, yesterday has-PRS.3SG the mum already the book bought
c. *Na, gester hòt schua de mama s puach kaft*
no, yesterday has-PRS.3SG already the mum the book bought
'No, it was mum who already bought the book yesterday'

Summing up, in this section I have demonstrated that the distribution of DP subjects with respect to the finite verb is governed by rules of information structure; in particular, DP subjects precede the finite verb when they are topicalised, whereas subject-verb inversion is restricted to the case in which the DP subject is a focus. In this case, the area involved in focalization is the low left periphery, whereas topicalised DP subject appear in the high left periphery. The fact that DP subjects must show up in a Spec of one of the two peripheries implies that all sentences involving an overt subject must be analysed as involving the presence of *pro* in Spec,AgrSP, which is consequently to be considered a position ruled out for overt subjects.

In the following subsection, I provide further evidence for this hypothesis, by examining wh-main interrogatives and sentences with a fronted focus.

5.3.2 DP subjects in sentences with a fronted operator

The aim of this subsection is to provide additional evidence from the syntax of sentences with a fronted operator in favour of the hypothesis that overt NP subjects must show up in an A'-position and are ruled out from Spec,AgrSP (where only a quasi-argumental or expletive *pro* can be licensed).

In my preliminary work on the syntax of Palù (Cognola 2010), I pointed out that subject-verb inversion is ruled out iff (i) an operator is fronted and (ii) the subject is realised by an NP. In sentences with a fronted operator, the DP subject must be dislocated, generally to the right. Some examples are given in (195).[10]

(195) a. *Benn hòt der Mario kaft a puach?
 when has-PRS.3SG the Mario bought a book
 b. (Der Mario$_j$), benn hòt=er$_j$ kaft a puach (der Mario$_j$)?
 the Mario when has=SBJ-CL.3.SG.M bought a book the Mario
 'When did Mario buy a book?'
 c. *Bo hòt der Nane kaft s puach?
 where has-PRS.3SG the John bought a book
 d. Bo hòt=er$_j$ kaft s puach der Nane$_j$?
 where has=SBJ-CL.3.SG.M bought s book the John
 'Where did John buy the book?'
 e. *Ver bem hòt der Nane kaft s puach?
 for whom has-PRS.3SG the John bought the book

---

10. As discussed in Cognola (2008:89), subject-verb inversion is possible only if in special interrogatives or in exclamative clauses. Two examples are given below.

 a. Benn hòt der Mario a bain za tschaina trog?!!
 when has-PRS.3SG the Mario a wine to dinner brought
 'When has Mario ever come to dinner with a bottle of wine?!'
 b. Bos hòt der Mario zok?!
 what has-PRS.3SG the Mario said
 'What has Mario said?!!'

The analysis of these sentences goes beyond the scopes of this work, but see Obernauer (1994, 2004), Benincà (1996), Poletto/Pollock (2004), and Zanuttini/Portner (2003) on this.

f. Ver bem   hòt=er$_j$ kaft   s puach   der Nane$_j$?
    for whom has=SBJ-CL.3.SG.M bought the book the John
    'For whom did John buy the book?'
g. *En biavle   kinder   hòt   der Nane kaft   a puach?
    to how many children has-PRS.3SG the John bought a book
h. En biavle   kinder   hòt=er$_j$ kaft   a puach der Nane$_j$?
    to how many children has=SBJ-CL.3.SG.M bought a book the John
    'To how many children did John buy a book?'
i. *En de bel   jor   hòt   der Nane pakemmp der Luca?
    in the what year has-PRS.3SG the John met   the Luca
j. En de bel   jor   hòt=er   pakemmp der Luca der Nane$_j$?
    in the what year has=SBJ-CL.3.SG.M met   the Luca   the John
    'In what year did John meet Luca?'
k. *En bem   hòt   der Nane kaft   s puach?
    to whom has-PRS.3SG the John bought the book
l. En bem   hòt=er$_j$ kaft   s puach   der Nane$_j$?
    to whom has=SBJ-CL.3.SG.M bought the book the John
    'Who did John buy a book for?'

In order to establish whether the distribution of DP subjects in sentences with a fronted operator found in the variety of Palù is shared by the other varieties, I consider the data from the questionnaires (sentences 1 and 2, see Appendix). As summarised in Table 5.3, in wh-main interrogative clauses the right-dislocation of the overt subject is the preferred way of realising the NP subject (i.e. the first choice in the translation) for 44 informants out of 45, and is judged grammatical by all of them. Subject-verb inversion in wh-main interrogatives is used by 1/45 consultant in the translation of the Italian sentence into Mòcheno and it is judged grammatical by 54/90 informants (60%).[11]

In Table 5.4, I examine the data on subject-verb inversion in more detail. Subject-verb inversion is accepted in each sentence by 27 informants out of 45 (60%); among them, 16/27 (59%) judge the construction marked, in particular they claim that it is not a real interrogative clause, but a special interrogative or an exclamative. Therefore, only a small percentage (22/90, 24%) of the consulted speakers accept subject-verb inversion as a pure alternative to subject right dislocation.

---

11. Note, that the numbers (16/27) are not the same for both types of interrogatives because the same speakers always reject subject-verb inversion in both interrogatives. Consultant are sensitive to the type of wh-element involved: some of them reject subject-verb inversion only in argument clauses, whereas others only in the adjunct one. This fact recalls observation made for Northern Italian dialects (see Munaro 1997), French (Aboch/Pfau 2011) and Mòcheno (Cognola 2010). This aspect cannot be further investigated in this work.

Table 5.3 Syntax of DP subjects in wh-main interrogatives

	RD	Subj-V inv
Obj interr	45/45	27/45
Temp interr	45/45	27/45
Total	90/90	54/90
Percentage	100%	60%

Table 5.4 Syntax of DP subjects in wh-main interrogatives

	Marked (special interrog)	Unmarked	Ungrammatical
Obj interr	16/27	11/27	18/45
Temp interr	16/27	11/27	18/45
Total	32/54	22/54	36/90
Percentage	59%	40%	40%

The data collected in the fieldwork confirm the conclusion reached in the preliminary work that subject-verb inversion in wh-main interrogatives is not in free distribution with subject right dislocation. Right dislocation is the unmarked way of realising NP subjects in wh-main interrogative clauses, whereas subject-verb inversion is restricted and rejected by most speakers as a real alternative to right dislocation.

I conclude this section by examining sentences with a fronted contrastive focus. As exemplified in (196), in the case in which the fronted operator is a contrastive focus, subject-verb inversion is ruled out.

(196) a. *Boas=o?*   *Der Mario hòt*   *a puach*
know=SBJ-CL.2.SG the Mario has-PRS.3SG a book
en de Maria kaft
to the Mary bought
'Do you know that Mario bought Mary a book?'
b. **Na, A HEFTL hòt*   *der Mario kaft*
no, a notebook has-PRS.3SG the Mario bought
en de Maria net a puach
to the Mary not a book
c. *Na, A HEFTL hòt=er$_j$*   *kaft der Mario$_j$*
no, a notebook has=SBJ-CL.3.SG.M bought the Mario
en de Maria, net a puach
to the Mary, not a book
'No, it was a notebook that Mario bought for Mary, not a book'

d. *Hait der Mario hòt de dai nuna pakemmp*
today the Mario has-PRS.3SG the your grandmother met
'Mario met your grandmother today'

e. **Na, GESTER hòt der Mario pakemmp*
no, yesterday has-PRS.3SG the Mario met
de mai nuna, net hait
the my grandmother, NEG today

f. *Na, GESTER hòt=er$_j$ pakemmp de mai nuna*
no, yesterday has=SBJ-CL.3.SG.M met the my grandmother
der Mario$_j$, net hait
the Mario, NEG today
'No, it was yesterday that Mario met my grandmother, not today'

The data discussed in this subsection are all expected within the theory put forward in this book. Overt subjects must appear in a Spec position of the high or of the low left periphery and can never appear in Spec,AgrSP (where the presence of *pro* must be assumed). The fact that subjects cannot appear in subject-verb inversion in sentences with a fronted operator follows straightforwardly from the fact that overt subjects can only follow the finite verb if they are new-information foci and two foci are ruled out in the same sentence (see Calabrese 1982; Rizzi 1997; Belletti 2004; Cognola 2012).

5.4 Conclusions

This chapter has provided empirical evidence for the hypothesis that Mòcheno is a partial *pro*-drop language.

With respect to the syntactic properties ascribed in the literature to null-subject languages, Mòcheno can be said to behave as a partial *pro*-drop language that displays all three properties of the implicational scale proposed by Holmberg/Roberts (2010: 38), see (197). Mòcheno allows for free inversion, does not have that-trace violations and licenses expletive null subjects.

(197) Free inversion > that-trace violations > expletive null subjects.

According to the above description, the only difference between Mòcheno and a consistent null-subject language is that only the latter can license a referential *pro*. As we have seen, this is not completely true, since in the Fierozzo and Roveda dialects a referential *pro* is licenced for the second person singular in all constructions in which the finite verb appears in CP. The conditions governing the licensing of referential *pro* in Mòcheno are summarised in (198).

(198) Licensing of referential *pro* I
    a. EPP has been checked by a fronted XP;
    b. the finite verb is in CP (Subj^0);
    c. the finite verb bears second person singular morphology.

Now, the licensing mechanism for referential *pro* found in Mòcheno (198), which is typical of Old Romance languages (Benincà 1984; Adams 1987) but is very restricted in the Mòcheno grammar, co-exists with another much more productive device through which *pro* can be licensed in Spec,AgrSP: the insertion of subject clitics. As discussed in this and in the previous chapters, subject clitics are syntactic heads whose function is to license *pro* in Spec,AgrSP. This means that languages with subject clitics are null-subject languages.

In Mòcheno, *pro* licensing through the mediation of a subject clitic is subject to the syntactic position of the finite verb. Subject clitics can only show up when the finite verb is in CP, as demonstrated in previous chapter, and must be enclitic to the finite verb. I propose that the *pro* licensed through the mediation of the subject enclitic pronoun must be considered to be quasi-argumental, only differing from referential *pro* in not being able to express the gender ϕ features. This is summarised in (199).

(199) Licensing of quasi-argumental *pro* I
    a. EPP has been checked by a fronted XP;
    b. the finite verb is in Subj^0;
    c. a subject clitic follows the finite verb.

The licensing mechanism for quasi-argumental *pro* assumed to be at work when subject clitics appear in the sentence must also be hypothesised for sentences with overt subjects. In the second part of the chapter, I provided evidence showing that in all the sentences involving an NP subject (preceding or following the finite verb, or appearing in free-inversion) *pro* is licensed in Spec,AgrSP and the nominal subject appears in a Spec position, either in the high left periphery or in the vP periphery. This leads to a refinement of the conditions governing the licensing of quasi-argumental *pro* given in (200), where a co-indexed subject can be either a subject clitic or an overt NP/strong pronoun. It is assumed that the latter have to appear in order to express the subject gender ϕ features that cannot be realised by the quasi-argumental *pro*.

(200) Licensing of quasi-argumental *pro* II
    a. EPP has been checked by a fronted XP;
    b. the finite verb is in Subj^0;
    c. the co-indexed subject appears in the sentence.

In the last part of the chapter, we saw that DP subjects cannot follow the finite verb in sentences with a fronted operator. In the account that we are proposing this is fully to be expected, since DP subjects cannot show up in Spec,AgrSP. It is particularly noteworthy that in this configuration *pro* cannot automatically be licensed in Spec,AgrSP, as in main declarative clauses. This gives rise to a right-dislocation construction. The syntax of wh-main interrogatives allows us a final refinement of the conditions under which *pro* is licensed by introducing a condition that affects Spec,SubjP.

If Spec,FocusP is empty.
(201) Licensing of quasi-argumental *pro* III
    a. Spec,FocusP is empty;
    b. the finite verb is in $Subj^0$;
    c. the co-indexed subject appears in either the left or the right periphery.

If Spec,FocusP is occupied.
(202) Licensing of quasi-argumental *pro* IV
    a. Spec,FocusP is occupied;
    b. the finite verb is in $Subj^0$;
    c. a subject clitic follows the finite verb.

The proposal of the definitive conditions for licensing quasi-argumental *pro* summarised in (201) and (202) may be seen as *ad-hoc* speculations, unsupported by empirical data. In particular, the assumption that even in sentences with an overt subject *pro* must be assumed to show up in Spec,AgrSP may appear implausible and counter-intuitive.

I think that this becomes less problematic when we consider Holmberg's (2005: 539) work on the partial null-subject language Finnish, where he notes that "a third person definite subject pronoun can be null when it is bound by a higher argument, under conditions that are rather poorly understood". This is illustrated by the following example (203, from Holmberg 2005: 539), where we see that *pro* can be licensed in an embedded clause if it is bound by a nominal subject appearing in the matrix sentence.

(203) Pekka$_j$ väittää [että hän$_i$ /$_j$ /pro$_i$ /*$_j$ puhuu englantia hyvin]
    'Pekka claims that he speaks English well'

What I assume for Mòcheno is that the licensing mechanism for *pro* found in bi-clausal structures in a partial *pro*-drop language such as Finnish and exemplified in (203) can even operate in single clauses.

This last idea leads us straight into the next chapter, where I consider the syntactic derivation of both sentences with multiple access to CP and embedded clauses, and attempt to answer any remaining questions. The central idea developed in the next chapter is that since *pro* is a maximal category (Cardinaletti 1997, 2004; Holmberg 2005) and can satisfy the EPP feature associated with Spec,SubjP.

CHAPTER 6

Multiple access to CP and asymmetric *pro*-drop

6.1 Introduction

This last chapter is devoted to completing my analysis of Mòcheno main clauses by trying to provide answers to some residual questions which have not yet been answered.

I investigate the derivation of sentences in which several constituents appear in the left periphery and demonstrate that they are characterised by a V2 rule. I go on to analyse the syntax of embedded clauses, which is only touched upon in previous chapters, providing evidence that in dependent clauses the finite verb does not move to the left periphery and *pro* cannot be licensed. This gives rise to a strong asymmetry between main and embedded clauses in the distribution of *pro*-drop which can be explained by the hypothesis that Mòcheno is an asymmetrical *pro*-drop language, like Old Romance (Benincà 1984, 2006). A comparison between main declarative clauses and embedded clauses with respect to the syntax of the finite verb and of *pro* licensing in Spec,AgrSP allows us to put forward a hypothesis for the derivation of sentences with a fronted subject and to precisely define the conditions for the licensing of *pro*.

In the first section of the chapter, I examine the syntax of main clauses with multiple access to CP, showing first that, as the literature on the V2 phenomenon indicates (Haegeman 1997; Roberts 2004; Benincà 2006; Jouitteau 2010; Holmberg 2012 a.o.) and as already partially demonstrated in Chapter 2, two constituents that can potentially satisfy the EPP feature cannot be fronted. This can be easily captured in terms of RM (Rizzi 1990; Roberts 2004; Holmberg 2012), according to which (A, A' or head) movement across an already filled A, A' or head position is blocked.

The fact that Mòcheno is not subject to the linear restriction, i.e. V3 and V4 word orders are possible, a typical characteristic of relaxed V2 languages, indicates that the RM explanation of the ungrammaticality of sentences involving two fronted constituents potentially able to satisfy EPP is only part of the story. In order to account for the distribution of V3/V4 word order patterns in Mòcheno, I test the predictions made by Benincà's (2006) analysis of Old Romance languages, according to which multiple access to the left periphery can only take place if the lowest constituent has satisfied the EPP feature (in Spec,FocusP in Beninca's system), by combining constituents that cannot satisfy EPP (that is HTs and LDs). This comparison produces a very clear preliminary result: in all cases in which EPP is satisfied by a fronted operator, Mòcheno behaves like Old Romance languages, since the operator can be preceded by several topics, all realised syntactically as LDs (pronominal doubling in IP is obligatory). These empirical facts indicate that operators can be combined with other constituents that cannot satisfy the EPP feature in Spec,SubjP, such as LDs and HTs.

Contrary to the predictions that a simple-preposed topic behaves like an operator, I show that SPs cannot be preceded by left-dislocated topics. I also demonstrate that,contrary to expectations, multiple SPs are possible. This unpredicted result leads me to reconsider the data supporting the claim that SPs can satisfy EPP discussed in Chapter 4 and to propose that the conclusion reached in that chapter is incorrect. The new hypothesis is that when simple-preposed topics appear in the left periphery, EPP is satisfied by *pro*.

The fact that EPP can be satisfied by *pro* under certain conditions leads me to reconsider the data in an attempt to explain why in a relaxed V2 language like Mòcheno all topics (whether realised as LDs or SPs) can skip Spec,SubjP and do not "count" for V2. In order to answer this question, I first examine Grewendorf/Poletto's (2010) splitting analysis of topics in the reduced V2 language Cimbrian, showing that their account, which connects the fact that topics can skip the Spec of an FP the head of which is associated with the EPP feature responsible for V2 with the presence of doubling in IP fails to fully account for the facts, since in Mòcheno SPs (topics that are not doubled by a clitic) do not "count" for V2 either.

The alternative analysis that I put forward is that what is responsible for V3/V4 word orders is that EPP can be satisfied by the silent category *pro*. This opens up the possibility of moving topicalised constituents to the left periphery without interfering with the EPP feature, which has already been satisfied. The predictions of this hypothesis are explored in the chapter, with a special focus on the RM effects between topics. I show that in all cases in which EPP is satisfied by the silent category *pro*, topics can be moved to those TopicPs appearing above Spec,SubjP, without interfering with the satisfaction of the EPP feature, but giving rise to RM effects between topics.

I then suggest an explanation for why it is possible to have V3 and V4 word orders with left-dislocated topics preceding the operator in terms of bi-clausal structure, as recently proposed by Ott (2011a, b). In this analysis, dislocation constructions appearing in the left periphery and involving a topic doubled by a clitic are analysed as the fragments of an independent elliptical clause (Merchant 2001) juxtaposed to a second clause in which the clitic copies appear. As we will see,

Ott's analysis allows us to account for the distribution of pronominal clitics in Mòcheno (assumed to function as anchors connecting two independent clauses), for the fact that a strong phonological break is needed after LDs but not after SPs and, lastly, for the form of the V2 rule. The bi-clausal analysis allows us to circumvent the problem of accounting for the fact that topics skip Spec,SubjP, since this is only an effect of the fact that two independent clauses, in which two different constituents satisfy EPP (*pro* in the higher and the operator in the lower), are juxtaposed. In the light of this new analysis of the V2 rule in Mòcheno, I reconsider some problematic data on the distribution of adverbials and weak subjects that could not be captured within the previous theoretical account (see Chapter 4).

In the second section of the chapter, I tackle the final residual question dealt with in this book: the syntax of embedded clauses, with a special focus on the syntax of the finite verb and the realization of the subject. As discussed in Chapter 2, the syntax of embedded clauses is crucially important for the understanding of the V2 phenomenon. The presence of a complementiser in CP is expected to interfere with either the syntactic position of the finite verb or the distribution of root phenomena. In German, for instance, main and embedded clauses are characterised by an asymmetry in the position of the finite verb (den Besten 1983; Tomaselli 1990, 2004; Haider 2010a a.o.); in Old Romance languages, on the other hand, the asymmetry between main and embedded clauses manifests itself in the distribution of *pro* drop. As discussed by Benincà (1984), in Old Romance *pro* is only licensed in Spec,AgrSP if the finite verb is in CP, i.e. in the main declarative clause, not when it is in an embedded clause, where it is assumed to remain in AgrS^0. In the latter case the subject is obligatory and is assumed to appear in Spec,AgrSP. Benincà calls this distribution of *pro*-drop, "asymmetric *pro*-drop".[1]

In the first part of the second section, I present a number of examples to illustrate the fact that in Mòcheno embedded clauses the finite verb moves above sentential adverbials, moving either to Subj^0 or AgrS^0.[2] The distribution of subject pronominal forms and of embedded topicalization in relation to the morphological form of the complementiser (Leu 2008, 2010) provides evidence that all varieties of Mòcheno are non-*pro*-drop languages with NP subjects. In other words, in embedded clauses the finite verb remains in AgrS^0 and the subject in Spec,AgrSP. With regard to subject pronouns, on the other hand, only the Roveda and Fierozzo varieties can be said to be non-*pro*-drop languages, whereas the dialect of Palù is

---

1. An asymmetry in the distribution of subjects similar to that found in Old Romance languages and in Mòcheno also partially exists in Brazilian Portuguese (see Sheehan 2007).

2. The analysis does not include sentences with strict OV syntax, which only appear consistently in the dialect of Palù, see below.

partially *pro*-drop in embedded clauses, too. According to this analysis, Mòcheno can be classified as an asymmetrical partial *pro*-drop language.

The chapter is organised in the following way. In Section 6.2, I consider the syntax of sentences in which several constituents appear in the left periphery. The goals of this section are to provide evidence in favour of the fact that two XPs that can potentially satisfy the EPP feature cannot co-occur in CP (6.2.1) and the only grammatical combinations are between one XP able to satisfy the EPP feature and one (or more) constituents that cannot (6.2.2). Unexpectedly, in main declarative clauses simple-preposed topics behave as constituents that cannot satisfy the EPP feature, since two or more SPs can co-occur in the left periphery of Mòcheno (6.2.3). After showing that the Mòcheno data cannot be captured by Grewendorf/Poletto's (2010) analysis of Cimbrian V2, I will propose an alternative account for Mòcheno that relies on the claim that topics can skip Spec,SubjP when the EPP feature is satisfied by *pro*. Sentences in which the EPP feature is satisfied by an operator, are shown to be derived through a bi-clausal structure, as proposed by Ott (2011b). In Section 6.3, I finally investigate the syntax of the finite verb and the realization of the subjects in Mòcheno embedded clauses, showing that when the finite verb stays put in Agr^0 and does not move to the left periphery, a *pro* cannot be licensed. This means on the one hand that movement of the finite verb to the left periphery is a precondition for licensing of *pro*, and, on the other, that Mòcheno is an asymmetric *pro*-drop language, as Old Romance.

6.2 Multiple access to CP and EPP

In this section, I examine sentences in which several constituents appear in the left periphery and try to account for their syntax within the hypothesis that Mòcheno is a V2 language with a split-CP, whose structure is repeated in (204). In this structure can be seen that fronted operators and simple-preposed topics are able to satisfy the EPP feature associated with $Subj^0$, whereas LDs and HTs are not.

(204) $[_{FRAME}$ [HT – Scene Setter] $[_{THEME}$ $[_{TOPIC\text{-}P}$ LD] $[_{TOPIC\text{-}P}$ SP_j] $[_{FOCUS\text{-}P}$ [wh_j/$focus_j$] $[_{SUBJ\text{-}P}$ t_j finite verb]]]]

The predictions that I test starting from the above structure are that two constituents potentially able to satisfy EPP cannot contemporarily appear in the left periphery (nothing can move through the already filled Spec,SubjP) and that constituents that can satisfy EPP can be combined with XPs that cannot. Moreover, the expectation is that constituents unable to satisfy EPP must precede operators and SPs.

6.2.1 Bottleneck effects

The aim of this subsection is to provide evidence for the fact that two XPs potentially able to satisfy EPP cannot appear contemporarily in the left periphery. This restriction is defined "bottleneck effect" by Poletto (2002) and is captured in terms of RM (Haegeman 1997; Roberts 2004; Grewendorf/Poletto 2010 a.o.).

Let us begin by considering whether two operators can co-occur in the left periphery of Mòcheno. In (205), I show that two operators cannot contemporarily appear (in any order) in CP. The ban on having two operators in the same sentence is not *per se* a piece of evidence supporting an analysis of Mòcheno as a V2 language, since this restriction is also found in many non-V2 languages (see Benincà 2001, 2006; Rizzi 1997; Benincà/Poletto 2004; Belletti 2004 a.o.).

(205) a. *Ber A PUACH hòt   kaft   ont net a penna?
         who a book   has-PRS.3SG bought and NEG a pen
     b. *A PUACH ber hòt   kaft   ont net a penna?
         a book who has-PRS.3SG bought and NEG a pen
     c. *Benn DER MARIO hòs=o   pakemmp ont net der Luca?
         when the Mario have=SBJ-CL.2.SG met   and NEG the Luca
     d. *DER MARIO benn hòs=o   pakemmp ont net der Luca
         the Mario when have=SBJ-CL.2.SG met   and NEG the Luca

In (206), I examine the combination of an operator and a simple-preposed topic, showing that a wh-interrogative element cannot be preceded by a simple-preposed topic (206b, d), identified as such on the basis of the context given in (206a, c).[3]

(206) a. *Boas=o?*   *Der Mario hòt*   *de dai muam pakemmp*
         know=SBJ-CL.2.SG the Mario has-PRS.3SG the your aunt met
         'Do you know that Mario has met your aunt?'
     b. **De mai muam bo*   *hòt=er*   *pakemmp?*
         the my aunt   where has=SBJ-CL.3.SG.M met
         'Where did he meet your aunt?'
     c. *Boas=o?*   *Der Mario hòt*   *a puach en de Maria*
         know=SBJ-CL.2.SG the Mario has-PRS.3SG a book   to the Mary
         kaft
         bought
         'Do you know that Mario bought Mary a book?'
     d. **En de Maria benn* *hòt=er$_j$*   *kaft*   *a puach der Mario$_j$?*
         to the Mary when has=SBJ-CL.3.SG.M bought a book   the Mario

---

3. The pattern illustrated in (206) is shared by all arguments, see Cognola (2010) on this.

As shown in (207) in a non-V2 language (Italian) a simple-preposed topic can precede an interrogative wh-element (207). This is expected since modern Italian is not a V2 language and confirms the fact that the syntactic behaviour of Mòcheno actually depends on its V2 rule.

(207) A Maria, cosa hai comprato?
to Mary what have-PRS.2SG bought
'What did you buy for Mary?'

The above data show that an operator and a simple-preposed topic cannot co-occur in Mòcheno. This is predicted from the hypothesis that they are both constituents able to satisfy the EPP feature associated with Subj^0.

As already discussed in Chapter 4, two simple-preposed constituents cannot appear in the left periphery, as repeated in (208). This restriction is expected within the hypothesis that two XPs able to satisfy EPP cannot contemporarily show up in CP.

(208) a. S puach hòt=er gester kaft
the book has=SBJ-CL.3.SG.M yesterday bought
'The book he bought yesterday'
b. *S puach der Mario hòt kaft
the book the Mario has-PRS.3SG bought

Finally, in (209) I show that weak subject pronouns are not compatible with simple-preposed constituents (209b, c) or with wh-interrogative pronouns (209d, e). Note, that a DP subject can precede an SP, since it cannot satisfy EPP (209b): this is evidence for the hypothesis that weak subject pronouns and DP subjects do not share the same syntax in Mòcheno.

(209) a. Benn hòt=sa$_j$ kaft s puach de mama$_j$?
when has=SBJ-CL.3.SG.F bought the book the mum
'When did mum buy the book?'
b. *De s puach hòt gester kaft
SBJ-WEAK.3.SG.F the book has-PRS.3SG yesterday bought
c. *S puach de hòt gester kaft
the book SBJ-WEAK.3.SG.F has-PRS.3SG yesterday bought
d. *De benn hòt kaft s puach?
SBJ-WEAK.3.SG.F has-PRS.3SG bought the book
e. *Benn de hòt kaft s puach?
when SBJ-WEAK.3.SG.F has-PRS.3SG bought the book

Summing up, in this subsection I examined some data already discussed in Chapter 4 showing that they perfectly fit into the theoretical account proposed for Mòcheno. In particular, it has been demonstrated that two constituents able to satisfy the EPP feature in Spec,SubjP cannot be fronted, as is typical of V2 languages.

Now, considered that Mòcheno is a V2 language of Old Romance type, in which LDs and HTs are unable to satisfy the EPP feature associated with Subj⁰, the prediction to be tested is that constituents able to move through Spec,SubjP can be combined with XPs that do not "count" for V2. This is immediately tested in the following subsection.

6.2.2 Combination of constituents in the left periphery

In what follows I test the prediction that constituents able to satisfy the EPP feature in Spec,SubjP can be combined with constituents that do not "count" for V2. The order of constituents in the left periphery is assumed to be fixed: constituents unable to satisfy EPP must precede operators and simple-preposed topics.

Let us consider first the combination of operators and left-dislocated topics. As repeated in (210), an LD can co-occur with an operator and the LD must precede the operator.

(210) a. *Boas=o?   Der Mario hòt   de dai muam pakemmp*
       know=SBJ-CL.2.SG the Mario has-PRS.3SG the your aunt met
       'Do you know that Mario has met your aunt?'
   b. *De dai muam$_j$ bo   hòt=er=en$_j$ pakemmp?*
       the your aunt where has=SBJ-CL.3.SG.M=OBJ-CL.3.SG.F met
   c. **Bo de dai muam$_j$ hòt=er=en$_j$ pakemmp?*
       where the your aunt has=SBJ-CL.3.SG.M=OBJ-CL.3.SG.F met
       'Where did he meet your aunt?'
   Context: My brother says he is going to buy the book for Maria's birthday in the bookshop, which would take him at least one hour; after ten minutes he is back with the book and says he bought it in the village shop. My mum is amased that he was so quick, since she thinks he had gone to far-away bookshop. I say: Someone says:
   Ah, s puach hòt=er en de libreria kaft (The book he bought in the bookshop)
   d. *S puach$_j$ EN DE BOTEIG hòt=er=s$_j$*
       the book   in the shop   has=SBJ-CL.3.SG.M=OBJ-CL.3.SG.N
       kaft, ont net en de libreria
       bought and NEG in the bookshop

e. *EN DE BOTEIG s puach$_j$ hòt=er=s$_j$
in the shop the book has=SBJ-CL.3.SG.M=OBJ-CL.3.SG.N
kaft, ont net en de libreria
bought and NEG in the bookshop
'It was in the shop where he bought the book, not in the bookshop'

The distribution of operators and left-dislocated topics is fully expected within the theoretical account proposed in this book. The lowest operator satisfies the EPP feature associated with Subj^0 and can be combined with a preceding constituent unable to move through Spec,SubjP.

Let us consider now the combination of simple-preposed topics and weak subject pronouns (both able to satisfy EPP) with left-dislocated constituents. Beginning with weak subject pronouns, in (211a, b) I show that a left-dislocated constituent must be followed by a strong or a weak subject pronominal form.

(211) a. S puach$_j$ si /de
the book SBJ-STRONG.3.SG.F SBJ-WEAK.3.SG.F
hòt=(*s$_j$) gester kaft
has-PRS.3SG=OBJ-CL.3.SG.N yesterday bought
'The book she bought yesterday'

b. En de Maria$_j$ si /de
to the Mary SBJ-STRONG.3.SG.F SBJ-WEAK.3.SG.F
hòt=en$_j$ gester kaft s puach
has-PRS.3SG=OBJ-CL.3.SG.F yesterday bought the book
'To Mary she bought a book'

The data above clearly indicate that the prediction made by the theory that constituents that satisfy EPP can be combined with XPs unable to satisfy EPP is confirmed.

In (212), I examine the case in which both constituents appearing in CP are topics: the prediction is that simple-preposed topics can be preceded by left-dislocated constituents. Recall that LDs can only realise accessible D-linked constituents, whereas both accessible and non-accessible D-linked XPs can be thematised through SP. In the examples can be seen that a simple-preposed DO can be preceded by a left-dislocated IO (212a), but a simple-preposed IO cannot be preceded by a left-dislocated DO. In this configuration, the higher verb argument must be doubled by the clitic pronoun and must therefore be analysed as an LD (212b).

(212) a. Benn hòst kaft s puach en de Maria?
when have-PRS.2SG bought the book to the Mary
'When did you buy Mary the book?'

b. *En de Maria$_j$ s puach hòn=e=en$_j$*
   to the Mary the book have=SBJ-CL.1.SG=OBJ-CL.3.SG.F
   gester   kaft
   yesterday bought
c. *S puach$_k$ en de Maria$_j$ hòn=e=s$_k$=*(en)$_j$*
   the book to the Mary have=SBJ-CL.1.SG=OBJ-CL.3.SG.N=OBJ-CL.3.SG.F
   gester   kaft
   yesterday bought
   'As for Mary's book, I bought it yesterday'

Restrictions are also found when other verb arguments are topicalised in the left periphery. As shown in (213a–c), the subject and the DO cannot be contemporarily topicalised in the left periphery. The IO and the subject can contemporarily appear in the left periphery (213d, e), but, contrary to the predictions, the highest argument (IO) cannot be doubled by the clitic.

(213) a. *Benn hòt=er$_j$ kaft   s puach der Mario$_j$?*
        when has=SBJ-CL.3.SG.M bought the book the Mario
        'When did Mario buy the book?'
     b. **S puach der Mario hòt=(s)   gester   kaft*
        the book the Mario has-PRS.3SG=OBJ-CL.3.SG.N yesterday bought
     c. **Der Mario s puach hòt   gester   kaft*
        the Mario the book has-PRS.3SG yesterday bought
     d. *Bos   hòt=er$_j$ kaft   der Mario$_j$ en de Maria?*
        what has=SBJ-CL.3.SG.M bought the Mario   to the Mary
        'What did Mario buy for Mary?'
     e. *En de Maria der Mario hòt=(*en)   a puach kaft*
        to the Mary the Mario has-PRS.3SG=OBJ-CL.3.SG.F a book bought
        'As for Mary, Mario bought her a book'

The above data indicate that when two topicalised verb arguments appear in the left periphery (one realised syntactically by an LD, the other by an SP) the prediction made by the theory (i.e. that only the order LD-SP is possible) is not borne out. Let us conclude by examining the combination of a verb argument and an adverbial in the left periphery. In (214a–c), I show that an IO only requires pronominal doubling when it precedes the adverbial: this follows straightforwardly from the hypothesis that the lower constituent is always an SP and the higher one an LD. When the adverbial is combined with the DO, as in (214d–f), we see that it cannot be doubled by the clitic in no word order pattern. This runs counter to the theory, which predicts that doubling is obligatory when the DO precedes the adverbial.

(214) a. *Bos hòst kaft en de Maria en de boteig?*
what have-PRS.SG bought to the Mary in the shop
'What did you buy for Mary in the shop?'
b. *En de boteig en de Maria hòn=e a puach kaft*
in the shop to the Mary have=SBJ-CL.1.SG a book bought
c. *En de Maria$_j$ en de boteig hòn=e=*(en$_j$)*
in the shop to the Mary have=SBJ-CL.1.SG=OBJ-CL.3.SG.F
a puach kaft
a book bought
'As for Mary, in the shop I bought a book for her'
d. *Ber hòt kaft s puach gester?*
who has-PRS.3SG bought the book yesterday
'Who bought the book yesterday?'
e. *Gester s puach hòt der Mario kaft*
yesterday the book has-PRS.3SG the Mario bought
f. *S puach gester hòt=(*s) der Mario kaft*
the book yesterday has-PRS.3SG=OBJ-CL.3.SG.N the Mario bought
'It was Mario who bought the book'

The data discussed in this subsection demonstrate that the syntactic behaviour of operators and topics is captured by the theory proposed for Mòcheno, whereas that of SPs and LDs is erratic. In particular, SPs do not behave as constituents able to satisfy the EPP feature when they are combined with LDs.

6.2.3 Again on simple-preposed topics and EPP

In this subsection, I provide evidence in favour of the hypothesis that SPs are unable to satisfy the EPP feature associated with Subj^0 and that in all cases in which a topic (realised syntactically by an SP or an LD) appears in the left periphery, EPP has been satisfied by a silent *pro*. I suggest that the asymmetries observed with SPs follow from this fact.

In (215), I reconsider the data that led me to hypothesise that SPs can satisfy the EPP feature. As shown in (215a, b), when the fronted XP is an SP the subject cannot be realised by a strong or a weak pronoun, but only by an enclitic pronoun. Moreover, the simple-preposed XP and the finite verb must form a Spec/head configuration (215c). Both these properties are typical of constituents able to satisfy EPP.

(215) Context: my friend was supposed to buy a book, but was always finding an excuse for not buying it. Finally he buys the book and I can say to another friend who knows the facts:
Bo hòt=er kaft s puach? (Where did he buy the book?)
   a. *S puach si   /de   hòt
       the book SBJ-STRONG.3.SG.F SBJ-WEAK.3.SG.F has-PRS.3SG
       si   /de   kaft   en de boteig
       SBJ-STRONG.3.SG.F SBJ-WEAK.3.SG.F bought in the shop
   b. S puach   hòt=se   kaft   en de boteig
       the book has=SBJ-CL.3.SG.F bought in the shop
   c. *S puach en de boteig hòt=se   kaft
       the book in the shop   has=SBJ-CL.3.SG.F bought
       'The book she bought in the shop'

The conclusion that SPs can satisfy the EPP feature in Spec,SubjP is challenged by the examples in (216), where can be seen that two accessible D-linked constituents can be realised syntactically by two SPs, and not by an LD followed by an SP as would be predicted by the theory.

(216) a. Benn hòt=er   kaft   s puach en de boteig?
       when has=SBJ-CL.3.SG.M bought the book in the shop
       'When did he buy the book in the shop?'
   b. S puach   en de boteig hòt=er   gester   kaft
       the book in the shop   has=SBJ-CL.3.SG.M yesterday bought
       'It was yesterday when he bought the book in the shop'
   c. Bos   hòt=er$_j$ kaft   der Mario$_j$ en de Maria?
       what has=SBJ-CL.3.SG.M bought the Mario   to the Mary
       'What did Mario buy for Mary?'
   d. En de Maria der Mario hòt=(*en)   a puach kaft
       to the Mary the Mario has-PRS.3SG=OBJ-CL.3.SG.F a book bought
       'It was a book that Mario bought for Mary'

In order to reconcile (215) with (216), I propose that the hypothesis that SPs can satisfy the EPP feature is wrong due to an incorrect interpretation of the data. In particular, I suggest that the data on the obligatory Spec/head configuration must be reevaluated by considering the informational status of the XP following the topic. In the examples in (215), the constituent following the SP is actually a new-information focus and not given/old information, as is typical of topics. This might indicate that what is ungrammatical is the sequence SP-focus and not the sequence SP-SP. That the simple-preposed topics cannot be followed by a new-information focus is confirmed by the following examples (217).

(217) a. Benn hòt=er   kaft   s puach en de boteig?
      when has=SBJ-CL.3.SG.M bought the book in the shop
      'When did he buy the book in the shop?'
   b. *S puach en de boteig gester   hòt=er   kaft
      the book in the shop yesterday has=SBJ-CL.3.SG.M bought
   c. Bos   hòt=er$_j$ kaft   der Mario$_j$ en de Maria?
      what has=SBJ-CL.3.SG.M bought the Mario   to the Mary
      'What did Mario buy for Mary?'
   d. *En de Maria der Mario a puach hòt=(en)   kaft
      to the Mary   the Mario a book   has-PRS.3SG=OBJ-CL.3.SG.F bought

The correct interpretation of the data allows us to reach the descriptive generalization given in (218).

(218) a. Topics cannot satisfy EPP, operators can;
   b. If FocusP hosts an operator, topics must be doubled in IP;
   c. If FocusP is empty, topics do not need to be doubled in IP.

Note, that the distribution of pronominal doublers in IP summed up in the descriptive generalization in (218) depends on purely syntactic constraints (i.e. the presence or the absence of an operator in Spec,FocusP) and not on the semantics of the topic construction involved (for instance, familiarity vrs contrastive topic).

Since the data discussed so far have shown that simple-preposed topics are actually unable to sastify the EPP feature in Spec,SubjP, we now have to tackle the issue of what satisfies EPP when the fronted XP is an SP. Building on the data discussed in the previous chapter, where it was shown that Mòcheno is a partial *pro*-drop language, I propose that in those cases in which the fronted XP cannot satisfy the EPP feature associated with Subj^0, EPP is satisfied by *pro*. This hypothesis is particularly relevant to the proposed theory because it allows us to reject the alternative analysis that assumes that EPP can be satisfied by a silent operator in all cases in which no constituent able to satisfy EPP is present in the left periphery, as in (215) above. The hypothesis that EPP can be satisfied by a null operator is unteneable, since as shown in (219), in all clauses for which the presence of a silent operator must be assumed in CP (such as yes/no main interrogatives), topics must be realised by LDs and not by SPs. This means that both overt and silent operators force the realization of topics as LDs, which runs counter to the hypothesis that SPs are compatible with a silent operator.

(219) a. S puach$_j$ hòt=er=s$_j$ kaft?
       the book   has=SBJ-CL.3.SG.M=OBJ-CL.3.SG.N bought

b. *S puach hòt-er kaft?
   the book has=SBJ-CL.3.SG.M bought
   'Did he buy the book?'
c. En de Maria$_j$ hòt=er=en$_j$ a puach gem?
   to the Mary has=SBJ-CL.3.SG.M=OBJ-CL.3.SG.F a book given
d. *En de Maria hòt=er a puach gem?
   to the Mary has=SBJ-CL.3.SG.M a book given
   'Did he give Mary a book?'

Summing up, I suggest that the EPP feature associated with Subj^0 is satisfied by *pro* in all cases in which no operator is fronted. When *pro* satisfies EPP, topics not doubled by a clitic can be moved to the left periphery without giving rise to bottleneck effects because SubjP hosts a silent category. Since in a language with split-CP there are multiple TopicPs (Rizzi 1997; Benincà 2001), when topics skip Spec,SubjP they have access to more than one position: therefore, multiple SPs are grammatical. Note that the hypothesis that *pro* can satisfy the EPP feature allows us to derive sentences with V3 and V4 word orders within a mono-clausal analysis[4] and makes the clear prediction that RM between topics not doubled by a clitic may take place. Before testing the predictions of my theory, in the following section I discuss the alternative analysis proposed for the derivation of V3 and V4 word orders in Cimbrian by Grewendorf/Poletto (2010).

6.2.4 Grewendorf/Poletto's account

As discussed above, the lack of V3 and V4 word orders in "strict" V2 languages can be accounted for in terms of RM (Rizzi 1990; Haegeman 1997; Poletto 2002; Roberts 2004): once the EPP feature has been satisfied, nothing can be moved through that filled position, since "like repels like" (Holmberg 2012: 38). The RM explanation is applicable only to the syntax of operators in relaxed V2 languages: two operators cannot be fronted, because both could potentially satisfy the EPP feature associated with Subj^0. The syntax of topics, which can appear in the left periphery together with operators and are multiple, is not part of the RM account.

Grewendorf/Poletto (2010: 34), building on work by Bidese (2008), Poletto/Tomaselli (2004, 2009), on Cecchetto's (1999, 2000) and Belletti's (2006) "big-DP" hypothesis and on Poletto's (2008) splitting analysis of doubling, propose that "V2 is relaxed when clitic doubling appears". Their hypothesis can be summed up as thus: topics can skip the Spec of the FP the head of which is associated with the

---

4. Following Ott (2011b), I assume that all sentences involving LDs are the result of an underlying bi-clausal structure. See below.

EPP feature responsible for the V2 phenomenon because the clitic realises the case features of the noun, thus making it possible for the constituent to be extracted from the TopicP internal to the DP. According to Grewendorf/Poletto (2010), therefore, in reduced V2 languages, topics appearing in the left periphery are a subpart of the extended DP layer, not full DPs. In strict V2 languages, on the other hand, a topic is moved as a whole DP (including the case projection) and cannot consequently skip the Spec of the FP whose head is associated with EPP.

There are, in my view, two conceptual problems with Grewendorf/Poletto's theory. According to their analysis, topics appearing in the left periphery and doubled by a clitic in IP (LDs from a syntactic point of view) lack case, since the splitting hypothesis predicts that the clitic realises case (as head of KP) and the element that is moved is only a subpart of the DP containing the noun and lacking the case projection.[5] If we accept Benincà's (1988, 2001) characterization of topics (see Chapter 2), Grewendorf/Poletto's (2010) theory appears untenable. Benincà shows that HTs are the only topic construction in which the thematised constituent lacks case (with nominative as a sort of default-case), whereas both left-dislocated and simple-preposed topics are assumed to bear case. In the examples in (220), I show that a theme must be doubled by a clitic independently of the presence of case (i.e. of the case-assigning preposition in a language with no case morphology on nouns such as Mòcheno).

(220) a. *Der Nane$_j$ benn hòt=er=*(en)$_j$ gem a puach?*
the John when has=SBJ-CL.3.SG.M=OBJ-CL.3.SG.M given a book
b. *En Nane$_j$ benn hòt=er=*(en)$_j$ gem a puach?*
to-the John when has=SBJ-CL.3.SG.M=OBJ-CL.3.SG.M given a book
'As for John, when did he give him the book'

The data discussed above indicate that, in the case of Mòcheno, the hypothesis that topics can skip Spec,SubjP when moved to the left periphery because they do not bear case (which is realised in IP by the clitic doubler) is untenable. The clitic doubler is, in fact, obligatory with both HTs and LDs, irrespective of whether or not the thematised constituent bears case.

The second conceptual problem in the splitting analysis of LD regards its use of the left periphery of the DP layer. Based on Giusti's (2006) proposal that the DP layer also has an articulated left periphery, Grewendorf/Poletto (2010) suggest that a left-dislocated constituent is marked as a topic within the DP and is then

---

5. Note, that in this respect Poletto's (2008) splitting analysis of doubling differs from the original proposals by Uriagereka (1995), Cecchetto (1999, 2000) and Belletti (2006), who solve the problem of case assignment by assuming that the big DP (clitic and DP) receives case from the verb as a complex constituent.

moved to the left periphery in order to check its discourse-features. Grewendorf/ Poletto's (2010) use of the left periphery internal to the DP is not standard: the evidence supporting the hypothesis of a left periphery within the DP comes from the fact that modifications of the noun can be topicalised/focused not the noun itself (see also Cinque 2010). The pragmatic marking of the noun is generally assumed to take place within the vP periphery and not within the DP (Belletti 2006; Cecchetto 1999, 2000). Therefore, in order to be convincing, their hypothesis needs to be supported by data on the structure of the DP in Cimbrian to show that D can be topicalised in the DP prior to any movement to the left periphery.

However, the most problematic aspect of Grewendorf/Poletto's (2010) analysis of topics in relaxed V2 languages in relation to Mòcheno is of empirical nature. Their account only considers topic constructions involving pronominal doubling (LDs) and can potentially account for sentences in which the topic preceding the operator is doubled by a clitic. Grewendorf/Poletto do not address cases in which the topic moved to the left periphery, skipping Spec,SubjP, is not doubled by a clitic, and is therefore simple-preposed. The Mòcheno data presented above show that in this relaxed V2 language simple-preposed constituents cannot satisfy the EPP feature associated with Spec,SubjP either – despite their lack of pronominal doubling. Within Grewendorf/Poletto's (2010) framework, this can only be accounted for by assuming that clitics are optional: an unwelcome result, in the light both of Benincà's (1988, 2001), Cardinaletti's (2002) and Cruschina's (2010) work on topic constructions, which demonstrates that pronominal doubling is not optional in topic constructions, and of the data discussed in this section.

Given the shortcomings of Grewendorf/Poletto's (2010) analysis of sentences with multiple access to CP in relaxed V2 languages, I propose an alternative analysis which accounts for the Mòcheno data, in the subsection below.

6.2.5 An alternative account for main declarative clauses

The alternative idea that I put forward in order to make sense of the data discussed in Sections 6.2.2 and 6.2.3 is that the core property that is responsible for the fact that topics can be moved to the left periphery without interfering with EPP is not the development of LD, but the possibility that *pro* satisfies EPP in Spec,AgrSP as any other maximal category. When EPP is satisfied by *pro*, which is an option available in the grammar of Mòcheno only in the particular case in which the (new-information) focus is left in the vP periphery and no operator is fronted (see above and Cognola 2012), fronting of topics to Spec,TopicPs is possible. Note, that in this configuration the linear word order we obtain is the same of strict V2 languages (221), but the underlying structure of Mòcheno is different, as I tried to demonstrate.

(221) a. *S puach hòt   der Mario kaft*
         the book has-PRS.3SG the Mario bought
      b. *Das Buch hat   Mario gekauft*
         the book has-PRS.3SG Mario bought

The structure of (221a) is given in (222) below.

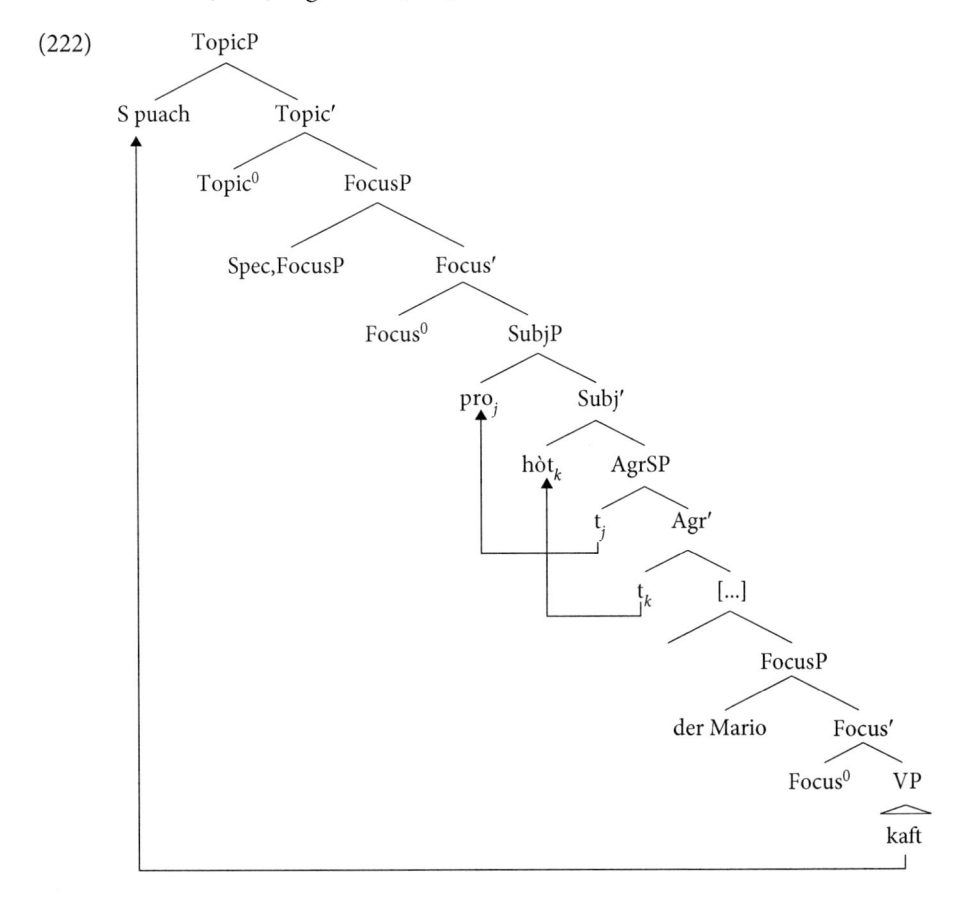

(222)
```
            TopicP
           /      \
      S puach    Topic'
                /      \
            Topic⁰    FocusP
                     /      \
               Spec,FocusP   Focus'
                            /      \
                        Focus⁰    SubjP
                                 /     \
                              proⱼ    Subj'
                                     /    \
                                  hòtₖ   AgrSP
                                         /    \
                                        tⱼ    Agr'
                                              /   \
                                            tₖ   [...]
                                                  /    \
                                                FocusP
                                               /      \
                                          der Mario  Focus'
                                                     /    \
                                                Focus⁰    VP
                                                          |
                                                         kaft
```

A simplified structure of (221b) is given in (223), where I show that in German, unlike Mòcheno, the fronted constituent satisfies the EPP feature responsible for the V2 phenomenon and forms a Spec/head configuration with the finite verb. The presence of *pro* does not need to be assumed for German, since this language is not a *pro*-drop language.[6]

---

6. This is a simplified structure. See Chapter 2 for a discussion of the German data.

(223)   CP
        ╱ ╲
   das Buch_j C'
            ╱ ╲
        kaufte_k VP
               ╱ ╲
              Hans V'
                  ╱ ╲
                 t_j   t_k

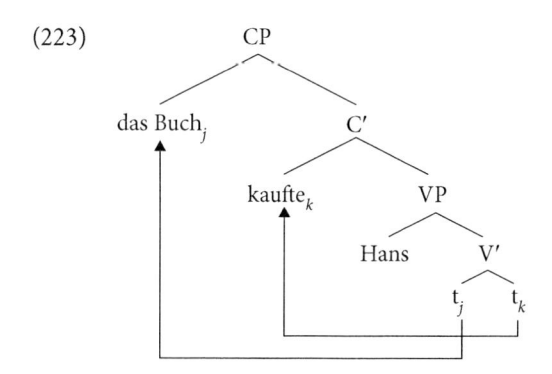

According to the proposed analysis, in sentences with a fronted SP *pro* satisfies the EPP feature in Spec,SubjP because no operator is fronted. In this configuration, movement of topics to the left periphery can take place, considered that Spec,SubjP hosts a silent category.[7]

Constituents that can be simple preposed when EPP is satisfied by *pro* are subject to RM in Mòcheno. According to the split-CP hypothesis (Rizzi 1997; Benincà 2001), several TopicPs are present in the left periphery which become accessible to D-linked constituents when *pro* satisfies the EPP feature in Spec,SubjP. The distribution of V3 and V4 word orders with simple-preposed topics is not unsystematic, but governed by RM. In the following examples, I exemplify these RM effects between simple-preposed topics and propose a tentative account along the lines of Rizzi (2004) and Friedmann/Belletti/Rizzi (2009). The relevant features are +/−topic; +/−argumental; +/−case (this feature allows us to distinguish PPs, that is constituents that have case morphology, even in the form of a preposition, from all other XPs that do not have any case morphology).

As exemplified in (224), no RM effects arise between an adverbial ([−arg]) and a DO or a subject ([+arg]).

(224) a. *Ber   hòt   kaft   s puach   gester?*
          who   has-PRS.3SG   bought   the book yesterday
          'Who bought the book yesterday?'
     b. *Gester   s puach   hòt   der Mario kaft*
          yesterday   the book   has-PRS.3SG   the Mario bought

---

7. RM violations between referential pro and a fronted constituent are only reported for impaired languages (aphasia, Grillo 2009; Garraffa/Grillo 2008), for child language (Friedmann/Belletti/Rizzi 2009; Guasti/Branchini/Arosio 2009; Cognola 2011a) and for the language of so-called semi-speakers (Padovan 2011). The fact that RM effects can arise between *pro* (generally in A-position) and a fronted XP (moved through A'-movement) represents a special case of RM probably due to the fact that in the impaired or reduced grammatical competence the difference between A and A' movement has gone lost.

c. S puach   gester   hòt=(*s)   der Mario kaft
    the book yesterday has-PRS.3SG=OBJ-CL.3.SG.N   the Mario bought
    'It was Mario who bought the book'
d. Bo   hòt=er$_j$ kaft   s puach   der Mario$_j$ gester?
    where   has=SBJ-CL.3.SG.M bought   the book the Mario   yesterday
    'Where did Mario buy the book yesterday?'
e. Gester   der Mario   hòt=s   en de boteig kaft
    yesterday   the Mario   has-PRS.3SG=OBJ-CL.3.SG.N in the shop   bought
f. Der Mario gester   hòt=s   en de boteig kaft
    the Mario yesterday has-PRS.3SG=OBJ-CL.3.SG.N in the shop   bought
    'He bought it in the shop'

Two [+arg; +topic] constituents cannot be simple-preposed, as repeated in (225a, b, c). Note, that the sentences would be ungrammatical even in the presence of pronominal doubling: this follows straightforwardly from the hypothesis that the possibility of being doubled by a clitic in IP is not a relevant condition for multiple access to CP to be possible. I take these examples to indicate that when both constituents share the same features [+arg; +topic], only one of them can appear in the left periphery (225d, e).[8]

(225) a. Benn   hòt=er$_j$ kaft   s puach   der Mario$_j$?
          when   has=SBJ-CL.3.SG.M bought the book the Mario
          'When did Mario buy the book?'
      b. *S puach$_j$ der Mario hòt=(s$_j$)   gester   kaft
          the book   the Mario has-PRS.3G=OBJ-CL.3.SG.N   yesterday bought
      c. *Der Mario$_j$ s puach$_k$ hòt=(er$_j$)=(s$_k$)
          the Mario   the book   has=SBJ-CL.3.SG.M=OBJ-CL.3.SG.N
          gester   kaft
          yesterday bought
      d. S puach   hòt=er   gester   kaft
          the book has=SBJ-CL.3.SG.M   yesterday bought
      e. Er   /Der Mario hòt=s   gester   kaft
          SBJ-STRONG.3.SG.M   the Mario   has=OBJ-CL.3.SG.N   yesterday bought
          'He/Mario bought it yesterday'

Let us consider the combination of subject and IO. As exemplified in (226), a subject, characterised by the features [+topic, +arg, −case] can appear in the left

---

8. The account in terms of RM does not allow us to make sense of all the data, in particular of the fact that a subject and a DO cannot co-occur (see above). The prediction of the RM account in this case is that the two XPs can co-occur and the subject must precede the DO. I leave this issue open for further research.

periphery with an IO. I propose that no RM violations arise between subject and IO because the IO is specified for the feature [+case], since it has a case-assigning preposition, whereas the subject does not bear case morphology.

(226) a. Bos   hòt=er$_j$ kaft   der Mario$_j$ en de Maria gester?
         what has=SBJ-CL.3.SG.M bought   the Mario   to the Mary   yesterday
         'What did Mario buy for Mary yesterday?'
   b. Gester   en de Maria der Mario hòt=(*en)
         yesterday to the Mary the Mario has-PRS.3SG=OBJ-CL.3.SG.F
         a puach kaft
         a book   bought
   c. Gester   der Mario en de Maria hòt   a puach kaft
         yesterday the Mario to the Mary has-PRS.3SG a book bought
         'Yesterday Mario bought a book for Mary'

The data discussed above show that the distribution of simple-preposed topics in Mòcheno left periphery can be captured if we assume that SPs are unable to satisfy the EPP feature in Spec,SubjP and when an SP shows up in the left periphery, EPP has been satisfied by *pro*. In this configuration, topics can skip Spec,SubjP and be moved to the TopicPs assumed to be universally present in the structure of the left periphery of all languages. Movement of topics is subject to RM; I have tried to capture the possible word orders by proposing that RM is sensitive to the following set of features: [+/−topic; +/−arg; +/−case]. My analysis sets itself within the mono-clausal analysis of topicalizations and moves from the assumption that topics are moved from their base-positions to the left periphery as full constituents.

The last question to be tackled in this subsection is whether fronting of a topic in sentences in which EPP has been satisfied by *pro* is simply possible or obligatory. I think that there is strong evidence in favour of the fact that fronting of an XP is obligatory.

In the examples in (227), I compare two constructions that do not "count" for V2: HTs and SPs. As shown in (227a), the HT cannot be adjacent to the finite verb, i.e. the finite verb cannot form a Spec/head configuration with *pro* in SubjP, whereas a simple-preposed topic can be followed by the finite verb (227b), assumed to appear in Subj^0, in whose Spec *pro* shows up.

(227) a. *Der Nane$_j$ hòt=en$_j$ der Mario a puach
         the John   has-PRS.3SG=OBJ-CL.3.SG.M   the Mario a book
         kaft   en sell tepp$_j$
         bought to that stupid

b. *En Nane hòt der Mario a puach kaft*
to John has-PRS.3SG the Mario a book bought
'To John Mario bought a book'

I suggest that the above data indicate that for the V2 constraint to be satisfied, an A'-moved constituent must be fronted to the left periphery. This requirement is fulfilled only by SPs and not by HTs. This means that *pro* cannot satisfy EPP in all sentences, but only in those in which an A'-moved XP appears in the left periphery. Note, that this finding recalls observations on Icelandic stylistic fronting (Franco 2009; Platzack 1987), whose function has been claimed precisely to be that of licensing *pro*.

The hypothesis that *pro* can satisfy the EPP feature in Spec,SubjP only if an XP has been A'-moved to the left periphery, allows us to make sense of the derivation of sentences with a fronted subject. In the previous chapters, I showed that DP subjects and strong pronouns cannot be dropped in Mòcheno, as repeated in (228a), which contrasts with the data in (228b) that point to the fact that fronted subjects are not able to satisfy the EPP feature in Spec,SubjP.

(228) a. *(Der Mario /Er) hòt a puach kaft*
the Mario SBJ-STRONG.3.SG.M has-PRS.3SG a book bought
b. *Der Mario /er en de boteig hòt*
the Mario SBJ-STRONG.3.SG.M in the shop has-PRS.3SG
a puach kaft
a book bought
'Mario bought a book in the shop'

The contrast in the above examples is only apparent. As shown in the structure in (229), in sentences with a fronted subject, *pro* satisfies the EPP feature in Spec,SubjP and the subject is simple-preposed to the left periphery as a consequence of the requirement of having an A'-moved constituent in the left periphery. This structure allows us to derive sentences with a fronted subject within the hypothesis that they involve a V2 structure: the subject and the finite verb are in CP, *pro* satisfies EPP. Therefore, the hypothesis that main declarative clauses may not involve V-to-C movement must be abandoned.

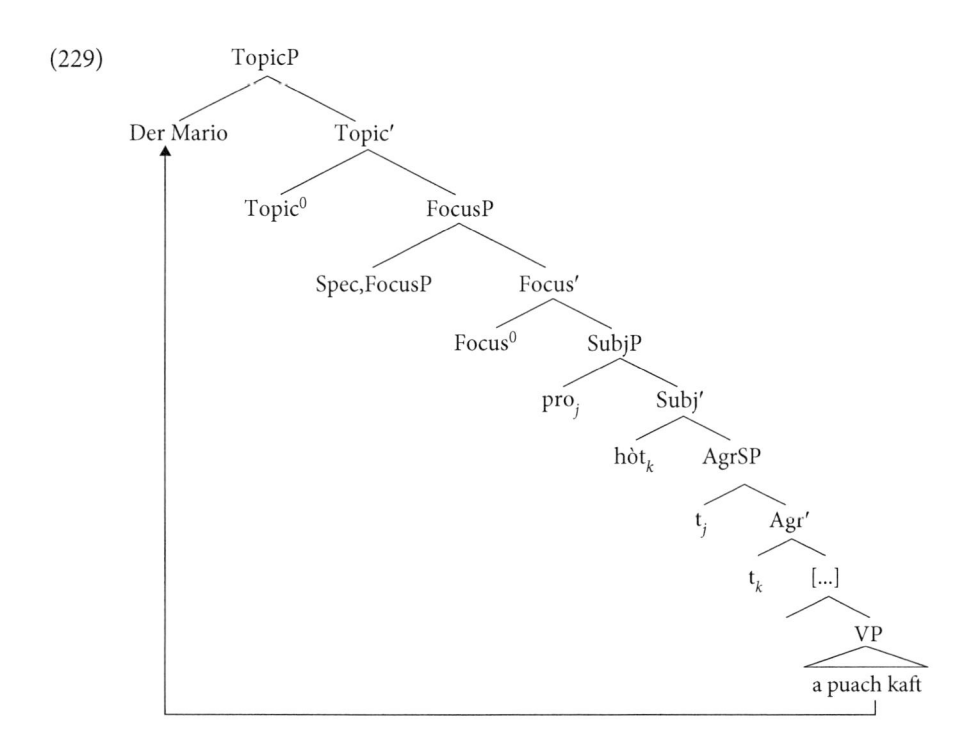

(229)
```
         TopicP
        /      \
   Der Mario   Topic'
              /     \
          Topic⁰   FocusP
                  /      \
            Spec,FocusP  Focus'
                        /      \
                   Focus⁰      SubjP
                              /     \
                          pro_j    Subj'
                                  /     \
                               hòt_k   AgrSP
                                      /     \
                                    t_j    Agr'
                                          /    \
                                        t_k   [...]
                                                \
                                                 VP
                                                  \
                                               a puach kaft
```

In this section, I proposed an analysis of Mòcheno main declarative clauses in which several simple-preposed constituents appear in the left periphery, building on the split-CP hypothesis and on the idea that *pro* can satisfy the EPP feature associated with Subj⁰. I consider now the syntactic derivation of main clauses in which the EPP feature is not satisfied by *pro*, i.e. of sentences with a fronted operator, which are characterised by the fact that all topics appearing in the left periphery must be realised by LDs.

6.2.6 Sentences with a fronted operator

As discussed in the previous section and in the previous chapters, Mòcheno is characterised by an asymmetry in the realization of topics in main declarative and in main interrogatives clauses. The relevant data are repeated in (230). When the EPP feature is satisfied by a fronted operator, all topics must be realised by an LD (230a); when EPP is satisfied by *pro*, topics must be realised syntactically by an SP (230b).

(230) a. Gester   der Mario$_j$ bo   hòt=er$_j$ kaft   s puach?
        yesterday the Mario   where   has=SBJ-CL.3.SG.M   bought the book
        'Where did Mario buy the book yesterday?'
    b. Gester   der Mario$_j$ hòt=*(er$_j$)   kaft   s puach
        yesterday the Mario   has=SBJ-CL.3.SG.M   bought the book
        'Yesterday Mario bought a book'

The asymmetry in (230) cannot be accounted for by assuming that all main clauses have the same structure with the only difference that topics must be doubled by a clitic when Spec,FocusP is filled. The idea that topics can skip Spec,SubjP also when this position is filled by an overt category (operator) runs counter to the analysis of main declarative clauses given in the previous section, where it was shown that the movement of topics to the left periphery across Spec,SubjP can only take place if this position hosts an empty category. Also Grewendorf/Poletto's (2010) theory seems unable to capture the asymmetry in the distribution of clitic doublers between main declarative and main interrogative clauses, since their claim is that topics can skip the Spec of the FP whose head is associated with the EPP feature because they are doubled by a clitic. This allows us to only make sense of the syntax of sentences in which LD is obligatory and not of sentences involving SPs.

The Mòcheno data may be accounted for by proposing that simple-preposed topics are moved, whereas LDs are base-generated (Cinque 1990; Benincà 2001; Frey 2004b). According to the base-generation analysis, the left-dislocated constituent is generated directly in CP: theta-role, case assignment and the connection between the LD and the clause are ensured by a chain mechanism. As discussed in Ott (2011a, b) for German (to whose work I refer the reader for the details of the analysis of LD in German) the approach to LD in terms of base-generation is descriptively, but not explicatively, adequate, since it fails to capture the asymmetries in the distribution of V2 and V3 word order patterns. In particular, it posits a special mechanism (base-generation) for the derivation of sentences with V3 word order, which is operative only with LD and absent in all other sentences. A similar argument is valid also for Mòcheno. The idea that topics can be directly base-generated in the left periphery and can be connected to the main clause through a chain mechanism between the fronted XP and the clitic pronoun in IP allows us to capture the syntax of main interrogative clauses, but fails to make sense of the impossibility of having left-dislocated topics, that is base-generation, in main declarative clauses (see previous section).

In order to account for the asymmetries observed in the realization of topics between sentences in which EPP has been satisfied by *pro* (only simple-preposed topics) and sentences in which EPP has been satisfied by an operator (only left-dislocated topics), I start from hypothesis that topics are always moved to the left periphery (as shown above) and never base-generated there. Following Ott (2011b), I propose that all topic constructions involving a constituent doubled by a clitic in IP involve an underlying bi-clausal structure, with IP ellipsis in the highest juxtaposed sentence. As shown in (231), Ott proposes to analyse German *Linksversetzung* (231a) by assuming that the dislocated XP is actually part of an independent clause in a bi-clausal structure (231b); "in the mapping to phonetic form, CP1 is reduced by ellipsis of the complement of the fronted XP" (Ott 2011b: 2) leading to the actual surface form (231c).

(231) a. Den Peter$_j$,   den$_j$ habe   ich
        the Peter-ACC SUBJ-PRON.ACC have-PRS.1SG SUBJ-PRON.NOM
        gestern   gesehen
        yesterday seen
        'Peter I saw yesterday'
     b. [CP1 [den Peter] habe ich gestern gesehen]] [CP2 den habe ich gestern gesehen]
     c. [CP1 [den Peter] ~~habe ich gestern gesehen~~] [CP2 den habe ich gestern gesehen]

Ott's ellipsis analysis (Merchant 2001) has the advantage of capturing the empirical properties of German *Linksversetzung* and its distribution. The assumption that the dislocated constituent is hosted in an independent clause allows us to account for theta-role and case assignment, which are both assigned by the verb in the highest clause (CP1). The bi-clausal analysis also makes sense of the loose relation between the fronted constituent and the clause, evidenced by the intonation break between the dislocated XP and its doubler and by the need to have a resumptive element in IP. The resumptive element actually ensures the connection between the two juxtaposed clauses and functions as an "anchor". Considering German *Linksversetzung* as the result of the juxtaposition of two independent clauses with ellipsis in the highest one also allows us to circumvent the problem of the violation of the V2 rule, i.e. of the presence of V3 word order. Since the juxtaposed clauses are two complete and independent clauses, the dislocated constituent satisfies the requirements of the V2 rule in the highest clause, whereas the doubler (the demonstrative pronoun, a maximal category in German) does the same in the lower one. This means that the linear V3 word order found in *Linksversetzung* is not a violation of the V2 rule, but the result of the juxtaposition of two sentences in which the V2 has been satisfied by two different fronted constituents.

I apply Ott's (2011b) analysis to the Mòcheno main interrogative clause in (232).

(232) *Der Mario$_j$ bo   hòt=er=en$_j$ tsechen*
      the Mario   where has=SBJ-CL.3.SG.M=OBJ-CL.3SG.M   seen?
      'Where did he see Mario?'

As shown in (233), I assume that the left-dislocated constituent is simple-preposed in the higher clause, in which EPP has been satisfied by *pro* and topics can be simple-preposed without interfering with Spec,SubjP. In the lower clause, EPP is satisfied by the moved operator; the subject clitic functions as an anchor between the two clauses.

(233) [CP1 [der Mario][pro$_k$] [IP t$_k$ hòt-er tsechen]] [CP2 bo hòt-er-en tsechen?]

Ott's ellipsis analysis of LDs allows us to maintain the hypothesis that topics are moved in both main declarative and main interrogative clauses, independently of the presence or of the absence of the clitic doubler. In the bi-clausal approach, the function of clitic doublers is simply that of connecting two juxtaposed sentences. Moreover, the ellipsis approach allows us to also capture the V2 facts in a straightforward way. In wh-main interrogative clauses EPP is satisfied by the moved operator, which actually blocks movement of any other constituent to the left periphery for RM reasons. Like in German, topics can only be expressed by juxtaposing another main clause in which the EPP feature has been satisfied by the silent category *pro* and movement of topics to the left periphery is therefore permitted.

There are two predictions made by this hypothesis that have to be tested. The ellipsis approach implies that the connection between the fronted topic and the main clause is rather loose in sentences derived by an underlying bi-clausal structure and tighter in those involving an underlying mono-clausal structure. This prediction is borne out. According to consultants, sentences involving a left-dislocated topic preceding an operator are only grammatical if an intonational break or a question mark separates the left-dislocated constituent from the operator. This requirement is not found with simple-preposed topics in main declarative clauses.

The second prediction is that the same RM effects between topics found in main declarative clauses arise in sentences with a fronted focus. This prediction is borne out, too, as exemplified in (234). Above we saw that in main clauses a DO and a subject cannot be simple-preposed, as repeated in (234a, b). The same effect is found also in main interrogative clauses (234c, d).

(234) a. *S puach$_j$ der Mario hòt=(s$_j$) gester kaft
        the book the Mario has-PRS.3SG=OBJ-CL.3.SG.N yesterday bought
    b. *Der Mario$_j$ s puach$_k$ hòt=(er$_j$)=(s$_k$)
        the Mario the book has=SBJ-CL.3.SG.M=OBJ-CL.3.SG.N
        s puach kaft
        the book bought
    c. ???Der Mario$_j$, s puach$_k$ benn hot-er$_j$-s$_k$
        the Mario the book when has=SBJ-CL.3.SG.M=OBJ-CL.3.SG.N
        kaft
        bought
    d. ???S puach$_k$ der Mario$_j$ benn hot-er$_j$-s$_k$ kaft
        the book the Mario when has=SBJ-CL.3.SG.M=OBJ-CL.3.SG.N bought

No RM violations arise between adverbials and verb arguments (235a, b) or between DO and IO (235c, d), like in main declarative clauses.

(235) a. Gester s puach$_k$ bo hòt=er=s$_k$ kaft
        yesterday the book where has=SBJ-CL.3.SG.M=OBJ-CL.3.SG.N bought
    b. S puach$_k$ gester bo hòt=er=s$_k$ kaft
        the book yesterday where has=SBJ-CL.3.SG.M=OBJ-CL.3.SG.N bought
        'Where did he buy the book yesterday?'
    c. Gester a puach$_j$ en de Maria$_k$, ber
        yesterday a book to the Mary who
        hòt=s$_j$=en$_k$ trog?
        has-PRS.3SGOBJ-CL.3.SG.N=OBJ-CL.3.SG.F brought
    d. Gester en de Maria$_k$ s puach$_j$ ber
        yesterday to the Mary a book who
        hòt=s$_j$=en$_k$ trog?
        has-PRS.3SGOBJ-CL.3.SG.N=OBJ-CL.3.SG.F brought
        'Who brought Mary the book yesterday?'

In this subsection, I have shown how the bi-clausal analysis can account for the syntax of wh-main interrogative clauses. This theory allows us to make sense of the syntactic data in an interesting way and also to account for the differences between Mòcheno and German with respect to the number of constituents that can precede the finite verb (V3 in German, V3/V4 in Mòcheno). In Mòcheno, the possibility of using the TopicPs above SubjP is shown to depend on the partial *pro*-drop character of this language; since German in not a *pro*-drop language, in it, EPP cannot be satisfied by *pro* and therefore nothing can skip the Spec of the head associated with the EPP feature.

6.2.7 Partial conclusions

In this section I analysed main declarative and main interrogative clauses with multiple access to CP, thus completing the investigation of the V2 rule in main clauses.

In (236), I summarise the characteristics of the Mòcheno V2 rule. For the V2 constraint to be satisfied, one maximal projection must move to Spec,SubjP, one constituent must be A'-moved to the left periphery and the finite verb must move to Subj^0. Fronted operators fulfill both requirements (236a, b), whereas fronted topics fulfill (236b), but not (236a). In this case, *pro* appears in Spec,SubjP.

(236) a. one maximal projection in Spec,SubjP (A position);
 b. one A'-moved fronted constituent;
 c. the finite verb in Subj^0.

My analysis predicts that the bi-clausal structure is only possible in sentences with a fronted operator. There are two exceptions to this. The first is the HT construction, which has been given a bi-clausal analysis (Garzonio 2004). The bi-clausal analysis of HTs and the theory proposed here can be reconciled if we assume that the structure of the elliptical sentence containing the HT is different from that of the juxtaposed sentence preceding wh-main interrogative clauses. For HTs, I assume that the higher sentence contains only the HT and the verb "to be" (since only nominative can be assigned) which is reduced by ellipsis. The structure of the HT construction according to this hypothesis is given in (237).

(237) a. *Der Mario$_j$ gester s puach hòn=e=en$_j$*
 the Mario yesterday the book have=SBJ-CL.1.SG=OBJ-CL.3.SG.M
 kaft en sell tepp$_j$
 bought to that stupid
 'As for Mario, I bought yesterday a book to that stupid'
 [CP1 Der Mario ist]] [CP2 [gester] [s puach][pro$_k$] hòne-en t$_k$ kaft en sell tepp]

The second exception to the hypothesis that the bi-clausal structure is only possible in sentences with a fronted operator is the syntax of the double-object construction. As shown in (238), when both objects are fronted, the higher must be doubled by a clitic; if this is the DO, the IO must be doubled, too (238c).

(238) a. *Benn hòst kaft s puach en de Maria?*
 when have-PRS.2SG bought the book to the Mary
 'When did you buy a book for Mary?'

b. *En de Maria$_j$ s puach hòn=e=*(en$_j$)*
   to the Mary the book have=SBJ-CL.1.SG=OBJ-CL.3.SG.F
   gester   kaft
   yesterday bought

c. *S puach   en de Maria$_j$ hòn=e=*(en$_j$)*
   the book to the Mary   have=SBJ-CL.1.SG=OBJ-CL.3.SG.F
   gester   kaft
   yesterday bought
   'As for Mary's book, I bought it yesterday'

For the case of the double-object construction, I assume that LDs must be derived through the bi-clausal structure, which is becoming a grammatical option in main clauses, starting precisely from the double-object construction (see Benincà 1994 on this).

A similar account might also explain the syntax of weak subject pronouns discussed in Chapters 3 and 4. As repeated in (239), all consultants agree that weak subject pronouns cannot follow the finite verb (239a) and are only compatible with the absolute sentence-initial position (239b). Both these restrictions are predicted by the account proposed in this book. The fact that an adverbial can precede a weak subject pronoun (239c) is although not predicted, since weak subject pronouns are assumed to realise Spec,SubjP and nothing can be moved across filled Spec,SubjP. I tentatively suggest that the fact that only half of the consulted speakers accept (239c) is evidence of a shift in the grammar of Mòcheno towards a widening of the possible usages of the bi-clausal structure, in which the higher clause has a reduced CP (as assumed for HT).

(239) a. **Gester   hòt   de   kaft   s puach*
        yesterday has-PRS.3SG   SBJ-WEAK.3.SG.F bought   the book

b. *De   hòt   kaft   s puach*
   SBJ-WEAK.3.SG.F   has-PRS.3SG   bought   the book
   'She bought the book'

c. *Gester   de   hòt   kaft   s puach*
   yesterday SBJ-WEAK.3.SG.F has-PRS.3SG   bought   the book
   'She bought the book yesterday'

This section concludes my analysis of the syntax of Mòcheno main clauses. I now tackle the syntax of embedded clauses in relation to the V2 rule and to the distribution of *pro*-drop. This final topic allows us to provide evidence for the hypothesis that *pro* can only be licensed when the finite verb moves from AgrS^0 to Subj^0.

6.3 On the syntax of embedded clauses

The whole theoretical account proposed so far builds on an analysis of the syntax of main declarative clauses, as being characterised by a V2 rule which manifests itself in the movement of the finite verb to Subj^0 and XP fronting to Spec,SubjP for EPP reasons.

In this last section, I return to an issue that has only been touched upon so far, but is very relevant to any discussion of V2: the syntax of embedded clauses. Den Besten's (1983) analysis of the V2 phenomenon in Continental Germanic is strongly supported by the asymmetry found in the syntax of finite verbs in main and embedded clauses (see Chapter 2). The fact that the finite verb has to appear in OV syntax in embedded clauses and in second position in main clauses has been taken as evidence that complementisers and finite verb compete for the same CP head, and consequently as evidence for the whole analysis of V2. In Chapter 2 we also saw that the distribution pattern of the finite verb in main and embedded clauses in Continental Germanic languages is not shared by the whole Germanic language family. Scandinavian languages, for instance, are all V2, but are not characterised by an asymmetry in the syntax of the finite verb between main and embedded clauses, since their base-word order is VO. Moreover, only Scandinavian languages permit embedded topicalization, which is ruled out in Continental Germanic languages.

The aim of this concluding section is to explore the syntax of Mòcheno embedded clauses, focusing on the syntax of the finite verb and its interactions with the realised complementiser, in order to establish whether Mòcheno behaves like Continental Germanic languages or like Scandinavian with respect to the aforementioned phenomena (syntax of the finite verb and embedded topicalization). I also investigate the syntax of subjects in embedded clauses, which does not usually give rise to asymmetries between main and embedded clauses in Germanic languages, but has been reported to do so in Old Romance. As first pointed out by Benincà (1984), Old Romance languages were characterised by an asymmetric *pro*-drop system (see Chapter 2) which contrasted main and embedded clauses.

There is strong evidence that in Mòcheno embedded clauses the finite verb leaves VP and moves past sentential adverbials, which indicates a similarity with Scandinavian rather than with Continental Germanic languages. In this last section, I investigate whether the finite verb moves to Agr^0 or to an FP in the left periphery in Mòcheno embedded clauses by considering Leu's (2008, 2010) analysis of embedded topicalization in Germanic, which he links to the morphological shape of the complementiser displayed by each language. His hypothesis that embedded topicalization is possible only in those languages in which the complementiser is reduced morphologically (*ass/att*) and that the full complementiser has to be derived compositionally, allows us to demonstrate that the finite verb does not move to the left periphery (that is to Subj⁰) in Mòcheno embedded clauses. The finite verb's lack of movement to Subj⁰ is shown to correlate with the absence of the conditions for *pro* licensing described in the previous chapters: this actually means that when the finite verb remains in AgrS⁰, *pro* cannot be licensed in Spec,AgrSP, as in Old Romance languages.

6.3.1 Position of the finite verb in embedded clauses

As discussed in Chapter 3, the syntax of Mòcheno is not characterised by the asymmetry between main and embedded clauses found in Continental Germanic languages.

In Mòcheno embedded clauses three word order patterns are possible (240): strict OV (240a), the so-called *Satzklammerstruktur* (240b) and adjacency between finite and non-finite verb forms, as in Romance (240c).

(240) a. I   boas   nèt, benn as
        SBJ-STRONG.1.SG know-PRS.1SG NEG when that
        de maina kamaroten a film tsechen hom
        the my friends   a film seen   have-PRS.3PL
     b. I   boas   nèt, benn as
        SBJ-STRONG.1.SG know-PRS.1SG NEG when that
        de maina kamaroten hom   a film tsechen
        the my friends   have-PRS.3PL a film seen
     c. I   boas   nèt, benn as
        SBJ-STRONG.1.SG know-PRS.1SG NEG when that
        de maina kamaroten hom   tsechen a film
        the my friends   have-PRS.3PL seen   a film
        'I don't know when my friends have seen a film'

As shown in Table 6.1, the three word order patterns in (240) do not show up with the same frequency in all varieties. They are all produced and accepted by the great majority of speakers in the village of Palù, whereas in the other two villages

Table 6.1 Word order patterns in embedded clauses

	OV	%	Satzklammer	%	VO	%
Palù	14/15	93%	12/13	92%	9/9	100%
Roveda	8/15	53%	8/10	80%	14/14	100%
Fierozzo	3/15	20%	8/15	53%	15/15	100%
Total	25/45	55%	28/38	73%	38/38	100%

the acceptance of strict OV and of the *Satzklammerstruktur* decreases – dramatically in the case of the OV word order pattern in the village of Fierozzo. VO syntax is universally accepted in embedded clauses (see Appendix).

The first thing to be examined is the position of the finite verb with respect to sentential adverbs and negation, which is the standard test used for detecting what the position of the finite verb is (Kratzer 1989; Pollock 1989; Belletti 1990; Holmberg/Platzack 1995; Diesing 1997 a.o.). As illustrated in (241), in embedded sentences with *Satzklammerstruktur* the finite verb has to precede the sentential adverb *òllbe*, "always" (241a, b). The same word order is found in sentences with VO syntax (241c, d).

(241) a. I   hòn=en   pfrok, abia's
         SBJ-STRONG.1.SG have-PRS.1SG=OBJ-CL.3.SG.F asked how that
         der Hons hòt   òllbe s zimmer putzt
         the John has-PRS.3SG always the room cleaned

      b. *I   hòn=en   pfrok, abia's
         SBJ-STRONG.1.SG have-PRS.1SG=OBJ-CL.3.SG.F asked how that
         der Hons òllbe   hòt   s zimmer putzt
         the John always has-PRS.3SG the room cleaned

      c. I   hòn=en   pfrok, abia's
         SBJ-STRONG.1.SG have-PRS.1SG=OBJ-CL.3.SG.F asked how that
         der Hons hòt   òllbe putzt s zimmer
         the John has-PRS.3SG always cleaned the room

      d. *I   hòn=en   pfrok, abia's
         SBJ-STRONG.1.SG have-PRS.1SG=OBJ-CL.3.SG.F asked how that
         der Hons òllbe   hòt   putzt s zimmer
         the John always has-PRS.3SG cleaned the room
         'I asked him how John has always cleaned his room'

The examples in (242) show that the position of the finite verb in embedded clauses with the *Satzklammerstruktur* and VO syntax is identical to its position in main declarative clauses.

(242) a. Der Mario hòt   òllbe s zimmer putzt
         the Mario has-PRS.3SG always the room cleaned
      b. *Der Mario òllbe   hòt   s zimmer putzt
         the Mario always has-PRS.3SG the room cleaned
         'Mario has always cleaned his room'

In order to detect whether in embedded clauses the finite verb moves to Subj^0 or AgrS^0, in what follows I consider the distribution of subject pronominal forms and of embedded topicalization.

6.3.2 Form of the complementiser and CP structure

In order to investigate the syntactic position the finite verb in embedded clauses, I start from Leu's (2010) recent proposal that complementisers are compositionally derived and involve two adjacent FPs in CP.

Building on the observation that Germanic languages can be split into two groups according to the morphological shape of their complementiser (those with a full complementiser composed by *d-* and *-ass* or *-att*, such as Afrikans, Dutch, Frisian and German, and those with the reduced form *ass*, such as Yiddish, Danish, Faroese, Icelandic, Norwegian and Swedish), Leu proposes that the full complementiser is composed of two independent morphemes heading their own FP. The full complementiser form is derived through head movement: *d-* heads its own FP and moves in order to incorporate *ass* (this order is consistent with the mirror principle, see Baker 1985; Brody 2000), as shown in (243).

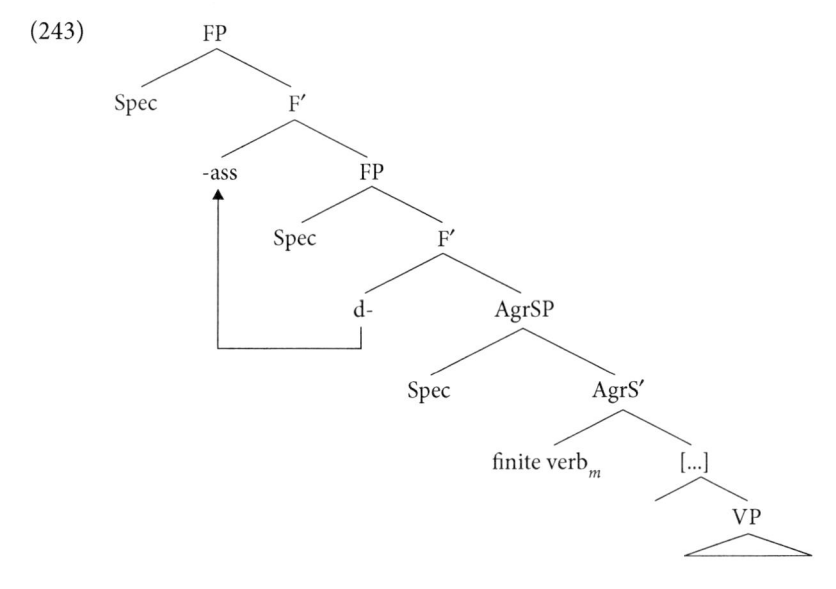

(243)
```
          FP
         /  \
       Spec   F'
             /  \
          -ass   FP
                /  \
              Spec   F'
                    /  \
                   d-    AgrSP
                        /    \
                      Spec    AgrS'
                             /    \
                       finite verb_m  [...]
                                      \
                                       VP
```

The morphological shape of the complementiser correlates with the distribution of embedded topicalization across Germanic (Leu 2010): all languages with the reduced complementiser permit embedded topicalization, which is ruled out in languages with the full complementiser.[9] This is exemplified in (244a, b from Leu 2010: 10 who adapts examples by Vikner 1995).

---

9. See Julien (2002) and Bentzen et al. (2007) for the distribution of embedded topicalization in Scandinavian.

(244) a. Wir   wissen   (*dass) dieses Buch hat
       SUBJ-PRON-1.PL know-PRS.1PL   that   this book   has-PRS.3SG
       Bo nicht gelesen
       Bo NEG   read
    b. Vir   ved   *(at) denne bog har
       SUBJ-PRON-1.PL know-PRS.1PL   that this book has
       Bo ikke lest
       Bo NEG read
       'We know that Bo did not read this book'

Leu captures the striking correlation between the morphological shape of the complementiser and the distribution of embedded topicalization across Germanic through the hypothesis that embedded topicalization is possible only in those languages in which the FP headed by *d-* does not have a syntactic realization. The fact that the head of this FP is not lexicalised by *d-* opens up the possibility that the finite verb moves to its head and an XP can be fronted to its Spec position, as illustrated in (245).

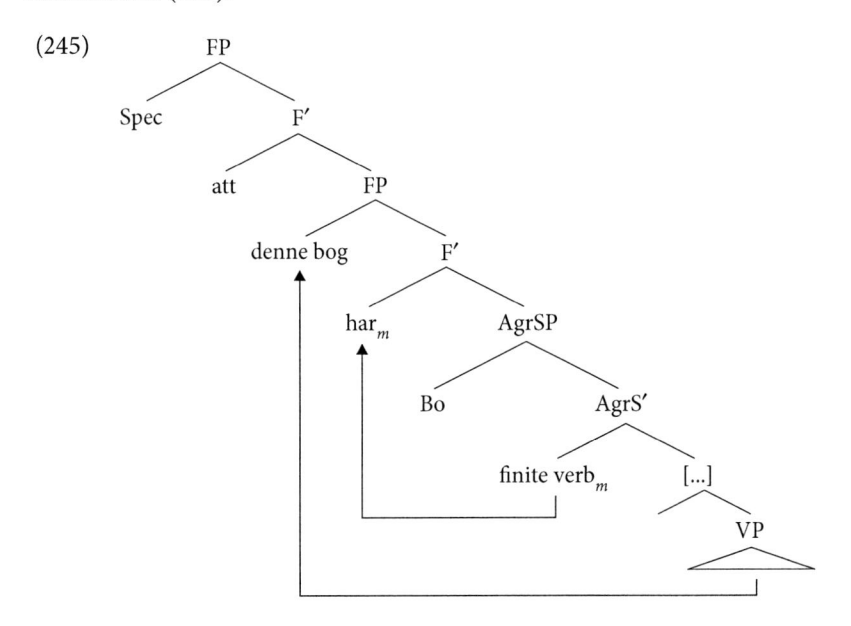

(245)
```
              FP
             /  \
          Spec   F'
                /  \
              att   FP
                   /  \
            denne bog  F'
                      /  \
                   har_m  AgrSP
                         /  \
                        Bo   AgrS'
                             /  \
                      finite verb_m [...]
                                    \
                                     VP
```

The whole story proposed by Leu (2010) can be summed up in the generalization in (246).

(246) F hosts *d-* OR attracts *x*

Leu does not put forward a specific hypothesis about which FPs are involved in the realization of the complementiser. I suggest here that the lowest FP hosting *d-* corresponds to Subj⁰, as shown in the structure in (247).

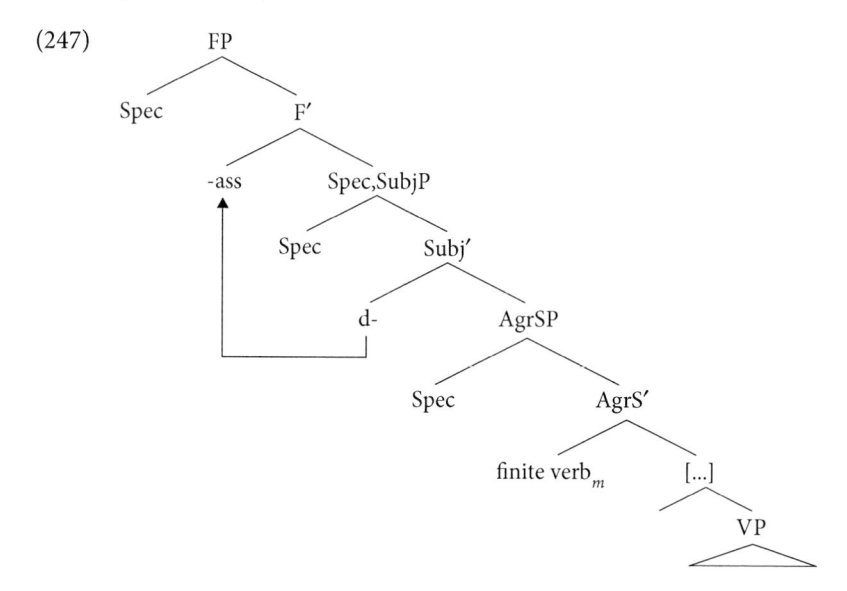

(247)

```
              FP
             /  \
          Spec   F'
                /  \
             -ass   Spec,SubjP
              ↑    /    \
                Spec    Subj'
                       /    \
                     d-      AgrSP
                            /    \
                          Spec    AgrS'
                                 /    \
                         finite verb_m  [...]
                                        \
                                         VP
```

Let us examine the Mòcheno data in the light of Leu's hypothesis, focusing first on the morphological shape of the complementiser. The data that I collected for this book show that the only complementiser form available in all varieties of Mòcheno is the reduced form *as*.[10] As to embedded topicalization, the data indicate that this construction is possible, but is restricted to a few verbs of saying and thinking and ruled out with all other verbs. In (248), I give some examples.

(248)   a.   Der Nane   hòt   mer   zok,   as   s puach
              the John   has-PRS.3SG   me-DAT   said   that   the book
              hòt=se   kaft
              has=SBJ-CL.3.SG.F bought
              'John told me that she bought the book'
   b.   I   hòn   gamuat   as   en de Maria
              SBJ-STRONG.1.SG   have-PRS.1SG   thought   that   to the Mary
              hòn=e   vourstellt   der dai kamarot
              have=SBJ-CL.1.SG introduced the your friend
              'I thought that I introduced Mary to your friend'

---

10. The form *tas/das* shows up in some examples in Rowley (2003:269ff.) and in Cognola (2006, Appendix).

c. *I   boas   as   s puach   hòt=se
   SBJ-STRONG.1.SG know-PRS.1SG that the book has=SBJ-CL.3.SG.F
   kaft
   bought

d. *Er   hòt   mer   pfrok, bo   as
   SBJ-STRONG.3.SG.M has-PRS.3SG me-DAT asked where that
   s puach   hòt=se   kaft
   the book has=SBJ-CL.3.SG.F   bought

Embedded topicalization is only possible if the topicalised XP(s) follow(s) the complementiser, as shown in (249). This means that the "Romance" embedded topicalization, in which topics can precede the complementiser (see Rizzi 1997 and Poletto 2002) is ruled out in Mòcheno.

(249) a. I   hòn   gamuat, as   en de Maria
         SBJ-STRONG.1.SG have-PRS.1SG thought that to the Mary
         der dai kamator   bar=e=sen   vourstelln
         the your friend   AUX-FUT=SBJ-CL.1.SG=OBJ-CL.3.SG.F introduce

      b. *I   hòn   gamuat, en de Maria
         SBJ-STRONG.1.SG have-PRS.1SG thought to the Mary
         der dai kamator as   bar=e=sen   vourstelln
         the your friend that AUX-FUT=SBJ-CL.1.SG=OBJ-CL.3.SG.F introduce
         'I thought that I would introduce your friend to Mary'

The data above indicate that the structural view proposed by Leu is only part of the story, since the presence of the reduced complementiser does not automatically imply that embedded topicalization is possible in all sentences. The Mòcheno data show that the lowest CP head lexicalised by *d-* is not accessible in all sentences in those Germanic languages with the reduced complementiser form. The distribution of embedded topicalization in Mòcheno, i.e. the impossibility of having this construction in Mòcheno except for a very reduced number of verbs, seems to indicate that the finite verb moves to AgrSP, and not to SubjP, in embedded clauses. This means that Mòcheno is not a generalised V2 language (differently from Yiddish and Icelandic, see Vikner 1995 and Heycock 2006 a.o.).

That SubjP is not accessible to the finite verb in embedded clauses is demonstrated by the syntax of subject pronouns. As shown in the previous chapters, in the main declarative clauses of all Mòcheno varieties, subject pronouns must be realised by the enclitic form in all cases in which the EPP feature has been satisfied by a fronted operator or by *pro* (when the fronted constituent is an SP). Enclisis is derived through movement of the finite verb to $Subj^0$. The relevant examples are repeated below in (250).

(250) a. *S puach si   /de   hòt
         the book SBJ-STRONG.3.SG.F SBJ-WEAK.3.SG.F has-PRS.3SG
         si   /de   kaft   en de boteig
         SBJ-STRONG.3.SG.F SBJ-WEAK.3.SG.F bought in the shop
    b. S puach [pro] hòt=se   kaft   en de boteig
         the book   has=SBJ-CL.3.SG.F bought in the shop
         'The book she bought in the shop'
    c. *Bos si   /de   hòt
         what SBJ-STRONG.3.SG.F SBJ-WEAK.3.SG.F has-PRS.3SG
         si   /de   kaft   en de boteig?
         SBJ-STRONG.3.SG.F SBJ-WEAK.3.SG.F bought in the shop
    d. Bos hòt=se [pro]   kaft   en de boteig?
         what has=SBJ-CL.3.SG.F bought in the shop
         'What did she buy the in the shop?'

The examples above indicate that the distribution of subject pronouns correlates with the syntactic position of the finite verb: in all cases in which the pronominal subject is realised by the clitic form, the finite verb is assumed to have moved to Subj^0.

Let us consider the syntax of subject pronouns in the Palù dialect. As exemplified in (251), in embedded clauses subject pronouns must be realised by the clitic forms, enclitic to the complementiser (251b, c). In embedded clauses, the clitic cannot encliticise to the finite verb in any word order pattern (251d–f).

(251) a. Er   hòt   mer   pfrok
         SBJ-STRONG.3.SG.M has-PRS.3SG me-DAT asked
         'He asked me'
    b. abia as=se   (hòt)   der compito   gamocht
         how that=SBJ-CL.3.SG.F has-PRS.3SG the homework done
         (hòt)
         has-PRS.3SG
    c. abia as=se   (hòt)   gamocht der compito
         how that=SBJ-CL.3.SG.F has-PRS.3SG done   the homework
         (hòt)
         has-PRS.3SG
    d. *abia as   gamocht der compito   hòt=se
         how that done   the homework has=SBJ-CL.3.SG.F
    e. *abia as   hòt=se   der compito   gamocht
         how that has=SBJ-CL.3.SG.F the homework done
    f. *abia as   hòt=se   gamocht der compito
         how that has=SBJ-CL.3.SG.F done   the homework
         'how she did her homework'

In the Palù dialect, the clitic forms enclitic to the complementiser are the only way in which a subject pronoun can be realised in embedded clauses, as repeated in (252).

(252) a. Er   hòt   mer   pfrok
         SBJ-STRONG.3.SG.M has-PRS.3SG me-DAT asked
         'He asked me'
     b. *abia as   si/   de
         how that SBJ-STRONG.3.SG.F SBJ-WEAK.3.SG.F
         (hòt)   der compito gamocht   (hòt)
         has-PRS.3SG the homework done   has-PRS.3SG
     c. *abia as   si/   de
         how that SBJ-STRONG.3.SG.F SBJ-WEAK.3.SG.F
         (hòt)   gamocht der compito (hòt)
         has-PRS.3SG done   the homework has-PRS.3SG

I take the data in (251) and (252) to indicate that in the embedded clauses of the Palù dialect the finite verb does not move to Subj⁰, but remains in AgrS⁰ or lower down in the structure, for the case of strict OV syntax.[11] Since the finite verb does not move to Subj⁰, subject clitics encliticise to the complementiser.

The fact that the finite cannot move to Subj⁰ in embedded clauses indicates that the finite verb and the complementiser compete for the same position – Subj⁰ – and when this position hosts the complementiser the movement of the finite verb is blocked. This means that the Palù dialect patterns like Continental Germanic languages in displaying an asymmetry between main and embedded clauses, which involves the realization of the subject and not the syntax of the finite verb.

Let us examine the data from the other two Mòcheno varieties repeated in (253). As discussed in Chapter 3, in the Fierozzo and Roveda dialects the most natural way of realising subject pronouns in embedded clauses is through the weak forms (253b). Alternatively, the strong forms can show up (253c). Crucially, clitic enclitic to the complementiser are ruled out in these two varieties (they are marginally accepted by few speakers, see discussion in Chapter 3 and the questionnaires given in the Appendix).

(253) a. Er   hòt   mer   pfrok
         SBJ-STRONG.3.SG.M has-PRS.3SG me-DAT asked
         'He asked me'

---

11. The analysis of OV/VO word order patterns goes beyond the scopes of this book, but see Cognola (2012) on this and on the hypothesis that strict OV syntax can be reconciled with the hypothesis that the finite verb moves to I (as in Hinterhölzl 2000; Haegeman 2000).

b. abia   as   si/   de
    how   that   SBJ-STRONG.3.SG.F   SBJ-WEAK.3.SG.F
    hòt   gamocht der compito
    has-PRS.3SG done   the homework
c. *abia as=se   (hòt)   gamocht der compito
    how   that=SBJ-CL.3.SG.F has-PRS.3SG done the homework
    'how she did her homework'

Recall, that the asymmetry observed in the realization of subject pronouns between the Palù dialect and the Fierozzo and Roveda varieties are limited to embedded clauses. In main declarative clauses, in fact, all three varieties behave as exemplified in (250) above: pronominal subjects must be realised by a subject clitic enclitic to the finite verb if EPP has been satisfied by an operator or *pro*. As exemplified in (254), a subject clitic can only show up in the embedded clauses of the Fierozzo and Roveda dialects if the complementiser *as* is missing and the sentence has the intonational pattern of a main declarative clause.

(254) a. Er   hòt   mer   pfrok
         SBJ-STRONG.3.SG.M   has-PRS.3SG   me-DAT   asked
         'He asked me'
     b. *abia as   hòt=se   gamocht der/en   der compito
         how   that has=SBJ-CL.3.SG.F   done   the-NOM/ACC   the homework
     c. abia   hòt=se   gamocht der/en   compito?
         how   has=SBJ-CL.3.SG.F   done   the-NOM/ACC   homework

The data above indicate that also in these two varieties, finite verb and *as* compete for the same position in CP: when a complementiser is present, the finite verb cannot move to CP and subject-verb inversion is ruled out. This allows us to conclude that in all three dialects movement of the finite verb to Subj⁰ is blocked when the complementiser is present. Typologically, Mòcheno patterns like Frisian and Mainland Scandinavian in allowing for limited embedded V2 with a reduced number of verbs and with German and Frisian in allowing V2 with all verbs with absent complementiser (Heycock 2006).

6.3.3 Realization of the subject and syntax of the finite verb

The aim of this subsection is to provide evidence for the hypothesis that in Mòcheno embedded clauses SubjP is not accessible to the finite verb (unless the complementiser is not present, see above) and that this leads to the impossibility of *pro* licensing in Spec,AgrSP.

Let us consider the data in (255), where I show that in an embedded interrogative clause in which both the wh-element and the complementiser are present (i.e. embedded topicalization is ruled out, see previous section) an NP subject must precede the finite verb in all varieties.

(255) a. De mama hòt   mer   pfrok, benn as
         the mum has-PRS.3SG me-DAT asked when that
         der Nane hòt   kaft   a puach
         the John has-PRS.3SG bought   a book
    b. De mama hòt   mer   pfrok, benn as
         the mum has-PRS.3SG me-DAT asked when that
         der Nane hòt   a puach kaft
         the John has-PRS.3SG a book   bought
    c. De mama hòt   mer   pfrok, benn as
         the mum has-PRS.3SG me-DAT asked when that
         der Nane a puach kaft   hòt
         the John a book bought   has-PRS.3SG
         'My mum asked me when John bought the book'

The above data are extremely relevant to the theory proposed in this chapter, since they indicate that in embedded clauses NP subjects have a different syntax from main clauses. As repeated in (256), in a main interrogative clause the NP subject cannot follow the finite verb, but must be right-dislocated.

(256) a. *Bo   hòt   der Nane kaft   s puach?
         where has-PRS.3SG   the John bought a book
    b. Bo   hòt=er$_j$ kaft   s puach der Nane$_j$?
         where has=SBJ-CL.3.SG.M   bought   s book the John
         'Where did John buy the book?'

Considered that embedded topicalization is always ruled out in embedded interrogative clauses, as repeated in (257), the syntax of NP subjects in embedded clauses cannot be accounted for by assuming that the subject appears in an FP of the left periphery. Therefore, the only position available for NP subjects is Spec,AgrSP.

(257) a. *Er   hòt   mer   pfrok abia as
         SBJ-STRONG.3.SG.M   has-PRS.3SG me-DAT asked how that
         de compiti   hòt=er   gamocht
         the homeworks   has=SBJ-CL.3.SG.M   done

b. *Er   hòt   mer   pfrok bo   as
   SBJ-STRONG.3.SG.M has-PRS.3SG me-DAT asked where that
   en de Maria hòt=er=(en)   kaft   a puach
   to the Mary has=SBJ-CL.3.SG.M=OBJ-CL.3.SG.F bought a book

I suggest that the asymmetry in the syntax of NP subjects found between main and embedded clauses depends on the fact that only in main clauses *pro* can be licensed. In embedded clauses, the finite verb cannot move to Subj⁰ and *pro* cannot be licensed: NP subjects appear therefore in Spec,AgrSP, as in the structure in (258).[12]

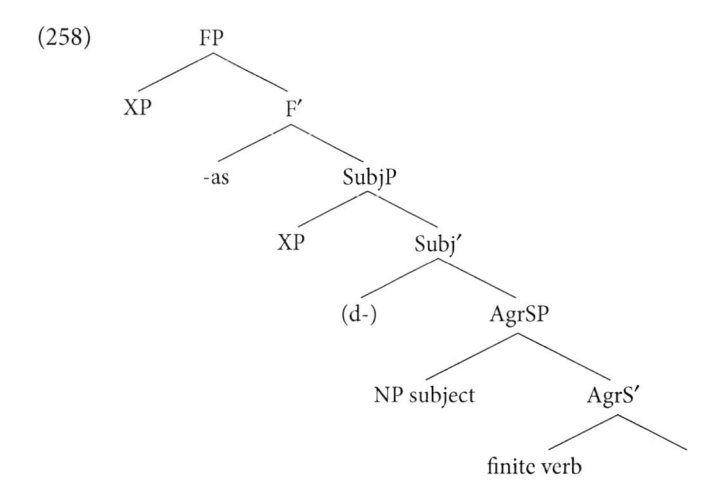

(258)
```
           FP
          /  \
         XP   F'
             /  \
           -as  SubjP
                /  \
               XP  Subj'
                   /  \
                (d-)  AgrSP
                      /   \
                NP subject AgrS'
                              \
                           finite verb
```

I take the syntax of NP subjects in main and embedded clauses to indicate that all Mòcheno varieties display asymmetric *pro*-drop.

Let us now reconsider the data on the syntax of subject pronouns. As repeated in (259), in the Fierozzo and Roveda dialects subject clitics are ruled out from embedded clauses and subject pronouns must be realised by either a strong or a weak from. These data are now fully expected within the hypothesis that Mòcheno is an asymmetric *pro*-drop language: in embedded clauses the finite verb cannot move to Subj⁰ and *pro* cannot be licensed (through the mediation of the clitic). Therefore, the subject pronoun is realised by a maximal category in Spec,AgrSP.

(259) a. Er   hòt   mer   pfrok
         SBJ-STRONG.3.SG.M has-PRS.3SG me-DAT asked
         'He asked me'

---

12. See below for the arguments supporting the hypothesis that the finite verb cannot move to Subj⁰ in embedded clauses.

b. abia as   si/   de   hòt
   how that SBJ-STRONG.3.SG.F   SBJ-WEAK.3.SG.F   has-PRS.3SG
   gamocht der compito
   done   the homework
c. *abia as=se   (hòt)   gamocht der compito
   how that=SBJ-CL.3.SG.F has-PRS.3SG done   the homework
   'how she did her homework'
d. Abia hòt=se   gamocht der compito?
   how has=SBJ-CL.3.SG.F done   the homework
   'How did she do her homework?'

What is not expected within the theory is the syntax of subjects pronouns in the Palù dialect, where the clitic forms are obligatory and the other forms ruled out (260). I propose that the Palù dialect is becoming a *pro*-drop language in embedded clauses, which manifests itself in the possibility of licensing *pro* in Spec,AgrSP without the movement of the finite verb to Subj⁰, but simply through the mediation of the subject clitic.

(260) a. abia as=se/   de mama hòt   gamocht
         how that=SBJ-CL.3.SG.F/ the mum has-PRS.3SG done
         der compito
         the homework
     b. *abia as   si/de   hòt   gamocht
         how that SBJ-STRONG.3.SG.F SBJ-WEAK.3.SG.F done
         der compito
         the homework
         'how she did her homework'

Summing up, I have provided evidence that Mòcheno is an asymmetric *pro*-drop language, in which *pro* can be licensed in main clauses because the finite verb moves to Subj⁰, but not in embedded clauses, because the finite verb cannot move to CP. This captures the syntax of NP subjects in all Mòcheno varieties and that of subject pronouns in the Fierozzo and Roveda dialects. The only exception is the syntax of subject pronouns in the Palù dialect, which I propose is determined by the fact that this variety has developed the possibility of licensing *pro* through the mediation of the clitic. This means that the Palù dialect is not an asymmetric but a symmetric *pro*-drop language with subject pronouns, in which although *pro* licensing takes place through different mechanisms: the movement of the finite verb to CP and the mediation of the clitic in main clauses, and the mediation of the clitic in embedded clauses.

In this last part of the section, I provide evidence for the hypothesis that the finite verb cannot move to Subj⁰ in embedded clauses, although Mòcheno only displays the reduced complementiser *as*. My suggestion is that the finite verb cannot move to the head of SubjP because this position hosts the silent *d-* (Leu 2008, 2010), which prevents movement of the finite verb to Subj^0 in all Mòcheno dialects and functions as a host for subject clitics in the Palù variety. The *d* morpheme remains silent in Mòcheno due to a deletion rule.

Let us see how this deletion rule functions. As shown in (261a), in the Fierozzo and Roveda dialects a preposition must be followed by the full article form *de*; in the Palù dialect *d-* disappears and the article is reduced to *e* (261b). This rule is very systematic as can be seen in the questionnaires in Cognola (2006).

(261) a. *I   hòn   kaft   a puach en de/ ver de Maria*
           SBJ-STRONG.1.SG have-PRS.1SG bought a book   to the   for the Mary
      b. *I   hòn   kaft   a puach ene/   vare Maria*
           SBJ-STRONG.1.SG have-PRS.1SG bought a book   to-the   for the Mary
         'I bought a book for Mary'

As shown in (262), there is evidence that the same deletion rule is operative at the CP level, where it affects the *d-* of the complementiser. In (262a, b) I give two sentences produced in a spontaneous conversation by an elderly speaker from Palù who has lived more that 50 years in Australia and whom I interviewed in August 2011. As can be seen in the examples, this speaker systematically uses the pronominal form *to* for the second person singular, whereas all other consultants use *o* (262c, d).

(262) a. *Bills=to   zucker ene   café?*
         want=SBJ-PRON.2.SG sugar in-the coffee
         'Would you like some sugar in your coffee?'
      b. *Er   hòt   mer   zok,*
         SBJ-STRONG.3.SG.M has-PRS.3SG   me-DAT   said
         as=to   kemmen tuast
         that=SBJ-PRON.2.SG come   do-PRS.2SG
         'He told me that you would come'
      c. *Bills=o   zucker ene   café?*
         want=SBJ-CL.2.SG   sugar in-the coffee
         'Would you like some sugar in your coffee?'
      d. *as=o   s puach kaft   host*
         that=SBJ-CL.2.SG the book bought have-PRS.2SG
         'that you bought the book'

In the Fierozzo and Roveda dialects, the morpheme *d-* can be optionally dropped in the DP, as exemplified in the examples in (263, from speakers ROVE-CF, aged 32, and ROVE-JP, aged 68). Note, that in the production of the same speaker both forms with and without *d* appear. When asked, consultants claim that the two forms are identical.

(263) a. En de boteig hòn=e   s puech   kaft   as
         in the shop have=SBJ-CL.1.SG the book bought that
         hòt   mer   tschoffn er Mario
         has-PRS.3SG me-DAT said   the Mario
         'In the shop I bought suggested by Mario'
      b. En de boteig (d)er Giani hòt   òllbe   kaft   s mel
         in the shop the John   has-PRS.3SG always bought the flour
         'In the shop Mario has always bought the flour'

At the CP level, it is possible to have a *d-* morpheme preceding the subject pronouns in the Roveda dialect, as shown in (264) from consultant (ROVE-RF). This form precedes the first person singular pronoun (*e*, see Chapter 3) and is preceded by the complementiser (264b). I claim that this form, traditionally analysed as an epenthetic consonant, is actually the lexicalization of Subj⁰. As expected from this hypothesis, *d-* can be deleted, as (264c).[13]

(264) a. De Maria hòt   mer   pfourst
         the Mary has-PRS.3SG me-DAT asked
         'Mary asked me'
      b. abia as   d=e   hòn   gamocht
         how that d=SBJ-WEAK.1.SG have-PRS.1SG done
         en compito
         the-ACC homework
      c. abia as   e   hòn   gamocht en compito
         how that SBJ-WEAK.1.SG have-PRS.1SG done   the-ACC homework
         'how I did my homework'

Summing up, I propose that in all Mòcheno dialects a silent *d* morpheme heads Subj⁰ in embedded clauses and blocks the movement of the finite verb to SubjP, as shown in (265).

---

13. According to the proposal put forward here, the form *de* is composed by *d+e* and is not an allomorphe of *e/i*.

(265)
```
              FP
             /  \
           XP    F'
                /  \
              -as   SubjP
                   /    \
                  XP    Subj'
                        /   \
                      (d-)   AgrSP
                             /    \
                  subject pronoun  AgrS'
                                   /   \
                              finite verb
```

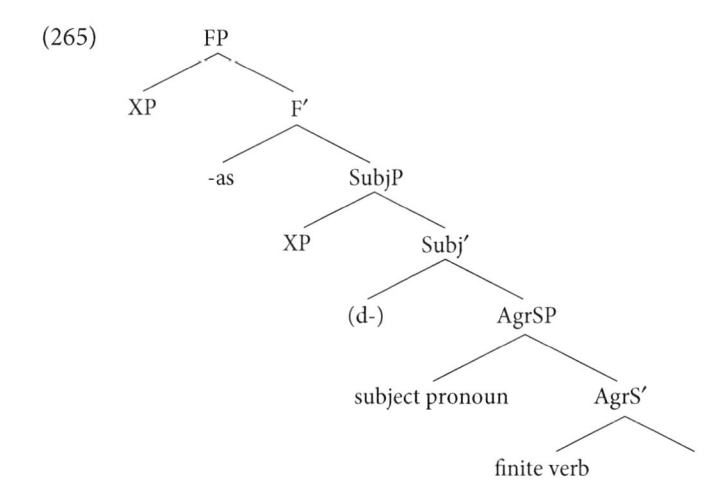

In this subsection, I provided evidence for the hypothesis that movement of the finite verb to Subj⁰ can only take place in main clauses if the complementiser is absent and in the embedded clauses selected by a verb belonging to the reduced class allowing for embedded topicalization.[14]

6.4 Conclusions

In this chapter, I discussed the syntax of main clauses with multiple access to CP and that of embedded clauses, completing the investigation of the characteristics of the V2 phenomenon in Mòcheno that I started in Chapter 2, where I introduced the empirical properties through which V2 manifests itself in this language.

In Chapter 2 we saw that one of the characteristics that Mòcheno shares with V2 Old Romance languages is the availability of an articulated left periphery, a property which has erroneously been taken to indicate the absence of the V2 rule. In this chapter, I demonstrate how multiple access to the left periphery can coexist with both the satisfaction of the EPP feature in SubjP and with the licensing of *pro*.

The proposed analysis is based on two core ideas. The first is that multiple access to CP is not an unsystematic and arbitrary phenomenon, but is ordered and structured and depends on the fact that in relaxed V2 languages constituents that can satisfy the EPP feature can co-occur with constituents unable to move through Spec,SubjP, exactly as in Old Romance (Benincà 2006). The second is

---

[14] Why the *d* morpheme does not interfere in the cases in which embedded topicalization is possible, is something that remains unexplained in this book.

that the empty category *pro* can satisfy EPP, which is not ruled out of the theory, since *pro* is a maximal category and evidence of its existence is provided in Chapter 5.

Building on these assumptions, in this chapter I showed that whether or not multiple access is permitted to the left periphery depends on the type of constituent satisfying the EPP feature in Spec,SubjP. When EPP is satisfied by a fronted operator, topics have to be realised syntactically as LDs, whereas if EPP is satisfied by *pro* and Spec,FocusP is empty, topics have to be realised syntactically as SPs. In this chapter it has been demonstrated that SPs cannot satisfy the EPP feature, contrary to the conclusion reached in Chapter 4. In both configurations (EPP satisfied by *pro* or by an operator) topics are subject to RM effects.

I accounted for the first type of configuration (LD-operator) by using Ott's (2011a, b) bi-clausal analysis of dislocation structures in German, according to which sentences involving LDs have to be analysed as fragments of an elliptical sentence, juxtaposed to a lower sentence. Resumptive pronouns connect the two sentences. The second configuration is accounted for by a mono-clausal analysis which assumes that the movement of topics to the left periphery is possible because EPP is satisfied by *pro*: the fact that EPP is satisfied by a silent category opens up the possibility of moving other constituents to the TopicPs of the left periphery without interfering with Spec,SubjP and satisfaction of EPP.

The proposed analysis has the advantage of accounting for sentences with multiple access to CP without the need to call for any special mechanism or extra FPs. It assumes that EPP can be satisfied in two ways in Mòcheno: by either a fronted operator or the silent category *pro*. In the former case Spec,SubjP is not accessible for further movement of constituents to the left periphery, as in strict V2 languages (that is languages with linear restriction) and this block can only be circumvented by juxtaposing an independent clause, in which EPP has been satisfied by *pro* and topics can move to the left periphery without interfering with Spec,SubjP. According to the proposed analysis, therefore, a reduced V2 language like Mòcheno and a strict V2 language like German have the same structure as far as sentences with a fronted operator are concerned, since for both languages it has to be assumed that EPP is satisfied by the fronted constituent in the Spec position of an FP in CP, to the head of which the finite verb moves.

The Mòcheno data allowed us to provide a new analysis of the difference between relaxed and strict V2 languages: only in the former can EPP be satisfied by *pro*, opening up the possibility of circumventing Spec,SubjP (no RM violations) and moving constituents to the TopicPs of the left periphery (which are assumed to be available in both Romance and Germanic languages, but cannot be used in strict V2 languages because they are not *pro*-drop).

In the second part of the chapter I examined the syntax of embedded clauses: my findings have allowed me to refine and complete the theory proposed for embedded clauses. I can now demonstrate that Mòcheno is an asymmetric *pro*-drop language, with the exception of sentences with subject pronouns in the Palù dialect. This conclusion, corroborated by strong evidence like the distribution of embedded topicalization in both embedded interrogatives and in sentences selected by a speech verb, makes the parallel between Mòcheno and Old Romance languages even more striking. In embedded clauses the absence of the partial *pro*-drop system identified for main clauses correlates with the lack of movement of the finite verb to the left periphery. In order to demonstrate that the finite verb does not move to the lowest portion of CP in embedded clauses, I started out from Leu's (2008, 2010) intuition that Germanic complementisers have to be split into two different morphemes, each heading its own FP. The predictions of Leu's theory have been tested in the case of Mòcheno, a language that only has the reduced complementiser form *as*. I proposed that the lowest FP involved in the realization of the complementiser is actually SubjP: an FP connected with definiteness/finiteness that manifests itself through the morpheme *d-* in embedded clauses and through subject clitics in main clauses. Evidence from both the Palù and Roveda dialects indicates that in embedded clauses a silent *d-* realises the head of SubjP, which blocks the movement of the finite verb to that position. I have demonstrated that *pro* cannot be licensed when the finite verb does not move to the head of SubjP and in this case the subject appears in Spec,AgrSP. This allows us to refine the description of the conditions governing the licensing of *pro* in main clauses, by establishing that *pro* is licensed only if the finite verb moves to $Subj^0$, which could not be done in Chapter 4.[15]

---

15. This clarification is particularly relevant for main declarative clauses with a fronted subject, for which the movement of the finite verb to $Subj^0$ and *pro* licensing could only be stipulated.

CHAPTER 7

Conclusions

This book has investigated the syntax of the finite verb in Mòcheno, a German dialect spoken in the Fersina valley, a linguistic speech island in Northern Italy.

The study is based on strong new empirical data collected during 26 single interviews with one informant (Cognola 2010) and extensive fieldwork involving 45 speakers from the three villages selected to obtain a statistically significant population group.[1] An important initial finding is that the kind of variation displayed by Mòcheno cannot be accounted for by either the contact hypothesis (Togni 1990; Rowley 2003) or the double-base hypothesis (Kroch 1989). This indirectly confirms similar conclusions reached for other similar languages characterised by syntactic variation (see the contributions in Putnam 2010, in particular Abraham 2010).

Even though specific arguments against the double-base hypothesis for Mòcheno are presented only in Chapter 2, where I show that Mòcheno does not behave as it should according to this hypothesis, the whole book is intended as a comprehensive counterargument to the double-base explanation of syntactic variation. The theory I develop places the complex Mòcheno data within the hypothesis that its syntactic variation emerges from a single grammar, in which the syntax of the finite verb and *pro* licensing interact in a very complex way. As has already been discussed in detail, the system identified for Mòcheno is not shared by either contact Romance varieties or standard or dialectal German.

Mòcheno differs from contact Romance varieties in two respects. First of all, unlike modern contact Romance, Mòcheno must be considered a V2 language – as were all Old Romance varieties until at least the XIV century (Benincà 1984, 2006). Secondly, despite the fact that both Mòcheno and contact Trentino dialect have developed a system of subject clitic pronouns and must therefore be classified as *pro*-drop languages (as proposed by Brandi/Cordin 1981, 1989; Poletto 2000; Roberts 2010 a.o.), the two languages differ from each other in several respects. In Mòcheno only, *pro* licensing is subject to the syntactic position of the finite verb, whereas in the local Trentino dialect *pro* is licensed independently of

---

1. See the Introduction for a description of the criteria used for selecting the participants and the Appendix for the questionnaires.

the position of the finite verb. I demonstrate that in Mòcheno only quasi-argumental, not referential, *pro* can be licensed (except for the very limited case of the second person singular in the Fierozzo and Roveda dialects). In Trentino, referential *pro* is always licensed. Finally, only Mòcheno displays an asymmetric *pro*-drop system, which is completely absent from the modern Trentino dialects, none of which are V2-languages.

Mòcheno is also shown to differ from standard German. As discussed in depth in Chapter 2, several constituents can precede the finite verb in the left periphery in Mòcheno: I demonstrated that this is not a violation of the German V2 rule, but rather a typical trait of the (Old Romance) type of V2 rule displayed by Mòcheno. Furthermore, Mòcheno has developed subject clitics (which supports the claim that it must be analysed as a partial *pro*-drop language) whereas German lacks subject clitics and only permits expletive *pro*. Although this aspect is not examined in any detail in this book, Mòcheno also seems to diverge from German dialects. Like Bavarian dialects (Bayer 1984; Gruber 2008), in Mòcheno *pro* licensing by the finite verb appearing in the left periphery is restricted to the second person; however, unlike these varieties, *pro* licensing for all persons can take place through the mediation of subject clitics, which is ruled out in Bavarian. Moreover, Mòcheno differs from Bavarian also in its use of the left periphery, since Bavarian is much closer to standard German in not allowing V4 and V5 word order patterns (see Guidolin 2011). The distribution of subject pronouns detected in Mòcheno is reminiscent of similar patterns in West Flemish noted by Haegeman (1990, 1992), although the two varieties are not fully comparable. Mòcheno has developed a class of subject clitics which coexist with weak and strong forms and whose function is to license *pro*; West Flemish just displays weak and strong forms and is not a *pro*-drop language. Consequently, in West Flemish weak and strong forms can both appear in subject-verb inversion (presumably in Spec,AgrSP), which is ruled out in Mòcheno, since Spec,AgrSP can only host *pro*. Finally, only Mòcheno is an asymmetric *pro*-drop language, whereas the other Bavarian dialects are not.

A detail discussion of a comprehensive body of very detailed Mòcheno data has allowed us to demonstrate that its grammar differs from the grammar of the contact Romance varieties and that of German and German dialects. This clear, strong result indicates that the asymmetries observed between Mòcheno and (standard) German, traditionally attributed to the effect of contact with modern Romance varieties, cannot be accounted for in these terms, since Mòcheno also differs from contact Romance. Therefore, both the contact and the double-base hypotheses have to be abandoned in the case of Mòcheno, in favour of an account of syntactic variation within a single grammar.

As discussed in the book, the type of syntactic variation displayed by Mòcheno resembles that of Old Romance languages and of some conservative Romance dialects (Poletto 2002; Roberts 2010). This finding is not, in my view, surprising, indicating, as it does, that the contact hypothesis traditionally put forward for Mòcheno must be refined by postulating that Mòcheno was shaped by its contact with Old rather than modern Romance varieties. According to this hypothesis, originally suggested by Benincà (1994) for Rhetoromance and applied to Mòcheno for the syntactic phenomenon of restructuring by Cognola (2009), contact does not manifest itself through the direct borrowing of syntactic constructions, or through the application of the abstract rules of one of the two languages in contact with each other, but through the reinforcement of those grammatical traits common to the contact languages. Explaining the exact role of Old Romance in the contact situation of Mòcheno is obviously beyond the scopes of this study, but the point I wish to convey is that Mòcheno has maintained those characteristics of its grammar that were shared by Old Romance. Almost nothing is known about the language spoken by the first settlers who moved to the Fersina valley between the XIII and XIV centuries, but it seems reasonable to assume that the Southern German variety they spoke behaved similarly to Old and Middle High German. In the context of the present discussion it is important to note that Old High German was a (partial) *pro*-drop V2 language (Axel 2007; Axel/Weiß 2007) in which both OV/VO word orders were permitted (Hinterhölzl 2009 a.o.). Old Romance languages also share these properties (see Benincà 1984, 2006; Adams 1987 for the idea that Old Romance languages were *pro*-drop and V2 languages; Poletto 2006 for evidence supporting the fact that OV word order patterns coexist with VO word order in Old Italian). This analysis of the role of Old Romance varieties in the contact situation of Mòcheno is still speculative; it could, however, develop into an interesting working hypothesis to be tested by future research, involving a full comparison between modern Mòcheno syntax and the diachronic syntax of Old Romance and older German varieties.

The Mòcheno data presented in this book contribute significantly to the debate on the triggers of language variation. They provide new evidence against the competing grammars explanation and enable us to reevaluate the role played by contact languages. They also contribute to our understanding of the V2 phenomenon by allowing insights into the grammar of a language whose syntax had never been described before. Above all, the Mòcheno data provide new empirical evidence for the definition of Old Romance V2, which can thus be classified as one specific type of V2 (see also Holmberg 2012).

An important characteristic that seems to be shared by Old Romance languages, an observation confirmed by the data presented in this book, is that not all fronted constituents "count" in the same way for V2: only fronted operators are able to satisfy the EPP feature responsible for the V2 effect (see Benincà 2006; Poletto 2002; Holmberg 2012 a.o.). Another typical trait of Old Romance languages results from this fact: the possibility of V3 and V4 word orders. As we also saw in Mòcheno, multiple access to the left periphery in Old Romance languages is not a chaotic phenomenon, but is controlled by precise requirements; in particular, topics must always precede foci. Therefore, these ordering restrictions are a constant of Romance V2 languages, which demonstrates that they form a coherent and autonomous group, different from and independent of other typologically different V2 languages, such as the Germanic ones.

Asymmetric *pro*-drop is the last property shared by the Old Romance languages and Mòcheno that I examined: when the finite verb is in CP, *pro* can be licensed, when it remains in $AgrS^0$, *pro* cannot be licensed. As discussed in Chapter 2, the investigation of the type of *pro*-drop displayed by Old Romance languages was central to the first generative work on these languages (Benincà 1984; Adams 1987) but has been neglected in recent studies. In this book, I defended the thesis that the *pro*-drop character of Mòcheno plays a central role in the empirical manifestation of the V2 phenomenon in this language. I suggest that this can be explained by considering *pro* in the derivation of V2 sentences as an XP able to satisfy the EPP feature.

From a comparative perspective, the V2 phenomenon must therefore be understood as a property of one FP of the left periphery ((267), Holmberg 2012: 39) and not necessarily as a constraint affecting the linear position of the finite verb, which is only typical of the subtype of V2 present in Germanic languages.

(267) a. A functional head in the left periphery attracts the finite verb.
 b. This functional head wants a constituent moved to its specifier position.

Both Old Romance and Germanic languages fit into the definition of V2 given in (267) and can be considered to be two subtypes of V2 languages which proceed from (267). The former are characterised by the *pro*-drop property and by the fact that only fronted operators can satisfy the EPP feature which means that operators can be combined with topics (constituents that can never satisfy the EPP feature responsible for V2). In V2 Germanic languages, movement of the finite verb to the left periphery coexists with very reduced *pro* licensing and with no difference in the ability of fronted constituents to satisfy the EPP feature.

Although the V2 rule displayed by Mòcheno is undoubtedly similar to the Old Romance subtype of V2, with which Mòcheno has been shown to share the three macro-features discussed above, this does not mean that Mòcheno is an Old Romance language and is simply replicating the abstract rules of Old Romance varieties. The most important asymmetry between Mòcheno and Old Romance languages is the presence of subject clitics in Mòcheno, whose distribution is tightly connected with *pro* licensing in Spec,AgrSP. As discussed by Vanelli (1987) and Poletto (1995, 2000), subject clitics are a relatively late development (after the Renaissance period) in Northern Italian dialects, which, as V2 languages, allowed only weak and strong subject pronoun forms.[2] This claim is also supported by the examples in (267, from Benincà 2006:68), where can be seen that in the older stages of Venetian and Milanese, two Northern Italian dialects which have now subject clitics, subject pronouns drop in main clauses when the finite verb is in CP (267a, b). This contrasts sharply with Mòcheno, where subject clitics are obligatory when the finite verb is in CP (267c).

(267) a. et levà   lo rem et de-   me sulo col
        and raised-PST.3SG the oar and hit-PST.3SG me on-the neck
        et menà-   me zo   per lo brazo, sì ch' el me
        and stroke-PST.3SG me down the arm,   so that he to me
        lo scavezà   (OldVen.; Lio Mazor, 18)
        it broke-PST.3SG
        'and he raised the oar and hit me on the neck, and struck my arm so that he broke it'
    b. Quand tu veniss   al mondo, se tu
        when you came-PST.2SG to the world, if you
        voliss   pensar, negota ge   portassi,   negota
        want-COND.2SG think, nothing there brought-PST.2SG nothing
        n   poi   portar   (Old Mil.; Bonvesin, 179)
        from-there can-PRS.2SG take
        'When you came into the world, if you think about it, you didn't bring anything and nothing you can take away'
    c. Bos hòt=*(er)   kaft?
        what has=SBJ-CL.3.SG.M bought
        'What did he buy?'

The above data and their analysis presented in this book show that the system of subject clitics developed by Mòcheno evolved independently within the language, since it is not shared by Old Romance languages, in which movement of the finite verb to CP was a sufficient condition for *pro* to be licensed. Subject pronouns in

---

2. Poletto (1995) suggests that the development of subject clitics in Northern Italian dialects is actually due to the loss of the V2 rule in these varieties: when the finite verb ceased to move to CP, subject clitics developed.

Mòcheno may develop into agreement markers; however, the data collected thus far clearly demonstrate that this shift has not yet occurred.

The presence of subject clitics in Mòcheno and their interaction with the V2 rule are the basis for the central tenet of the hypothesis put forward in this study: that the FP whose head is associated with the EPP feature responsible for the V2 phenomenon in Mòcheno is SubjP. The hypothesis that the functional head associated with the EPP feature is $Subj^0$ is not a standard assumption, nevertheless, I have shown it to be backed up by strong empirical evidence. Building on Rizzi's (2006) intuition that the head of SubjP is lexicalised by subject clitics in Northern Italian dialects, I showed that in Mòcheno the distribution of subject clitics depends on whether the fronted constituent is able to satisfy the EPP feature: in all cases in which the fronted XP is an operator (that is it "counts" for V2), subject clitics are obligatory and both strong and weak forms are ruled out. I have captured these facts by proposing that $Subj^0$ is the head associated with the EPP feature and that in all cases in which a constituent moves to (or through) Spec,SubjP the finite verb moves to $Subj^0$ in order to function as a host for the subject clitics, whose function is to license *pro* in Spec,AgrSP.

That SubjP must be involved in the derivation of main clauses and in the movement of the finite verb is also indicated by the syntax of embedded clauses. Within a compositional theory of Germanic complementisers (Leu 2010), it has been demonstrated that SubjP lexicalises the *d-* morpheme, whose presence prevents movement of the finite verb to $Subj^0$ in embedded clauses. Since the finite verb cannot move to SubjP, *pro* cannot be licensed.

Drawing on the work of Leu (2008), in Chapter 6 I put forward the hypothesis that the *d-* morpheme appearing in $Subj^0$ in embedded clauses lexicalises some features connected to the finiteness of the sentence, which are therefore expressed by subject clitic pronouns in main declarative clauses. It is tempting to hypothesise that the FP assumed to host clitics and the *d-* morpheme has some relation with FinP (Rizzi 1997), which is generally held to be the FP involved in the V2 rule. Since in Leu's hypothesis, Germanic complementisers are compositionally derived, I tentatively propose that FinP is composed of two FPs: a higher FP lexicalised by *as-* and a lower one headed by the *d-* morpheme. The question of whether the highest FP (in the head of which *as* is found), is also present in main clauses, and of whether it corresponds to ForceP, is an issue that could not be dealt with in this book.

Central to this book is the proposition that a necessary condition for the development of V3 and V4 word order patterns in Mòcheno is the fact that the EPP feature can be satisfied by *pro*. As discussed in Chapter 6, V3 word order patterns are not excluded in standard German, where they are restricted to some dislocation structures. Ott's (2011a, b) theory shows these dislocation structures do not violate the V2 rule of German, since they derive from an underlying bi-clausal structure. Therefore, V3 word orders do not represent a reduction or a weakening of the V2 rule. In this book, I propose that the possibility of V4 or V5 word orders depends on the fact that in Mòcheno *pro* can satisfy the EPP feature associated with Subj^0, which permits constituents to skip Spec,SubjP and not give rise to RM (as discussed in Chapter 6, RM violations between *pro* and a moved XP arise only in impaired or child language). Therefore, the real asymmetry between a V2 language such as standard German and Mòcheno lies in the fact that *pro* can satisfy the EPP feature, which leads to V4 and V5 word orders when a sentence with two simple-preposed topics is juxtaposed with a main clause in which a fronted operator satisfies the EPP feature. This new proposal differs radically from previous suggestions (Grewendorf/Poletto 2010), since it does not link the presence of V4 and V5 word orders to the development of object clitics. The Mòcheno data strongly support this theory and it is to be hoped that future research will be able to test its validity for other V2 languages.

To sum up, in this book I demonstrated that Mòcheno has a V2 rule of Old Romance type, which means that the movement of the finite verb to the left periphery coexists with a system of *pro* licensing and with multiple access to CP. Unlike Old Romance languages, Mòcheno has developed a system of subject clitics, whose function is to license *pro* in Spec,AgrSP; *pro* cannot simply be licensed by the finite verb in CP – as it can in Old Romance. In Mòcheno, multiple access to CP has been shown to depend directly on the fact that *pro* can satisfy the EPP feature in Spec,SubjP; when this happens, topics can be simple-preposed to the TopicPs of the left periphery, skipping Spec,SubjP. When the EPP feature has been satisfied by a moved operator, V4 and V5 word orders are derived through a bi-clausal analysis, as proposed by Ott (2011b).

Needless to say, many questions remain unsolved. For instance, why LDs (bi-clausal structures) are not fully ruled out in main declarative clauses, counter to the predictions of my theory. In Chapter 6, I try to account for the presence of LDs in main declarative clauses where EPP is satisfied by *pro* by assuming that they are innovative traits of the Mòcheno grammar, but more work is needed to support this claim. Another aspect which needs to be investigated in more detail is the derivation of the hanging-topic construction, in particular when HTs appear with LDs in wh-main interrogative clauses. We need to understand whether HTs are part of the higher clause or of an independent one. The syntax of object clitics and object pronouns in general is an area which has not even been touched upon in this book. Finally, as mentioned above, the exact nature of the lowest FPs of CP, those constituting FinP, also need to be better understood, particularly their link with the V2 rule.

Despite the several remaining issues, I think that the approach to syntactic variation adopted in this book has allowed the provision of convincing answers to crucial questions on language variation and has contributed to our understanding of the V2 phenomenon, in general, and of the various types of V2 languages, in particular. It has to be hoped that the promising results of this study can be developed and extended in future research on a wider set of languages.

References

Aboch, Enoch Oladé. 2004. *The Morphosyntax of Complement-Head Sequences. Clause Structure and Word Order Patterns in Kwa*. Oxford: OUP.

Aboch, Enoch Oladé & Pfau, Roland. 2011. What-s a wh-word got to do with it? In *Mapping the Left Periphery. The Cartography of Syntactic Structures*, Vol. 5, Paola Benincà & Nicola Munaro (eds), 91–124. Oxford: OUP.

Abraham, Werner. 1992. Text-grammatical considerations for German. Or: Theme – rheme constituency in German and the question of configurationality. *Milwaukee Studies on Language (MISL)* 6: 1–28.

Abraham, Werner. 2010. Spoken syntax in Cimbrian of the linguistic islands in Northern Italy – and what they (do not) betray about language universals and change under areal contact with Italo-Romance. In *Studies on German-Language Islands* [Studies in Language Companion Series 123], Michael T. Putnam (ed.), 233–278. Amsterdam: John Benjamins.

Abraham,Werner. 2012. Das Oberdeutschdifferential: Bairisch/österreichisch-(hoch-)alemannische Hauptunterschiede – zum methodischen Status der Mikrolinguistik. Handout for the *Syntax des Bairischen workshop*, Frankfurt, 29–30 June.

Abraham, Werner & Cornadie, Jac. 2001. *Präteritumschwund und Diskursgrammatik. Präteritumschwund in gesamteuropäischen Bezügen: Areale Ausbreitung, heterogene Entstehung, Parsing sowie diskursgrammatische Grundlagen und Zusammenhänge*. Amsterdam: John Benjamins.

Adams, Marianne. 1987. Old French, Null Subjects and Verb Second Phenomena. PhD dissertation, UCLA.

Alber, Birgit. 2010. Past participles in Mòcheno: Allomorphy and alignment. In *Studies on German-Language Islands* [Studies in Language Companion Series 123], Michael T. Putnam (ed.), 33–63. Amsterdam: John Benjamins.

Altmann, Hans. 1981. *Formen der Herausstellung im Deutschen: Rechtsversetzung, Linksversetzung, freies Thema und verwandte Konstruktionen*. Tübingen: Niemeyer.

Antinucci, Francesco & Cinque, Guglielmo. 1977. Sull'ordine delle parole in italiano: l'emarginazione. *Studi di Grammatica Italiana* 6: 121–146.

Axel, Karin. 2007. *Studies on Old High German Syntax. Left Sentence Periphery, Verb Placement and Verb Second* [Linguistik Aktuell/Linguistics Today 112]. Amsterdam: John Benjamins.

Axel, Karin & Weiß, Helmut. 2011. Pro-drop in the history of German. From Old High German to the modern dialects. In *Null Pronouns*, Peter Gallmann & Melani Wratil (eds), 21–52. Berlin: Mouton de Gruyter.

Baker, Mark. 1985. The mirror principle and morphosyntactic explanation. *Linguistic Inquiry* 16: 373–415.

Battisti, Carlo. 1925. Appunti toponomastici ed onomastici sull'oasi tedesca dei mòcheni (Alto perginese, Trentino). Venezia: Reale Deputazione, Estratto da *Archivio veneto-tridentino*.

Bauer, Ingeborg. 1962. Sprachliche Monographie der Fersentaler Deutschen Gemeinden im Trentino. PhD dissertation, University of Innsbruck.

Barbosa, Pilar. 1995. Null Subjects. PhD dissertation. MIT.

Bayer, Josef. 1984. COMP in Bavarian. *The Linguistic Review* 3: 209–274.

Bayer, Josef. 1990. Notes on the ECP in English and German. *Groninger Arbeiten zur germanischen Linguistik* 30: 1–55.

Bayer, Josef. 2004. Decomposing the left periphery. Dialectal and crosslinguistic evidence. In *The Syntax and Semantics of the Left Periphery*, Horst Lohnstein & Susanne Trissler (eds), 59–95. Berlin: Mouton de Gruyter.

Belletti, Adriana. 1990. *Generalized Verb Movement*. Turin: Rosenberg and Sellier.

Belletti, Adriana. 2001. Inversion as focalization. In *Inversion in Romance and the Theory of Universal Grammar*, Aafke Hulk & Jean-Yves Pollock (eds), 60–90. Oxford: OUP.

Belletti, Adriana. 2004. Aspects of the low IP area. In *The Structure of CP and IP. The Cartography of Syntactic Structure*, Vol. 2, Luigi Rizzi (ed.), 16–51. Oxford: OUP.

Belletti, Adriana. 2006. Extended doubling and the VP periphery. *Probus* 17: 1–35.

Benincà, Paola. 1984. Un'ipotesi sulla sintassi delle lingue romanze medievali. *Quaderni Patavini di Linguistica* 4: 3–19. Reprinted in Benincà, Paola. 1994. *La Variazione Sintattica*, 177–194. Bologna: Il Mulino.

Benincà, Paola. 1988. Costruzioni con ordini marcati degli elementi. In *Grande Grammatica Italiana di Consultazione*, Vol. 1, Lorenzo Renzi (ed.), 115–195 (pp. 119–129 in collaboration with Giampaolo Salvi). Bologna: Il Mulino.

Benincà, Paola. 1994. L'interferenza sintattica: di un aspetto della sintassi ladina considerato di origine tedesca. In *La variazione sintattica*, Paola Benincà, 89–103. Bologna: Il Mulino.

Benincà, Paola. 1995. Complement clitics in medieval Romance: The Tobler-Mussafia law. In *Clause Structure and Language Change*, Adrian Battye & Ian Roberts (eds), 325–344. Oxford: OUP.

Benincà, Paola. 1996. La struttura della frase esclamativa alla luce del dialetto padovano. In *Italiano e dialetti nel tempo. Saggi di grammatica per Giulio C. Lepschy*, Paola Benincà, Guglielmo Cinque, Tullio De Mauro & Nigel Vincent (eds), 23–42. Roma: Bulzoni.

Benincà, Paola. 2001. The position of Topic and Focus in the left periphery. In *Current Studies in Italian Syntax: Essays Offered to Lorenzo Renzi*, Guglielmo Cinque & Giampaolo Salvi (eds), 39–64. Amsterdam: Elsevier.

Benincà, Paola. 2006. A detailed map of the left periphery of Medieval Romance. In *Crosslinguistic Research in Syntax and Semantics. Negation, Tense and Clausal Architecture*, Raffaella Zanuttini, Hector Campos, Elena Herburger & Paul Portner (eds), 53–86. Washington DC: Georgetown University Press.

Benincà, Paola & Cinque, Guglielmo. 1993. Su alcune differenze fra enclisi e proclisi. In *Omaggio a Gianfranco Folena*, 2313–2326. Padova: Programma.

Benincà, Paola & Poletto, Cecilia. 2004. Topic, Focus and V2: Defining the CP sublayers. In *The Structure of CP and IP. The Cartography of Syntactic Structures*, Vol. 2, Luigi Rizzi (ed.), 52–75. Oxford: OUP.

Bennis, Hans & Haegeman, Liliane. 1984. On the status of agreement and relative clauses in West-Flemish. In *Sentential Complementation*, Wim de Geest & Yvon Putseys (eds), 33–55. Dordrecht: Foris.

Bentzen, Kristine & Hrafnbjargarson, Gunnan Hrafn, Hróarsdóttir, Thorbjörg & Wiklund, Anna-Lena. 2007. The Tromsø guide to the Force behind V2. *Working Papers in Scandinavian Syntax* 79: 93–118.

Berruto, Gaetano. 1995. *Fondamenti di Sociolinguistica*. Bari: Laterza.
den Besten, Hans. 1983. On the interaction of root transformations and lexical delective rules. In *On Formal Syntax of the Westgermania* [Linguistik Aktuell/Linguistics Today 3], Werner Abraham (ed.), 47–131. Amsterdam: John Benjamins.
Biberauer, Theresa (ed.). 2008. *The Limits of Syntactic Variation* [Linguistik Aktuell/Linguistics Today 132]. Amsterdam: John Benjamins.
Biberauer, Theresa. 2010. Semi null-subject languages, expletives and expletive *pro* reconsidered. In *Parametric Variation: Null Subjects in Minimalist Theory*, Theresa Biberauer, Anders Holmberg, Ian Roberts & Michelle Sheehan (eds), 153–199. Cambridge: CUP.
Biberauer, Theresa, Holmberg, Anders, Roberts, Ian & Sheehan, Michelle. 2010. *Parametric Variation: Null Subjects in Minimalist Theory*. Cambridge: CUP.
Biberauer, Theresa & Richards, Marc. 2006. True optionality: When the grammar doesn't mind. In *Minimalist Essays* [Linguistik Aktuell/Linguistics Today 91], Cedric Boeckx (ed.), 35–67. Amsterdam: John Benjamins.
Biberauer, Theresa & Roberts, Ian. 2006. Loss of residual head final orders and remnant fronting in Late Middle English: Causes and consequences. In *Comparative Studies in Germanic Syntax* [Linguistik Aktuell/Linguistics Today 97], Jutta M. Haartmann & László Molnarfi (eds), 263–297. Amsterdam: John Benjamins.
Bidese, Ermenegildo. 2008. *Die Diachronische Syntax des Zimbrischen*. Tübingen: Gunter Narr.
Bidese, Ermenegildo & Tomaselli, Alessandra. 2005. Formen der "Herausstellung" und Verlust der V2-Restriktion im Zimbrischen. In Das *Zimbrische zwischen Germanisch und Romanisch*, Ermenegildo Bidese, John Down & Thomas Stolz (eds), 71–92. Bochum: Brockmeyer.
Bocci, Giuliano. 2007. Criterial positions and left periphery in Italian. *Nanzan Linguistics* (Special issue) 3: 35–70.
Borer, Hagit. 1989. Anaphoric AGR. In *The Null Subject Parameter*, Osvaldo Jaeggli & Ken Safir (eds), 69–110. Dordrecht: Kluwer.
Brandi, Luciana & Cordin, Patrizia. 1981. Dialetti e italiano: Un confronto sul parametro del soggetto nullo. *Rivista di Grammatica Generativa* 6: 33–88.
Brandi, Luciana & Cordin, Patrizia. 1989. Two Italian dialects and the null subject parameter. In *The Null Subject Parameter*, Osvaldo Jaeggli & Ken Safir (eds), 111–142. Dordrecht: Kluwer.
Brandner, Ellen. 2004. Head-movement in minimalism and V2 as Forcemarking. In *The Syntax and Semantics of the Left Periphery*, Horst Lohnstein & Susanne Trissler (eds), 97–138. Berlin: Mouton de Gruyter.
Branigan, Philip. 1996. Verb second and the A bar Status of Subjects. *Studia Linguistica* 50: 50–79.
Brody, Michael. 2000. Mirror theory. *Linguistic Inquiry* 31: 29–56.
Cabredo Hofherr, Patricia. 2006. Arbitrary pro and the theory of pro-drop. In *Agreement and Arguments*, Peter Ackema, Patrick Brandt, Maaike Schoorlemmer & Fred Weerman (eds), 230–258. Oxford: OUP.
Calabrese, Andrea. 1982. Alcune ipotesi sulla struttura informazionale della frase in italiano e sul suo rapporto con la struttura fonologica. *Rivista di Grammatica Generativa* 5: 65–115.
Cardinaletti, Anna. 1990. *Impersonal Constructions and Sentential Arguments in German*. Padova: Unipress.
Cardinaletti, Anna. 1997. Subjects and clause structure. In *The New Comparative Syntax*, Liliane Haegeman (ed.), 56–95. London: Longman.

Cardinaletti, Anna. 2002. Against optional and zero clitics. Right dislocation versus marginalization. *Studia Linguistica* 56: 29–57.
Cardinaletti, Anna. 2004. Towards a cartography of subject positions. In *The Structure of CP and IP. The Cartography of Syntactic Structure*, Vol. 2, Luigi Rizzi (ed.), 115–165. Oxford: OUP.
Cardinaletti, Anna & Giusti, Giuliana. 1996. *Problemi di sintassi tedesca*. Padova: Unipress.
Cardinaletti, Anna & Roberts, Ian. 2002. Clause structure and X-second. In *Functional Structure in DP and IP. The Cartography of Syntactic Structure*, Vol. 1, Guglielmo Cinque (ed.), 123–166. Oxford: OUP.
Cardinaletti, Anna & Starke, Michal. 1999. The typology of structural deficiency: A case study of three classes of pronouns. In *Clitics in the Languages of Europe. Empirical Approaches to Language Typology*, Henk van Riemsdijk (ed.), 145–233. Berlin: Mouton de Gruyter.
Carstens, Vicky. 2003. Rethinking complementizer agreement: Agree with a case-checked goal. *Linguistic Inquiry* 34: 393–412.
Cecchetto, Carlo. 1999. A comparative analysis of left and right dislocation in Romance. *Studia Linguistica* 53: 40–67.
Cecchetto, Carlo. 2000. Doubling structures and reconstruction. *Probus* 12: 93–126.
Chafe, Wallace. 1987. Cognitive constrains on information flow. In *Coherence and Grounding in Discourse* [Typological Studies in Language 11], Russell Tomlin (ed.), 21–51. Amsterdam: John Benjamins.
Chomsky, Noam. 1977. On wh-movement. In *Formal Syntax*, Paul W. Culicover, Thomas Wasow & Adrian Akmaljian (eds), 71–132. New York NY: Academic Press.
Chomsky, Noam. 1995. *The Minimalist Program*. Cambridge MA: The MIT Press.
Chomsky, Noam. 2001. Derivation by phase. In *Ken Hale: A Life in Language*, Michael Kenstowicz (ed.), 1–52. Cambridge MA: The MIT Press.
Cinque, Guglielmo. 1977. The movement nature of left dislocation. *Linguistic Inquiry* 8: 397–423.
Cinque, Guglielmo. 1990. *Types of A'-dependencies*. Cambridge MA: The MIT Press.
Cinque, Guglielmo. 1999. *Adverbs and Functional Heads*. Oxford: OUP.
Cinque, Guglielmo. 2010. *The Syntax of Adjectives. A Comparative Study*. Cambridge MA: The MIT Press.
Cognola, Federica. 2006. Costruzioni infinitivali e fenomeni di trasparenza in varietà standard e dialettali tedesche, con particolare riguardo al dialetto della Valle del Fersina. MA thesis, University of Padua.
Cognola, Federica. 2008. OV/VO word orders in Mocheno main declarative clauses. In *Selected Proceedings of the XXXIV Incontro di Grammatica Generativa*, Paola Benincà, Federico Damonte & Nicoletta Penello (eds), 83–97. Padova: Unipress.
Cognola, Federica. 2009. Dinamiche del contatto germanico-romanzo: La ristrutturazione nel dialetto tedesco della valle del Fersina. In *Alloglossie e comunità alloglotte nell'Italia contemporanea*, Paolo Consani, Paola Desideri, Francesca Guazzelli & Carmela Perta (eds), 65–79. Roma: Bulzoni.
Cognola, Federica. 2010. Word Order and Clause Structure in a German Dialect of Northern Italy: On the Interaction between High and Low Left Periphery. PhD dissertation, University of Padua.
Cognola, Federica. 2011a. *Acquisizione plurilingue e bilinguismo sbilanciato: Uno studio sulla sintassi dei bambini mocheni in età prescolare*. Padova: Unipress.

Cognola, Federica. 2011b. Alcune considerazioni per un'analisi unitaria del prefisso ge- del tedesco. In *I Preverbi: Tra sintassi e diacronia*, Davide Bertocci & Elena Triantafillis (eds), 35–65. Padova: Unipress.

Cognola, Federica. 2012. The mixed OV/VO syntax of Mòcheno main clauses: On the interaction between high and low left periphery. To appear in *Theoretical Approaches to Disharmonic Word Orders*, Theresa Biberauer & Michelle Sheehan (eds). Oxford: OUP.

Contreras, Heles. 1991. On the position of subjects. In *Perspectives on Phrase Structure: Heads and Licensing*, Susan D. Rothstein (ed.), 63–79. New York NY: Academic Press.

van Craenenbroeck, Jeroen & Haegeman, Liliane. 2007. The derivation of subject-initial V2. *Linguistic Inquiry* 38: 167–178.

Cruschina, Silvio. 2006. Informational focus and in Sicilian and the left periphery. In *Phases of Interpretation* [Studies in Generative Grammar 91], Mara Frascarelli (ed.), 363–385. Berlin: Mouton de Gruyter.

Cruschina, Silvio. 2010. Syntactic extraposition and clitic resumption in Italian. *Lingua* 120: 50–73.

De Crousaz, Isabelle & Shlonsky, Ur. 2003. The distribution of a subject clitic pronoun in a Franco-Provençal dialect and the licensing of pro. *Linguistic Inquiry* 34: 413–442.

Diesing, Molly. 1992. *Indefinites*. Cambridge MA: The MIT Press.

Diesing, Molly. 1997. Yiddish VP order and the typology of object movement in Germanic. *Natural Language and Linguistic Theory* 15: 369–427.

Featherston, Sam. 2005. That-trace effects in German. *Lingua* 115: 1277–1302.

Figueiredo Silva, Maria. 2000. Main and embedded null subjects in Brazilian Portuguese. In *Brazilian Portuguese and the Null Subject Parameter*, Mary Kato & Esmeralda Negroão (eds), 127–146. Frankfurt: Vervuert-Ibero Americana.

Fischer, Susann. 2002. *The Catalan Clitic System: A Diachronic Perspective on its Syntax and Phonology*. Berlin: Mouton de Gruyter.

Fontana, Joseph. 1993. Phrase Structure and the Syntax of Clitics in the History of Spanish. PhD dissertation, University of Pennsylvania, Philadelphia.

Franco, Irene. 2009. Verb, Subjects and Stylistic Fronting. A Comparative Analysis of the Interaction of CP Properties with Verb Movement and Subject Positions in Icelandic and Old Romance. PhD dissertation, University of Siena.

Frascarelli, Mara. 2000. *The Syntax-Phonology Interface in Topic and Focus Constructions in Italian*. Dordrecht: Kluwer.

Frascarelli, Mara. 2004. Dislocation, clitic resumption and minimality: A comparative analysis of left and right topic constructions in Italian. In *Romance Languages and Linguistic Theory 2002* [Current Issues in Linguistic Theory 256], Reineke Bok-Bennema, Bart Hollebrandse, Brigitte Kampers-Manhe & Petra Sleeman (eds), 99–118. Amsterdam: John Benjamins.

Frascarelli, Mara & Hinterhölzl, Roland. 2007. Types of topics in German and Italian. In *On Information Structure. Meaning and Form* [Linguistik Aktuell/Linguistics Today 100], Kerstin Schwabe & Susanne Winkler (eds), 87–116. Amsterdam: John Benjamins.

Frey, Werner. 2004a. A medial topic position for German. *Linguistische Berichte* 198: 153–190.

Frey, Werner. 2004b. Notes on the syntax and the pragmatics of German left-dislocation. In *The Syntax and Semantics of the Left Periphery*, Horst Lohnstein & Susanne Trissler (eds), 203–233. Berlin: Mouton de Gruyter.

Frey, Werner & Pittner, Karin. 1999. Adverbialpositionen im deutschenglischen Vergleich. In *Sprachspezifische Aspekte der Informationsverteilung*, Monika Doherty (ed.), 14–41. Berlin: Akademie-Verlag.

Friedmann, Naama, Belletti, Adriana & Rizzi, Luigi. 2009. Relativized relatives: Types of intervention in the acquisition of A-bar dependencies. *Lingua* 119: 67–88.
Fuß, Eric. 2008. Word Order and Language Change. On the Interface between Syntax and Morphology. Habilitationsschrift, University of Frankfurt am Main.
Garraffa, Maria & Grillo, Nino. 2008. Canonicity effects as grammatical phenomena. *Journal of Neurolinguistics* 21: 177–197.
Garzonio, Jacopo. 2004. Interrogative types and the left periphery: Some data from the Fiorentino dialect. In *Quaderni di lavoro dell'ASIS*, Barbara Patruno & Chiara Polo (eds). <www.maldura.unipd.it/ddlcs>
Gerola, Berengario. 1929. *Ricerche sull'antica oasi tedesca di Pinè*. Trento: Scottoni.
Gilligan, Gary. 1987. A Cross-linguistic Approach to the Pro-Drop Parameter. PhD dissertation, University of Southern California.
Giusti, Giuliana. 2006. Parallels in clausal and nominal periphery. In *Phases of Interpretation*, Mara Frascarelli (ed.), 163–184. Berlin: Mouton de Gruyter.
Grewendorf, Günther. 1988. *Aspekte der deutschen Syntax*. Tübingen: Narr.
Grewendorf, Günther. 2005. The discourse configurationality of scrambling. In *The Free Word Order Phenomenon*, Joachim Sabel & Mamoru Saito (eds), 75–135. Berlin: Mouton de Gruyter.
Grewendorf, Günther. 2008. The left clausal periphery: Clitic left-dislocation in Italian and left-dislocation in German. In *Dislocated Elements in Discourse: Syntactic, Semantic, and Pragmatic Perspectives*, Benjamin Shaer, Philippa Cook, Werner Frey & Claudia Mainborn (eds), 49–94. London: Routledge.
Grewendorf, Günther & Poletto, Cecilia. 2010. Hidden verb second: The case of Cimbrian. In *Studies on German-Language Islands* [Studies in Language Companion Series 123], Michael Putnam (ed.), 301–346. Amsterdam: John Benjamins.
Grillo, Nino. 2009. Generalized minimality: Feature impoverishment and comprehension deficits in agrammatism. *Lingua* 119: 1426–1443.
Gruber, Bettina. 2008. Complementiser Agreement. New Evidence from the Upper Austrian Variant of Gmunden. MA thesis, University of Vienna.
Guasti, Maria Teresa, Branchini, Chiara & Arosio, Fabrizio. 2009. Agreement in the production of Italian subject and object wh-questions. In *Proceedings of the XXXV Incontro di Grammatica Generativa*, Vincenzo Moscati & Emiliano Servidio (eds), 104–117. MIT Working papers.
Guidolin, Silvia. 2011. The Split-CP hypothesis applied to Germanic languages. *Quaderni Patavini di Linguistica*. Padova: Unipress.
Haegeman, Liliane. 1990. Subject pronouns and subject clitics in West Flemish. *The Linguistic Review* 7: 333–363.
Haegeman, Liliane. 1992. *Theory and Description in Generative Syntax: A Case Study in West Flemish*. Cambridge: CUP.
Haegeman, Liliane. 1997. Verb second, the split CP and null subjects in early Dutch finite clauses. *GenGenP* 4(2): 133–175.
Haegeman, Liliane. 2000. Remnant movement and OV order. In *The Derivation of VO and OV* [Linguistik Aktuel/Linguistics Today 31], Peter Svenonius (ed.), 69–96. Amsterdam: John Benjamins.
Haider, Hubert. 1983. Connectedness effects in German. *Groninger Arbeiten zur Germanistischen Linguistik* 23: 82–119.

Haider, Hubert. 1986. V-second in German. In *Verb Second Phenomena in Germanic Languages*, Hubert Haider & Martin Prinzhorn (eds), 49–75. Dordrecht: Foris.
Haider, Hubert. 1993. *Deutsche Syntax – Generativ*. Tübingen: Narr.
Haider, Hubert. 2010a. *The Syntax of German*. Cambridge: CUP.
Haider, Hubert. 2010b. Wie wurde Deutsch OV? Ms, University of Salzburg.
Haider, Hubert & Prinzhorn, Martin (eds). 1986. *Verb Second Phenomena in Germanic Languages*. Dordrecht: Foris.
Heller, Katrin. 1979. Alcuni problemi linguistici del dialetto dei Mòcheni sulla base di testi dialettali. In *La Valle del Fersina e le isole linguistiche tedesche del Trentino. Atti del convegno di S. Orsola, 1–3 Settembre 1978*, Giovan Battista Pellegrini (ed.), 113–120. San Michele all'Adige: Pubblicazioni del museo degli usi e costumi della gente trentina.
Heycock, Caroline. 2006. Embedded root phenomena. In *The Blackwell Companion to Syntax*, Vol. II, Martin Everaert & Henk van Riemsdijk (eds), 174–209. Malden MA: Blackwell.
Hinterhölzl, Roland. 2000. Movement and stranding in Germanic OV languages. In *The Derivation of VO and OV* [Linguistik Aktuel/Linguistics Today 31], Peter Svenonius (ed.), 293–326. Amsterdam: John Benjamins.
Hinterhölzl, Roland. 2006. *Scrambling, Remnant Movement, and Restructuring in West Germanic*. Oxford: OUP.
Hinterhölzl, Roland. 2009. The role of information structure in word order variation and word order change. In *New Approaches to Word Order Variation in Germanic*, Roland Hinterhölzl & Svetlana Petrova (eds), 45–66. Berlin: Mouton de Gruyter.
Hirschbühler, Paul & Junker, Marie-Odile. 1988. Remarques sur les sujets nuls en subordonnées en ancien et en moyen francais. *Revue Québécoise de Linquistique Théorique et Appliquée* 7(3): 63–84.
Holmberg, Anders. 1986. Word Order and Syntactic Features in the Scandinavian Languages. PhD dissertation, University of Stockholm.
Holmberg, Anders. 1991. The distribution of Scandinavian weak pronouns. In *Clitics and their Hosts* [EurotypWorking Papers], Henk van Riemsdijk & Luigi Rizzi (eds), 155–174. Strasbourg: European Science Foundation.
Holmberg, Anders. 2005. Is there a little pro? Evidence from Finnish. *Linguistic Inquiry* 36: 533–564.
Holmberg, Anders. 2012. Verb second. To appear in *Syntax. An International Handbook of Contemporary Syntactic Research*, 2nd edn [HSK Series], Tibor Kiss & Artemis Alexiadou (eds). Berlin: Walter de Gruyter.
Holmberg, Anders & Platzack, Christer. 1995. *The Role of Inflection in Scandinavian Syntax*. Oxford: OUP.
Holmberg, Anders & Roberts, Ian. 2010. Introduction. In *Parametric Variation: Null Subjects in Minimalist Theory*, Theresa Biberauer, Anders Holmberg, Ian Roberts & Michelle Sheehan (eds), 1–57. Cambridge: CUP.
Holmberg, Anders & Sheehan, Michelle. 2010. Control into finite clauses in partial null-subject languages. In *Parametric Variation: Null Subjects in Minimalist Theory*, Theresa Biberauer, Anders Holmberg, Ian Roberts & Michelle Sheehan (eds), 125–152. Cambridge: CUP.
Hornung, Maria. 1979. La particolare posizione del dialetto tedesco della Valle del Fèrsina nel quadro delle isole linguistiche tedesche dell'Italia settentrionale. In *La Valle del Fersina e le isole linguistiche tedesche del Trentino. Atti del Convegno di S. Orsola, 1–3 settembre 1978*, Giovan Battista Pellegrini (ed.), 25–31. San Michele all'Adige: Pubblicazioni del Museo degli usi e costumi della gente trentina.

Huang, James. 1984. On the distribution and reference of empty pronouns. *Linguistic Inquiry* 15: 531–574.

Jaeggli, Osvaldo. 1982. *Topics in Romance Syntax*. Dordrecht: Foris.

Jayaseelan, Karattuparambil. 2001. IP-internal Topic and Focus phrases. *Studia Linguistica* 55(1): 39–75.

Jouitteau, Mélanie. 2010. Introduction. In *A Typology of V2 with Regard to V1 and V2 Phenomena*, Mélanie Jouitteau (ed.), 197–209. Special Issue of *Lingua* 120(2): 197–209.

Julien, Marit. 2002. *Syntactic Heads and Word Formation*. Oxford: OUP.

Kayne, Richard S. 1975. *French Syntax*. Cambridge MA: The MIT Press.

Kayne, Richard S. 1983. Connectedness. *Linguistic Inquiry* 14: 223–249. Reprinted in 1984 in *Connectedness and Binary Branching*. Dordrecht: Foris.

Kayne, Richard S. 1994. *The Antisymmetry of Syntax*. Cambridge MA: The MIT Press.

Kayne, Richard S. 1998. Overt vs. covert movement. *Syntax* 1: 128–191.

Kolmer, Agnes. 2005. Subjektklitika als Kongruenzmarkierer: Ein Vergleich zwischen bairischen und alemannischen Sprachinseldialekten in Norditalien (Zimbrisch und Walserdeutsch). In *Das Zimbrische zwischen Germanisch und Romanisch*, Ermenegildo Bidese, John Down & Thomas Stolz (eds), 164–189. Bochum: Brockmeyer.

Koeneman, Olaf & Zeijstra, Edde. 2012. One law for the rich and another for the poor: The Rich Agreement Hypothesis rehabilitated. Ms, University of Amsterdam. <http://ling.auf.net/lingBuzz/001462>

Koopman, Hilda. 1984. *The Syntax of Verbs: From Verb Movement Rules in the Kru Language to Universal Grammar*. Dordrecht: Foris.

Koopman, Hilda & Sportiche, Dominique. 1991. The position of subjects. *Lingua* 85: 211–258.

van Koppen, Marjo. 2005. One Probe – two Goals: Aspects of Agreement in Dutch Dialects. PhD dissertation, Leiden University.

Koster, Jan. 1994. Predicate incorporation and the word order of Dutch. In *Paths towards Universal Grammar: Studies in Honor of Richard S. Kayne*, Guglielmo Cinque, Jan Koster, JeanYves Pollock, Luigi Rizzi & Raffaella Zanuttini (eds), 255–276. Washington DC: Georgetown University Press.

Kranzmayer, Eberhard. 1956. *Historische Lautgeographie des gesamtbairischen Dialektraumes*. Wien: Verlag Böhlau.

Kratzer, Angelika. 1989. Stage-level and individual-level predicates. In *The Generic Book*, Gregory N. Carlson & Francis Jeffry Pelletier (eds), 125–175. Chicago IL: University of Chicago Press.

Kroch, Anthony. 1989. Reflexes of grammar in patterns of language change. *Language Variation and Change* 1: 199–244.

Kroch, Anthony & Taylor, Ann. 2000. Verb-object order in early Middle English. In *Diachronic Syntax: Models and Mechanisms*, Susan Pintzuk, George Tsoulas & Anthony Warner (eds), 132–163. Oxford: OUP.

Labov, William. 1966. *The Social Stratification of English New York City*. Washington DC: CAL.

Labov, William. 1972. *Sociolinguistic Patterns*. Philadelphia PA: University of Philadelphia.

Labov, William. 2001. *Principles of Linguistic Change*. Oxford: Blackwell.

Lenerz, Jürgen. 1985. Diachronic syntax: Verb position and COMP in German. In *Studies in German Grammar*, Jindrich Toman (ed.), 103–132. Dordrecht: Foris.

Leu, Thomas. 2008. The Internal Syntax of Determiners. PhD dissertation, University of New York.

Leu, Thomas. 2010. Generalized x-to-C in Germanic. Handout EGG summer school. <http://egg.auf.net/>
Lohnstein, Horst. 2000. *Satzmoduskompositionell. Zur Parametrisierung der Modusphrase im Deutschen*. Berlin: Akademie Verlag.
Lohnstein, Horst & Bredel, Ursula. 2004. Inflectional morphology and sentence mood in German. In *The Syntax and Semantics of the Left Periphery*, Horst Lohnstein & Susanne Trissler (eds), 235–264. Berlin: Mouton de Gruyter.
Lohndal, Terje. 2009. That-t in Scandinavian and elsewhere: Variation in the position of C. *Studia Linguistica* 63: 204–232.
Longobardi, Giuseppe. 1994. La posizione del verbo gotico e la sintassi comparata dei complementatori germanici: Alcune riflessioni preliminari. In *Miscellanea di studi linguistici in onore di Walter Belardi*, Palmira Cipriani, Paolo Di Giovine & Marco Mancini (eds), 353–373. Roma: Il Calamo.
Lopez, Luis. 2009. *A Derivational Syntax for Information Structure*. Oxford: OUP.
Lutz, Uli. 1996. Some notes on extraction theory. In *On Extraction and Extraposition in German* [Linguistik Aktuell/Linguistics Today 11], Uli Lutz & Jürgen Pafel (eds), 1–44. Amsterdam: John Benjamins.
Merchant, Jason. 2001. *The Syntax of Silence. Sluicing, Islands and the Theory of Ellipsis*. Oxford: OUP.
Munaro, Nicola. 1997. *Proprietà strutturali e distribuzionali dei sintagmi interrogativi in alcuni dialetti Italiani settentrionali*. Padova: Unipress.
Munaro, Nicola. 2010. La frase interrogativa. In *Grande grammatica dell'italiano antico*, Lorenzo Renzi (ed.), 1147–1185. Bologna: Il Mulino.
Müller, Gereon. 2004. Verb-second as vP-first. *Journal of Comparative Germanic Linguistics* 7: 179–234.
Nicolis, Marco. 2008. The null subject parameter and correlating properties: The case of creole languages. In *The Limits of Syntactic Variation* [Linguistik Aktuell/Linguistics Today 132], Theresa Biberauer (ed.), 271–294. Amsterdam: John Benjamins.
Nilsen, Øystein. 2003. Eliminating Positions. PhD dissertation, University of Utrecht.
Obenauer, Hans Georg. 1994. Aspects de la syntaxe A-barre. Effects de intervention et mouvements des quantifieurs. Thèse d'Etat, Université de Paris VII.
Obenauer, Hans Georg. 2004. Non standard wh-questions and alternative checkers in Pagotto. In *The Left Periphery of Germanic Languages*, Horst Lohnstein & Susanne Trissler (eds), 343–384. Berlin: Mouton de Gruyter.
Ott, Dennis. 2011a. Local Instability: The Syntax of Split Topics. PhD dissertation, Harvard University. <http://ling.auf.net/lingBuzz/001255>
Ott, Dennis. 2011b. An ellipsis approach to constrastive left dislocation. Ms, University of Groningen. <http://ling.auf.net/lingBuzz/001415>
Padovan, Andrea. 2011. Il progetto CimbroLang. Ms, University of Trento.
Perlmutter, David. 1971. *Deep and Surface Structure Constraints in Syntax*. New York NY: Holt, Rinehart & Winston.
Pesetzky, David. 1987. Wh-in-situ: Movement and unselective binding. In *The Linguistic Representation of (In)definiteness*, Eric J. Reuland & Alice ter Meulen, 98–129. Cambridge MA: The MIT Press.
Piatti, Salvatore. 1996. *Palù/Palae. Frammenti di storia*. Palù del Fersina: Pubblicazioni dell'Istituto Mòcheno.

Pintzuk, Susan. 1999. *Phrase Structures in Competition: Variation and Change in Old English Word Order*. New York NY: Garland.

Pintzuk, Susan, Tsoulas, George & Warner, Anthony (eds). 2001. *Diachronic Syntax: Models and Mechanisms*. Oxford: OUP.

Pittner, Karin. 1999. *Adverbiale im Deutschen. Untersuchungen zu ihrer Stellung und Interpretation*. Tübingen: Stauffenburg.

Platzack, Christer. 1986. The position of the finite verb in Swedish. In *Verb Second Phenomena in Germanic Languages,* Hubert Haider & Martin Prinzhorn (eds), 27–47. Dordrecht: Foris.

Platzack, Christer. 1987. The Scandinavian languages and the null-subject parameter. *Natural Language and Linguistic Theory* 5: 377–401.

Poletto, Cecilia. 1993. Subject clitic verb inversion in Northern Eastern Italian dialects. In *Syntactic Theory and the Dialects of Italy*, Adriana Belletti (ed.), 204–251. Turin: Rosenberg & Sellier.

Poletto, Cecilia. 1995. The diachronic development of subject clitics in North Eastern Italian dialects. In *Clause Structure and Language Change*, Adrian Battye & Ian Roberts (eds), 295–324. Oxford: OUP.

Poletto, Cecilia. 2000. *The Higher Functional Field. Evidence from North Italian Dialects*. Oxford: OUP.

Poletto, Cecilia. 2002. The left periphery of a V2-Rhaetoromance dialect: A new perspective on V2 and V3. In *Syntactic Microvariation. Proceedings of the Workshop on Syntactic Microvariation, Amsterdam, August 2000*, Sjef Barbiers, Leonie Cornips & Susanne van der Kleij (eds), 214–242. Amsterdam: Meertens Institute. <http://www.mertens.knaw.nl/books/synmic/pdf/poletto.pdf>

Poletto, Cecilia. 2006. Parallel phases: A study of the high and low left periphery of Old Italian. In *Phases of Interpretation* [Studies in Generative Grammar 91], Mara Frascarelli (ed.), 261–294. Berlin: Mouton de Gruyter.

Poletto, Cecilia. 2008. Doubling as a spare movement strategy. In *Microvariation in Syntactic Doubling*, Sjef Barbiers, Olaf Koeneman, Marika Lekakou & and Margreet van der Ham (eds), 38–68. Bingley: Emerald.

Poletto, Cecilia & Pollock, Jean-Yves. 2004. On the left periphery of some Romance wh-questions. In *The Structure of CP and IP. The Cartography of Syntactic Structures*, Vol. 2, Luigi Rizzi (ed.), 251–296. Oxford: OUP.

Poletto, Cecilia & Tomaselli, Alessandra. 1995. Verso una definizione di elemento clitico. In *Studi di grammatica tedesca e comparata*, Roberto Dolci & Giuliana Giusti (eds), 159–224. Venezia: La Tipografica.

Poletto, Cecilia & Tomaselli, Alessandra. 2002. La sintassi del soggetto nullo nelle isole tedescofone del Veneto: Cimbro e Sappadino a confronto. In *La dialettologia oltre il 2001. Atti del convegno di Sappada/Plodn (Belluno), 1–5 luglio 2001*, Gianna Marcato (ed.), 237–252. Padova: Unipress.

Poletto, Cecilia & Tomaselli, Alessandra. 2004. Le frasi interrogative in sappadino e altre varietà germaniche conservative. In *I dialetti e la Montagna. Atti del convegno di Sappada/Plodn (Belluno), 2–6 luglio 2003,* Gianna Marcato (ed.), 255–268. Padova: Unipress.

Poletto, Cecilia & Tomaselli, Alessandra. 2009. Die Syntax der Pronominalobjekte und die Form des Partizips. Konservative Merkmale in der Sprachgeschichte des Zimbrischen. In *Perspektiven Drei, Akten der 3. Tagung Deutsche Sprachwissenschaft in Italien (Rom, 14.–16.2.2008)*, Claudio di Meola (ed.), 263–274. Frankfurt: Peter Lang.

Pollock, Jean Yves. 1989. Verb movement, universal grammar, and the structure of IP. *Linguistic Inquiry* 20: 365–424.
Puskas, Genoveva. 2000. *Word Order in Hungarian. The Syntax of Ā-positions* [Linguistik Aktuell/Linguistics Today 33]. Amsterdam: John Benjamins.
Putnam, Michael T. 2010. Introduction. In *Studies on German-Language Islands* [Studies in Language Companion Series 123], Michael T. Putnam (ed.), 1–9. Amsterdam: John Benjamins.
Reinhart, Tanya. 1981. Pragmatics and linguistics: An analysis of sentence topics. *Philosophica* 27: 53–94.
Reis, Marga. 1985. Satzeinleitende Strukturen im Deutschen. Über COMP, Haupt- und Nebensätze, w-Bewegungen und die Doppelkopfanalyse. In *Erklärende Syntax des Deutschen*, Werner Abraham (ed.), 271–312. Tübingen: Narr.
Ribeiro, Ilza. 1995. Evidence for a verb-second phrase in Old Portuguese. In *Clause Structure and Language Change*, Adrian Battye & Ian Roberts (eds), 110–139. Oxford: OUP.
van Riemsdijk, Henk. 1997. Left-dislocation. In *Materials on Left-dislocation* [Linguistik Aktuell/Linguistics Today 14], Elena Anagnostopoulou, Henk van Riemsdijk & Frans Zwarts (eds), 110. Amsterdam: John Benjamins.
Rivero, María Luisa. 1986. Parameters in the typology of clitics in Romance and Old Spanish. *Language* 62: 774–807.
Rizzi, Luigi. 1982. *Issues in Italian Syntax*. Dordrecht: Foris.
Rizzi, Luigi. 1986. Null objects in Italian and the theory of pro. *Linguistic Inquiry* 17: 501–577.
Rizzi, Luigi. 1990. *Relativized Minimality*. Cambridge MA: The MIT Press.
Rizzi, Luigi. 1991. Residual verb second and the wh-criterion. *Geneva Generative Papers* 2. Reprinted in *Parameters and Functional Heads*, Adriana Belletti & Luigi Rizzi (eds), 63–90. Oxford: OUP.
Rizzi, Luigi. 1997. The fine structure of the left periphery. In *Elements of Grammar. A Handbook of Generative Syntax*, Liliane Haegeman (ed.), 281–337. Dordrecht: Kluwer.
Rizzi, Luigi. 2001. The position of Inter(rogative)P in the left periphery of the clause. In *Current Studies in Italian Syntax: Essays offered to Lorenzo Renzi*, Guglielmo Cinque & Giampaolo Salvi (eds), 287–296. Amsterdam: Elsevier.
Rizzi, Luigi. 2004. Locality and left periphery. In *Structures and Beyond. The Cartography of Syntactic Structure*, Vol. 3, Adriana Belletti (ed.), 223–251. Oxford: OUP.
Rizzi, Luigi. 2005. On some properties of subjects and topics. In *Contributions to the 30th Incontro di Grammatica Generative*, Laura Brugè, Giuliana Giusti, Nicola Munaro, Walter Schweikert & Giuseppina Turano, 203–224. Venezia: Libreria Editrice Cafoscarina.
Rizzi, Luigi. 2006. On the form of chains: Criterial positions and ECP effects. In *Wh-movement Moving On*, Lisa Cheng & Norbert Corver (eds), 97–134. Cambridge MA: The MIT Press.
Rizzi, Luigi & Ian, Roberts. 1989. Complex inversion in French. *Probus* 1: 1–30.
Rizzi, Luigi & Shlonsky, Ur. 2007. Strategies of subject extraction. In *Interfaces + Recursion = Language?*, Uli Sauerland & Hans Martin Gärtner (eds), 115–160. Berlin: Mouton de Gruyter.
Roberts, Ian. 1993. *Verbs and Diachronic Syntax: A Comparative History of English and French*. Dordrecht: Kluwer.
Roberts, Ian. 1996. Remarks on the Old English C-system and the diachrony of V2. In *Language Change and Generative Grammar*, Ellen Brandner & Gisella Ferraresi (eds), 154–167. *Linguistische Berichte*: Sonderheft 7.

Roberts, Ian. 1997. Directionality and word order change in the history of English. In *Parameters of Morphosyntactic Change*, Ans van Kemenade & Nigel Vincent (eds), 423–460. Cambridge: CUP.

Roberts, Ian. 2004. The C-System in Brythonic Celtic languages, V2 and the EPP. In *The Structure of CP and IP. The Cartography of Syntactic Structures*, Vol. 2, Luigi Rizzi (ed.), 297–328. Oxford: OUP.

Roberts, Ian. 2010. Varieties of French and the null subject parameter. In *Parametric Variation: Null Subjects in Minimalist Theory*, Theresa Biberauer, Anders Holmberg, Ian Roberts & Michelle Sheehan (eds), 303–327. Cambridge: CUP.

Roberts, Ian & Roussou, Anna. 2002. The Extended Projection Principle as a condition on the tense dependency. In *Subjects, Expletives and the EPP*, Peter Svenonius (ed.), 125–155. Oxford: OUP.

Rogger, Iginio. 1979. Dati storici sui mòcheni e i loro stanziamenti. In *La Valle del Fersina e le isole linguistiche tedesche del trentino. Atti del Convegno di S. Orsola, 1–3 settembre 1978*, Giovan Battista Pellegrini (ed.), 153–173. San Michele all'Adige: Pubblicazioni del Museo degli usi e costumi della gente trentina.

Röngvaldsson, Eiríkur & Höskuldur, Thráinsson. 1990. On Icelandic word order once more. In *Modern Icelandic Syntax*, Joan Maling & Annie Zaenen (Eds), 3–40. San Diego CA: Academic Press.

Rowley, Anthony. 1982. *Fersentaler Wörterbuch – Vocabolario del dialetto tedesco della Valle del Fersina nel Trientino*. Hamburg: Buske.

Rowley, Anthony. 1986. *Fersental (Val Fèrsina bei Trient/Oberitalien). Untersuchung einer Sprachinselmundart*. Tübingen: Max Niemeyer.

Rowley, Anthony. 2003. *Liacht as de sproch: grammatica della lingua mochena*. Palù del Fersina: Pubblicazioni dell'istituto mòcheno di cultura.

Salvi, Giampaolo. 1990. La sopravvivenza della legge di Wackernagel nei dialetti occidentali della Penisola Iberica. *Medioevo Romanzo* 15: 177–210.

Santorini, Beatrice. 1995. Two types of verb-second in the history of Yiddish. In *Clause Structure and Language Change*, Adrian Battye & Ian Roberts (eds), 53–79. Oxford: OUP.

Schirmunski, Viktor. 1962. *Deutsche Mundarten. Vergleichende Laut- und Formenlehre der deutschen Mundarten*. Berlin: Akademie Verlag.

Sheehan, Michelle. 2007. The EPP and Null Subjects in Romance. PhD dissertation, University of Newcastle.

Shlonsky, Ur. 2009. Hebrew as a partial null-subject language. *Studia Linguistica* 63: 133–157.

Sportiche, Dominique. 1996. Clitic constructions. In *Phrase Structure and the Lexicon*, Johan Rooryck & Laurie Ann Zaring (eds), 213–276. Dordrecht: Kluwer.

Sportiche, Dominique. 1998. *Partitions and Atoms of Clause Structure*. London: Routledge.

von Stechow, Arnim & Sternefeld, Werner. 1989. *Bausteine syntaktischen Wissens*. Opladen: Westdeutscher Verlag.

Svenonius, Peter. 2000. Quantifier movement in Icelandic. In *The Derivation of VO and OV* [Linguistik Aktuell/Linguistics Today 31], Peter Svenonius (ed.), 255–291. Amsterdam: John Benjamins.

Tarallo, Fernando. 1983. Relativization Strategies in Brazilian Portuguese. PhD dissertation, University of Pennsylvania, Philadelphia.

Taylor, Ann & Pintzuk, Susan. 2012. The effect of information structure on object position in the history of English. To appear in *Information Structure and Syntactic Change* [Oxford Studies in the History of English 1], Anneli Meurman-Solin, Maria Jose Lopez-Couso & Bettelou Los (eds). Oxford: OUP.

Thiersch, Crain. 1978. Topics in German Syntax. PhD dissertation, MIT.

Togni, Lucia. 1990. Per un'analisi di alcuni fenomeni linguistici del dialetto della Valle del Fersina: Un confronto con la sintassi tedesca. MA thesis, University of Trento.

Tomaselli, Alessandra. 1990. *La sintassi del verbo finito nella lingue germaniche*. Padova: Unipress.

Tomaselli, Alessandra. 1995. Cases of V3 in Old High German. In *Clause Structure and Language Change*, Adrian Battye & Ian Roberts (eds), 345–369. Oxford: OUP.

Tomaselli, Alessandra. 2004. *Introduzione alla sintassi del tedesco*. Bari: B.A. Graphis.

Travis, Lisa. 1984. Parameters and Effects of Word Order Variation. PhD dissertation, MIT.

Travis, Lisa. 1994. Parameters of phrase structure and verb-second phenomena. In *Principles and Parameters in Comparative Grammar*, Robert Freidin (ed.), 339–364. Cambridge MA: The MIT Press.

Truckenbrodt, Hubert. 2006. On the semantic motivation of syntactic verb movement to C in German. *Theoretical Linguistics* 32: 257–306.

Trudgill, Peter. 1992. *Introducing Language and Society*. London: Penguin.

Uriagereka, Juan. 1995. Aspects in the syntax of clitic placement in Western Romance. *Linguistic Inquiry* 26: 79–123.

Vallduví, Enric. 1992. *The Informational Component*. New York NY: Garland.

Vance, Barbara. 1989. Null Subjects and Syntactic Change in Medieval French. PhD dissertation, Cornell University.

Vanelli, Laura. 1987. I pronomi soggetto nei dialetti italiani settentrionali dal Medio Evo ad oggi. *Medioevo Romanzo* XIII: 173–211.

Vanelli, Laura, Renzi, Lorenzo & Benincà, Paola. 1985. Tipologia dei pronomi soggetto nelle lingue romanze. *Quaderni Patavini di Linguistica* 5: 49–66.

Vikner, Sten. 1995. *Verb Movement and Expletive Subjects in the Germanic Languages*. Oxford: OUP.

Westergaard, Marit. 2009. *The Acquisition of Word Order: Micro-cues, Information Structure and Economy* [Linguistik Aktuell/Linguistics Today 145]. Amsterdam: Benjamins.

Wiklund, Anna-Lena, Bentzen, Kristine, Hrafnbjargarson, Gunnar Hrafn & Hróarsdóttir, Thorbjörg. 2009. On the distribution and illocution of V2 in Scandinavian that-clauses. *Lingua* 119: 1914–1938.

Wurzer, Bernhard 1977. *Die deutschen Sprachinsel in Oberitalien*. Bozen: Athesia Verlag.

Zamboni, Alberto. 1979. Fenomeni di interferenza nelle isole linguistiche tedesche del Trentino (con particolare riguardo all'area mòchena). In *La Valle del Fersina e le isole linguistiche tedesche del trentino. Atti del Convegno di S. Orsola, 1–3 settembre 1978*, Giovan Battista Pellegrini (ed.), 83–111. San Michele all'Adige: Pubblicazioni del Museo degli usi e costumi della gente trentina.

Zanuttini, Raffaella & Portner, Paul. 2003. Exclamative Clauses: At the Syntax-Semantics Interface. *Language* 79(1): 39–81.

Zwart, Jan Wouter. 1997. *Morphosyntax of Verb Movement. A Minimalist Approach to the Syntax of Dutch*. Dordrecht: Kluwer.

Appendix

Questionnaires from Palai

PALÙ-FM

- Age: 24
- Sex: M
- Variety: Palù, Tural (auserpòch)
- Date of the interview: 11th August 2011
- Place of the interview: Istitute for the promotion of the Mòcheno language and culture, Palù del Fersina

1. Translation into Mòcheno: Cosa ha comprato (lei)?
   Bos hòt-se kaft si?
   Alternatives (judgment task)
   *Bos hòt-se si kaft? – no
   *Bos se-hòt kaft? – no
   *Bos de hòt kaft? – no
   *Bos si hòt kaft? – no
   *Bos hòt de kaft? – no
   *Bos hòt si kaft? – no
   *Bos hòt de mama kaft? – no, only: Bos hòt-se kaft de mama?

2. Translation into Mòcheno: Quando ha comprato il libro (lui)?
   Benn hòt-er er s puach kaft?
   Alternatives (judgment task)
   Benn hòt-er s puach kaft? – ok
   Benn hòt-er kaft s puach? – ok
   *Benn er/der hòt kaft s puach? – no
   *Benn hòt-ar/der kaft s puach? – no
   *Benn hòt der tata kaft s puech? – no, only: Benn hòt-er kaft s puech der tata?
   Benn hòt der tata s puech kaft? – ok

3. Translation into Mòcheno: Maria mi ha chiesto come hai fatto il compito
   De Maria hòt-mar pfrok,
   abia hos=o s prufung gamocht
   Alternatives (judgment task)
   abia as=o s prufung gamocht host – ok
   abia as=o host s prufung gamocht – ok
   abia as=o host gamocht s prufung – ok

abia du host gamocht s prufung – ok
*abia as du host gamocht s prufung – no
abia as=o du host gamocht s prufung – ok

Translation into Mòcheno: Maria mi ha chiesto come (lei) ha fatto il compito
abia si hòt s prufung gamocht
Alternatives (judgment task)
abia=se (si) hòt s prufung gamocht – ok
*abia as si hòt s prufung gamocht – no
*abia as de hòt s prufung gamocht – no
*abia=se de hòt s prufung gamocht – no

Translation into Mòcheno: Maria mi ha chiesto come Gianni ha fatto il compito
abia der Giani hòt s prufung gamocht
Alternatives (judgment task)
abia as der Giani hòt s prufung gamocht – ok
*abia as er hòt s prufung gamocht der Gianni – no

4. **Translation into Mòcheno: Ieri ha comprato un libro (lei)**
   Gester hòt-se (si) a puach kaft
   Alternatives (judgment task)
   Gester si hòt a puach kaft – ok, focus on SI
   *Gester se hòt a puach kaft – no
   *Gester de hòt a puach kaft – no
   *Gester hòt de a puach kaft – no
   Gester de mama hòt a puach kaft – ok
   Gester hòt de mama a puach kaft – ok

5. **Judgment task**
   S puach hòt-er gester kaft – ok: the fronted XP is an SP
   *S puach gester hòt-er kaft – no
   *S puach der Mario hòt kaft – no

6. **Judgment task**
   Bos hòt-er kaft – ok
   *Bos gester hòt-er kaft – no, only: Bos hòt-er kaft gester? or Gester, bos hòt-er kaft?

7. **Judgment task**
   A PUACH hòt-er kaft ont net an quaderno – ok
   *A PUACH gester hòt-er kaft ont net a quaderno – no, only: Gester A PUACH hòt-er kaft, ont net an quaderno

8. **Judgment task**
   *Gester s puach er hòt-s kaft – no

9. **Judgment task**
   De mama hòt a puach kaft – ok

10. **Judgment task**
    De mama ene boteig hòt a puach kaft – ok

11. **Judgment task**
    *De mama ene boteig hòt-se a puach kaft – no

12. Judgment task
    Gester s puach ber hòt-s kaft? – ok

13. Judgment task
    *Ber s puach hòt-s kaft? – no

14. Judgment task
    *S puach ber hòt kaft? – no, S obligatory

15. Judgment task
    *Ber s puach hòt kaft? – no

PALÙ-LB

- Age: 29
- Sex: F
- Variety: Palù, Tolar (inderpòch)
- Date of the interview: 29th July 2011
- Place of the interview: kitchen of the consultant

1. Translation into Mòcheno: Cosa ha comprato (lei)?
   Bos hòt-se kaft?
   Alternatives (judgment task)
   *Bos se hòt kaft? – no
   *Bos de hòt kaft? – no
   *Bos si hòt kaft? – no
   *Bos hòt de kaft? – no
   *Bos hòt si kaft? – no, only: Bos hòt-se kaft si?
   *Bos hòt de mama kaft? – no, only: Bos hòt-se kaft de mama?

2. Translation into Mòcheno: Quando ha comprato il libro (lui)?
   Benn hòt-er kaft s puach?
   Alternatives (judgment task)
   *Benn ar/er/der hòt s puach kaft? – no
   *Benn hòt-ar/der s puach kaft? – no
   *Benn hòt der tata kaft s puech? – no, only: Benn hòt-er kaft s puech der tata?
   *Benn hòt der tata s puech kaft? – no

3. Translation into Mòcheno: Maria mi ha chiesto come hai fatto il compito
   De Maria hòt mer pfrok,
   abias-o (du) gamocht host de compite
   Alternatives (judgment task)
   *abia du gamocht host de compite – no

   Translation into Mòcheno: Maria mi ha chiesto come (lei) ha fatto il compito
   abiase hòt gamocht de compite
   Alternatives (judgment task)
   *abia (as) de hòt gamocht de compite – no
   abiase si hòt gamocht de compite – ok
   *abia si hòt gamocht de compite – no

Translation into Mòcheno: Maria mi ha chiesto come Gianni ha fatto il compito
abia der Giani gamocht hòt de compite
Alternatives (judgment task)
abias-ar gamocht hòt de compite der Giani – ok

4. Translation into Mòcheno: Ieri ha comprato un libro (lei)
   Gester hòt-se a puach kaft
   Alternatives (judgment task)
   Gester si hòt a puach kaft – ok, focus on SI
   *Gester se hòt a puach kaft – no
   *Gester de hòt a puach kaft – no
   *Gester hòt de a puach kaft – no
   Gester de mama hòt a puach kaft – ok
   Gester hòt de mama a puach kaft – ok
   Gester hòt de mama kaft a puech – ok

5. Judgment task
   S puach hòt-er gester kaft – ok, the fronted XP is an SP
   *S puach gester hòt-er kaft – no
   *S puach der Mario hòt kaft – no

6. Judgment task
   Bos hòt-er kaft – ok
   *Bos gester hòt-er kaft – no, only: Bos hòt-er kaft gester? and Gester bos hòt-er kaft?

7. Judgment task
   Na, A PUACH hòt-er kaft ont net an quaderno – ok
   *A PUACH gester hòt-er kaft ont net a quaderno – no

8. Judgment task
   *Gester s puach er hòt-s kaft – no

9. Judgment task
   De mama hòt a puach kaft – ok

10. Judgment task
    De mama ene boteig hòt a puach kaft – ok

11. Judgment task
    *De mama ene boteig hòt-se a puach kaft – no

12. Judgment task
    Gester s puach ber hòt-s kaft? – ok

13. Judgment task
    *Ber s puach hòt-s kaft? – no

14. Judgment task
    *S puach ber hòt kaft? – no

15. Judgment task
    *Ber s puach hòt kaft? – no

PALÙ-NI

- Age: 16
- Sex: M
- Cariety: Palù, Tolar (inderpòch)
- Date of the interview: 7th June 2011
- Place of the interview: Istitute for the promotion of the Mòcheno language and culture, Palù del Fersina

1. Translation into Mòcheno: Cosa ha comprato (lei)?
   Bos hòt-se kaft ?
   Alternatives (judgment task)
   *Bos se hòt kaft –no
   *Bos de hòt kaft? – no
   ??Bos si hòt kaft?
   *Bos si hòt kaft? – no

2. Translation into Mòcheno: Quando ha comprato il libro (lui)?
   Benn hòt-er kaft s puach?
   Alternatives (judgment task)
   *Benn ar/er/der hòt-ar/der kaft s puach? – no
   Benn hòt der tata kaft s puach? – ok
   Benn hòt-er kaft s puach der tata? – ok
   Benn hòt der tata s puach kaft? – ok

3. Translation into Mòcheno: Maria mi ha chiesto come hai fatto il compito
   De Maria de hòt-me pfrok,
   abia do host gamocht der compito
   Alternatives (judgment task)
   abia as-o der compito gamocht host – ok
   abia as du der compito gamocht host – ok
   abia aso du der compito gamocht host – ok

   Translation into Mòcheno: Maria mi ha chiesto come (lei) ha fatto il compito
   abia de hòt si gamocht der compito – sua traduzione
   Alternatives (judgment task)
   abia as-se der compito gamocht hòt – ok
   abia as-de der compito gamocht hòt – ok
   abia as-si der compito gamocht hòt – ok

   Translation into Mòcheno: Maria mi ha chiesto come Gianni ha fatto il compito
   abia as hòt der Nane gamocht der compito
   Alternatives (judgment task)
   abia as der Nane der compito gamocht hòt – ok

4. Translation into Mòcheno: Ieri ha comprato un libro (lei)
   Gester hòt-se kaft a puach – ok, also OV
   Alternatives (judgment task)
   Gester si hòt a puach kaft –ok
   *Gester se hòt a puach kaft – no

Gester de hòt a puach kaft –ok
*Gester hòt de a puach kaft – no
Gester de mama hòt a puach kaft – ok
Gester hòt de mama a puach kaft – ok

5. Judgment task
   S puach hòt-er gester kaft – ok
   S puach gester hòt-er kaft – ok
   S puach der Mario hòt kaft – ok

6. Judgment task
   Bos hòt-er kaft?
   *Bos gester hòt-er kaft? – no, only Bos hòt-er gester kaft? and Gester, bos hòt-er kaft?

7. Judgment task
   A PUACH hòt-er kaft, ont net a quaderno – ok
   A PUACH gester hòt-er kaft – ok

8. Judgment task
   Gester s puach er hòt-s kaft – ok, focus on ER

9. Judgment task
   De mama hòt a puach kaft – ok

10. Judgment task
    De mama en de boteig hòt a puach kaft –ok

11. Judgment task
    *De mama en de boteig hòt-se a puach kaft – no

12. Judgment task
    Gester s puach ber hòt-an kaft? – ok

13. Judgment task
    *Ber s puach hòt-an kaft? – no

14. Judgment task
    *S puach ber hòt kaft? – no

15. Judgment task
    *Ber s puach hòt kaft? – no

PALÙ-ST

- age: 18
- sex: F
- variety: Palù, Simeter (auserpoch)
- date of the interview: 12th July 2011
- Place of the interview: Istitute for the promotion of the Mòcheno language and culture, Palù del Fersina

1. Translation into Mòcheno: Cosa ha comprato (lei)?
   Bos hòt-se kaft?

Alternatives (judgment task)
*Bos se hòt kaft? – no
Bos de hòt kaft? – ok as an esclamative, not as a real interrogative
Bos der/ar hòt kaft? – ok as an esclamative, not as a real interrogative
*Bos si hòt kaft –no
*Bos hòt-de kaft? – no
*Bos hòt si kaft? – no, only: Bos hòt se si kaft?
Bos hòt de mama kaft? – ok
Bos hòt-se kaft de mama? – ok

2. **Translation into Mòcheno: Quando ha comprato il libro (lui)?**
Benn hòt-er kaft s puach?
Alternatives (judgment task)
*Benn ar hòt kaft s puach? – no
*Benn er/der hòt kaft s puach? – no
*Benn hòt-ar kaft s puach? – no
*Benn hòt-der kaft s puach? – no
Benn hòt der tata kaft s puach? – ok
Benn hòt-er kaft s puach der tata? – ok
Benn hòt der tata s puach kaft? – ok

3. **Translation into Mòcheno: Maria mi ha chiesto come hai fatto il compito**
Maria de hòn mar pfrok
abiaso host gamocht de hausaufgabe –1
abia hoso gamocht de hausaufgabe – 2
Alternatives (judgment task)
abiaso host de hausaufgabe gamocht – ok
abiaso de hausaufgabe gamocht host – ok
abia du host gamocht de hausaufgabe – ok
*abia as du host gamocht de hausaufgabe – ok
*abia as host gamocht de hausaufgaben – ok

Translation into Mòcheno: Maria mi ha chiesto come (lei) ha fatto il compito
abia si hòt gamocht de hausaufgaben
Alternatives (judgment task)
abiase hòt gamocht de hausaufgaben – ok
abia de hòt gamocht de hausaufgaben – ok
abiase si hòt gamocht de hausaufgaben – ok

Translation into Mòcheno: Maria mi ha chiesto come Gianni ha fatto il compito
abia Giani de hausaufgaben gamocht hòt
Alternatives (judgment task)
abia ar er de hausaufgaben gamocht hòt – ok

4. **Translation into Mòcheno: Ieri ha comprato un libro (lei)**
Gester hòt-se a puach kaft
Alternatives (judgment task)
Gester si hòt a puach kaft – ok
*Gester se hòt a puach kaft – no
Gester de hòt a puach kaft – ok

*Gester hòt de a puach kaft – no
Gester de mama hòt a puach kaft – ok
Gester hòt de mama a puach kaft – ok

5. Judgment task
   S puach hòt-er gester kaft – ok, fronted XP is an SP
   *S puach gester hòt-er kaft – no
   *S puach der Mario hòt kaft – no

6. Judgment task
   Bos hòt-er kaft? – ok
   *Bos gester hòt-er kaft? – no

7. Judgment task
   A PUACH hòt-er kaft (net a quaderno) – ok
   A PUACH gester hòt-er kaft, net a quaderno – ok, also Gester A PUACH hòt-er kaft, net an quaderno

8. Judgment task
   Gester s puach er hòt-s/an kaft – ok

9. Judgment task
   De mama hòt a puach kaft – ok

10. Judgment task
    De mama en de boteig hòt a puach kaft – ok

11. Judgment task
    *De mama en de boteig hòt-se a puach kaft – no

12. Judgment task
    Gester s puach ber hòt-an/s kaft? – ok

13. Judgment task
    *Ber s puach hòt-s kaft? –no

14. Judgment task
    *S puach ber hòt kaft? – no

15. Judgment task
    *Ber s puach hòt kaft? – no

PALÙ-VL

- Age: 14
- Sex: F
- Variety: Palù, Orastòll (auserpòch)
- Date of the interview: 21st June 2011
- Place of the interview: Istitute for the promotion of the Mòcheno language and culture, Palù del Fersina

1. Translation into Mòcheno: Cosa ha comprato (lei)?
   Bos hòt-se kaft (de mama)?

Alternatives (judgment task)
   Bos hòt de mama kaft? – ok
   Bos se hòt kaft? – ok
   Bos de hòt kaft? – ok
   *Bos si hòt kaft –no
   *Bos hòt-de kaft? – no
   Bos hòt si kaft? – ok, also: Bos hòt se si kaft

2. Translation into Mòcheno: Quando ha comprato il libro (lui)?
   Benn hòt-er er kaft s puach?
   Alternatives (judgment task)
   Benn der/er hòt kaft s puach? – ok
   *Benn ar hòt kaft s puach? – no
   *Benn hòt-ar kaft s puach? – no
   Benn hòt der tata kaft s puach? – ok
   Benn hòt-er kaft s puach der tata? – ok
   Benn hòt-er s puach kaft? – ok

3. Translation into Mòcheno: Maria mi ha chiesto come hai fatto il compito
   Maria de hòn mar pfrok
   abia hoso tu der compito – 1
   bia aso der compito tu – 2
   Alternatives (judgment task)
   bia hoso gamocht der compito – ok
   *bia aso der compito gamocht host – no

   Translation into Mòcheno: Maria mi ha chiesto come (lei) ha fatto il compito
   bia hòt-se gamocht der compito
   Alternatives (judgment task)
   *bia de hòt der compito gamocht – no
   bia si hòt der compito gamocht – ok

   Translation into Mòcheno: Maria mi ha chiesto come Gianni ha fatto il compito
   bia hòt-er gamocht der compito Giani

4. Translation into Mòcheno: Ieri ha comprato un libro (lei)
   Gester hòt-se a puach kaft
   Alternatives (judgment task)
   Gester si hòt a puach kaft – ok
   Gester de hòt a puach kaft – ok
   *Gester se hòt a puach kaft – ok
   *Gester hòt de a puach kaft – no
   Gester de mama hòt a puach kaft – ok
   Gester hòt de mama a puach kaft – ok

5. Judgment task
   S puach hòt-er gester kaft – ok, fronted XP is an SP
   *S puach gester hòt-er kaft – no
   S puach der Mario hòt kaft – ok

6. Judgment task
   Bos hòt-er kaft? – ok
   *Bos gester hòt-er kaft? – no

7. Judgment task
   A PUACH hòt-er kaft (net a quaderno) – ok
   A PUACH gester hòt-er kaft, net a quaderno – ok

8. Judgment task
   xxx

9. Judgment task
   De mama hòt a puach kaft – ok

10. Judgment task
    De mama en de boteig hòt a puach kaft – ok

11. Judgment task
    *De mama en de boteig hòt-se a puach kaft – no

12. Judgment task
    Gester s puach ber hòt-an kaft? – ok

13. Judgment task
    Ber s puach hòt-an kaft? – ok

14. Judgment task
    *S puach ber hòt kaft? – no

15. Judgment task
    Ber s puach hòt kaft? – ok

PALÙ-GL

- Age: 55
- Sex: F
- Variety: Palù, Steffener (auserpòch)
- Date of the interview: 12th July 2011
- Place of the interview: kitchen of the consultant

1. **Translation into Mòcheno: Cosa ha comprato (lei)?**
   Bos hòt-se kaft?
   Alternatives (judgment task)
   *Bos se hòt kaft? – no
   *Bos de hòt kaft? – no
   *Bos si hòt kaft? – no
   *Bos hòt de kaft? – no
   *Bos hòt si kaft? – no
   Bos hòt de mama kaft? – ok
   Bos hòt-se kaft de mama? – ok

2. **Translation into Mòcheno: Quando ha comprato il libro (lui)?**
   Benn hòt-er kaft s puach?

Alternatives (judgment task)
*Benn ar/er/der hòt kaft s puach? – no
*Benn hòt-ar kaft s puach? – no
*Benn hòt-der kaft s puach? – no
Benn hòt der tata kaft s puach? – ok
Benn hòt der tata s puach kaft? – ok
Benn hòt-er kaft s puech der tata? – ok

3. Translation into Mòcheno: Maria mi ha chiesto come hai fatto il compito
De Maria hòt mar pfrok,
abiaso der compito gamocht host
Alternatives (judgment task)
abia der compito gamocht host – ok
*abia du der compito gamocht host – no
abiaso du der compito gamocht host – ok
abiaso der compito host gamocht – ok
abiaso host der compito gamocht – ok

Translation into Mòcheno: Maria mi ha chiesto come (lei) ha fatto il compito
abiase si der compito gamocht hòt
Alternatives (judgment task)
abia de hòt gamocht der compito – ok
abia si hòt gamocht der compito – ok
abia der Mario hòt-an gamocht der compito – ok

4. Translation into Mòcheno: Ieri ha comprato un libro (lei)
Gester si hòt a puach kaft
Alternatives (judgment task)
Gester hòt-se a puach kaft – ok
*Gester hòt de a puach kaft – no
*Gester se hòt a puach kaft – no
Gester de hòt a puach kaft – ok
Gester de mama hòt a puach kaft – ok
Gester hòt de mama a puach kaft – ok

5. Judgment task
S puach hòt-er gester kaft – ok
S puach gester hòt-er kaft – ok
S puach der Mario hòt kaft – ok

6. Judgment task
Bos hòt-er kaft? – ok
Bos gester hòt-er kaft? – ok

7. Judgment task
A PUACH hòt-er kaft ont net a quaderno – ok
A PUACH gester hòt-er kaft ont net a quaderno – ok

8. Judgment task
Gester s puach er hòt-s kaft – ok

9. Judgment task
   De mama hòt a puach kaft – ok
10. Judgment task
    De mama ene boteig hòt a puach kaft – ok
11. Judgment task
    *De mama en de boteig hòt-se a puach kaft – no
12. Judgment task
    Gester s puach ber hòt-s kaft? – ok
13. Judgment task
    Ber s puach hòt-s kaft? – ok
14. Judgment task
    *S puach ber hòt kaft? – no
15. Judgment task
    *Ber s puach hòt kaft? – no

PALÙ-HN

- Age: 59
- Sex: F
- Variety: Palù, Jorgar (inderpòch)
- Date of the interview: 21st July 2011
- Place of the interview: Istitute for the promotion of the Mòcheno language and culture, Palù del Fersina

1. **Translation into Mòcheno: Cosa ha comprato (lei)?**
   Bos hòt-se kaft?
   Alternatives (judgment task)
   Bos hòt-se kaft de mama? – ok
   *Bos se hòt kaft? – no
   *Bos de/si hòt kaft? no
   *Bos hòt de/si kaft? – no
   Bos hòt de mama kaft? – no

2. **Translation into Mòcheno: Quando ha comprato il libro (lui)?**
   XXX

3. **Translation into Mòcheno: Maria mi ha chiesto come hai fatto il compito**
   De Maria hòt-mer pfrok,
   bia-so gamocht hòst der compito

   Translation into Mòcheno: Maria mi ha chiesto come (lei) ha fatto il compito
   bia-se der compito gamocht hòt
   Alternatives (judgment task)
   *bia de der compito gamocht hòt – no
   *bia si der compito gamocht hòt – no

bia se si der compito gamocht hòt – ok
*bia se de der compito gamocht hòt – no

Translation into Mòcheno: Maria mi ha chiesto come Gianni ha fatto il compito
abia der Giani der compito gamocht hòt

4. **Translation into Mòcheno: Ieri ha comprato un libro (lei)**
   Gester hòt-se a puach kaft
   Alternatives (judgment task)
   Gester si hòt a puach kaft – ok
   *Gester se hòt a puach kaft – no
   *Gester de hòt a puach kaft – no
   *Gester hòt de a puach kaft – no
   Gester de mama hòt a puach kaft – ok
   Gester hòt de mama a puach kaft – ok

5. **Judgment task**
   S puach hòt-er gester kaft – fronted is an SP
   *S puach gester hòt-er kaft – no
   *S puach der Mario hòt kaft – no

6. **Judgment task**
   Bos hòt-er kaft? – no
   *Bos gester hòt-er kaft? – no, only: Bos hòt-er kaft gester? and Gester, bos hòt-er kaft der Mario?

7. **Judgment task**
   A PUACH hòt-er kaft (ont net a quaderno) – ok
   *A PUACH gester hòt-er kaft (ont net a quaderno) – no, only: A PUACH hòt-er kaft gester, net a quaderno

8. **Judgment task**
   xxxx

9. **Judgment task**
   De mama hòt a puach kaft – ok

10. **Judgment task**
    De mama en de boteig hòt a puach kaft – ok

11. **Judgment task**
    *De mama en de boteig hòt-se a puach kaft – no

12. **Judgment task**
    S puach ber hòt-s kaft gester? ok

13. **Judgment task**
    *Ber s puach hòt-s kaft? – no

14. **Judgment task**
    *S puach ber hòt kaft? -no

15. **Judgment task**
    *Ber s puach hòt kaft? – no

PALÙ-MP

- Age: 55
- Sex: M
- Variety: Palù, Steffener, auserpòch
- Date of the interview: 19th August 2011
- Place of the interview: kitchen of the consultant

1. **Translation into Mòcheno: Cosa ha comprato (lei)?**
   Bos hòt-se kaft?
   Alternatives (judgment task)
   *Bos se hòt kaft? – no, only in embedded clauses (free relatives)
   *Bos hòt de mama kaft? – no, only: Bos hòt-se kaft de mama?
   *Bos de hòt kaft? – no
   *Bos si hòt kaft? – no
   *Bos hòt de kaft? – no
   *Bos hòt si kaft? – no, only: Bos hòt-se si kaft?

2. **Translation into Mòcheno: Quando ha comprato il libro (lui)?**
   Benn hòt-er kaft s puach?
   Alternatives (judgment task)
   *Benn ar/er/der hòt kaft s puach? – no
   *Benn hòt-ar kaft s puach? – no
   *Benn hòt-der kaft s puach? – no
   *Benn hòt der tata kaft s puach? – no, only: Benn hòt-er kaft s puech der tata?
   *Benn hòt-er s puech kaft? – no
   *Benn hòt der tata s puach kaft? – no

3. **Translation into Mòcheno: Maria mi ha chiesto come hai fatto il compito**
   De Maria hòt me pfrok,
   biaso tun za mochen de compiti – 1
   biaso tun host za mochn de compiti – 2
   Alternatives (judgment task)
   *biaso tun host za mochn de compiti – no
   biaso du tun host za mochn de compiti – ok

   Translation into Mòcheno: Maria mi ha chiesto come (lei) ha fatto il compito
   biase si tun hòt za mochen de compiti
   Alternatives (judgment task)
   biase tun hòt za mochen de compiti – ok
   *bia si tun hòt za mochen de compiti – no
   *bia de tun hòt za mochen de compiti – no

   Translation into Mòcheno: Maria mi ha chiesto come Gianni ha fatto il compito
   bias der Giani tun hòt za mochen de compiti
   Alternatives (judgment task)
   bias-ar tun hòt za mochen de compiti der Giani – ok
   bias tun hòt za mochen de compiti der Giani – ok

4. Translation into Mòcheno: Ieri ha comprato un libro (lei)
   Gester hòt-se kaft a puach
   Alternatives (judgment task)
   Gester si hòt kaft a puach – ok
   *Gester hòt de kaft a puach – no
   *Gester se hòt kaft a puach – no
   Gester hòt de mama kaft a puach – ok
   *Gester de hòt kaft a puach – no
   Gester de mama hòt kaft a puach – ok
   Gester hòt de mama a puach kaft – ok

5. Judgment task
   S puach hòt-er gester kaft – ok, fronted XP is an SP
   *S puach gester hòt-er kaft – no
   *S puach der Mario hòt kaft – no

6. Judgment task
   Bos hòt-er kaft – ok
   *Bos gester hòt-er kaft – no

7. Judgment task
   A PUACH hòt-er kaft ont net a heftl – ok
   ??A PUACH gester hòt-er kaft ont net a heftl – no, only: Gester A PUACH hòt-er kaft, net a heftl

8. Judgment task
   Gester s puach er hòt-s kaft – ok

9. Judgment task
   De mama hòt a puach kaft – ok

10. Judgment task
    De mama ene boteig hòt a puach kaft – ok

11. Judgment task
    *De mama en de boteig hòt-se a puach kaft – no

12. Judgment task
    Gester s puach ber hòt-s kaft? – ok

13. Judgment task
    *Ber s puach hòt-s kaft? – no

14. Judgment task
    *S puach ber hòt kaft? – no

15. Judgment task
    *Ber s puach hòt kaft? – no

PALÙ-MO

- Age: 38
- Sex: M

- Variety: Palù, Lenzer (auserpòch)
- Date of the interview: 12^(th) July 2011
- Place of the interview: kitchen of the consultant

1. **Translation into Mòcheno:** Cosa ha comprato (lei)?
   Bos hòt-se kaft?
   Alternatives (judgment task)
   *Bos se hòt kaft? – no
   *Bos de/si hòt kaft? – no
   *Bos hòt-de/si kaft? – no, only: Bos hòt-se kaft si?
   *Bos hòt de mama kaft? , no, only: Bos hòt-se kaft de mama?

2. **Translation into Mòcheno:** Quando ha comprato il libro (lui)?
   Benn hòt-er kaft s puach?
   Alternatives (judgment task)
   *Benn er hòt kaft s puach? – no
   *Benn ar hòt kaft s puach? – no
   *Benn der hòt kaft s puach? – no
   *Benn hòt ar kaft s puach? – no
   *Benn hòt der kaft s puach? – no
   *Benn hòt der tata kaft s puach? – no, only: benn hòt-er kaft s puach der tata?
   *Benn hòt-er s puach kaft der tata? – no
   *Benn hòt der tata s puach kaft? – no

3. **Translation into Mòcheno:** Maria mi ha chiesto come hai fatto il compito
   De Maria hòt-mar pfrok,
   abiaso der compito gamocht host
   Alternatives (judgment task)
   *abia du der compito gamocht host – no
   *abia der compito gamocht host – no
   abiaso (du) der compito gamocht host (du) – ok

   Translation into Mòcheno: Maria mi ha chiesto come (lei) ha fatto il compito
   abiase si der compito gamocht hòt
   Alternatives (judgment task)
   *abia si der compito gamocht hòt – no
   *abia de der compito gamocht hòt – no
   *abiase de der compito gamocht hòt – no

   Translation into Mòcheno: Maria mi ha chiesto come Gianni ha fatto il compito
   abia as hòt gamocht der compito der Giani – 1
   abia's der Giani der compito gamocht hòt – 2
   Alternatives (judgment task)
   abia as-ar hòt gamocht der compito de Giani – ok

4. **Translation into Mòcheno:** Ieri ha comprato un libro (lei)
   Gester hòt-se a puach kaft
   Alternatives (judgment task)
   Gester si hòt a puach kaft – ok, focus on SI
   *Gester se hòt a puach kaft – no

*Gester de hòt a puach kaft – no
*Gester hòt de a puach kaft – no
Gester de mama hòt a puach kaft – no
Gester hòt de mama a puach kaft – ok, only as an answer to the question hòt der tata a puach kaft? na, gester hòt de mama a puach kaft
Gester hòt de mama kaft a puach, net der tata
*Gester hòt de mama schua a puach kaft – no, only: gester hòt schua de mama a puach kaft and S hòt schua de mama s puach kaft

5. Judgment task
   S puach hòt-er gester kaft – ok
   *S puach gester hòt-er kaft – no
   *S puach der Mario hòt kaft – no

6. Judgment task
   Bos hòt-er kaft? – ok
   *Bos gester hòt-er kaft? -no

7. Judgment task
   A PUACH hòt-er kaft, ont net an quaderno – ok
   *A PUACH gester hòt-er kaft, ont net an quaderno – no, only: A PUACH hòt-er kaft gester or Gester? A PUACH hòt-er kaft, net an quaderno

8. Judgment task
   *Gester s puach er hòt-s kaft – no

9. Judgment task
   De mama hòt a puach kaft – ok

10. Judgment task
    De mama ene boteig hòt a puach kaft – ok

11. Judgment task
    *De mama ene boteig hòt-se a puach kaft – no

12. Judgment task
    Gester # s puach, ber hòt-s kaft? – ok, only with a break before the DO

13. Judgment task
    *Ber s puach hòt-s kaft? – no

14. Judgment task
    *S puach ber hòt kaft? – no

15. Judgment task
    *Ber s puach hòt kaft? – no

PALÙ-PB

- Age: 31
- Sex: F
- Variety: Palù, Steffener (auserpòch)
- Date of the interview: 12th July 2011

- Place of the interview: Istitute for the promotion of the Mòcheno language and culture, Palù del Fersina

1. Translation into Mòcheno: Cosa ha comprato (lei)?
   Bos hòt-se kaft?
   Alternatives (judgment task)
   *Bos se hòt kaft? – no
   *Bos de hòt kaft? – no
   *Bos si hòt kaft? – no
   *Bos hòt de kaft? – no
   *Bos hòt si kaft? – no
   Bos hòt de mama kaft? – ok, it would be better: Bos hòt-se kaft de mama?

2. Translation into Mòcheno: Quando ha comprato il libro (lui)?
   Benn hòt-er s puach kaft? – 1
   Benn hòt-er-s kaft s puach? – 2
   Alternatives (judgment task)
   *Benn ar/er/der hòt s puach kaft? – no
   *Benn hòt ar/der s puach kaft? – no
   Benn hòt der tata s puach kaft? – only as a special interrogative/esclamative; the real interrogative would be: Benn hòt-er-s kaft s puech der tata?

3. Translation into Mòcheno: Maria mi ha chiesto come hai fatto il compito
   De Maria hòt mer pfrok,
   abiaso der compito gamocht host
   Alternatives (judgment task)
   *abia as du der compito gamocht host -no
   *abiaso host gamocht der compito – no
   abiaso host der compito gamocht – ok
   *abia as de der compito gamocht host – no

   Translation into Mòcheno: Maria mi ha chiesto come (lei) ha fatto il compito
   abiase (si) der compito gamocht hòt – ok, focus on SI with the doubling construction
   Alternatives (judgment task)
   *abia si compito gamocht hòt – no
   abiase si der compito gamocht hòt/ hòt gamocht – doubling solo con il pronome, non con il DP soggetto

   Translation into Mòcheno: Maria mi ha chiesto come Gianni ha fatto il compito
   abia as der Giani der compito gamocht hòt/ hòt gamocht
   Alternatives (judgment task)
   *abia asar der Giani der compito gamocht hòt/ hòt gamocht
   *abia asse de mama der compito gamocht hòt/ hòt gamocht
   abia as de mama der compito gamocht hòt/ hòt gamocht

4. Translation into Mòcheno: Ieri ha comprato un libro (lei)
   Gester hòt-se a puach kaft
   Alternatives (judgment task)
   *Gester si hòt a puach kaft – no, only: Gester hòt-se si a puach kaft net er
   *Gester se hòt a puach kaft – no

```
*Gester se hòt a puach kaft – no
*Gester de hòt a puach kaft – no
*Gester hòt de a puach kaft – no
Gester de mama hòt a puach kaft – ok
Gester hòt de mama a puach kaft – ok
```

5. Judgment task
   S puach hòt-er gester kaft – ok, fronted XP is an SP
   *S puach gester hòt-er kaft – no
   *S puach der Mario hòt kaft – no

6. Judgment task
   Bos hòt-er kaft – ok
   *Bos gester hòt-er kaft – no

7. Judgment task
   A PUACH hòt-er kaft ont net a quaderno – ok
   *A PUACH gester hòt-er kaft ont net a quaderno – no

8. Judgment task
   *Gester s puach er hòt-s kaft – no

9. Judgment task
   De mama hòt a puach kaft – ok

10. Judgment task
    De mama en de boteig hòt a puach kaft – ok

11. Judgment task
    *De mama en de boteig hòt-se a puach kaft – no

12. Judgment task
    S puach gester, ber hòt-s kaft? – ok

13. Judgment task
    *Ber s puach hòt-s kaft? – no

14. Judgment task
    *S puach ber hòt kaft? – no

15. Judgment task
    *Ber s puach hòt kaft? – no

PALÙ-ET

- Age: 60
- Sex: M
- Variety: Palù, Battister (inderpòch)
- Date of the interview: 12th July 2011
- Place of the interview: Istitute for the promotion of the Mòcheno language and culture, Palù del Fersina

1. Translation into Mòcheno: Cosa ha comprato (lei)?
   Bos hòt-se kaft?

Alternatives (judgment task)
   *Bos se hòt kaft? – no
   *Bos de hòt kaft – no
   *Bos si hòt kaft? – no
   *Bos hòt de kaft? – no
   *Bos hòt si kaft? – no, only Bos hòt-se si kaft?
   *Bos hòt de mama kaft? – no, solo: Bos hòt-se kaft de mama?

2. **Translation into Mòcheno: Quando ha comprato il libro (lui)?**
   Benn hòt-er kaft s puech?
   Alternatives (judgment task)
   *Benn ar hòt kaft s puech? – no
   *Benn er hòt kaft s puech? – no
   *Benn der hòt kaft s puech? – no
   *Benn hòt-ar kaft s puech? – no
   *Benn hòt-der kaft s puech? – no
   *Benn hòt der tata kaft s puech? – no, only: Der tata, benn hòt-er kaft s puech?
   Benn hòt-er kaft s puech der tata? – ok
   Benn hòt-er s puech kaft? – ok

3. **Translation into Mòcheno: Maria mi ha chiesto come hai fatto il compito**
   De Maria hòt-mer pfrok,
   abiaso de compite gamocht host

   Translation into Mòcheno: Maria mi ha chiesto come (lei) ha fatto il compito
   abias' de Lucia de compite gamocht hòt
   Alternatives (judgment task)
   *abia de compite gamocht hòt – no
   *abia si de compite gamocht hòt – no
   abiase si de compite gamocht hòt – ok

   Translation into Mòcheno: Maria mi ha chiesto come Gianni ha fatto il compito
   abia der Nane de compite gamocht hòt
   Alternatives (judgment task)
   *abia er/ar der Nane de compite gamocht hòt – no

4. **Translation into Mòcheno: Ieri ha comprato un libro (lei)**
   Gester hòt-se a puach kaft
   Alternatives (judgment task)
   Gester si hòt a puach kaft – ok
   *Gester se hòt a puach kaft – no
   Gester de hòt a puach kaft – ok
   *Gester hòt de a puach kaft – no
   Gester de mama hòt a puach kaft – ok
   Gester hòt de mama a puach kaft – ok

5. **Judgment task**
   S puach hòt-er gester kaft – fronted XP is an SP, answer to: Benn hòt-er kaft s puach?
   *S puach gester hòt-er kaft – no
   *S puach der Mario hòt kaft – no

6. **Judgment task**
    Bos hòt-er kaft? – ok
    *Bos gester hòt-er kaft? – no

7. **Judgment task**
    A PUACH hòt-er kaft (ont net a quaderno) – ok
    *A PUACH gester hòt-er kaft (ont net a quaderno) – no: Gester hòt-er a puach kaft, or Gester A PUACH hòt-er kaft, net a quaderno

8. **Judgment task**
    *Gester s puech er hòt-s kaft – no

9. **Judgment task**
    De mama hòt a puach kaft – ok

10. **Judgment task**
    De mama en de boteig hòt a puach kaft – ok

11. **Judgment task**
    *De mama en de boteig hòt-se a puach kaft – no

12. **Judgment task**
    ?Gester s puach ber hòt-s kaft? – ok, better: Gester ber hòt-s kaft s puach?

13. **Judgment task**
    *Ber s puach hòt-s kaft? – no

14. **Judgment task**
    *S puach ber hòt kaft? – no

15. **Judgment task**
    *Ber s puach hòt kaft? – no

PALÙ-EO

- Age: 67
- Sex: F
- Variety: Palù, Battister (inderpòch)
- Date of the interview: 20th July 2011
- Place of the interview: kitchen of the consultant

1. **Translation into Mòcheno: Cosa ha comprato (lei)?**
    Bos hòt-se kaft?
    Alternatives (judgment task)
    *Bos se hòt kaft? – no
    *Bos de hòt kaft? – no
    *Bos si hòt kaft? – no
    *Bos hòt de kaft? – no
    *Bos hòt-si kaft? – no, only: bos hòt-se si kaft?
    *Bos hòt de mama kaft? – no, only: Bos hòt-se kaft de mama?

2. **Translation into Mòcheno: Quando ha comprato il libro (lui)?**
   Benn hòt-er kaft s puach?
   Alternatives (judgment task)
   *Benn er hòt kaft s puech? – no
   *Benn ar hòt kaft s puech? – no
   *Benn der hòt kaft s puech? – no
   *Benn hòt-ar kaft s puach? – no
   *Benn hòt-der kaft s puach? – no
   *Benn hòt der tata kaft s puach? – no, only: Benn hòt-er kaft der tata s puach?
   Benn hòt der tata s puach kaft? – ok

3. **Translation into Mòcheno: Maria mi ha chiesto come hai fatto il compito**
   De Maria hòt me pfrok,
   abia aso du der compito gamocht host
   Alternatives (judgment task)
   *abia as du der compito gamocht host – no

   Translation into Mòcheno: Maria mi ha chiesto come (lei) ha fatto il compito
   biase si gamocht hòt der compito
   Alternatives (judgment task)
   *bia si gamocht hòt der compito – no
   *bia de gamocht hòt der compito – no

   Translation into Mòcheno: Maria mi ha chiesto come Gianni ha fatto il compito
   bia (as) der Giani gamocht hòt der compito

4. **Translation into Mòcheno: Ieri ha comprato un libro (lei)**
   Gester hòt-se kaft a puach
   Alternatives (judgment task)
   Gester si hòt a puach kaft – ok, focus reading on SI
   *Gester se hòt a puach kaft – no
   Gester de hòt a puach kaft – ok
   *Gester hòt de a puach kaft – no
   Gester de mama hòt a puach kaft – ok
   Gester hòt de mama a puach kaft – ok

5. **Judgment task**
   S puach hòt-er gester kaft – ok, fronted XP is an SP, answer to Benn hòt-er kaft s puech?
   or hòt-er kaft s puech?
   *S puach gester hòt-er kaft – no
   *S puach der Mario hòt kaft – no, only: Der Mario hòt s puech kaft

6. **Judgment task**
   Bos hòt-er kaft? – ok
   *Bos gester hòt-er kaft? – no, Gester bos hòt-er kaft?

7. **Judgment task**
   A PUACH hone kaft, net a heft – ok
   *A PUACH gester hone kaft, net a heft – no: Gester hòt-er a puach kaft ont net a heft

8. **Judgment task**
   *Gester s puach er hòt-s kaft – no

9. Judgment task
   De mama hòt a puach kaft – ok

10. Judgment task
    De mama en de boteig hòt a puach kaft – ok

11. Judgment task
    *De mama en de boteig hòt-se a puach kaft – no

12. Judgment task
    Gester s puach ber hòt-s kaft? – ok

13. Judgment task
    *Ber s puach hòt-s kaft? – no

14. Judgment task
    S puach ber hòt kaft? – ok

15. Judgment task
    *Ber s puach hòt kaft? – no

PALÙ-IP

- Age: 79
- Sex: F
- Variety: Palù, Steffener (auserpòch)
- Date of the interview: 21st June 2011
- Place of the interview: kitchen of the consultant

1. Translation into Mòcheno: Cosa ha comprato (lei)?
   Bos hòt-se kaft?
   Alternatives (judgment task)
   *Bos se hòt kaft? -no
   *Bos de hòt kaft? – no
   *Bos si hòt kaft? – no, only: Bos hòt-se si kaft?
   *Bos hòt-si kaft? – no
   *Bos hòt de kaft? – no
   Bos hòt de mama kaft? – ok
   De mama, bos hòt-se kaft? -ok
   *De mama, bos hòt kaft? – no

2. Translation into Mòcheno: Quando ha comprato il libro (lui)?
   Benn hòt-er kaft s puach (der tata)?
   Alternatives (judgment task)
   Benn hòt der tata kaft s puach? – ok
   *Benn hòt er s puach kaft – no

3. Translation into Mòcheno: Maria mi ha chiesto come hai fatto il compito
   De Maria hòt me pfrok,
   bia hoso gamocht de compete – [FC: with the same intonation as a main interrogative clause]

Alternatives (judgment task)
*bia aso de compete gamocht host – no

Translation into Mòcheno: Maria mi ha chiesto come Gianni ha fatto il compito
bia der Hans der compito hòt gamocht

4. **Translation into Mòcheno: Ieri ha comprato un libro (lei)**
Gester de mama hòt a puach kaft – 1
De mama gester hòt a puach kaft – 2
Alternatives (judgment task)
Gester hòt-se a puach kaft – ok
Gester si hòt a puach kaft – ok
*Gester se hòt a puach kaft – no
Gester de hòt a puach kaft – ok
*Gester hòt de a puach kaft – no
Gester hòt de mama a puach kaft – ok

5. **Judgment task**
xxx

6. **Judgment task**
S puach hòne gester kaft – ok, fronted XP is an SP
*S puach gester hòt-er kaft – no
*S puach der Mario hòt kaft – no, only: Der Mario hòt s puach kaft

7. **Judgment task**
Bos hòt-er kaft? – ok
*Bos gester hòt-er kaft? – no

8. **Judgment task**
A PUACH hone kaft, net a quaderno
*A PUACH gester hone kaft, net a quaderno – no

9. **Judgment task**
*Gester s puach er hòt-s kaft – no

10. **Judgment task**
De mama hòt a puach kaft – ok

11. **Judgment task**
De mama en de boteig hòt a puach kaft – ok

12. **Judgment task**
*De mama en de boteig hòt-se a puach kaft

13. **Judgment task**
*Gester s puach ber hòt-s kaft? – no

14. **Judgment task**
*Ber s puach hòt-s kaft?

15. **Judgment task**
*S puach ber hòt kaft – no

16. **Judgment task**
*Ber s puach hòt kaft? – no

PALÙ-LT

- Age: 75
- Sex: M
- Variety: Palù, Simeter (auserpòch)
- Date of the interview: 11th August 2011
- Place of the interview: kitchen of the consultant

1. Translation into Mòcheno: Cosa ha comprato (lei)?
   Bos hòt-se kaft?
   Alternatives (judgment task)
   *Bos se hòt kaft? – no
   *Bos de hòt kaft? – no
   *Bos si hòt kaft? – no
   *Bos hòt de kaft? – no
   *Bos hòt-si kaft? – no
   Bos hòt-se kaft de mama? – ok
   Bos hòt de mama kaft? – ok

2. Translation into Mòcheno: Quando ha comprato il libro (lui)?
   Benn hòt-er s puach kaft?
   Benn hòt-er s puach kaft der tata?
   Alternatives (judgment task)
   Benn hòt-er kaft s puach? – ok
   *Benn er hòt kaft s puech? – no
   *Benn ar hòt kaft s puech? – no
   *Benn der hòt kaft s puech? – no
   *Benn hòt-ar kaft s puach? – no
   *Benn hòt-der kaft s puach? – no
   Benn hòt-er kaft s puech der tata? – ok
   Benn hòt der tata kaft s puech? – ok
   Benn hòt der tata s puach kaft? – ok

3. Translation into Mòcheno: Maria mi ha chiesto come hai fatto il compito
   De Maria hòt me pfrok,
   biado-sa du gamocht host de compite
   Alternatives (judgment task)
   *bia du gamocht host de compite – no
   biado-sa gamocht host de compito – ok

   Translation into Mòcheno: Maria mi ha chiesto come (lei) ha fatto il compito
   biase sa gamocht hòt de compite
   Alternatives (judgment task)
   abia ase-sa gamocht hòt de compite – ok
   abia ase-sa si gamocht hòt de compite – ok
   *abia sa gamocht hòt de compite – no

   Translation into Mòcheno: Maria mi ha chiesto come Gianni ha fatto il compito
   bia der Giani de compiti hòt gamocht

Alternatives (judgment task)
bia as der Giani de compiti hòt gamocht – ok
bia as-ar de compiti hòt gamocht der Giani – ok
biar de compiti hòt gamocht der Giani – ok
*bia de compiti hòt gamocht der Giani – no

4. Translation into Mòcheno: Ieri ha comprato un libro (lei)
Gester hòt-se kaft a puach
Alternatives (judgment task)
Gester si hòt kaft a puach – ok
*Gester se hòt kaft a puach – no
Gester de hòt kaft a puach – ok
*Gester hòt de kaft a puach – no
Gester de mama hòt (kaft) a puach (kaft) – ok
Gester hòt de mama kaft a puach – ok

5. Judgment task
S puach hòne gester kaft – ok, fronted XP is an SP
*S puach gester hone kaft – no
*S puach der Mario hòne kaft – no, only: Der Mario hòt s puech kaft

6. Judgment task
Bos hòt-er kaft? – ok
*Bos gester hòt-er kaft? – no, only: Bos hòt-er kaft gester? or Gester bos hoso kaft?

7. Judgment task
A PUACH hòt-er kaft, ont net a heft – ok
A PUACH gester hòt-er kaft, ont net a heft – ok, also: Gester A PUACH hòt-er kaft ont net....

8. Judgment task
Gester s puach er hòt-s kaft – ok

9. Judgment task
De mama hòt a puach kaft – ok

10. Judgment task
De mama ene boteig hòt a puach kaft – ok

11. Judgment task
*De mama en de boteig hòt-se a puach kaft – no

12. Judgment task
Gester s puach ber hòt-s kaft? – ok

13. Judgment task
*Ber s puach hòt-s kaft? – no

14. Judgment task
*S puach ber hòt kaft? – no

15. Judgment task
*Ber s puach hòt kaft? – no

PALÙ-MT

- Age: 75
- Sex: F
- Variety: Palù, Orastòll (auserpòch)
- Date of the interview: 11th August 2011
- Place of the interview: kitchen of the consultant

1. Translation into Mòcheno: Cosa ha comprato (lei)?
   Bos hòt-se kaft dai mama?
   Alternatives (judgment task)
   Bos hòt se kaft? – ok
   *Bos se hòt kaft? – no
   *Bos hòt de kaft? – no
   *Bos si hòt kaft? – no
   *Bos de hòt kaft? – no
   *Bos hòt si kaft? – no, Bos hòt-se kaft si? – ok, focus on SI
   *Bos hòt de mama kaft? – no: only: Bos hòt-se kaft de mama?

2. Translation into Mòcheno: Quando ha comprato il libro (lui)?
   Benn hòt-er kaft s puach?
   Alternatives (judgment task)
   *Benn ar hòt kaft s puech? – no
   *Benn er hòt kaft s puech? – no
   *Benn der hòt kaft s puech? – no
   *Benn hòt-ar kaft s puach? – no
   *Benn hòt-der kaft s puach? – no
   *Benn hòt der tata kaft s puach? – no, only: Benn hòt-er kaft s puach der tata?
   *Benn hòt der tata s puach kaft? – no
   *Benn hòt-er s puach kaft? – no

3. Translation into Mòcheno: Maria mi ha chiesto come hai fatto il compito
   De Maria hòt me pfrok,
   biaso host gamocht der compito
   Alternatives (judgment task)
   biaso der compito gamocht host – ok
   biaso host der compito gamocht – ok
   biaso du host gamocht der compito – ok
   *abia host gamocht der compito – no, only: abia hoso gamocht der compito

   Translation into Mòcheno: Maria mi ha chiesto come (lei) ha fatto il compito
   bia hòt-se gamocht der compito de sell/dai kamarote? [FC: clear intonational pattern of a main interrogative clause]
   abiase hòt gamocht der compito – ok
   abiase si hòt gamocht der compito – ok
   *abia hòt gamocht der compito – no

   Translation into Mòcheno: Maria mi ha chiesto come Gianni ha fatto il compito
   bia hòt-er gamocht der compito der Giani

Alternatives (judgment task)
bias der compito gamocht hòt der Giani – ok
bias der Giani der compito gamocht hòt – ok

4. Translation into Mòcheno: Ieri ha comprato un libro (lei)
Gester hòt-se a puach kaft
Alternatives (judgment task)
Gester si hòt a puach kaft – ok, focus on SI
*Gester se hòt a puach kaft – no
Gester de hòt a puach kaft – ok
Gester de mama hòt a puach kaft – ok
*Gester hòt de a puach kaft – no
Gester hòt de mama a puach kaft – ok

5. Judgment task
S puach hòt-er gester kaft – ok, fronted XP is an SP, answer to: Benn hòt-er kaft s puach?
*S puach gester hòt-er kaft – no
*S puach der Mario hòt kaft – no, Der Mario hòt kaft s puech

6. Judgment task
Bos hòt-er kaft? – ok
*Bos gester hòt-er kaft? – no, only: Gester, bos hòt-er kaft?

7. Judgment task
A PUACH hòt-er kaft, ont net an quaderno – ok
*A PUACH gester hone kaft, net an quaderno – no: Gester A PUACH hòt-er kaft, ont net...

8. Judgment task
*Gester s puach er hòt-s kaft – no

9. Judgment task
De mama hòt a puach kaft – ok

10. Judgment task
De mama ene boteig hòt a puach kaft – ok

11. Judgment task
*De mama ene boteig hòt-se a puach kaft – no

12. Judgment task
Gester s puach ber hòt-s kaft? – ok

13. Judgment task
*Ber s puach hòt-s kaft? – no

14. Judgment task
*S puach ber hòt kaft? – no, S is obligatory

15. Judgment task
*Ber s puach hòt kaft? – no

Questionnaires from Fierozzo

FIER-AP

- Age: 27
- Sex: M
- Variety: Fierozzo, S.Felice/Auserpèrg, Unterroudlern
- Date of the interview: 16th September 2011
- Place of the interview: kitchen of the consultant

1. Translation into Mòcheno: Cosa ha comprato (lei)?
   Bos de hòt kaft?
   Alternatives (judgment task)
   Bos hòt-se kaft? – ok
   *Bos se hòt kaft? – no
   Bos hòt-se kaft de mama? – ok
   Bos de hòt kaft de mama? – ok
   *Bos hòt de mama kaft? – no
   *Bos hòt-de kaft? – no
   *Bos si hòt kaft? – no
   *Bos hòt si kaft? – no, only: Bos hòt-se si kaft?

2. Translation into Mòcheno: Quando ha comprato il libro (lui)?
   Benn hòt-er kaft der puech?
   Alternatives (judgment task)
   *Benn der hòt kaft der puech? – no
   *Benn ar hòt kaft der puech? – no
   *Benn er hòt kaft der puech? – no
   Benn hòt-er kaft der puech der tata? – ok
   *Benn hòt der tata kaft der puech? – no
   *Benn hòt der tata der puech kaft? – no
   *Benn hòt-ar/der kaft der puech? – no

3. Translation into Mòcheno: Maria mi ha chiesto come hai fatto il compito
   Der Mario hòt-mer pfrok
   bi host-en gamocht der compito
   Alternatives (judgment task)
   *bi as host-en gamocht der compito – no
   *bi host der compito gamocht – no
   *bi der compito gamocht host – no
   bie de host gamocht der compito – ok
   bie de host du gamocht der compito net si – ok
   *bi host-en du gamocht der compito net si – no

   Translation into Mòcheno: Maria mi ha chiesto come (lei) ha fatto il compito
   bie de hòt-en si gamocht der compito
   Alternatives (judgment task)
   *bie hòt si gamocht der compito – no

Translation into Mòcheno: Maria mi ha chiesto come Gianni ha fatto il compito
abie der Giani hòt gamocht der compito
Alternatives (judgment task)
abie der hòt gamocht der compito der Giani – ok
*abie hòt gamocht der compito der Giani – no

4. Translation into Mòcheno: Ieri ha comprato un libro (lei)
   Gester de hòt kaft an puech
   Alternatives (judgment task)
   *Gester hòt-se kaft an puech – no, only: Gester de hòt-se kaft an puech
   Gester de mama hòt kaft an puech – ok
   Gester si hòt kaft an puech – ok
   *Gester se hòt kaft an puech – no
   *Gester hòt de kaft an puech – no
   *Gester hòt de mama kaft an puech – no
   *Gester hòt der mama an puech kaft – no

5. Judgment task
   S puech hone gester kaft – ok, only VO
   *S puech gester hone kaft – no
   S puech der Mario hòt kaft – ok

6. Judgment task
   Bos hòt-er kaft? – ok, better: Bos der hòt kaft?
   *Bos gester hòt-er kaft? – no, only: Bos hòt-er kaft gester? and Gester, bos hòt-er kaft?

7. Judgment task
   AN PUECH i hon kaft, net an quaderno – ok
   *AN PUECH gester i hon kaft, net an quaderno – no

8. Judgment task
   Gester der puech er hòt-en kaft – ok

9. Judgment task
   De mama hòt kaft an puech – ok

10. Judgment task
    De mama en de boteig hòt kaft an puech – ok

11. Judgment task
    *De mama en de boteig hòt-se kaft a puach – no

12. Judgment task
    Gester der puech ber hòt-en kaft? – ok

13. Judgment task
    *Ber der puech hòt-en kaft? – no

14. Judgment task
    *Der puech ber hòt kaft? – no

15. Judgment task
    *Ber der puech hòt kaft? – no

16. Judgment task
    *Gester hòt-er a puach kaft – no

17. Judgment task
    Gester hòt-er kaft a puech – ok

FIER-CP

- Age: 19
- Sex: F
- Variety: Fierozzo, S.Felice-Mitterperg, Boler
- Date of the interview: 29th July 2011
- Place of the interview: pub of Fierozzo

1. Translation into Mòcheno: Cosa ha comprato (lei)?
   Bos hòt-se kaft?
   Alternatives (judgment task)
   *Bos se hòt kaft? – no
   *Bos de hòt kaft? – no
   *Bos si hòt kaft? – no
   *Bos hòt-de kaft? – no
   *Bos hòt si kaft? – no, only: Bos hòt-se kaft si?
   Bos hòt de mama kaft? – ok
   Bos hòt-se kaft de mama? – ok

2. Translation into Mòcheno: Quando ha comprato il libro (lui)?
   Benn hòt-er der puech kaft?
   Alternatives (judgment task)
   Benn hòt-er kaft der puech? – ok
   *Benn ar hòt kaft der puech – no
   *Benn er hòt kaft der puech – no
   *Benn der hòt kaft der puech? – no
   *Benn hòt-ar/der kaft der puech – no
   Benn hòt der tata kaft der puech? – ok
   Benn hòt-er kaft der puech der tata? – ok
   Benn hòt der tata der puech kaft? – ok

3. Translation into Mòcheno: Maria mi ha chiesto come hai fatto il compito
   De Mario hòt-mer pfrott,
   abia (as) de host gamocht der compito
   Alternatives (judgment task)
   *abia host gamocht der compito – no
   abia de host du gamocht der compito – ok, focus on DU
   *abia DE host gamocht der compito – no

   Translation into Mòcheno: Maria mi ha chiesto come (lei) ha fatto il compito
   abia si hòt gamocht der compito

Alternatives (judgment task)
abia si hòt gamocht der compito – ok
*abiase hòt gamocht der compito – no
abia (as) de hòt gamocht der compito – ok
abia de hòt si gamocht der compito – focus on SI

Translation into Mòcheno: Maria mi ha chiesto come Gianni ha fatto il compito
abia as der Giani hòt gamocht der compito
Alternatives (judgment task)
*abia as er/der hòt gamocht der compito der Giani – no

4. Translation into Mòcheno: Ieri ha comprato un libro (lei)
Gester de hòt an puech kaft
Alternatives (judgment task)
Gester hòt-se an puech kaft – ok
Gester si hòt an puech kaft – ok, focus on SI
*Gester se hòt an puech kaft – no
*Gester hòt de an puech kaft – no
Gester de mama hòt an puech kaft – ok
Gester hòt de mama an puech kaft – ok

5. Judgment task
S puach hòt-er gester kaft – ok
*S puach gester hòt-er kaft – no
S puach der Mario hòt kaft – ok

6. Judgment task
Bos hòt-er kaft? – ok
*Bos gester hòt-er kaft? – no, only: Bos hòt-er kaft gester? or Gester bos hòt-er kaft?

7. Judgment task
A PUACH hòt-er kaft, net an quaderno – ok
A PUACH gester hòt-er kaft, net an quaderno – ok

8. Judgment task
*Gester s puech er hòt-s kaft – no

9. Judgment task
De mama hòt an puech kaft – ok

10. Judgment task
De mama en de boteig hòt an puech kaft – ok

11. Judgment task
*De mama en de boteig hòt-se kaft a puach – no

12. Judgment task
Gester der/der doi puech ber hòt-s kaft? – ok

13. Judgment task
*Ber der puech hòt-s kaft? – no

14. Judgment task
*Der puech ber hòt kaft? –no

15. **Judgment task**
    *Ber s puech hòt kaft? – no

16. **Judgment task**
    Gester hòt-er an/s puech kaft – ok

17. **Judgment task**
    Gester hòt-er kaft s puech – ok

FIER-GP

- Age: 20
- Sex: M
- Variety: Fierozzo, S.Felice-Mitterperg, Simeter
- Date of the interview: 9th September 2011
- Place of the interview: Istitute for the promotion of the Mòcheno language and culture, Palù del Fersina

1. **Translation into Mòcheno: Cosa ha comprato (lei)?**
    Bos hòt-se kaft?
    Alternatives (judgment task)
    *Bos se hòt kaft? – no
    Bos hòt-se kaft de mama? – ok
    *Bos hòt de mama kaft? – no
    *Bos si hòt kaft? – no
    *Bos hòt-de kaft? – no
    *Bos de hòt kaft? – no
    *Bos hòt si kaft? – no, only: Bos hòt-se si kaft?

2. **Translation into Mòcheno: Quando ha comprato il libro (lui)?**
    Benn hòt-er kaft s puech?
    Alternatives (judgment task)
    Benn hòt-er s puech kaft? – ok
    Benn hòt der tata s puech kaft? – ok
    Benn hòt-er kaft s puech der tata? – ok
    *Benn er hòt kaft s puech? – no
    *Benn hòt-ar/der kaft s puech? – no
    *Benn ar hòt kaft s puech? – no
    *Benn der hòt kaft s puech? – no
    Benn hòt der tata kaft s puech? – ok

3. **Translation into Mòcheno: Maria mi ha chiesto come hai fatto il compito**
    De Maria hòt-mer pfrok
    abia as de host gamocht der compito
    Alternatives (judgment task)
    abia de host gamocht der compito – ok
    abia du host gamocht der compito – ok
    abia as du host gamocht der compito – ok

abia as de host du gamocht der compito – ok
*abia as host du gamocht der compito – no
*abia ase host gamocht der compito – no

Translation into Mòcheno: Maria mi ha chiesto come (lei) ha fatto il compito
abia (as) de hòt gamocht der compito
Alternatives (judgment task)
*abia ase hòt gamocht der compito – no
abia as de hòt si gamocht der compito – ok, focus on SI
*abia as hòt si gamocht der compito – no

Translation into Mòcheno: Maria mi ha chiesto come Gianni ha fatto il compito
abia s hòt der Giani der compito gamocht
*abia der Giani hòt gamocht der compito – no
abia der Giani hòt der compito gamocht – ok
abia as der/er hòt der compito gamocht der Giani – ok
abia as hòt der compito gamocht der Giani – ok

4. Translation into Mòcheno: Ieri ha comprato un libro (lei)
   Gester hòt-se kaft a puech
   Alternatives (judgment task)
   Gester si hòt kaft a puech – ok
   Gester de mama hòt kaft a puech – ok
   *Gester se hòt kaft a puech – no
   *Gester de hòt kaft a puech – no
   Gester hòt de mama kaft a puech – ok
   *Gester hòt de kaft a puech – no

5. Judgment task
   S puech hone gester kaft – ok
   *S puech gester hone kaft – no
   *S puech der Mario hòt kaft – no, only: S puech hòt kaft der Mario or S puech hòt-er kaft der Mario

6. Judgment task
   Bos hòt-er kaft? – ok
   *Bos gester hòt-er kaft? – no, only: Bos hòt-er kaft gester? or Gester bos hòt-er kaft?

7. Judgment task
   A PUACH hone kaft, net an quaderno – ok
   *A PUACH gester hone kaft, net an quaderno – no, only: Gester A PUACH hòt-er kaft, net...

8. Judgment task
   *Gester s puech er hòt-s kaft – no

9. Judgment task
   De mama hòt kaft a puech – ok

10. Judgment task
    De mama en de boteig hòt kaft a puech – ok

11. Judgment task
    *De mama en de boteig hòt-se kaft a puach- no

12. Judgment task
    Gester s puech ber hòt-s kaft? – ok

13. Judgment task
    *Ber s puech hòt-s kaft? – no

14. Judgment task
    *S puech ber hòt kaft? – no, only: S puech ber hòt-s kaft?

15. Judgment task
    *Ber s puech hòt kaft? – no

16. Judgment task
    *Gester hòt-er a puach kaft – no

17. Judgment task
    Gester hòt-er kaft a puech – ok

FIER-MG

- Age: 19
- Sex: M
- Variety: Fierozzo, S.Felice/Mitterperg, Simeter
- Date of the interview: 19th August 2011
- Place of the interview: Istitute for the promotion of the Mòcheno language and culture, Palù del Fersina

1. Translation into Mòcheno: Cosa ha comprato (lei)?
   Bos hòt-se kaft?
   Alternatives (judgment task)
   *Bos se hòt kaft? – no
   *Bos de hòt kaft? – no
   *Bos hòt de mama kaft? – no, only: Bos hòt-se kaft de mama?
   *Bos hòt si kaft? – no
   *Bos hòt-de kaft? – no
   *Bos si hòt kaft? – no
   Bos hòt-se kaft si? -ok

2. Translation into Mòcheno: Quando ha comprato il libro (lui)?
   Benn hòt-er kaft s puech?
   Alternatives (judgment task)
   *Benn hòt der tata kaft der puech? – no, only: Benn hòt-er kaft s puech der tata?
   *Benn er hòt kaft s puech – no
   *Benn ar hòt kaft s puech – no
   *Benn der hòt kaft s puech? – no
   *Benn hòt-ar/der kaft s puech – no
   *Benn hòt der tata s puech kaft? – no

3. Translation into Mòcheno: Maria mi ha chiesto come hai fatto il compito
   De Maria hòt-mer pfrok
   abia as du host gamocht der compito – 1
   abia ase host gamocht der compito – 2
   Alternatives (judgment task)
   *abia as de host gamocht der compito – no
   abia ase host du gamocht der compito – ok

   Translation into Mòcheno: Maria mi ha chiesto come (lei) ha fatto il compito
   abia as si hòt gamocht der compito
   Alternatives (judgment task)
   abia as de hòt gamocht der compito – ok
   abia ase hòt gamocht der compito – ok
   abia ase hòt si gamocht der compito – ok
   *abia as hòt si gamocht der compito – no
   *abia ase de compiti gamocht hòt – no
   *abia ase hòt de compiti gamocht – no

   Translation into Mòcheno: Maria mi ha chiesto come Gianni ha fatto il compito
   abia as der hòt gamocht de compiti der Giani
   Alternatives (judgment task)
   abia as der Giani hòt gamocht de compiti – ok

4. Translation into Mòcheno: Ieri ha comprato un libro (lei)
   Gester si hòt kaft a puech
   Gester hòt-se kaft a puech – ok
   *Gester hòt de mama kaft a puech – no, only: Gester de mama hòt kaft a puech
   *Gester hòt de kaft a puech – no
   *Gester se hòt kaft a puech – no
   Gester de hòt kaft a puech – ok

5. Judgment task
   S puech hone kaft gester – ok
   *S puech gester hone kaft – no
   *S puech der Mario hòt kaft – no

6. Judgment task
   Bos hòt-er kaft? – ok
   *Bos gester hòt-er kaft? – no, only: Bos hòt-er kaft gester? or Gester bos hòt-er kaft?

7. Judgment task
   A PUACH hone kaft, net an quaderno – ok
   A PUACH gester hone kaft, net an quaderno – ok

8. Judgment task
   *Gester s puech er hòt-s kaft – no

9. Judgment task
   De mama hòt kaft a puech – ok

10. Judgment task
    De mama en de boteig hòt kaft a puech – ok

11. Judgment task
    *De mama en de boteig hòt-se kaft a puach – no

12. Judgment task
    Gester s puech ber hòt-s kaft? – ok

13. Judgment task
    *Ber s puech hòt-s kaft? – no

14. Judgment task
    *S puech ber hòt kaft? – no

15. Judgment task
    *Ber s puech hòt kaft? – no

16. Judgment task
    *Gester hòt-er a puach kaft – no

17. Judgment task
    Gester hòt-er kaft a puech – ok

FIER-SB

- Age: 27
- Sex: M
- Variety: Fierozzo, S.Felice/Mitterperg, Groan
- Date of the interview: 11th July 2011
- Place of the interview: University of Trento

1. **Translation into Mòcheno: Cosa ha comprato (lei)?**
   Bos hòt-se kaft (si)?
   Alternatives (judgment task)
   Bos hòt-se kaft de mama? – ok
   *Bos se hòt kaft? – no
   *Bos de hòt kaft? – no
   *Bos si hòt kaft? – no
   *Bos hòt-de kaft? – no
   *Bos hòt si kaft? – no
   *Bos hòt de mama kaft? – no, only: Bos hòt-se kaft de mama?

2. **Translation into Mòcheno: Quando ha comprato il libro (lui)?**
   Benn hòt-er kaft s puech?
   Alternatives (judgment task)
   *Benn er/der/ar hòt kaft s puech – no
   *Benn hòt-der/ar kaft s puech – no
   *Benn hòt der tata kaft s puech? – no, only: Benn hòt-er kaft s puech der tata?
   Benn hòt-er s puech kaft der tata? – ok

3. **Translation into Mòcheno: Maria mi ha chiesto come hai fatto il compito**
   De Mario hòt-mer pfrok,
   abie de host gamocht de compite

Alternatives (judgment task)
*abie host gamocht de compite – no
*abie aso host gamocht de compite – no
abie as de (du) host gamocht (du) de compite – ok
*abie as de host de compite gamocht – no
abie as de de compite gamocht host – ok
*abie de de compite gamocht host – no

Translation into Mòcheno: Maria mi ha chiesto come (lei) ha fatto il compito
abie si hòt gamocht de compite
Alternatives (judgment task)
*abie hòt gamocht de compite – no
abie as de hòt gamocht de compite – ok
abie ase hòt gamocht de compite – ok
*abie as si hòt gamocht de compite
abie asse si hòt gamocht de compite – ok

Translation into Mòcheno: Maria mi ha chiesto come Gianni ha fatto il compito
abie der Giani hòt gamocht de compite – first version
abie der Giani de compite gamocht hòt – second version
Alternatives (judgment task)
*abie der Giani hòt de compite gamocht – no
abie as der Giani hòt gamocht de compite – ok
*abie as-der hòt gamocht de compite der Giani– no
abie er hòt gamocht de compite – ok

4. **Translation into Mòcheno: Ieri ha comprato un libro (lei)**
   Gester hòt-er/se kaft a puech
   Alternatives (judgment task)
   Gester si hòt kaft a puach – ok
   *Gester se hòt kaft a puach – no
   Gester de hòt kaft a puach – ok
   *Gester hòt de kaft a puach – no
   Gester de mama hòt kaft a puach – ok
   Gester hòt de mama kaft a puach – no

5. **Judgment task**
   S puach hòt-er gester kaft – ok, fronted XP is an SP, answer to Benn hòt-er kaft s puech?
   *S puach gester hòt-er kaft – no
   *S puach der Mario hòt kaft – no, only: Der Mario hòt kaft s puech

6. **Judgment task**
   Bos hòt-er kaft? – ok
   *Bos gester hòt-er kaft? – no, only: bos hòt-er kaft gester?

7. **Judgment task**
   A PUACH hòt-er kaft ont net eppas onders – ok
   *A PUACH gester hòt-er kaft – no, only: Gester A PUACH hòt-er kaft, net an quaderno

8. **Judgment task**
   *Gester s puech er hòt-s kaft – no

9. Judgment task
   De mama hòt kaft a puech – ok, only VO, OV is out

10. Judgment task
    De mama en de boteig hòt kaft a puech – ok, only VO, OV is out

11. Judgment task
    *De mama en de boteig hòt-sa kaft a puach – no

12. Judgment task
    *Gester s puech ber hòt-s kaft? – no

13. Judgment task
    *Ber s puach hòt-s kaft? – no

14. Judgment task
    *S puach ber hòt kaft? – no

15. Judgment task
    *Ber s puach hòt kaft? – no

16. Judgment task
    xxx

17. Judgment task
    xxx

FIER-GG

- Age: 39
- Sex: M
- Variety: Fierozzo, S.Felice/Mitterperg, Casar
- Date of the interview: 29th July 2011
- Place of the interview: kitchen of the consultant

1. Translation into Mòcheno: Cosa ha comprato (lei)?
   Bos hòt-se kaft?
   Alternatives (judgment task)
   *Bos se hòt kaft? – no
   *Bos de hòt kaft? – no
   *Bos si hòt kaft? – no
   *Bos hòt-de kaft? – no
   *Bos hòt si kaft? – no, only: Bos hòt-se kaft si?
   *Bos hòt de mama kaft? – no, only: Bos hòt-se kaft de mama?

2. Translation into Mòcheno: Quando ha comprato il libro (lui)?
   En benn hòt-er kaft s puech?
   Alternatives (judgment task)
   *En benn ar hòt kaft s puech? – no
   *En benn er hòt kaft s puech? – no
   *En benn der hòt kaft s puech – no
   *En benn hòt-ar kaft s puech? – no

*En benn hòt-der kaft s puech? – no
*En benn hòt der tata kaft s puech? – no
En benn hòt-er kaft s puech der tata – ok
*En benn hòt der tata s puech kaft? – no

3. Translation into Mòcheno: Maria mi ha chiesto come hai fatto il compito
   De Maria hòt-mer pfrok,
   abia (as) de host gamocht de compite
   Alternatives (judgment task)
   *abia de host de compite gamocht – no
   *abia de de compite gamocht host – no
   *abia host gamocht de compite – no
   abia de host du gamocht de compite – ok, focus on DU
   *abia de host gamocht du de compite – no

   Translation into Mòcheno: Maria mi ha chiesto come (lei) ha fatto il compito
   abia (as) de hòt si gamocht de compite
   Alternatives (judgment task)
   *abiase hòt si gamocht de compite – no

   Translation into Mòcheno: Maria mi ha chiesto come Gianni ha fatto il compito
   abia as der Giani hòt gamocht de compite
   Alternatives (judgment task)
   abia as der hòt gamocht de compite der Gianni – ok

4. Translation into Mòcheno: Ieri ha comprato un libro (lei)
   Gester hòt-se kaft a puech – also OV
   Alternatives (judgment task)
   Gester si hòt kaft a puech – ok, focus on SI
   *Gester se hòt kaft a puech – no
   *Gester de hòt kaft a puech – no
   *Gester hòt de kaft a puech – no
   Gester de mama hòt kaft a puech – ok
   *Gester hòt de mama kaft a puech – no
   Gester hòt de mama a puech kaft – ok

5. Judgment task
   S puech hòt-er gester kaft – ok, also VO
   *S puech gester hòt-er kaft – no, only: Gester hòt-er kaft s puech
   *S puech der Mario hòt kaft – no

6. Judgment task
   Bos hòt-er kaft? – ok
   *Bos gester hòt-er kaft? – no

7. Judgment task
   A PUACH hòt-er kaft ont net an quaderno – ok
   *A PUACH gester hòt-er kaft ont net an quaderno – no

8. Judgment task
   *Gester s puech er hòt-s kaft – no

9. Judgment task
   De mama hòt a puech kaft – ok

10. Judgment task
    De mama en de boteig hòt a puech kaft – ok

11. Judgment task
    *De mama en de boteig hòt-se a puach kaft – no

12. Judgment task
    Gester s puech ber hòt-s kaft? – ok

13. Judgment task
    *Ber s puach hòt-s kaft? – no

14. Judgment task
    *S puach ber hòt kaft? – no

15. Judgment task
    *Ber s puach hòt kaft – no

16. Judgment task
    Gester hòt-er a puech kaft – ok

17. Judgment task
    Gester hòt-er kaft a puech – ok

FIER-GAM

- Age: 38
- Sex: F
- Variety: Fierozzo, S.Felice/Inderperg, Markl
- Date of the interview: 20th July 2011
- Place of the interview: kitchen of the consultant

1. Translation into Mòcheno: Cosa ha comprato (lei)?
   Bos hòt-se kaft (si)?
   Alternatives (judgment task)
   *Bos se hòt kaft? – no
   Bos de hòt kaft? – ok
   Bos si hòt kaft? – ok
   *Bos hòt-de kaft? – no
   Bos hòt si kaft? – ok
   Bos hòt de mama kaft? – ok
   Bos hòt-se kaft de mama? – ok

2. Translation into Mòcheno: Quando ha comprato il libro (lui)?
   Benn hòt-er kaft s puech der tata?
   Alternatives (judgment task)
   Benn hòt-er kaft s puech? – ok
   Benn er hòt kaft s puech? – ok
   *Benn ar hòt kaft s puech? – no

*Benn der hòt kaft s puech – no
*Benn hòt-der kaft s puech? – no
*Benn hòt-ar kaft s puech? – no
Benn hòt der tata kaft s puech? – ok
Benn hòt-er kaft s puech der tata? – ok
Benn hòt der tata s puech kaft? – ok

3. Translation into Mòcheno: Maria mi ha chiesto come hai fatto il compito
   Maria hòt-mer pfrok,
   abia de host gamocht der compito
   Alternatives (judgment task)
   abia de host du gamocht der compito – ok
   abia du host gamocht der compito – ok

   Translation into Mòcheno: Maria mi ha chiesto come (lei) ha fatto il compito
   abia si hòt gamocht der compito
   Alternatives (judgment task)
   *abiase hòt gamocht der compito – no
   abia de hòt gamocht der compito – ok
   abia de hòt gamocht (si) der compito – ok

   Translation into Mòcheno: Maria mi ha chiesto come Gianni ha fatto il compito
   abia Giani hòt gamocht der compito
   Alternatives (judgment task)
   *abia de der compito gamocht host – no
   abia de host der compito gamocht – ok

4. Translation into Mòcheno: Ieri ha comprato un libro (lei)
   Gester hòt-se kaft a puech
   Alternatives (judgment task)
   Gester si hòt kaft a puech – ok
   *Gester se hòt kaft a puech – no
   Gester de hòt kaft a puech – ok
   *Gester hòt de kaft a puech – no
   Gester de mama hòt kaft a puech – ok
   Gester hòt de mama a puech kaft – ok
   Gester hòt de mama kaft a puech – ok

5. Judgment task
   S puach hòt-er gester kaft – ok, fronted XP is an SP
   S puach gester hòt-er kaft – ok
   S puach der Mario hòt kaft – ok

6. Judgment task
   Bos hòt-er kaft? – ok
   *Bos gester hòt-er kaft? – no, only: bos hòt-er kaft gester?

7. Judgment task
   A PUACH hòt-er kaft ont net an quaderno – ok
   A PUACH gester hòt-er kaft ont net an quaderno – ok

8. Judgment task
   Gester s puech er hòt-s kaft – ok

9. Judgment task
   De mama hòt a puech kaft – ok

10. Judgment task
    De mama en de boteig hòt a puech kaft – ok

11. Judgment task
    *De mama en de boteig hòt-se a puach kaft – no

12. Judgment task
    Gester s puech ber hòt-s kaft? – ok

13. Judgment task
    *Ber s puach hòt-s kaft? – no

14. Judgment task
    ??S puach ber hòt kaft? – not perfect

15. Judgment task
    ??Ber s puach hòt kaft – not perfect

16. Judgment task
    Gester hòt-er a puech kaft – ok

17. Judgment task
    Gester hòt-er kaft a puech – ok

FIER-PM

- Age: 51
- Sex: M
- Variety: Fierozzo, S.Francesco/auserperg, Joppereck
- Date of the interview: 11th August 2011
- Place of the interview: kitchen of the consultant

1. Translation into Mòcheno: Cosa ha comprato (lei)?
   Bos hòt-se kaft (si)?
   Alternatives (judgment task)
   *Bos se hòt kaft? – no
   *Bos de hòt kaft – no
   *Bos si hòt kaft? – no
   *Bos hòt-de kaft? – no
   *Bos hòt si kaft? – no, only: Bos hòt-se si kaft?
   Bos hòt-se kaft de muiter – his translation
   *Bos hòt de muiter kaft? – no

2. Translation into Mòcheno: Quando ha comprato il libro (lui)?
   En benn hòt-er kaft s puech?

Alternatives (judgment task)
*En benn ar hòt kaft s puech – no
*En benn er hòt kaft s puech – no
*En benn der hòt kaft s puech – no
*En benn hòt-ar kaft s puech – no
*En benn hòt-der kaft s puech – no
En benn hòt-er kaft s puech der voter? – his translation
En benn hòt der voter kaft s puech? – ok
En benn hòt der voter s puech kaft? – ok

3. Translation into Mòcheno: Maria mi ha chiesto come hai fatto il compito
   De Maria hòt-mer pfrok,
   abia de host gamocht de compiti
   Alternatives (judgment task)
   *abia host gamocht de compiti – no
   abia de host de compiti gamocht – ok
   *abia de de compiti gamocht host – no

   Translation into Mòcheno: Maria mi ha chiesto come (lei) ha fatto il compito
   abia ase si hòt gamocht de compite
   Alternatives (judgment task)
   *abia si hòt gamocht de compite
   abia de hòt gamocht de compite – ok
   abia de hòt si gamocht de compite – ok, focus on SI
   *abia hòt gamocht de compite – no
   abia hòt-se gamocht de compite – ok
   *abia ase de hòt gamocht de compite – no

   Translation into Mòcheno: Maria mi ha chiesto come Gianni ha fatto il compito
   abie der Nane hòt gamocht de compiti
   Alternatives (judgment task)
   abie as der Nane hòt gamocht de compiti – ok
   abie as der hòt gamocht de compiti der Nane – ok
   abie hòt gamocht de compiti der Nane – ok

4. Translation into Mòcheno: Ieri ha comprato un libro (lei)
   Gester hòt-se kaft a puech
   Alternatives (judgment task)
   Gester si hòt kaft a puech – ok, focus on SI
   *Gester se hòt kaft a puech – no
   Gester de hòt kaft a puech – ok
   Gester hòt de mama kaft a puech – ok, only if *de mama* is focused
   *Gester hòt de kaft a puech – no
   Gester de mama hòt kaft a puech – ok, unmarked

5. **Judgment task**
   S puach hone gester kaft – ok, fronted XP is an SP, answer to Benn host kaft s puech?
   *S puach gester hone kaft – no
   *S puach der Mario hòt kaft – no

6. **Judgment task**
   Bos hòt-er kaft? – ok
   *Bos gester hòt-er kaft? – no, only: Gester, bos hòt-er kaft?

7. **Judgment task**
   A PUACH hòt-er kaft ont net an quaderno/heft – ok
   *A PUACH gester hòt-er kaft ont net an quaderno – no, only: Gester A PUACH hone kaft, ont net an quaderno/a heft

8. **Judgment task**
   Gester s puech er hòt-s kaft – ok

9. **Judgment task**
   De muiter hòt a puech kaft – ok

10. **Judgment task**
    De muiter en de boteig hòt a puech kaft – ok

11. **Judgment task**
    *De mama en de boteig hòt-se kaft a puech – no

12. **Judgment task**
    Gester s puech ber hòt-s kaft? – ok

13. **Judgment task**
    *Ber s puech hòt-s kaft? – no

14. **Judgment task**
    *S puech ber hòt kaft? – no

15. **Judgment task**
    *Ber s puech hòt kaft? – no

16. **Judgment task**
    Gester hòt-er a puech kaft – ok

17. **Judgment task**
    Gester hòt-er kaft a puech – ok

FIER-RB

- Age: 47
- Sex: M
- Variety: Fierozzo, S.Felice/inderperg, Markl
- Date of the interview: 29th July 2011
- Place of the interview: kitchen of the consultant

1. **Translation into Mòcheno: Cosa ha comprato (lei)?**
   Bos hòt-se kaft (si)?
   Alternatives (judgment task)
   *Bos se hòt kaft (si)? – no
   *Bos de hòt kaft? – no
   *Bos si hòt kaft? – no

*Bos hòt-de kaft? – no
*Bos hòt si kaft? – no, only: Bos hòt-se kaft si?
Bos hòt de mama kaft? – ok
Bos hòt-se kaft de mama? – ok

2. Translation into Mòcheno: Quando ha comprato il libro (lui)?
Benn hòt-er kaft s puech?
Alternatives (judgment task)
*Benn er hòt kaft s puech? – no
*Benn ar hòt kaft s puech? – no
*Benn der hòt kaft s puech? – no
*Benn hòt-ar kaft s puech? – no
*Benn hòt-der kaft s puech? – no
Benn hòt der tata kaft s puech? – ok
Benn hòt-er kaft s puech der tata? – ok
*Benn hòt der tata s puech kaft? – no

3. Translation into Mòcheno: Maria mi ha chiesto come hai fatto il compito
De Mario hòt-mer pfrok,
abia de host gamocht de compite
Alternatives (judgment task)
abia host gamocht de compite – ok
*abiaso host gamocht de compite – no
*abia de host de compite gamocht – no
*abia de de compite gamocht host – no
abia de host du gamocht de compite – ok
abia de host gamocht du de compite – ok
*abia de host gamocht de compite du – no

Translation into Mòcheno: Maria mi ha chiesto come (lei) ha fatto il compito
abia (as) de hòt gamocht si de compite
Alternatives (judgment task)
*abia hòt gamocht si de compite – no
*abiase hòt gamocht de compite – no

Translation into Mòcheno: Maria mi ha chiesto come Gianni ha fatto il compito
abia (as) der Giani hòt gamocht de compite
Alternatives (judgment task)
*abia as der hòt gamocht de compite der Giani – no

4. Translation into Mòcheno: Ieri ha comprato un libro (lei)
Gester hòt-se kaft a puech
Alternatives (judgment task)
Gester si hòt kaft a puech – ok
*Gester se hòt kaft a puech – no
Gester de hòt kaft a puech – ok
*Gester hòt de kaft a puech – no
Gester de mama hòt kaft a puech – ok
Gester hòt de mama kaft a puech – ok

5. Judgment task
   S puach hòt-er gester kaft – ok, fronted XP is an SP
   *S puach gester hòt-er kaft – no
   *S puach der Mario hòt kaft – no, only: Der Mario hòt kaft s puech

6. Judgment task
   Bos hòt-er kaft? – ok
   *Bos gester hòt-er kaft? – no, only: Bos hòt-er kaft gester? or Gester, bos hòt-er kaft?

7. Judgment task
   A PUACH hòt-er kaft ont net an quaderno – ok
   A PUACH gester hòt-er kaft ont net an quaderno – ok

8. Judgment task
   *Gester s puech er hòt-s kaft – no

9. Judgment task
   De mama hòt a puech kaft – ok

10. Judgment task
    De mama en de boteig hòt a puech kaft – ok

11. Judgment task
    *De mama en de boteig hòt-se kaft a puach – no

12. Judgment task
    Gester s puech ber hòt-s kaft? – ok

13. Judgment task
    *Ber s puach hòt-s kaft? – no

14. Judgment task
    *S puach ber hòt kaft? – no

15. Judgment task
    *Ber s puach hòt kaft? – no

16. Judgment task
    Gester hòt-er a puech kaft – ok

17. Judgment task
    Gester hòt-er kaft a puech – ok

FIER-RR

- Age: 38
- Sex: F
- Variety: Fierozzo, S.Francesco/auserpèrg, Ouberroudlern
- Date of the interview: 29th July 2011
- Place of the interview: kitchen of the consultant

1. Translation into Mòcheno: Cosa ha comprato (lei)?
   Bos hòt-se kaft?

Alternatives (judgment task)
*Bos se hòt kaft? – no
*Bos de hòt kaft? – no
*Bos si hòt kaft? – no
*Bos hòt-de kaft? – no
*Bos hòt si kaft? – no
Bos hòt de mama kaft? – ok
Bos hòt-se kaft de mama? – ok

2. **Translation into Mòcheno: Quando ha comprato il libro (lui)?**
En benn hòt-er kaft s puech?
Alternatives (judgment task)
*En benn er hòt kaft s puech? – no
*En benn ar hòt kaft s puech? – no
*En benn der hòt kaft s puech – no
*En benn hòt-ar kaft s puech? – no
*En benn hòt-der kaft s puech? – no
*En benn hòt der tata kaft s puech? – no, only: En benn hòt-er kaft s puech der tata?
*En benn hòt der tata s puech kaft? – no

3. **Translation into Mòcheno: Maria mi ha chiesto come hai fatto il compito**
De Maria hòt-mer pfrok,
abia (as) de host gamocht de compite
Alternatives (judgment task)
*abia host gamocht de compite – no
abia de host gamocht du de compite – ok

Translation into Mòcheno: Maria mi ha chiesto come (lei) ha fatto il compito
abia si hòt gamocht de compite – first version
abia si hòt de compite gamocht – second version
Alternatives (judgment task)
abiase hòt gamocht de compite – ok
abia de hòt gamocht de compite – ok
*abiase hòt gamocht de compite si – no
*abia de hòt gamocht de compite si – no

Translation into Mòcheno: Maria mi ha chiesto come Gianni ha fatto il compito
abia der Giani hòt gamocht de compite
Alternatives (judgment task)
*abia er hòt gamocht de compite der Giani – no

4. **Translation into Mòcheno: Ieri ha comprato un libro (lei)**
Gester hòt-se kaft a puech
Alternatives (judgment task)
Gester si hòt kaft a puech – ok
*Gester se hòt kaft a puech – no
*Gester de hòt kaft a puech – no
*Gester hòt de kaft a puech – no
Gester de mama hòt kaft a puech – ok
*Gester hòt de mama kaft a puech – no

5. Judgment task
   S puech hòt-er gester kaft – ok, the fronted XP is an SP
   *S puech gester hòt-er kaft – no
   *S puech der Mario hòt kaft – no, only: Der Mario hòt kaft s puech

6. Judgment task
   Bos hòt-er kaft? – ok
   *Bos gester hòt-er kaft? – no, only: Bos hòt-er kaft gester?

7. Judgment task
   A PUACH hòt-er kaft ont net an quaderno – ok
   *A PUACH gester hòt-er kaft ont net an quaderno – no

8. Judgment task
   *Gester s puech er hòt-s kaft – no

9. Judgment task
   De mama hòt kaft a puech – ok

10. Judgment task
    De mama en de boteig hòt kaft a puech – ok

11. Judgment task
    *De mama en de boteig hòt-se a puach kaft – no

12. Judgment task
    ?Gester s puech ber hòt-s kaft? – not perfect

13. Judgment task
    *Ber s puach hòt-s kaft? – no

14. Judgment task
    *S puach ber hòt kaft? – no

15. Judgment task
    *Ber s puach hòt kaft – no

16. Judgment task
    ?Gester hòt-er a puech kaft – not perfect

17. Judgment task
    Gester hòt-er kaft a puech – ok

FIER-AS

- Age: 77
- Sex: F
- Variety: Fierozzo, S.Felice/inderpèrg, Tuneger
- Date of the interview: 11th August 2011
- Place of the interview: kitchen of the consultant

1. Translation into Mòcheno: Cosa ha comprato (lei)?
   Bos hòt-se kaft?

Alternatives (judgment task)
*Bos se hòt kaft? – no
*Bos de hòt kaft? – no
*Bos si hòt kaft? – no
*Bos hòt de kaft? – no
*Bos hòt si kaft? – no
Bos hòt-se kaft si? – ok, focus on SI
Bos hòt de mama kaft? – ok
Bos hòt-se kaft de mama? – ok

2. **Translation into Mòcheno: Quando ha comprato il libro (lui)?**
Benn hòt-er kaft s puech (der pare)?
Alternatives (judgment task)
*Benn ar hòt kaft s puech? – no
*Benn er hòt kaft s puech? – no
*Benn der hòt kaft s puech? – no
Benn hòt der tata kaft s puech? – ok
Benn hòt-er kaft s puech der tata? – ok
Benn hòt der tata s puech kaft? – ok
*Benn hòt-ar kaft s puech? – no
*Benn hòt-der kaft s puech? – no

3. **Translation into Mòcheno: Maria mi ha chiesto come hai fatto il compito**
De Maria hòt-mer pfrok,
abia de host gamocht der compito
Alternatives (judgment task)
abia du host gamocht der compito – ok
abia host gamocht der compito – ok

Translation into Mòcheno: Maria mi ha chiesto come (lei) ha fatto il compito
abia (as) de hòt gamocht der compito
Alternatives (judgment task)
*abia ase hòt gamocht der compito – no

Translation into Mòcheno: Maria mi ha chiesto come Gianni ha fatto il compito
abia der Giani hòt-en gamocht der compito

4. **Translation into Mòcheno: Ieri ha comprato un libro (lei)**
Geister hòt-se kaft a puech
Alternatives (judgment task)
Geister si hòt kaft a puach – ok
*Geister se hòt kaft a puech – no
Geister de hòt kaft a puech – ok
*Geister hòt de kaft a puech – no
Geister de mama hòt kaft a puech – ok
Geister hòt de mama kaft a puech – ok

5. **Judgment task**
S puech hòt-er geister kaft – ok, the fronted XP is an SP
S puech geister hòt-er kaft – ok
*S puech der Mario hòt kaft – no, only: Der Mario hòt kaft a puech

6. Judgment task
   Bos hòt-er kaft – ok
   Bos geister hòt-er kaft? – ok

7. Judgment task
   A PUACH hòt-er kaft, net a quaderno – ok
   A PUACH gester hòt-er kaft, net a quaderno – ok

8. Judgment task
   Geister s puech er hòt-s kaft – ok

9. Judgment task
   De mai mare hòt kaft a puech – ok

10. Judgment task
    De mai mare en de boteig hòt kaft a puech – ok

11. Judgment task
    *De mai mare en de boteig hòt-se kaft a puech – no

12. Judgment task
    Geister s puech ber hòt-s kaft? – ok

13. Judgment task
    *Ber s puech hòt-s kaft? – no

14. Judgment task
    *S puech ber hòt kaft? – no

15. Judgment task
    *Ber s puech hòt kaft? – no

16. Judgment task
    Gester hòt-er a puach kaft – ok

17. Judgment task
    Gester hòt-er kaft a puech – ok

FIER-AM

- Age: 67
- Sex: M
- Variety: Fierozzo, S.Felice/Mittelpèrg, Simeter
- Date of the interview: 16th September 2011
- Place of the interview: kitchen of the consultant

1. **Translation into Mòcheno: Cosa ha comprato (lei)?**
   Bos hòt-se kaft
   Alternatives (judgment task)
   *Bos se hòt kaft? – no
   Bos hòt-se kaft de mama? – ok
   Bos hòt de mama kaft? – ok
   *Bos de hòt kaft? – no

*Bos si hòt kaft? – no, only: Bos hòt-se kaft si?
*Bos hòt de kaft? – no
*Bos hòt si kaft? – no, only: Bos hòt-se si kaft?

2. **Translation into Mòcheno: Quando ha comprato il libro (lui)?**
Benn hòt-er kaft s puech?
Alternatives (judgment task)
*Benn er hòt kaft s puech? – no
*Benn hòt-ar kaft s puech? – no
Benn hòt-er kaft s puech der tata? – his translation
*Benn hòt der tata kaft s puech? – no
*Benn hòt der tata s puech kaft? – no
*Benn ar hòt kaft s puech? – no
*Benn der hòt kaft s puech? – no
*Benn hòt-der kaft s puech? – no

3. **Translation into Mòcheno: Maria mi ha chiesto come hai fatto il compito**
De Maria hòt-mer pfrok,
abia do host gamocht der compito
Alternatives (judgment task)
*abia do der compito gamocht host – no
*abia do host der compito gamocht – no
abia host gamocht der compito – ok [FC: same intonation as a main interrogative clause]
abie do host du gamocht der compito, net si – ok
abie du host du gamocht der compito, net si – ok
*abie host du gamocht der compito – ok

Translation into Mòcheno: Maria mi ha chiesto come (lei) ha fatto il compito
abie de si hòt gamocht der compito
Alternatives (judgment task)
abie as de si hòt gamocht der compito – ok
*abie ase hòt gamocht der compito – no
abie si hòt gamocht der compito – ok
*abie hòt si gamocht der compito – no

Translation into Mòcheno: Maria mi ha chiesto come Gianni ha fatto il compito
abie der Giani hòt gamocht der compito
Alternatives (judgment task)
abie der hòt gamocht der compito der Giani – ok
*abie hòt gamocht der compito der Giani – no

4. **Translation into Mòcheno: Ieri ha comprato un libro (lei)**
Geister hòt-se kaft s puech
Alternatives (judgment task)
Geister si hòt kaft a puech – ok
*Geister se hòt kaft a puech – no
Geister de mama hòt kaft a puech – his translation
*Geister hòt de mama kaft a puech – no
Geister de hòt kaft a puech – ok
*Geister hòt de kaft a puech – no

5. Judgment task
   S puech hone geister kaft – ok, also with OV syntax
   *S puech geister hòt-er kaft – no
   *S puech der Mario hòt kaft – no

6. Judgment task
   Bos hòt-er kaft – ok
   *Bos gester hòt-er kaft? – no, only: Bos hòt-er kaft geister?

7. Judgment task
   A PUACH hone kaft, net a quaderno za schraim – ok
   *A PUACH gester hone kaft, net a quaderno za schraim – no

8. Judgment task
   *Geister s puech er hòt-s kaft – no

9. Judgment task
   De mama hòt kaft s puech – ok

10. Judgment task
    De mama en de boteig hòt kaft a puech – ok

11. Judgment task
    *De mama en de boteig hòt-se kaft a puech – no

12. Judgment task
    Geister s puech ber hòt-s kaft? – ok

13. Judgment task
    *Ber s puech hòt-s kaft? – no

14. Judgment task
    *S puech ber hòt kaft? – no

15. Judgment task
    *Ber s puech hòt kaft? – no

16. Judgment task
    Gester hòt-er a puach kaft – ok

17. Judgment task
    Gester hòt-er kaft a puech – ok

FIER-COP

- Age: 78
- Sex: M
- Variety: Fierozzo, S.Felice/Inderpèrg, Soa
- Date of the interview: 18th August 2011
- Place of the interview: kitchen of the consultant

1. Translation into Mòcheno: Cosa ha comprato (lei)?
   Bos hòt-se kaft si?

Alternatives (judgment task)
Bos hòt-se si kaft? – ok
*Bos se hòt kaft? – no
*Bos de hòt kaft? – no
*Bos si hòt kaft? – no
*Bos hòt de kaft? – no
*Bos hòt si kaft? – no
Bos hòt-se kaft de mama? – his translation
Bos hòt de mama kaft? – ok

2. **Translation into Mòcheno: Quando ha comprato il libro (lui)?**
Benn hòt-er kaft s puech?
Alternatives (judgment task)
*Benn er hòt kaft s puech? – no
*Benn ar hòt kaft s puech? – no
*Benn der hòt kaft s puech? – no
*Benn hòt-ar kaft s puech? – no
*Benn hòt-der kaft s puech? – no
Benn hòt-er kaft s puech der tata? – his translation
Benn hòt der tata kaft s puech? – ok only as a special interrogative
Benn hòt der tata s puech kaft? – ok only as a special interrogative

3. **Translation into Mòcheno: Maria mi ha chiesto come hai fatto il compito**
De Maria hòt-mer pfrok,
abie du host gamocht de compite
Alternatives (judgment task)
abie host gamocht de compite – ok [FC: same intonation as a main interrogative]
abie de host-sa gamocht de compite – ok

Translation into Mòcheno: Maria mi ha chiesto come (lei) ha fatto il compito
abie de hòt-sa gamocht de compite
Alternatives (judgment task)
abie de si hòt-sa gamocht de compite – ok, focus on SI

Translation into Mòcheno: Maria mi ha chiesto come Gianni ha fatto il compito
abia as der Giani hòt-sa gamocht de compite

4. **Translation into Mòcheno: Ieri ha comprato un libro (lei)**
Geister hòt-se a puech kaft
Alternatives (judgment task)
Geister si hòt a puech kaft – ok
*Geister se hòt a puech kaft – no
Geister de hòt a puech kaft – ok
Geister hòt de mama a puech kaft – ok
Geister de mama hòt a puech kaft – ok
*Geister hòt de a puech kaft – no
Gester hòt de mama kaft a puech – ok

5. Judgment task
   S puech hone geister kaft – ok, fronted XP is an SP, answer to Benn hòt-se kaft s puech?
   *S puech geister hone kaft – ok
   *S puech der Mario hòt kaft – no, only: S puech hòt-se der Mario kaft

6. Judgment task
   Bos hòt-er kaft – ok
   *Bos geister hòt-er kaft? – no, only: Gester, bos hòt-er kaft?

7. Judgment task
   A PUECH hone kaft, net a heft – ok
   A PUECH gester hone kaft, net a heft – ok

8. Judgment task
   Geister s puech er hòt-s kaft – ok

9. Judgment task
   De mama hòt a puech kaft – ok

10. Judgment task
    De mama en de boteig hòt a puech kaft – ok

11. Judgment task
    *De mama en de boteig hòt-se a puech kaft – no

12. Judgment task
    *Geister s puech ber hòt-s kaft? – no, only: Gester, ber hòt kaft s doi puech?

13. Judgment task
    *Ber s puech hòt-s kaft? – no

14. Judgment task
    *S puech ber hòt kaft?

15. Judgment task
    *Ber s puech hòt kaft? – no

16. Judgment task
    Gester hòt-er a puach kaft – ok

17. Judgment task
    Gester hòt-er kaft a puech – ok

FIER-EI

- Age: 70
- Sex: M
- Variety: Fierozzo, S.Francesco/auserpèrg, Gaiger
- Date of the interview: 11th August 2011
- Place of the interview: kitchen of the consultant

1. Translation into Mòcheno: Cosa ha comprato (lei)?
   Bos hòt-se kaft si geister?

Alternatives (judgment task)
*Bos se hòt kaft geister? – no
*Bos de hòt kaft? – no
*Bos si hòt kaft? – no
*Bos hòt de kaft? – no
*Bos hòt si kaft? – no, only: Bos hòt-se si kaft?
Bos hòt-se kaft de mama? – his translation
*Bos hòt de mama kaft? – no

2. **Translation into Mòcheno: Quando ha comprato il libro (lui)?**
Benn hòt-er kaft s puech?
Alternatives (judgment task)
*Benn er hòt kaft s puech? – no
*Benn ar hòt kaft s puech? – no
*Benn hòt-ar kaft s puech? – no
*Benn hòt-der kaft s puech? – no
Benn hòt-er kaft s puech der tata? – ok
*Benn hòt der tata kaft s puech? – no
*Benn hòt der tata s puech kaft? – no

3. **Translation into Mòcheno: Maria mi ha chiesto come hai fatto il compito**
De Maria hòt-me pfrok,
abia de host gamocht der compito
Alternatives (judgment task)
abia de host der compito gamocht – ok
abia de der compito gamocht host – ok
abia host gamocht der compito – ok
abia host-en gamocht du der compito – ok

Translation into Mòcheno: Maria mi ha chiesto come (lei) ha fatto il compito
abia de hòt-en gamocht si der compito
Alternatives (judgment task)
abia de hòt-en gamocht der compito – ok
*abia hòt-en gamocht der compito – no
*abia si hòt-en gamocht der compito – no
abia as de hòt-en gamocht der compito – ok
*abia ase hòt-en gamocht der compito – no

Translation into Mòcheno: Maria mi ha chiesto come Gianni ha fatto il compito
abia der hòt gamocht der Giani der compito
Alternatives (judgment task)
*abia as der hòt gamocht der Giani der compito – no

4. **Translation into Mòcheno: Ieri ha comprato un libro (lei)**
Geister hòt-se a puech kaft
Alternatives (judgment task)
Geister si hòt kaft a puech – ok
*Geister se hòt kaft a puech – no
*Geister hòt de kaft a puech – no
Geister de hòt kaft a puech – ok

Geister de mama hòt kaft a puech – ok
Geister hòt de mama kaft a puech – ok

5. Judgment task
S puech hòt-er geister kaft- ok, fronted XP is an SP
*S puech geister hòt-er kaft – no
*S puech der Mario hòt kaft – no

6. Judgment task
Bos hòt-er kaft – ok
*Bos geister hòt-er kaft? – no, only: Bos hòt-er kaft geister? or Gester bos hòt-er kaft

7. Judgment task
A PUACH hòt-er kaft, net a quaderno – ok
*A PUACH gester hòt-er kaft, net a quaderno – no, only: Gester A PUACH hòt-er kaft

8. Judgment task
*Geister s puech er hòt-s kaft – no

9. Judgment task
De mama hòt kaft a puech – ok

10. Judgment task
De mama ene boteig hòt kaft a puech – ok

11. Judgment task
*De mama ene boteig hòt-se kaft a puech – no

12. Judgment task
Geister s puech ber hòt-s kaft? – ok

13. Judgment task
*Ber s puech hòt-s kaft? – no

14. Judgment task
*S puech ber hòt kaft? – no

15. Judgment task
*Ber s puech hòt kaft? – no

16. Judgment task
??Gester hòt-er a puach kaft – no

17. Judgment task
Gester hòt-er kaft a puech – ok

FIER-GM

- Age: 68
- Sex: M
- Variety: Fierozzo, S.Felice/Mittelperg, Meidln
- Date of the interview: 29th July 2011
- Place of the interview: kitchen of the consultant

1. **Translation into Mòcheno: Cosa ha comprato (lei)?**
   Bos hòt-se kaft si?
   Alternatives (judgment task)
   Bos hòt-se si kaft? – ok
   *Bos se hòt kaft? – no
   *Bos de hòt kaft? – no
   *Bos si hòt kaft? – no
   *Bos hòt de kaft? – no
   *Bos hòt si kaft? – no, only: Bos hòt-se si kaft?
   Bos hòt de mama kaft? – ok
   Bos hòt-se kaft de mama? – ok

2. **Translation into Mòcheno: Quando ha comprato il libro (lui)?**
   Benn hòt-er kaft s puech (er)?
   Alternatives (judgment task)
   *Benn er hòt kaft s puech? – no
   *Benn ar hòt kaft s puech? – no
   *Benn der hòt kaft s puech? – no
   *Benn hòt-ar kaft s puech? – no
   *Benn hòt-der kaft s puech? – no
   Benn hòt der tata kaft s puech? – ok
   Benn hòt-er kaft s puech der tata? – ok
   Benn hòt der tata s puech kaft? – ok

3. **Translation into Mòcheno: Maria mi ha chiesto come hai fatto il compito**
   De Maria hòt-mer pfrok,
   abia de host gamocht der compito
   Alternatives (judgment task)
   abia de host der compito gamocht – ok
   abia de der compito gamocht host – ok
   abia host gamocht der compito – ok
   abia de host gamocht du der compito – ok

   Translation into Mòcheno: Maria mi ha chiesto come (lei) ha fatto il compito
   abia si hòt gamocht der compito
   Alternatives (judgment task)
   abia (as) de hòt gamocht der compito – ok
   abia-se hòt gamocht der compito – ok
   abia de hòt gamocht der compito si – ok
   *abia hòt gamocht der compito si – no
   *abia-se hòt gamocht der compito si – no

   Translation into Mòcheno: Maria mi ha chiesto come Gianni ha fatto il compito
   abias der Giani hòt gamocht der compito
   Alternatives (judgment task)
   abia der hòt gamocht der compito der Gianni – ok

4. Translation into Mòcheno: Ieri ha comprato un libro (lei)
   Geister si hòt kaft a puech
   Alternatives (judgment task)
   Geister hòt-se a puech kaft – ok
   *Geister se hòt a puech kaft – no
   Geister de hòt a puech kaft – ok
   *Geister hòt de a puech kaft – no
   Geister de mama hòt kaft a puech – ok
   Geister hòt de mama kaft a puech – ok

5. Judgment task
   S puech hone geister kaft – ok, fronted XP is an SP
   S puech geister hòt-er kaft – ok
   *S puech der Mario hòt kaft – no, only: S puech hòt kaft der Mario

6. Judgment task
   Bos hòt-er kaft – ok
   *Bos geister hòt-er kaft? – no, only: Bos hòt-er kaft geister?

7. Judgment task
   A PUACH hòt-er kaft, net a quaderno – ok
   A PUACH gester hone kaft, net a quaderno – ok

8. Judgment task
   Geister s puech er hòt-s kaft – ok

9. Judgment task
   De mama hòt a puech kaft – ok

10. Judgment task
    De mama en de boteig hòt kaft a puech – ok

11. Judgment task
    *De mama en de boteig hòt-se kaft a puech – no

12. Judgment task
    Geister s puech ber hòt-s kaft? – ok

13. Judgment task
    *Ber s puech hòt-s kaft? – no

14. Judgment task
    S puech ber hòt kaft? – ok

15. Judgment task
    *Ber s puech hòt kaft? – no

16. Judgment task
    Gester hòt-er a puach kaft – ok

17. Judgment task
    Gester hòt-er kaft a puech – ok

Questionnaires from Roveda

ROVE-AF

- Age: 16
- Sex: F
- Variety: Roveda, Ouberpèrg, Kairo
- Date of the interview: 16th September 2011
- Place of the interview: kitchen of the consultant

1. Translation into Mòcheno: Cosa ha comprato (lei)?
   Bos hòt-se kaft?
   Alternatives (judgment task)
   *Bos se hòt kaft? – no
   Bos hòt-se kaft de mama? – ok, real interrogative
   Bos hòt de mama kaft? – ok, only as a special interrogative
   *Bos hòt de kaft? – no
   *Bos si hòt kaft? – no
   ?Bos hòt si kaft? – not perfect, better: Bos hòt-se si kaft?
   *Bos de hòt kaft? – no

2. Translation into Mòcheno: Quando ha comprato il libro (lui)?
   Benn hòt-er kaft s puech?
   Alternatives (judgment task)
   *Benn er/ar/der hòt kaft s puech? – no
   Benn hòt-er kaft s puech der tata? – her translation
   Benn hòt der tata kaft s puech? – ok
   Benn hòt der tata s puech kaft? – ok
   *Benn hòt der/ar kaft s puech? – no

3. Translation into Mòcheno: Maria mi ha chiesto come hai fatto il compito
   De Maria hòt mer pfrokt,
   abia de host gatun en compito
   Alternatives (judgment task)
   *abia de en compito gatun host – no
   abia de host en compito gatun – ok
   abia du host gatun en compito – ok
   *abia host gatun en compito – no
   abia de host du gatun en compito – ok
   *abia host du gatun en compito – no

   Translation into Mòcheno: Maria mi ha chiesto come (lei) ha fatto il compito
   abia de hòt gamocht en compito
   Alternatives (judgment task)
   abia as de hòt gamocht en compito – ok
   *abia ase hòt gamocht en compito – no
   abia de hòt si gamocht en compito – ok
   *abia hòt si gamocht en compito – no

Translation into Mòcheno: Maria mi ha chiesto come Gianni ha fatto il compito
abia Giani hòt gamocht en compito
Alternatives (judgment task)
?abia hòt gamocht en compito der Giani – not perfect
abia der hòt gamocht en compito der Giani – ok

4. Translation into Mòcheno: Ieri ha comprato un libro (lei)
   Geister hòt-se kaft a puech
   Alternatives (judgment task)
   Geister si hòt kaft a puech – ok
   Geister de hòt kaft a puech – ok
   Geister de mama hòt kaft a puech – her translation
   Gester hòt de mama kaft a puech – ok
   Geister hòt de mama a puech kaft – ok
   *Geister se hòt kaft a puech – no
   *Geister hòt de kaft a puech – no

5. Judgment task
   S puech hòt-er geister kaft – ok
   *S puech geister hone kaft – no
   *S puech der Mario hòt kaft – no

6. Judgment task
   Bos hòt-er kaft – ok
   *Bos geister hòt-er kaft – no, only: Bos hòt-er kaft geister? or Geister, bos hòt-er kaft?

7. Judgment task
   A PUACH hòt-er kaft, net a quaderno – ok
   *A PUACH geister hòt-er kaft net a quaderno – no

8. Judgment task
   *Geister s puech er hòt-s kaft – no

9. Judgment task
   De mama hòt a puech kaft – ok

10. Judgment task
    De mama en de boteig hòt a puech kaft – ok

11. Judgment task
    *De mama en de boteig hòt-se kaft a puech – no

12. Judgment task
    Geister s puech ber hòt-s kaft? – ok

13. Judgment task
    *Ber s puech hòt-s kaft? – no

14. Judgment task
    *S puech ber hòt kaft? – no

15. Judgment task
    *Ber s puech hòt kaft? – no

16. **Judgment task**
    Geister hòt-er a puach kaft – ok

17. **Judgment task**
    Geister hòt-er kaft a puech – ok

ROVE-EF

- Age: 18
- Sex: F
- Variety: Roveda, Ouberpèrg, Kairo
- Date of the interview: 16th September 2011
- Place of the interview: kitchen of the consultant

1. **Translation into Mòcheno: Cosa ha comprato (lei)?**
    Bos hòt-se kaft?
    Alternatives (judgment task)
    *Bos se hòt kaft? – no
    Bos hòt-se kaft de mama? – her translation, real interrogative
    Bos hòt de mama kaft? – ok only as a special interrogative
    *Bos de hòt kaft? – no
    *Bos hòt si kaft? – no
    *Bos si hòt kaft? – no
    *Bos hòt de kaft? – no
    Bos hòt-se si kaft? – ok

2. **Translation into Mòcheno: Quando ha comprato il libro (lui)?**
    Benn hòt-er kaft s puech?
    Alternatives (judgment task)
    *Benn er/ar hòt kaft s puech – no
    Benn hòt der tata kaft s puech – ok
    Benn hòt-er kaft s puech der tata – ok
    Benn hòt der tata s puech kaft – ok
    *Benn hòt der/ar kaft s puech – no

3. **Translation into Mòcheno: Maria mi ha chiesto come hai fatto il compito**
    De Maria hòt mer pfrok,
    abia de host gamocht en compito
    Alternatives (judgment task)
    *abia de en compito gamocht host – no
    abia de host en compito gamocht – ok
    *abia host gamocht en compito – no
    abia de host du gamocht en compito, net si – ok
    *abia host du gamocht en compito, (net si) – no
    abia as de host gamocht en compito – ok

    Translation into Mòcheno: Maria mi ha chiesto come (lei) ha fatto il compito
    abia de hòt (si) en compito gamocht

Alternatives (judgment task)
abia si hòt en compito gamocht – ok
*abia hòt si en compito gamocht – no, only: abia de hòt si en compito gamocht
*abia ase hòt gamocht en compito – no

Translation into Mòcheno: Maria mi ha chiesto come Gianni ha fatto il compito
abia der Giani hòt gamocht en compito
Alternatives (judgment task)
abia der hòt gamocht en compito der Giani – ok
*abia hòt gamocht en compito der Giani – no

4. **Translation into Mòcheno: Ieri ha comprato un libro (lei)**
   Geister hòt-se kaft a puech
   Alternatives (judgment task)
   Geister si hòt kaft a puech – ok, focus on SI
   *Geister se hòt kaft a puech – no
   Geister de mama hòt kaft a puech – ok
   Gester hòt de mama kaft a puech – ok
   Geister hòt de mama a puech kaft – ok
   *Geister de hòt kaft a puech – no
   *Geister hòt de kaft a puech – no

5. **Judgment task**
   S puech hone geister kaft – ok, fronted XP is an SP, answer to: *Benn host kaft s puech?*
   *S puech geister hone kaft – no
   *S puech der Mario hòt kaft – no

6. **Judgment task**
   Bos hòt-er kaft – ok
   *Bos geister hòt-er kaft – no, only: Bos hòt-er kaft geister? or Geister, bos hòt-er kaft?

7. **Judgment task**
   A PUACH hòt-er kaft, net a quaderno – ok
   *A PUACH geister hòt-er kaft net a quaderno – no

8. **Judgment task**
   *Geister s puech er hòt-s kaft – no

9. **Judgment task**
   De mama hòt a puech kaft -ok, also VO

10. **Judgment task**
    De mama en de boteig hòt a puech kaft – ok, also VO

11. **Judgment task**
    *De mama en de boteig hòt-se kaft a puech – no

12. **Judgment task**
    Geister s puech ber hòt-s kaft? – ok

13. **Judgment task**
    *Ber s puech hòt-s kaft? – no

14. Judgment task
    *S puech ber hòt kaft? – no

15. Judgment task
    *Ber s puech hòt kaft? – no

ROVE-IP

- Age: 27
- Sex: M
- Variety: Roveda, Ouberpèrg, Tingerla
- Date of the interview: 24th June 2011
- Place of the interview: garden of the consultant

1. Translation into Mòcheno: Cosa ha comprato (lei)?
   Bos hòt-se kaft?
   Alternatives (judgment task)
   *Bos se hòt kaft? – no
   Bos de hòt kaft? – ok
   *Bos hòt de kaft – no
   *Bos si hòt kaft? – no
   *Bos hòt si kaft? – no, only: Bos hòt-se kaft si?
   Bos hòt de mama kaft? – ok, but would be better: De mama, bos hòt-se kaft? or
   Bos hòt-se kaft de mama?

2. Translation into Mòcheno: Quando ha comprato il libro (lui)?
   Benn hòt-er kaft s puech?
   Alternatives (judgment task)
   *Benn er/der/ar hòt kaft s puech? – no
   *Benn hòt-der/ar kaft s puech? – no
   *Benn hòt der tata kaft s puech? – no, only: Benn hòt-er kaft s puech der tata?
   *Benn hòt-er s puech kaft? – no, only: Benn hòt-er kaft s puech?

3. Translation into Mòcheno: Maria mi ha chiesto come hai fatto il compito
   De Maria hòt-mer pfourst,
   abia host gamocht de compite
   Alternatives (judgment task)
   *abia du/di host gamocht de compite – no

   Translation into Mòcheno: Maria mi ha chiesto come (lei) ha fatto il compito
   abia hòt-sa gamocht du de compite – fist version
   abia hòt-se gamocht si de compite – second version
   Alternatives (judgment task)
   abia de hòt gamocht de compite – ok
   *abia as de de compete gamocht hòt – no

4. Translation into Mòcheno: Ieri ha comprato un libro (lei)
   Geister hòt-se kaft a puech

Alternatives (judgment task)
Geister si hòt kaft a puech – ok
*Geister se hòt kaft a puech – no
*Geister de hòt kaft a puech – no
*Geister hòt de kaft a puech – no
*Geister se hòt kaft a puech – no
Geister de mama hòt kaft a puech – ok
Geister hòt de mama kaft a puech – ok, but *de mama* is given a focus reading

5. Judgment task
S puach hòt-er geister kaft – ok
*S puech geister hòt-er kaft – no
*S puech der Mario hòt kaft – no

6. Judgment task
Bos hòt-er kaft? – ok
*Bos geister hòt-er kaft? – no, only: Bos hòt-er kaft geister?

7. Judgment task
A PUECH hòt-er kaft, net a quaderno – ok
*A PUECH geister hòt-er kaft – no, only: Geister hòt-er kaft a puech or Geister A PUECH hòt-er kaft

8. Judgment task
*Geister s puech er hòt-s kaft – no

9. Judgment task
De mama hòt kaft a puech -ok, only with VO word order: OV is ruled out

10. Judgment task
De mama en de boteig hòt kaft a puech – ok

11. Judgment task
*De mama en de boteig hòt-se kaft a puech – no

12. Judgment task
Geister s puech ber hòt-s kaft – ok

13. Judgment task
*Ber s puech hòt-s kaft – no

14. Judgment task
*S puech ber hòt kaft – no

15. Judgment task
*Ber s puech hòt kaft – no

ROVE-LF

- Age: 27
- Sex: F
- Variety: Roveda, Oberpèrg, Kamavrunt

- Date of the interview: 8th September 2011
- Place of the interview: kitchen of the consultant

1. **Translation into Mòcheno: Cosa ha comprato (lei)?**
    Bos hòt-se kaft?
    Alternatives (judgment task)
    *Bos se hòt kaft? – no
    Bos hòt-se kaft de mama? – her translation, real interrogative
    Bos hòt de mama kaft? – ok only as a special interrogative
    *Bos de hòt kaft? – no
    *Bos si hòt kaft? – no
    *Bos hòt de kaft? – no
    *Bos hòt si kaft? – no, only: Bos hòt-se si kaft?

2. **Translation into Mòcheno: Quando ha comprato il libro (lui)?**
    Benn hòt-er kaft s puech?
    Alternatives (judgment task)
    Benn hòt-er s puech kaft? – ok
    *Benn er hòt kaft s puech? – no
    *Benn hòt-ar kaft s puech? – no
    Benn hòt-er kaft s puech der tata? – her translation, real interrogative
    Benn hòt der tata kaft s puech? – ok only as a special interrogative
    Benn hòt der tata s puech kaft? – ok
    *Benn der hòt kaft s puech? – no
    *Benn hòt-der kaft s puech? – no

3. **Translation into Mòcheno: Maria mi ha chiesto come hai fatto il compito**
    De Maria hòt-mer pfrok,
    abia-s-e host gamocht en compito
    Alternatives (judgment task)
    abia de host gamocht en compito – ok
    *abia-s-e de host gamocht en compito – no
    abia-s-e host du gamocht en compito – ok
    abia du host gamocht en compito – ok
    *abia host du gamocht en compito – no
    abiase en compito gamocht host – ok
    abiase host en compito gamocht – ok

    Translation into Mòcheno: Maria mi ha chiesto come (lei) ha fatto il compito
    abia-se hòt si gamocht en compito
    Alternatives (judgment task)
    abia de hòt gamocht en compito – ok
    abia de hòt si gamocht en compito – ok
    *abia hòt si gamocht en compito – no

    Translation into Mòcheno: Maria mi ha chiesto come Gianni ha fatto il compito
    abia der Giani hòt gamocht en compito
    Alternatives (judgment task)
    abia der hòt gamocht en compito der Giani – ok
    *abia hòt gamocht en compito der Giani – no

4. Translation into Mòcheno: Ieri ha comprato un libro (lei)
   Geister hòt-se kaft a puech
   Alternatives (judgment task)
   *Geister de hòt kaft a puech – no
   Geister de mama hòt kaft a puech – ok, also OV
   Geister si hòt kaft a puech – ok
   Geister hòt de mama kaft a puech – ok, also OV
   *Geister hòt de kaft a puech – no
   *Geister se hòt kaft a puech – no

5. Judgment task
   S puech hòt-er geister kaft – ok, fronted XP is an SP
   *S puech geister hòt-er kaft – no, only: Geister s puech hòt-er kaft
   *S puech der Mario hòt kaft – no

6. Judgment task
   Bos hòt-er kaft? – ok
   *Bos geister hòt-er kaft? – no, only: Bos hòt-er kaft geister? or Geister bos hòt-er kaft?

7. Judgment task
   A PUECH hòt-er kaft, net a quaderno – ok
   A PUECH geister hòt-er kaft – ok

8. Judgment task
   *Geister s puech er hòt-s kaft – no

9. Judgment task
   De mama hòt a puech kaft – ok, also VO

10. Judgment task
    De mama en de boteig hòt kaft a puech – ok, also OV

11. Judgment task
    *De mama en de boteig hòt-se kaft a puech – no

12. Judgment task
    Geister s puech ber hòt-s kaft? – ok

13. Judgment task
    *Ber s puech hòt-s kaft? – no

14. Judgment task
    *S puech ber hòt kaft? – no

15. Judgment task
    *Ber s puech hòt kaft? – no

ROVE-SO

- Age: 13
- Sex: F
- Variety: Roveda, Ouberpèrg, Kamavrunt

- Date of the interview: 20th July 2011
- Place of the interview: kitchen of the consultant

1. Translation into Mòcheno: Cosa ha comprato (lei)?
   Bos hòt-se kaft?
   Alternatives (judgment task)
   *Bos se hòt kaft? – no
   *Bos de hòt kaft? – no
   *Bos si hòt kaft? – no
   *Bos hòt de kaft? – no
   *Bos hòt si kaft? – no, only: Bos hòt-se kaft si?
   *Bos hòt de mama kaft? – no
   Bos hòt-se kaft de mama? – ok

2. Translation into Mòcheno: Quando ha comprato il libro (lui)?
   Benn hòt-er kaft s puech?
   Alternatives (judgment task)
   Benn hòt-er s puech kaft? – ok
   *Benn er/der/ar hòt kaft s puech – no
   *Benn hòt der/ar kaft s puech – no
   *Benn hòt der tata kaft s puech – no
   Benn hòt-er kaft s puech der tata – ok
   *Benn hòt der tata s puech kaft – no

3. Translation into Mòcheno: Maria mi ha chiesto come hai fatto il compito
   De Maria hòt mer pfourst,
   abia as de host gamocht de compiti
   Alternatives (judgment task)
   *abia as host gamocht de compiti – no
   *abia as de host gamocht de compiti du – no
   abia as de host (du) gamocht (du) de compiti – ok

   Translation into Mòcheno: Maria mi ha chiesto come (lei) ha fatto il compito
   abia si hòt gamocht de compiti
   Alternatives (judgment task)
   abiase hòt gamocht de compiti – ok
   *abiase si hòt gamocht de compiti – no
   *abiase hòt si gamocht de compiti – no
   abiase hòt gamocht si de compiti – ok
   abia as de hòt gamocht de compiti – ok
   *abia as de hòt gamocht si de compiti – no

   Translation into Mòcheno: Maria mi ha chiesto come Gianni ha fatto il compito
   abia as er Giani hòt gamocht de compiti
   Alternatives (judgment task)
   *abia as er hòt gamocht de compiti er Giani – no

4. Translation into Mòcheno: Ieri ha comprato un libro (lei)
   Geister hòt-se kaft a puech – ok, also OV
   Geister si hòt kaft a puech – ok

*Geister se hòt kaft a puech – no
*Geister de hòt kaft a puech – no
*Geister hòt de kaft a puech – no
Geister de mama hòt kaft a puech – ok
Geister hòt de mama a puech kaft – ok, also VO

5. Judgment task
S puech hòt-er geister kaft – ok, fronted XP is an SP
*S puach geister hòt-er kaft – no
*S puech der Mario hòt kaft – no

6. Judgment task
Bos hòt-er kaft – ok
*Bos geister hòt-er kaft – no

7. Judgment task
A PUACH hòt-er kaft, net a quaderno – ok
A PUACH geister hòt-er kaft net a quaderno – ok

8. Judgment task
*Geister s puech er hòt-s kaft – no

9. Judgment task
De mama hòt a puech kaft – ok, also VO

10. Judgment task
De mama en de boteig hòt a puech kaft – ok

11. Judgment task
*De mama en de boteig hòt-se kaft a puech – no

12. Judgment task
Geister s puech ber hòt-s kaft? – ok

13. Judgment task
*Ber s puech hòt-s kaft? – no

14. Judgment task
*S puech ber hòt kaft? – no

15. Judgment task
*Ber s puech hòt kaft? – no

16. Judgment task
Geister hòt-er kaft a puech – ok

17. Judgment task
Geister hòt-er a puech kaft – ok

ROVE-BL

– Age: 37
– Sex: F
– Variety: Roveda, Ouberpèrg, Kamavrunt

- Date of the interview: 20th July 2011
- Place of the interview: kitchen of the consultant

1. **Translation into Mòcheno: Cosa ha comprato (lei)?**
   Bos hòt-se kaft?
   Alternatives (judgment task)
   *Bos se hòt kaft? – no
   *Bos de hòt kaft? – no
   *Bos si hòt kaft? -no
   *Bos hòt de kaft? -no
   *Bos hòt si kaft? -no, only: Bos hòt-se si kaft?
   Bos hòt de mama kaft? – ok as a special interrogative, real interrogative would be
   Bos hòt-se kaft de mama?

2. **Translation into Mòcheno: Quando ha comprato il libro (lui)?**
   Benn hòt-er kaft s puech?
   Alternatives (judgment task)
   *Benn er/der/ar hòt kaft s puech – no
   *Benn hòt der/ar kaft s puech – no
   Benn hòt der tata kaft s puech – ok, focus on *der tata*
   Benn hòt-er kaft s puech der tata – ok
   Benn hòt der tata s puech kaft -ok

3. **Translation into Mòcheno: Maria mi ha chiesto come hai fatto il compito**
   De Maria hòt mer pfourst,
   abia (as) de host gamocht en compito
   Alternatives (judgment task)
   % abia de en compito gamocht host – no
   abia de host en compito gamocht – ok
   *abia host gamocht en compito – no

   Translation into Mòcheno: Maria mi ha chiesto come (lei) ha fatto il compito
   abia (as) de hòt gamocht en compito
   Alternatives (judgment task)
   *abia as si hòt gamocht en compito – no, only: abia de hòt si gamocht en compito
   *abiase de hòt gamocht en compito – no

   Translation into Mòcheno: Maria mi ha chiesto come Gianni ha fatto il compito
   abia as hòt gatun der Mario za mochen en compito

4. **Translation into Mòcheno: Ieri ha comprato un libro (lei)**
   Geister hòt-se kaft a puech
   Alternatives (judgment task)
   ??Geister si hòt kaft a puech – no, better: Geister hòt-se kaft a puech si
   *Geister se hòt kaft a puech – no
   *Geister de hòt kaft a puech – no
   *Geister hòt de kaft a puech – no
   Geister de mama hòt a puech kaft – ok
   *Geister hòt de mama kaft a puech – no, ruled out also: *Geister hòt de mama a puech kaft

5. Judgment task
   S puech hòt-er geister kaft – ok, fronted XP is an SP
   *S puach geister hòt-er kaft -no, only: Geister hòt-er kaft s puech
   *S puech der Mario hòt kaft – no

6. Judgment task
   Bos hòt-er kaft? – ok
   *Bos geister hòt-er kaft? – no

7. Judgment task
   A PUACH hòt-er kaft, net a quaderno – ok
   *A PUACH geister hòt-er kaft net a quaderno – no

8. Judgment task
   *Geister s puech er hòt-s kaft – no

9. Judgment task
   De mama hòt a puech kaft -ok, also OV

10. Judgment task
    De mama en de boteig hòt a puech kaft – ok

11. Judgment task
    *De mama en de boteig hòt-se a puech kaft – no

12. Judgment task
    *Geister s puech ber hòt-s kaft? – no

13. Judgment task
    *Ber s puech hòt-s kaft? – no

14. Judgment task
    *S puech ber hòt kaft? – no

15. Judgment task
    *Ber s puech hòt kaft? – no

16. Judgment task
    Geister hòt-er kaft a puech – ok

17. Judgment task
    Geister hòt-er a puech kaft – ok

ROVE-CF

- Age: 32
- Sex: F
- Variety: Roveda, Ouberpèrg, Balschn
- Date of the interview: 8th September 2011
- Place of the interview: pub of Fierozzo

1. Translation into Mòcheno: Cosa ha comprato (lei)?
   Bos hòt-se kaft (si)?

Alternatives (judgment task)
*Bos hòt-se si kaft? – no
*Bos se hòt kaft? – no
Bos hòt kaft de mama? – her translation
Bos hòt-se kaft de mama? – ok
Bos hòt de mama kaft? – ok
*Bos hòt de kaft? – no
*Bos de hòt kaft? – no
*Bos si hòt kaft? – no
*Bos hòt si kaft? – no

2. Translation into Mòcheno: Quando ha comprato il libro (lui)?
Benn hòt-er kaft s puech?
Alternatives (judgment task)
*Benn hòt-er s puech kaft? – no
*Benn er/der/ar hòt kaft s puech? – no
*Benn hòt-der/ar kaft s puech? – no
Benn hòt-er kaft s puech er tata? – her translation
Benn hòt er tata kaft s puech? – ok
Benn hòt er tata s puech kaft? – ok

3. Translation into Mòcheno: Maria mi ha chiesto come hai fatto il compito
De Maria hòt mer pfrok,
abia (as) de host(-en) gamocht en compito
Alternatives (judgment task)
abia de host du gamocht en compito – ok
abia de host gamocht en compito du – ok
*abia de en compito gamocht host – no
*abia de host en compito gamocht – no
abia du host gamocht en compito – ok
abia host gamocht en compito – ok

Translation into Mòcheno: Maria mi ha chiesto come (lei) ha fatto il compito
abia si hòt gamocht en compito
Alternatives (judgment task)
?abia-se hòt gamocht en compito – ok
abia de hòt gamocht en compito – ok
abia de hòt-(en) (si) gamocht en compito (si) – ok

Translation into Mòcheno: Maria mi ha chiesto come Gianni ha fatto il compito
abia der Giani hòt gamocht en compito
Alternatives (judgment task)
abia-er hòt gamocht en compito der Giani – ok
abia hòt gamocht en compito der Giani – ok
*abia as der Giani hòt gamocht en compito – no

4. Translation into Mòcheno: Ieri ha comprato un libro (lei)
Geister hòt-se kaft a puech

Alternatives (judgment task)
Geister si hòt kaft a puech – ok
*Geister se hòt kaft a puech – no
*Geister hòt de kaft a puech – no
Geister de mama hòt kaft a puech – ok
*Geister hòt de mama kaft a puech – no
*Geister hòt de mama a puech kaft – no
Geister de hòt kaft a puech – ok

5. Judgment task
S puech hòt-er geister kaft – ok
*S puach geister hòt-er kaft – no
*S puech der Mario hòt kaft – no

6. Judgment task
Bos hòt-er kaft – ok
*Bos geister hòt-er kaft – no, only: Bos hòt-er kaft geister or Gester, bos hòt-er kaft

7. Judgment task
A PUACH hòt-er kaft, net a quaderno – ok
*A PUACH geister hòt-er kaft net a quaderno – no, only: Geister A PUECH hòt-er kaft, ont net an quaderno

8. Judgment task
*Geister s puech er hòt-s kaft – no

9. Judgment task
De mama hòt a puech kaft – ok

10. Judgment task
De mama en de boteig hòt a puech kaft – ok

11. Judgment task
*De mama en de boteig hòt-se a puech kaft – no

12. Judgment task
Geister s puech ber hòt-s kaft? – ok

13. Judgment task
*Ber s puech hòt-s kaft? – no

14. Judgment task
*S puech ber hòt kaft? – no

15. Judgment task
*Ber s puech hòt kaft? – no

16. Judgment task
Geister hòt-er kaft a puech – ok

17. Judgment task
Geister hòt-er a puech kaft – ok

ROVE-MP

- Age: 38
- Sex: M
- Variety: Roveda, Ouberpèrg, Balschn
- Date of the interview: 12th July 2011
- Place of the interview: Istitute for the promotion of the Mòcheno language and culture, Palù del Fersina

1. Translation into Mòcheno: Cosa ha comprato (lei)?
   Si, bos hòt-se kaft? – first version
   Bos hòt-se kaft si? – second version
   Alternatives (judgment task)
   *Bos se hòt kaft? – no
   *Bos de hòt kaft? – no
   *Bos si hòt kaft? – no
   Bos hòt de kaft? – ok
   Bos hòt si kaft? – ok
   *Bos hòt de mama kaft? – no, only: Bos hòt-se kaft de mama?

2. Translation into Mòcheno: Quando ha comprato il libro (lui)?
   Benn hòt-er kaft s puech?
   Alternatives (judgment task)
   *Benn er hòt kaft s puach? – no
   *Benn ar hòt-ar kaft s puach? – no
   *Benn der hòt-der kaft s puach? – no
   *Benn hòt-ar kaft s puech – no
   *Benn hòt- der kaft s puech – no
   *Benn hòt der tata kaft s puech? – no
   *Benn hòt der tata s puech kaft? – no

3. Translation into Mòcheno: Maria mi ha chiesto come hai fatto il compito
   De Maria hòt mer pfrok,
   abia de host gamocht de compite
   Alternatives (judgment task)
   abia host gamocht de compite – ok
   *abia as host gamocht de compite – no
   abia (as) du host gamocht de compite – ok
   abia (as) de host gamocht de compite – ok
   *abia aso du host gamocht de compite – no
   *abia as de du host gamocht de compite – no

   Translation into Mòcheno: Maria mi ha chiesto come (lei) ha fatto il compito
   abia (as) si hòt gamocht de compite
   Alternatives (judgment task)
   abia-se hòt gamocht de compite – ok
   ?abia-se si hòt gamocht de compite – not perfect
   *abia as de si hòt gamocht de compite – no

*abia as de hòt gamocht de compite – no
*abiase de hòt gamocht de compite – no

Translation into Mòcheno: Maria mi ha chiesto come Gianni ha fatto il compito
abia der Giani hòt gamocht de compite

4. **Translation into Mòcheno: Ieri ha comprato un libro (lei)**
   Geister hòt-se kaft a puech
   Alternatives (judgment task)
   Geister si hòt kaft a puech – ok
   *Geister se hòt kaft a puech – no
   *Geister de hòt kaft a puech – no
   *Geister hòt-de kaft a puech – no
   Geister de mama hòt kaft a puech – ok
   *Geister hòt de mama kaft a puech – no
   Geister hòt de mama a puach kaft – ok

5. **Judgment task**
   S puech hòt-er kaft geister – ok, fronted XP is an SP; OV is ruled out
   *S puech geister hòt-er kaft – no
   *S puech der Mario hòt kaft – no, only: Der Mario hòt kaft s puech

6. **Judgment task**
   Bos hòt-er kaft? – ok
   *Bos gester hòt-er kaft? – no, only: Bos hòt-er kaft geister?

7. **Judgment task**
   A PUECH hòt-er kaft, ont net an quaderno – ok
   *A PUECH geister hòt-er kaft, ont net.. – no, only: A PUECH hòt-er kaft geister, ont net..

8. **Judgment task**
   *Geister s puach er hòt-s kaft – no

9. **Judgment task**
   De mama hòt a puech kaft – ok

10. **Judgment task**
    De mama en de boteig hòt a puech kaft – ok

11. **Judgment task**
    *De mama en de boteig hòt-se a puach kaft – no

12. **Judgment task**
    Geister s puech ber hòt-s kaft? – ok, only with a break after *gester*

13. **Judgment task**
    *Ber s puach hòt-s kaft? – no

14. **Judgment task**
    *S puach ber hòt kaft? – no

15. **Judgment task**
    *Ber s puach hòt kaft? – no

ROVE-MB

- Age: 33
- Sex: F
- Variety: Roveda, Mitterperg
- Date of the interview: 24th June 2011
- Place of the interview: kitchen of the consultant

1. **Translation into Mòcheno: Cosa ha comprato (lei)?**
   Bos hòt-se kaft?
   Alternatives (judgment task)
   *Bos se hòt kaft? – no
   *Bos de hòt kaft? – no
   *Bos si hòt kaft? – no
   *Bos hòt de kaft? – no
   *Bos hòt si kaft? – only: Bos hòt-se si kaft?, focus on SI
   Bos hòt de mama kaft? – ok only as a special interrogative

2. **Translation into Mòcheno: Quando ha comprato il libro (lui)?**
   Benn hòt-er kaft s puech?
   Alternatives (judgment task)
   *Benn er hòt kaft s puach? – no
   *Benn ar hòt-ar kaft s puach? – no
   *Benn der hòt-der kaft s puach? – no
   *Benn hòt der tata kaft s puech? – no, only: Benn hòt-er kaft s puech der tata?

3. **Translation into Mòcheno: Maria mi ha chiesto come hai fatto il compito**
   De Maria hòt-mer pfourst,
   abia de host gamocht en compito – 1
   abia host gamocht en compito – 2
   Alternatives (judgment task)
   *abia as host gamocht en compito – no
   abia as de host gamocht en compito – ok
   abia as de du host gamocht en compito – ok
   abia as du en compito gamocht host – ok
   *abia as en compito gamocht host – no

4. **Translation into Mòcheno: Ieri ha comprato un libro (lei)**
   Geister hòt-se kaft a puech
   Alternatives (judgment task)
   Geister si hòt kaft a puech – ok
   *Geister se hòt kaft a puech – no
   *Geister de hòt kaft a puech – no
   *Geister hòt-de kaft a puech – no
   Geister de mama hòt kaft a puech – ok
   Geister hòt de mama kaft a puech – ok

5. **Judgment task**
   S puach hòt-er geister kaft – ok, fronted XP is an SP
   *S puach geister hòt-er kaft – no
   *S puach der Mario hòt kaft – no

6. **Judgment task**
   Bos hòt-er kaft? – ok
   *Bos geister hòt-er kaft? – no, only: Bos hòt-er kaft geister?

7. **Judgment task**
   A PUACH hone kaft, net a quaderno – ok
   *A PUACH geister hone kaft, net a quaderno – no

8. **Judgment task**
   *Geister s puach er hòt-s kaft – no

9. **Judgment task**
   De mama hòt a puech kaft – ok

10. **Judgment task**
    De mama en de boteig hòt a puech kaft – ok

11. **Judgment task**
    *De mama en de boteig hòt-se a puach kaft – no

12. **Judgment task**
    Geister s puach ber hòt-s kaft? – ok

13. **Judgment task**
    *Ber s puach hòt-s kaft? – no

14. **Judgment task**
    *S puach ber hòt kaft? – no

15. **Judgment task**
    *Ber s puach hòt kaft? – no

ROVE-RF

- Age: 45
- Sex: F
- Variety: Roveda, Ouberpèrg, Kamavrunt
- Date of the interview: 21st June 2011
- Place of the interview: kitchen of the consultant

1. **Translation into Mòcheno: Cosa ha comprato (lei)?**
   Bos hòt-se kaft?
   Alternatives (judgment task)
   *Bos se hòt kaft? – no
   *Bos de hòt kaft? – no
   *Bos si hòt kaft? – no
   *Bos hòt de kaft? – no

*Bos hòt si kaft? – no, only: Bos hòt-se si kaft?
  *bos hòt-se de kaft? – no
  Bos hòt de mama kaft? – ok

2. Translation into Mòcheno: Quando ha comprato il libro (lui)?
   Benn hòt-er kaft s puech er?
   Alternatives (judgment task)
   Benn er hòt kaft s puech – ok
   *Benn hòt-der/ar kaft s puach? – no
   Benn hòt-er kaft der tata s puech? – ok
   Benn hòt der tata kaft s puech? – ok
   ???Geister hòt der tata kaft s puech – not perfect

3. Translation into Mòcheno: Maria mi ha chiesto come hai fatto il compito
   De Maria hòt mar pfourst,
   abia as du host gamocht de compete
   Alternatives (judgment task)
   *abia aso (du) host gamocht de compete – no
   abia di host gamocht (du) de compete – ok

   Translation into Mòcheno: Maria mi ha chiesto come (lei) ha fatto il compito
   abia de hòt-sa si gamocht de compete
   Alternatives (judgment task)
   abia hòt-se si gamocht de compete – ok

   Translation into Mòcheno: Maria mi ha chiesto come Gianni ha fatto il compito
   abia der hòt gamocht der Giani de compete

4. Translation into Mòcheno: Ieri ha comprato un libro (lei)
   Geister hòt-se kaft a puach
   Alternatives (judgment task)
   Geister si hòt kaft a puach – ok
   *Geister se hòt kaft a puach – no
   Geister de hòt kaft a puach – ok
   *Geister hòt de kaft a puach – no
   Geister de mama hòt kaft a puach – ok
   ??Geister hòt de mama kaft a puach – not perfect

5. Judgment task
   S puach hòt-er geister kaft – ok
   *S puach geister hòt-er kaft – no
   *S puach der Mario hòt kaft – no, only: Der Mario hòt kaft s puech

6. Judgment task
   Bos hòt-er kaft – ok
   *Bos geister hòt-er kaft? – no, only: Bos hòt-er kaft geister?

7. Judgment task
   A PUACH hone kaft, net a quaderno – ok
   A PUACH gester hone kaft, net a quaderno – ok

8. Judgment task
   *Geister s puech er hòt-s kaft – no

9. Judgment task
   De mama hòt a puach kaft – ok, also: De mama hòt kaft a puech
10. Judgment task
    De mama en de boteig hòt a puech kaft – ok
11. Judgment task
    *De mama en de boteig hòt-se a puach kaft – no
12. Judgment task
    Geister s puech ber hòt-s kaft – ok
13. Judgment task
    *Ber s puach hòt-s kaft – no
14. Judgment task
    *S puech ber hòt kaft? – no
15. Judgment task
    *Ber s puach hòt kaft? – no

ROVE-DP

- Age: 63
- Sex: M
- Variety: Roveda, Ouberpèrg, Vrunt
- Date of the interview: 20th July 2011
- Place of the interview: kitchen of the consultant

1. Translation into Mòcheno: Cosa ha comprato (lei)?
   Bos hòt-se kaft (si)?
   Alternatives (judgment task)
   *Bos se hòt kaft? – no
   *Bos de hòt kaft? – no
   *Bos si hòt kaft – no
   *Bos hòt de kaft? – no
   *Bos hòt si kaft? – no, only: Bos hòt-se si kaft?
   Bos hòt de mama kaft? – ok, only as a special interrogative
   Bos hòt-se kaft de mama? – ok, unmarked interrogative
2. Translation into Mòcheno: Quando ha comprato il libro (lui)?
   Benn hòt-er s puech kaft?
   Alternatives (judgment task)
   Benn hòt-er kaft s puech? – ok
   *Benn er/ar/der hòt kaft s puech? – no
   *Benn hòt-ar kaft s puech? – no
   *Benn hòt der kaft s puech? – no
   *Benn hòt der tata kaft s puech – no, only: Benn hòt der tata s puech kaft
   Benn hòt-er kaft s puech der tata? – ok

3. Translation into Mòcheno: Maria mi ha chiesto come hai fatto il compito
   De Maria hòt-mer pfrok,
   bia du en compito/s augem gamocht host
   Alternatives (judgment task)
   *bia de en compito/s augem gamocht host – no

   Translation into Mòcheno: Maria mi ha chiesto come (lei) ha fatto il compito
   bia si en compito gamocht hòt
   Alternatives (judgment task)
   *biase en compito gamocht hòt – no
   *bia de en compito gamocht hòt – no

   Translation into Mòcheno: Maria mi ha chiesto come Gianni ha fatto il compito
   bia der Hons s augem gamocht hòt

4. Translation into Mòcheno: Ieri ha comprato un libro (lei)
   Geister hòt-se a puech kaft
   Alternatives (judgment task)
   Geister si hòt a puech kaft – ok
   *Geister se hòt a puech kaft – no
   *Geister de hòt a puech kaft – no
   *Geister hòt de kaft a puech – no
   Geister de mama hòt a puech kaft – ok
   Geister hòt de mama a puech kaft – ok

5. Judgment task
   S puech hòt-er geister kaft – ok, fronted XP is an SP
   *S puech geister hòt-er kaft -no, only: Geister hòt-er s puech kaft
   *S puech der Mario hòt kaft – no, only: S puech hòt der Mario kaft

6. Judgment task
   Bos hòt-er kaft – ok
   *Bos geister hòt-er kaft? – no

7. Judgment task
   A PUACH hòt-er kaft, net a quaderno – ok
   *A PUACH geister hone kaft, net a quaderno – no, only: Gester hòt-er A PUACH kaft, ont net an quaderno

8. Judgment task
   *Geister s puech er hòt-s kaft- no

9. Judgment task
   De mama hòt a puech kaft – ok

10. Judgment task
    De mama en de boteig hòt kaft a puech – ok

11. Judgment task
    *De mama en de boteig hòt-se kaft a puech – no

12. Judgment task
    *Geister s puech ber hòt-s kaft? – no

13. Judgment task
    *Ber s puech hòt-s kaft? – no
14. Judgment task
    *S puech ber hòt kaft? – no
15. Judgment task
    *Ber s puech hòt kaft? – no

ROVE-JP

- Age: 71
- Sex: F
- Variety: Roveda, Unterperg
- Date of the interview: 20th July 2011
- Place of the interview: kitchen of the consultant

1. Translation into Mòcheno: Cosa ha comprato (lei)?
   Bos hòt-se kaft (si)?
   Alternatives (judgment task)
   *Bos se hòt kaft? – no
   *Bos de hòt kaft? – no
   *Bos si hòt kaft? – no
   *Bos hòt de kaft? – no
   *Bos hòt si kaft? – no, only: Bos hòt-se si kaft?
   *Bos hòt de mama kaft? – no, only: Bos hòt-se kaft de mama?

2. Translation into Mòcheno: Quando ha comprato il libro (lui)?
   Benn hòt-er kaft s puech?
   Alternatives (judgment task)
   *Benn er/ar hòt kaft s puech – no
   Benn der hòt kaft s puech – no
   *Benn hòt-ar kaft s puech – no
   *Benn hòt der kaft s puech – no
   *Benn hòt der tata kaft s puech – no, only: benn hòt-er-s kaft der tata?
   *Benn hòt der tata s puech kaft – no, only: benn hòt-er kaft s puech der tata?

3. Translation into Mòcheno: Maria mi ha chiesto come hai fatto il compito
   De Maria hòt-mer pfrok,
   abia de host gamocht en compito
   Alternatives (judgment task)
   *abia du host gamocht en compito – no
   abia de host gamocht du en compito – ok

   Translation into Mòcheno: Maria mi ha chiesto come (lei) ha fatto il compito
   abia de hòt si gamocht en compito
   Alternatives (judgment task)
   *abiase hòt gamocht en compito – no
   abia ase hon gemocht en compito – ok
   abia as de hon gamocht en compito – ok

Translation into Mòcheno: Maria mi ha chiesto come Gianni ha fatto il compito
abia(s) der hòt gamocht en compito der Giani

4. Translation into Mòcheno: Ieri ha comprato un libro (lei)
   Geister hòt-se kaft a puech
   Alternatives (judgment task)
   Geister si hòt kaft a puech – ok
   *Geister se hòt kaft a puech – no
   Geister de hòt kaft a puech – ok
   *Geister hòt de kaft a puech – no
   Geister de mama hòt kaft a puech – ok
   *Geister hòt de mama kaft a puech – no

5. Judgment task
   S puech hòt-er geister kaft – ok (also VO), the fronted XP is an SP, answer to the question: Benn hòt-er kaft s puech?
   *S puech geister hòt-er kaft – no
   *S puech der Mario hòt kaft – no, only: Der Mario hòt kaft s puech

6. Judgment task
   Bos hòt-er kaft – ok
   *Bos geister hòt-er kaft? – no, only: Bos hòt-er kaft geister

7. Judgment task
   A PUACH hòt-er kaft, net a quaderno – ok
   *A PUACH geister hone kaft, net a quaderno – no

8. Judgment task
   *Geister s puech er hòt-s kaft- no

9. Judgment task
   De mama hòt kaft a puech – ok, OV is ruled out

10. Judgment task
    De mama en de boteig hòt kaft a puech – ok

11. Judgment task
    *De mama en de boteig hòt-se kaft a puech – no

12. Judgment task
    *Geister s puech ber hòt-s kaft? – no

13. Judgment task
    *Ber s puech hòt-s kaft? – no

14. Judgment task
    *S puech ber hòt kaft? – no

15. Judgment task
    *Ber s puech hòt kaft? – no

ROVE-MO

- Age: 69
- Sex: M
- Variety: Roveda, Ouberpèrg, Tingerla
- Date of the interview: 24th June 2011
- Place of the interview: kitchen of the consultant

1. Translation into Mòcheno: Cosa ha comprato (lei)?
   Bos hòt-se kaft de mama?
   Alternatives (judgment task)
   *Bos se hòt kaft? – no
   *Bos de hòt kaft? – no
   *Bos si hòt kaft? – no
   *Bos hòt de kaft? – no
   *Bos hòt si kaft? – no, only: Bos hòt-se si kaft?
   *Bos hòt de mama kaft? – no

2. Translation into Mòcheno: Quando ha comprato il libro (lui)?
   XX

3. Translation into Mòcheno: Maria mi ha chiesto come hai fatto il compito
   De Maria hòt-mer pfrok,
   abia di (du) host gamocht en compito

4. Translation into Mòcheno: Ieri ha comprato un libro (lei)
   Geister hòt-se kaft a puech
   Alternatives (judgment task)
   Geister si hòt kaft a puech – ok
   *Geister se hòt kaft a puech – no
   *Geister de hòt kaft a puech – no
   *Geister hòt de kaft a puech – no
   Geister de mama hòt kaft a puech – ok
   *Geister hòt de mama kaft a puech – no

5. Judgment task
   S puech hòt-er geister kaft – ok, fronted XP is an SP
   *S puech geister hòt-er kaft –no
   *S puech der Mario hòt kaft – no, only: S puech hòt der Mario kaft

6. Judgment task
   Bos hòt-er kaft – ok
   *Bos geister hòt-er kaft? – no, only: Bos hòt-er kaft geister

7. Judgment task
   A PUACH hòt-er kaft, net a quaderno – ok
   *A PUACH geister hone kaft, net a quaderno – no

8. Judgment task
   *Geister s puech er hòt-s kaft – no

9. Judgment task
   De mama hòt a puech kaft – ok, also OV
10. Judgment task
    De mama en de boteig hòt kaft a puech – ok
11. Judgment task
    *De mama en de boteig hòt-se kaft a puech – no
12. Judgment task
    Geister s puech ber hòt-s kaft? – ok
13. Judgment task
    *Ber s puech hòt-s kaft? – no
14. Judgment task
    *S puech ber hòt kaft? – no
15. Judgment task
    *Ber s puech hòt kaft? – no

ROVE-RP

- Age: 68
- Sex: F
- Variety: Roveda, Unterpèrg, Taufner
- Date of the interview: 19th August 2011
- Place of the interview: garden of the consultant

1. Translation into Mòcheno: Cosa ha comprato (lei)?
   Bos hòt-se kaft?
   Alternatives (judgment task)
   *Bos se hòt kaft? – no
   Bos hòt de mama kaft? – ok
   Bos hòt-se kaft de mama? – ok
   *Bos de hòt kaft? – no
   *Bos si hòt kaft? – no
   *Bos hòt de kaft? – no
   *Bos hòt si kaft? – no, only: Bos hòt-se kaft si?
2. Translation into Mòcheno: Quando ha comprato il libro (lui)?
   Benn hòt-er kaft s puech?
   Alternatives (judgment task)
   *Benn er hòt kaft s puech? – no
   *Benn ar hòt kaft s puech? – no
   *Benn der hòt kaft s puech? – no
   *Benn hòt-der kaft s puech? – no
   *Benn hòt-ar kaft s puech? – no
   Benn hòt-er tata kaft s puech? – ok
   Benn hòt-er kaft s puech der tata? – ok
   Benn hòt er tata s puech kaft – ok

3. Translation into Mòcheno: Maria mi ha chiesto come hai fatto il compito
   De Maria hòt-mer pfourst,
   abia du host gamocht en compito
   Alternatives (judgment task)
   abia de host gamocht en compito – ok
   abia de host du gamocht en compito – ok
   *abia host gamocht en compito – no

   Translation into Mòcheno: Maria mi ha chiesto come (lei) ha fatto il compito
   abia de si hòt gamocht en compito
   Alternatives (judgment task)
   abia as de hòt gamocht en compito – ok
   abia si hòt gamocht en compito – ok
   *abia hòt gamocht en compito – no

   Translation into Mòcheno: Maria mi ha chiesto come Gianni ha fatto il compito
   abia der Giani hòt gamocht en compito
   Alternatives (judgment task)
   abia der hòt gamocht en compito der Giani – ok
   *abia hòt gamocht en compito der Giani – no

4. Translation into Mòcheno: Ieri ha comprato un libro (lei)
   Geister hòt-se kaft a puech
   Alternatives (judgment task)
   Geister si hòt kaft a puech – ok
   Geister hòt de mama kaft a puech – ok
   *Geister de hòt kaft a puech – no
   *Geister se hòt kaft a puech – no
   Geister de mama hòt kaft a puech – ok
   *Geister hòt de kaft a puech – no

5. Judgment task
   S puech hone kaft gester – ok, only with VO
   *S puech geister hone kaft – no
   *S puech der Mario hòt kaft – no, only: Er Mario hòt kaft s puech

6. Judgment task
   Bos hòt-er kaft – ok
   *Bos geister hòt-er kaft? – no, only: Bos hòt-er kaft geister or Geister, bos host kaft?

7. Judgment task
   A PUACH hòt-er kaft, net a quaderno – ok
   A PUACH geister hone kaft, net a quaderno – ok

8. Judgment task
   Geister s puech er hòt-s kaft – ok

9. Judgment task
   De mama hòt kaft a puech – ok, only VO

10. Judgment task
    De mama en de boteig hòt kaft a puech – ok

11. Judgment task
    *De mama en de boteig hòt-se kaft a puech – no
12. Judgment task
    Geister s puech ber hòt-s kaft? – ok
13. Judgment task
    *Ber s puech hòt-s kaft? – no
14. Judgment task
    S puech ber hòt kaft? – ok
15. Judgment task
    *Ber s puech hòt kaft? – no
16. Judgment task
    Geister hòt-er a puech kaft – ok
17. Judgment task
    Geister hòt-er kaft a puech – ok

ROVE-EO

- Age: 59
- Sex: F
- Variety: Roveda, Mittelperg
- Date of the interview: 24th June 2011
- Place of the interview: kitchen of the consultant

1. Translation into Mòcheno: Cosa ha comprato (lei)?
   Bos hòt-se kaft?
   Alternatives (judgment task)
   *Bos se hòt kaft? – no
   *Bos de hòt kaft? – no
   *Bos si hòt kaft? – no
   *Bos hòt de kaft? – no
   *Bos hòt si kaft? -no, only: Bos hòt-se si kaft?
   Bos hòt de mama kaft? – ok
2. Translation into Mòcheno: Quando ha comprato il libro (lui)?
   Benn hòt-er kaft s puech der tata? – first version, unmarked interrogative
   Benn hòt der tata s puech kaft? – second version, only as a special interrogative/exclamative
   Alternatives (judgment task)
   *Benn hòt der tata kaft s puech? – no
   *Benn der/ar hòt kaft s puech? – no
   *Benn hòt der/ar kaft s puech? – no
3. Translation into Mòcheno: Maria mi ha chiesto come hai fatto il compito
   De Maria hòt mer pfourst,
   abia de du host en compito gamocht

Translation into Mòcheno: Maria mi ha chiesto come (lei) ha fatto il compito
abia as si en compito gamocht hòt

Translation into Mòcheno: Ieri ha comprato un libro (lei)
abia der Nane hòt gamocht en compito

4. Translation into Mòcheno: Ieri ha comprato un libro (lei)
   Geister hòt-se kaft a puech
   Alternatives (judgment task)
   Geister si hòt kaft a puech – ok also with OV
   *Geister de hòt kaft a puech – no
   *Geister se hòt kaft a puech – no
   *Geister hòt de kaft a puech – no
   Geister de mama hòt a puech kaft – ok
   Geister hòt de mama a puech kaft – ok

5. Judgment task
   S puech hòt-er geister kaft – ok, the fronted XP is an SP, answer to the question: Benn hòt-er kaft s puech?
   *S puach geister hòt-er kaft -no
   *S puech der Mario hòt kaft – no, only: Der Mario hòt kaft s puech

6. Judgment task
   Bos hòt-er kaft – ok
   *Bos geister hòt-er kaft – no

7. Judgment task
   xxx

8. Judgment task
   De mama hòt a puech kaft -ok, also VO

9. Judgment task
   De mama en de boteig hòt a puech kaft – ok

10. Judgment task
    *De mama en de boteig hòt-se a puech kaft – no

11. Judgment task
    *Geister s puech hòt-er-s kaft – no

12. Judgment task
    *Geister s puech ber hòt-s kaft? – no

13. Judgment task
    *Ber s puech hòt-s kaft? – no

14. Judgment task
    *S puech ber hòt kaft? – no

15. Judgment task
    *Ber s puech hòt kaft? – no

Index

A
Afrikaans   140, 142
age   4–8, 73–74, 92
agreement features   42
agreement morphology   139
   see also agreement system; case morphology; morphology
agreement system   144
antisymmetric approach   27
   see also cartographic approach
articulated left periphery   9–12, 75, 180, 209
   see also contrastive focus; contrastive topic; hanging-topic construction; Italian; left-dislocation; simple-preposing; Old Romance language; split CP
articulated structure of the left periphery   9, 35, 50, 63, 67
asymmetric pro-drop   32, 167, 169–170, 194, 205–206, 211, 214, 216
   see also asymmetry between main and embedded clauses
asymmetry between main and embedded clauses   20–21, 25, 30, 33, 45, 48–49, 167, 169, 195, 202
   see also embedded topicalization

B
Bavarian   71, 152, 214
   see also complementiser agreement
bi-clausal analysis   16, 169, 189, 191–192, 210, 219

big DP   180
   see also clitic doubling; splitting analysis
big-DP hypothesis   179
bilingualism   3
Brazilian Portuguese   140
Breton   21

C
cartographic approach   67
case morphology   51, 180, 183, 185
child language   183, 219
Cimbrian   94, 168, 170, 179, 181
clitic doubling   59, 156, 179
clitic pronouns   46, 80, 87, 89, 102
   see also subject pronouns
complementiser   25–27, 71, 98–99, 101, 142, 144, 148, 194, 197–204, 207–209
   see also deletion rule
complementiser agreement   96
reduced complementiser   197, 200, 211
consistent null-subject languages   140, 142, 144
contrastive topic   35, 58, 156, 178
contact hypothesis   9, 22, 67, 213, 215
Continental Germanic   26
   see also Germanic languages
contrastive focus   35, 122, 158, 161
core properties of the V2 phenomenon   15, 21–23, 43, 77
correlated properties of the V2 phenomenon   19, 21
CP expletives   21

D
Danish   197
   see also Germanic languages
deletion rule   207
diatopic variables   5
discourse features   181
   see also topic/focus features; contrastive topic; new information focus
distribution of pro-drop   19–20, 32–33, 167, 169, 193
double-base hypothesis   3, 9, 70, 115, 213
doubling construction   71, 105, 108–110
Dutch   28, 140, 142, 197
   see also Germanic languages

E
ellipsis   16, 189–190, 192
   see also bi-clausal analysis; mono-clausal analysis
embedded topicalization   169, 194, 197–200, 204, 209, 211
enclisis   36, 38, 90–91, 110, 114–115, 117–118, 125, 130, 136, 201
English   2, 10, 19
   see also double-base hypothesis; residual V2
EPP feature   21, 39, 41, 114, 116–118, 131–137, 153, 176–183, 185–188, 190–191
exclamative clauses   159–160
expletive subject pronoun
   see also CP expletives   40, 143, 147–148

F
Faroese   197
   see also Germanic languages

features   39, 109, 116–117, 147, 180, 183–185, 216, 218
  see also agreement features; discourse features; EPP feature, strong features; subject φ features; topic/focus features
fieldwork   4, 6, 8, 78, 91, 94, 96–98, 103, 108, 120, 128, 131, 155, 161
Finnish   139–140, 142, 164
  see also partial pro-drop languages
Flemish   28
  see also symmetric V2
freies Thema   50
  see also hanging-topic construction; nominativus pendens
French   9, 30
Frisian   197, 203
full complementiser   194, 197–198

G
gender   4–5, 116, 153, 163
German   23–26, 43, 48–51, 58, 66–71, 140, 148–151, 182, 188–191, 203
  see also Germanic languages
Germanic languages   19–23, 28–30, 34–35, 39–41, 45, 69, 71, 74–75, 77, 142, 145–146, 194–195, 197–198, 200, 202

H
hanging-topic construction   50, 125, 219
  HT   35–36, 38, 51–58, 66, 126–127, 170, 185, 192–193
head
  head-final   26
  head-initial   28
  head movement   20, 28–29, 197

I
Icelandic   21, 28, 40, 143, 186, 197, 200
illocutionary force   23, 40
impaired language   183

impersonal passive   143
information structure   3, 114, 158
inversion   see also OV syntax, OV word order
  free inversion   32, 139–141, 144–145, 147–148, 150–151, 162
  subject-verb inversion   24, 27, 30–33, 35–36, 45–49, 147, 155–156, 158–162, 203
Italian   21, 44–45, 51–53, 72–73, 139, 141–142, 144, 150, 172
  see also Romance languages

L
language contact   3
  see also bilingualism; contact hypothesis; double-base hypothesis; fieldwork; regional variety of Italian; single grammar; Trentino dialect
language variation   3, 215, 220
  see also age; diatopic variables; fieldwork; gender; micro-variation; optionality; scattered farms; sociolinguistic variables; variation
left-dislocation   32, 127
  see also Linksversetzung; contrastive topic
  LD   36, 38, 52–54, 56–61, 63, 65–66, 130–132, 173–177, 180–181, 187–188
linear restriction   19–20, 24, 30, 34, 41, 44, 49, 66, 70, 75, 77, 167, 210
Linksversetzung   58–59, 189
low left periphery   107, 124, 158, 162
  see also vP periphery

M
micro variation   7
Middle English   3
Middle High German   215
mirror principle   197
mono-clausal analysis   179, 185, 210

morphology   51, 139, 151, 163, 180, 183, 185

N
new information focus   157, 162, 177
nominativus pendens   50
Northern Italian dialects   13, 94, 114, 139, 217–218
  see also Trentino dialect
Norwegian   197
null-subject languages   140, 142–144, 150–151, 162–163

O
Old English   3, 10
Old French   9, 30
Old High German   3, 215
Old Italian   31, 32, 34, 66, 215
Old Milanese   31, 34
Old Portuguese   30–31
Old Romance languages   29–36, 77, 136, 152, 163, 194–195, 209, 211, 215–217
Old Venetian   31
optionality   1, 19, 67–68, 70, 72, 74–75, 77
OV syntax   49, 73, 194, 202
  see also new information focus

P
partial pro-drop languages   138, 140–142, 145, 148, 154, 162, 164, 170, 178
pragmatically-marked reading   72, 102, 104, 108, 144, 147, 154
proclisis   36–37, 91, 114, 136
pro   see also asymmetric pro-drop; distribution of pro-drop; partial pro-drop language
  pro-drop   32–33, 39, 72, 90, 137–142, 144–145, 148, 150–151, 169–170, 193–194, 205–206
  pro licensing   39, 141, 148, 154, 167, 170, 211
  quasi-argumental pro   140, 153–154, 163–164

referential pro 139–140, 145, 151–154, 162–163, 214
Provençal 30

R
regional variety of Italian 2
Relativised Minimality 41
  see also child language; impaired language; features; bi-clausal analysis; mono-clausal analysis
  RM 122, 167–168, 171, 179, 183, 185, 190–191, 210
Rhetoromance 9–10, 215
right dislocation 160–161
Romance contact varieties 2, 22, 48, 71
  see also Trentino dialect; regional variety of Italian
Romance languages 19–20, 22–23, 46, 51, 55, 57, 61, 74–75, 215
root phenomenon 25

S
Satzklammerstruktur 22, 49, 69, 195–196
Scandinavian 3, 20, 42, 194, 203
  see also Germanic languages
scattered farms 6
semi speakers 183
sentential adverbs 107–108, 158, 195
simple preposing 127–129
  see also Topikalisierung
  SP 56–61, 63, 66, 131–132, 135, 172, 174–178, 183, 185–187, 201
single grammar 3, 11, 15, 67, 69, 71, 74–75, 115
sociolinguistic criteria 4
sociolinguistic variables 2–4, 92
South Tyrolean 80
Spec/head configuration 115, 118–120, 122, 124–130, 132–137, 176–177, 182, 185
  see also core properties of the V2 phenomenon; EPP feature

special interrogative clauses 73, 159
split-CP 27, 33–34, 36, 39–41, 50, 68, 170, 179, 187
splitting analysis 168, 179–180
stylistic fronting 186
subject *see also* subject φ features; subject-verb inversion
  DP subjects 137, 139, 141, 157–161, 164, 172, 186
  NP subjects 46, 94–95, 118, 133, 135–137, 145, 154–155, 158–159, 169
  pragmatic subject 13, 116
  quirky subject 13
  syntactic subject 116–117, 154
subject pronouns *see also* distribution of pro-drop; enclisis; subject φ features; Wackernagelposition
  strong subject pronouns 46, 78–79, 82, 84, 99, 104–106, 118, 135, 137, 144, 186
  subject clitic pronouns 94–95, 98–99, 115–117, 121–122, 125, 132–134, 153, 163–164, 203, 206
  weak subject pronouns 78–80, 82, 84, 89, 92, 113, 136–137
subject φ features 13–16, 109, 116–117, 147, 153, 163
strong features 39
subtype of V2 48, 216
Swedish 197
syntactic variation 2–4, 6, 8–9, 15, 17, 19, 22, 43, 67, 69–70, 72, 74–75, 131, 213–215
  see also variation

T
"third-type" language 2, 140
topic/focus features 63, 107
Topikalisierung 58
Trentino dialect 2, 144, 213

V
variation 21–22, 33, 67–74, 87, 97, 99, 115, 132, 155

VO syntax 4, 22, 70, 72–73, 75, 195–196
vP periphery 16, 106–110, 158, 163, 181
V2-languages 39, 214
  see also asymmetry between main and embedded clauses; core properties of the V2 phenomenon; correlated properties of the V2 phenomenon; linear restriction; subject-verb inversion; XP movement; head movement
  asymmetrical V2 28
  relaxed V2 languages 136, 167, 179, 181, 209
  residual-V2 languages 41
  symmetrical analysis of V2 28

W
Wackernagelposition 71, 78, 89–91, 94, 98, 102, 105–106, 109–110, 113
Walser 94
West Flemish 71, 214
word order *see also* VO syntax; OV syntax; pragmatically-marked reading
  OV/VO word orders 2, 73, 215
  OV word order 26, 70, 73, 195, 215
  unmarked word order 122, 195
  V3 word order 31, 188–189, 218–219
  VO word order 215
  VP word order 116
  word order patterns 4, 155, 167, 188, 195–196, 214–215, 218

X
XP movement 20–21, 28

Y
yes/no questions 157
Yiddish 28, 144, 197, 200